犬夜叉

INUYASHA

ANI-MANGA™

Vol. 21

CREATED BY
RUMIKO TAKAHASHI

Inuyasha Ani-Manga™
Vol. #21

Created by
Rumiko Takahashi

Translation based on the VIZ anime TV series
Translation Assistance/Katy Bridges
Lettering & Editorial Assistance/John Clark
Cover Design & Graphics/Hidemi Sahara
Editor/Ian Robertson

Editorial Director/Elizabeth Kawasaki
Editor in Chief, Books/Alvin Lu
Editor in Chief, Magazines/Marc Weidenbaum
Sr. Director of Acquisitions/Rika Inouye
Sr. VP of Marketing/Liza Coppola
Exec. VP of Sales & Marketing/John Easum
Publisher/Hyoe Narita

Printed in the U.S.A.

Published by VIZ Media, LLC
P.O. Box 77010
San Francisco, CA 94107

10 9 8 7 6 5 4 3 2 1
First printing, June 2007

www.viz.com
store.viz.com

Story thus far

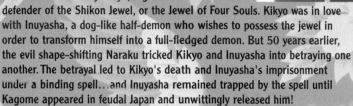

Kagome's mundane teenage existence was turned upside down when she was transported into a mythical version of Japan's medieval past! Kagome is the reincarnation of Lady Kikyo, a great warrior and the defender of the Shikon Jewel, or the Jewel of Four Souls. Kikyo was in love with Inuyasha, a dog-like half-demon who wishes to possess the jewel in order to transform himself into a full-fledged demon. But 50 years earlier, the evil shape-shifting Naraku tricked Kikyo and Inuyasha into betraying one another. The betrayal led to Kikyo's death and Inuyasha's imprisonment under a binding spell...and Inuyasha remained trapped by the spell until Kagome appeared in feudal Japan and unwittingly released him!

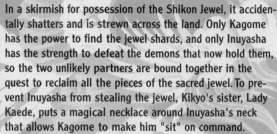

In a skirmish for possession of the Shikon Jewel, it accidentally shatters and is strewn across the land. Only Kagome has the power to find the jewel shards, and only Inuyasha has the strength to defeat the demons that now hold them, so the two unlikely partners are bound together in the quest to reclaim all the pieces of the sacred jewel. To prevent Inuyasha from stealing the jewel, Kikyo's sister, Lady Kaede, puts a magical necklace around Inuyasha's neck that allows Kagome to make him "sit" on command. Inuyasha's greatest tool in the fight to recover the sacred jewel shards is his father's sword, the Tetsusaiga, but Inuyasha's half-brother Sesshomaru covets the mighty blade and has tried to steal it more than once.

Kagome and Inuyasha are dealt a crushing blow when Kikyo, resurrected through witchcraft, steals all the shards of the sacred jewel that have been collected. Although Kikyo has grown to hate Naraku, she gives him all the jewel shards.

In his quest to kill Kagome, Naraku seeks a new ally— Tsubaki, a dark priestess who specializes in curses. Tsubaki agrees to help Naraku, but only after he promises her the nearly complete Jewel of the Four Souls, which she has long thirsted for. Can Inuyasha's friends break Tsubaki's curse, before it forces him to relive a nightmarish experience from his past?

INUYASHA™

ANI-MANGA™ VOL. 21

Contents

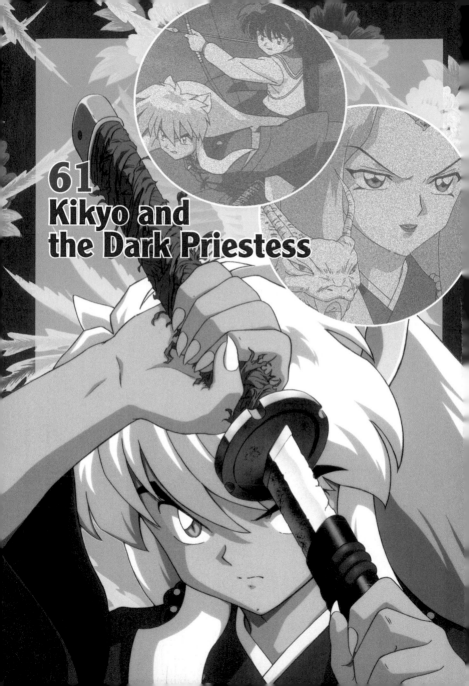

61
Kikyo and
the Dark Priestess

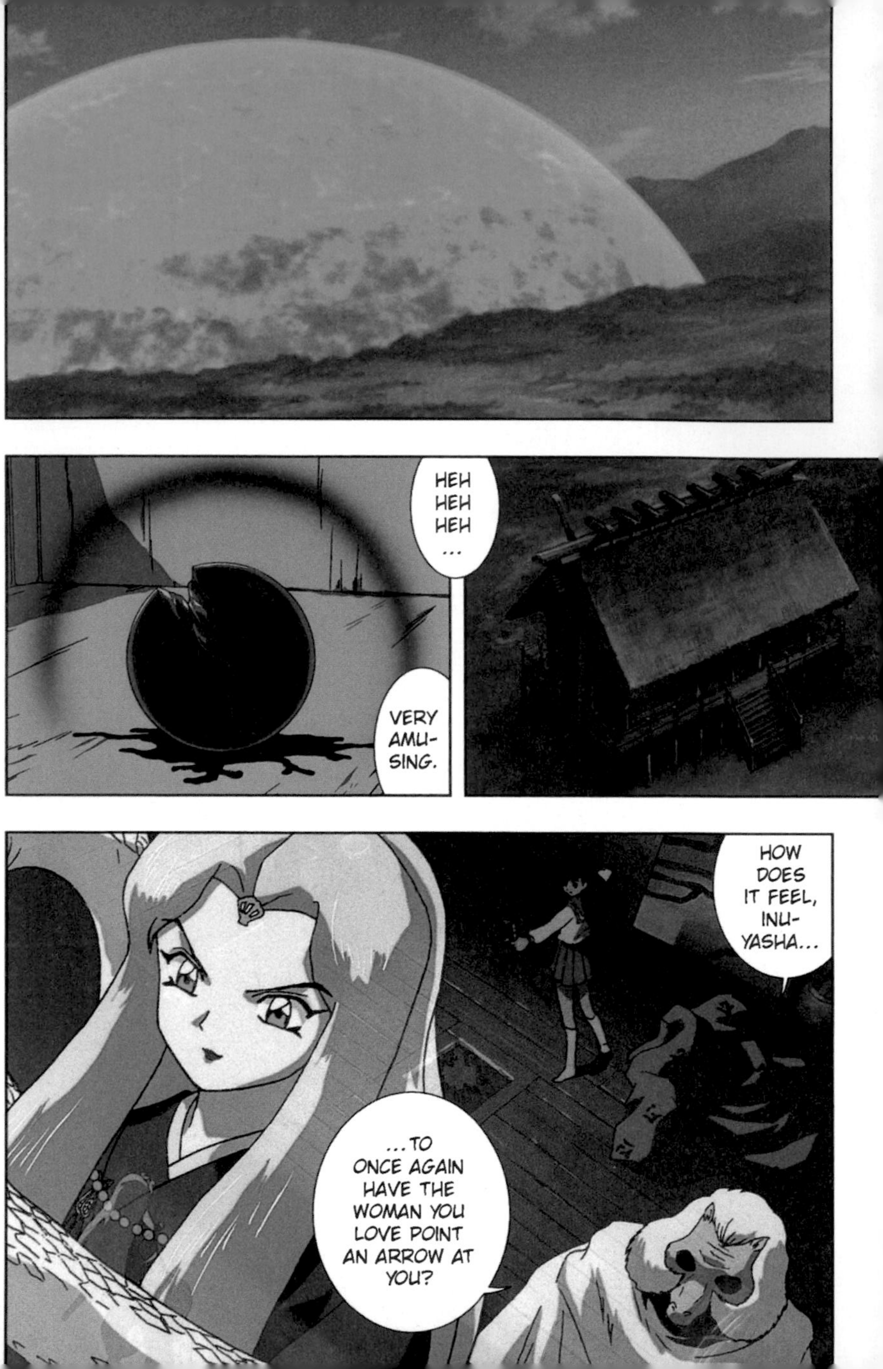
HEH HEH HEH ...
VERY AMUSING.
HOW DOES IT FEEL, INU-YASHA...
...TO ONCE AGAIN HAVE THE WOMAN YOU LOVE POINT AN ARROW AT YOU?

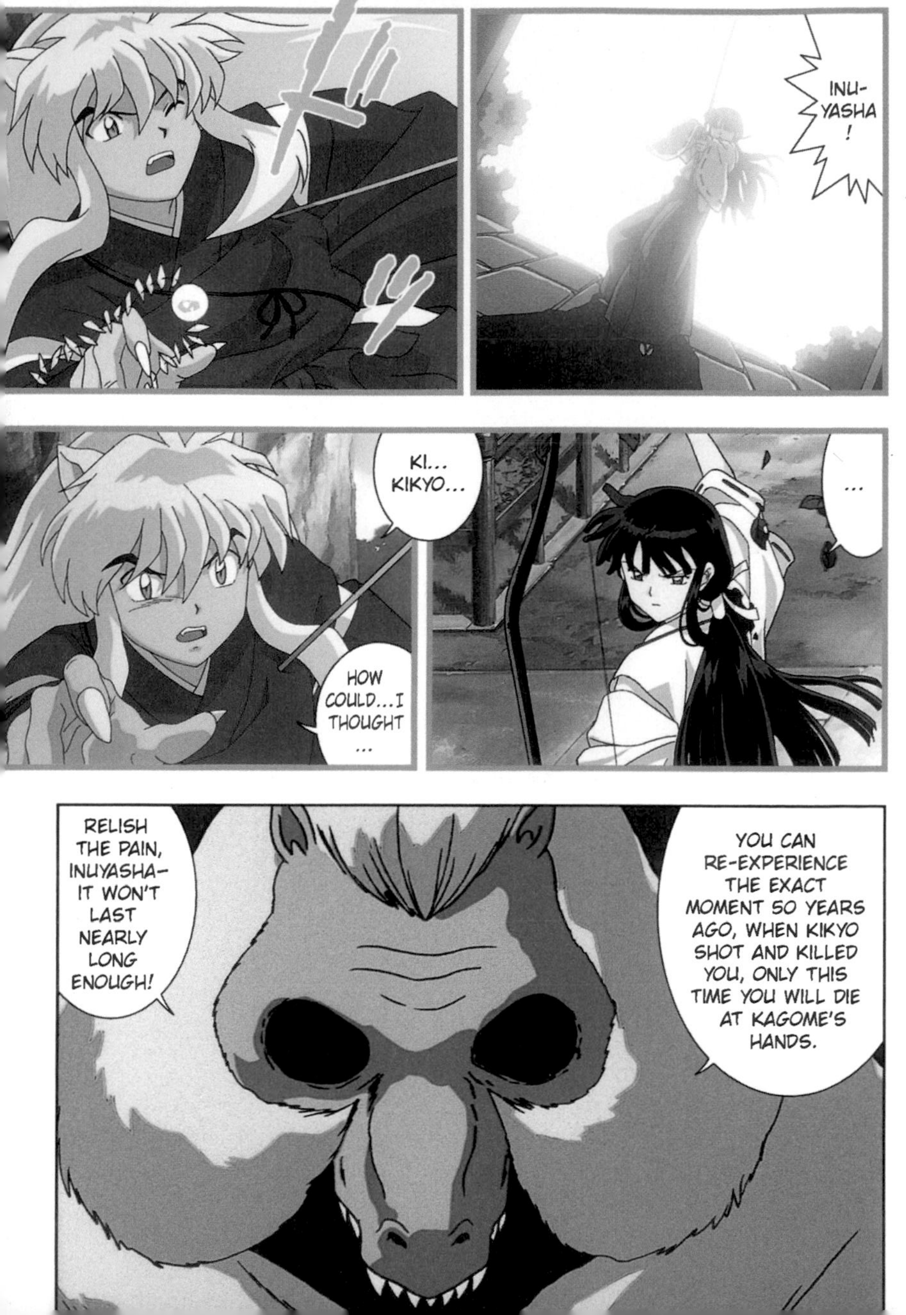
INU-YASHA!
...
KI... KIKYO...
HOW COULD...I THOUGHT...
YOU CAN RE-EXPERIENCE THE EXACT MOMENT 50 YEARS AGO, WHEN KIKYO SHOT AND KILLED YOU, ONLY THIS TIME YOU WILL DIE AT KAGOME'S HANDS.
RELISH THE PAIN, INUYASHA--IT WON'T LAST NEARLY LONG ENOUGH!

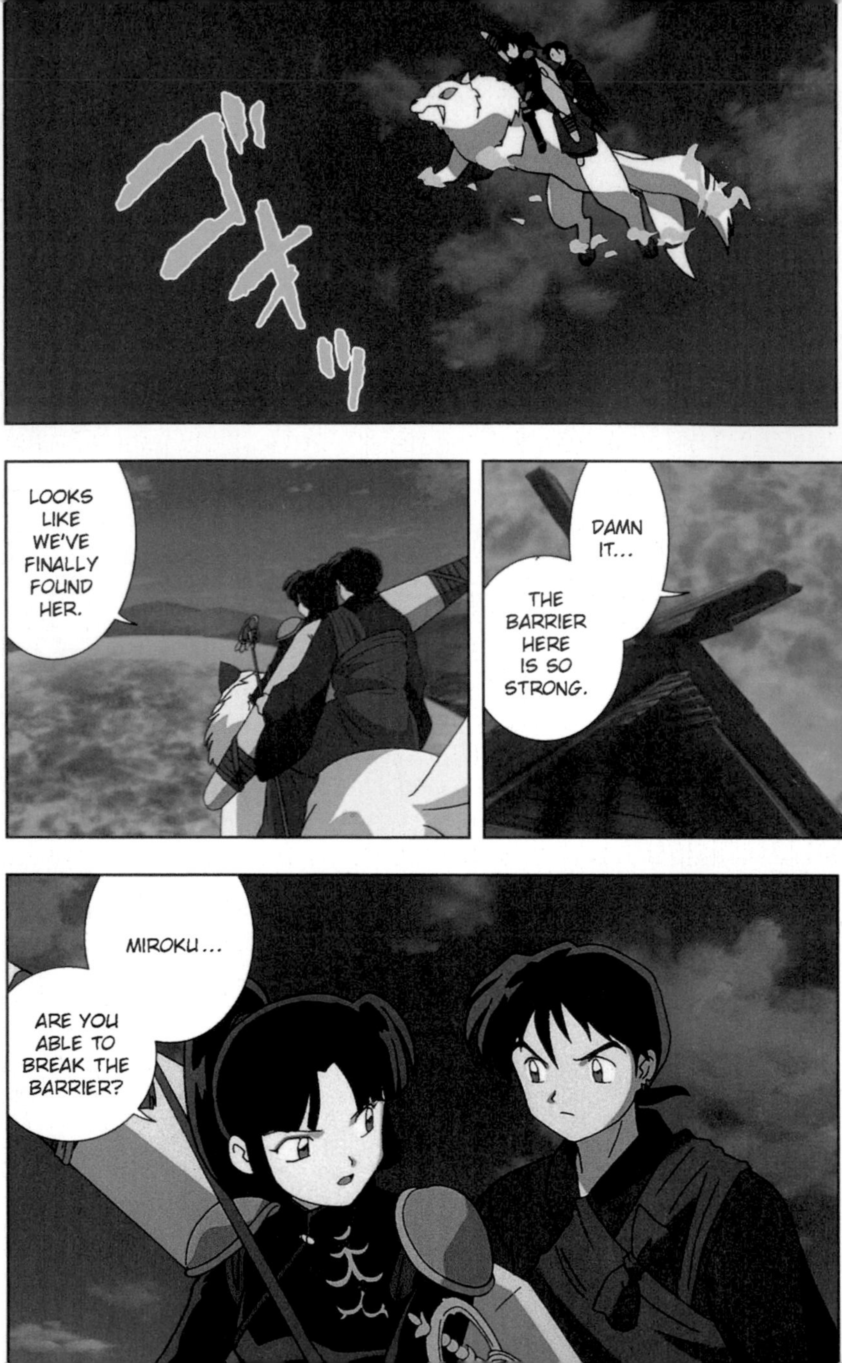
ゴオッ
DAMN IT...
THE BARRIER HERE IS SO STRONG.
LOOKS LIKE WE'VE FINALLY FOUND HER.
MIROKU...
ARE YOU ABLE TO BREAK THE BARRIER?

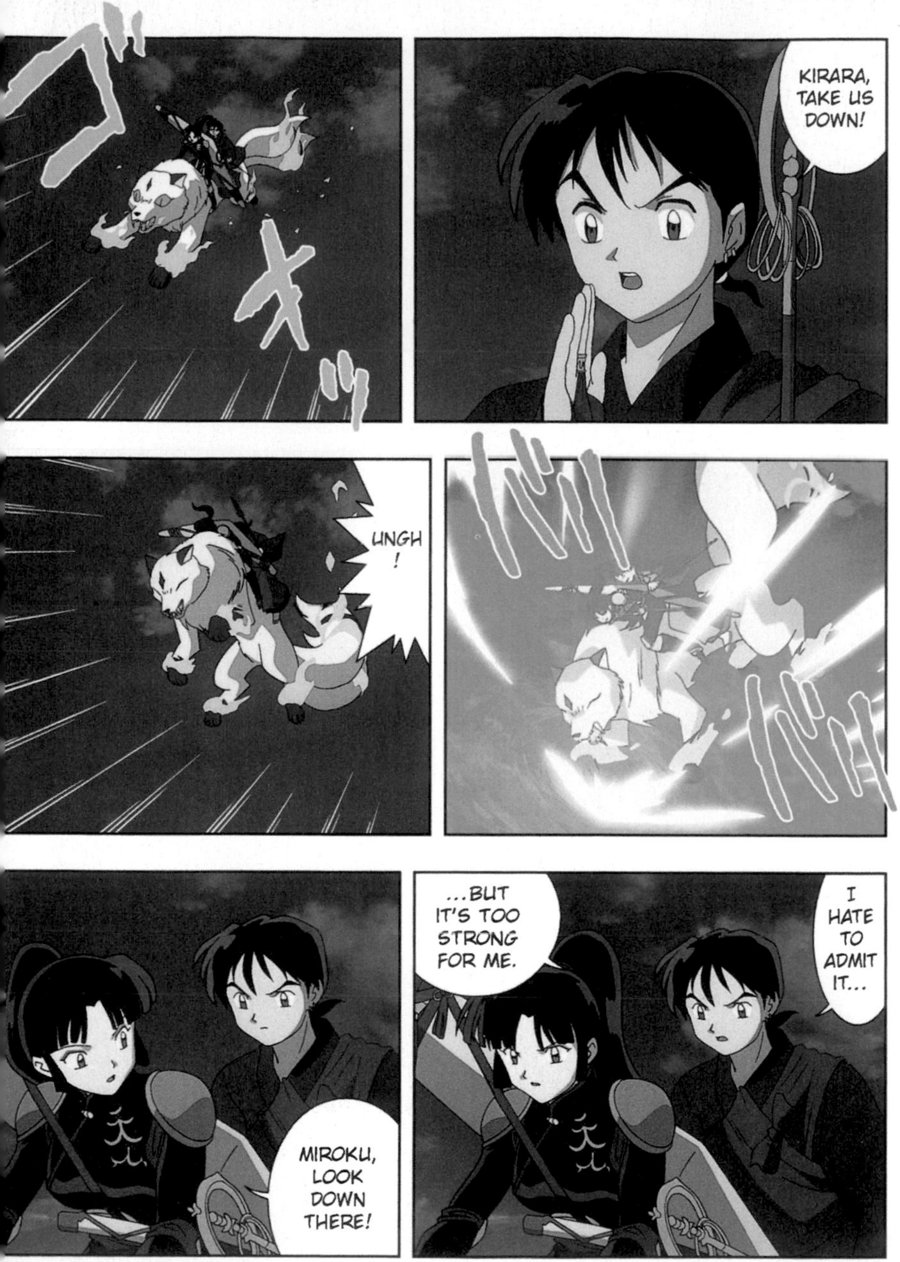
KIRARA, TAKE US DOWN!
UNGH!
I HATE TO ADMIT IT...
...BUT IT'S TOO STRONG FOR ME.
MIROKU, LOOK DOWN THERE!

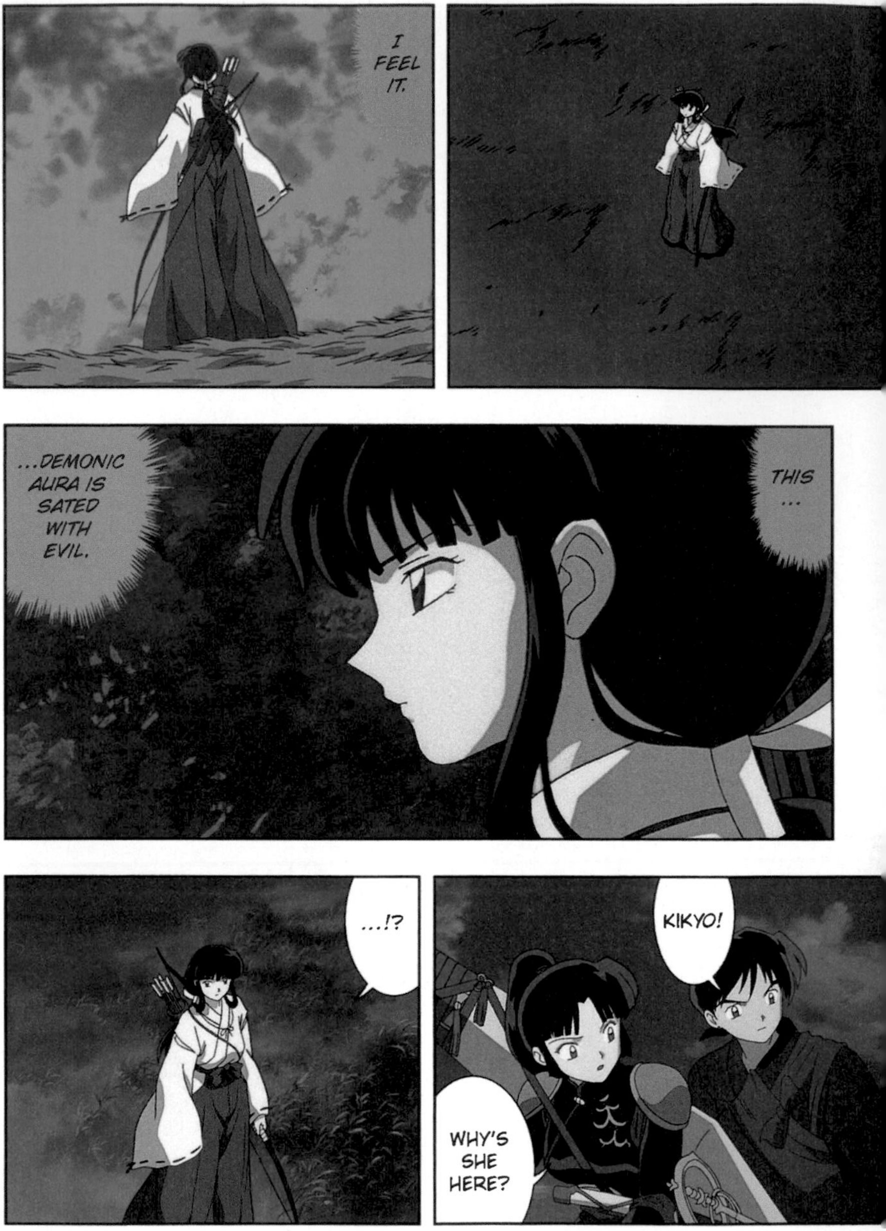
I FEEL IT.
THIS...
...DEMONIC AURA IS SATED WITH EVIL.
KIKYO!
WHY'S SHE HERE?
...!?

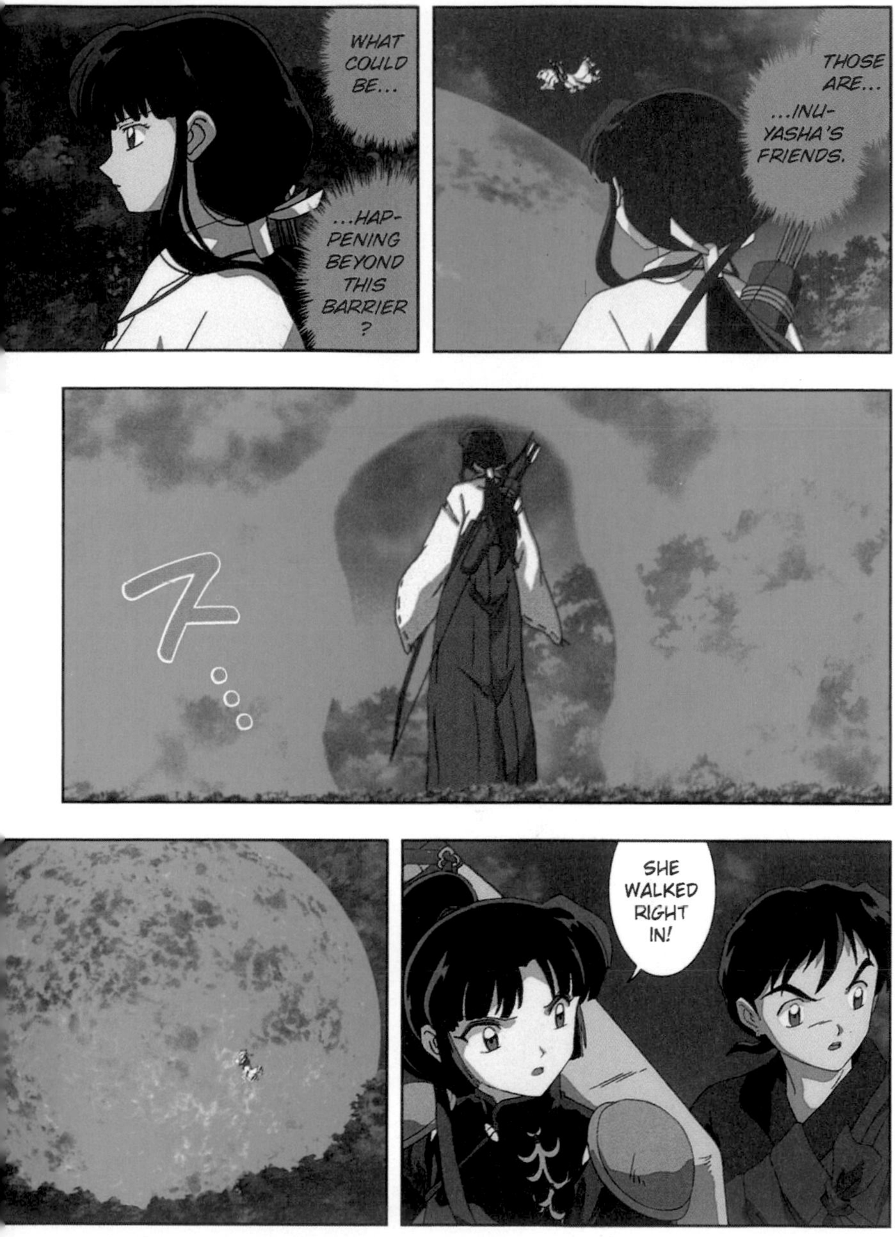
THOSE ARE... ...INU-YASHA'S FRIENDS.
WHAT COULD BE...
...HAP-PENING BEYOND THIS BARRIER?
フ
SHE WALKED RIGHT IN!

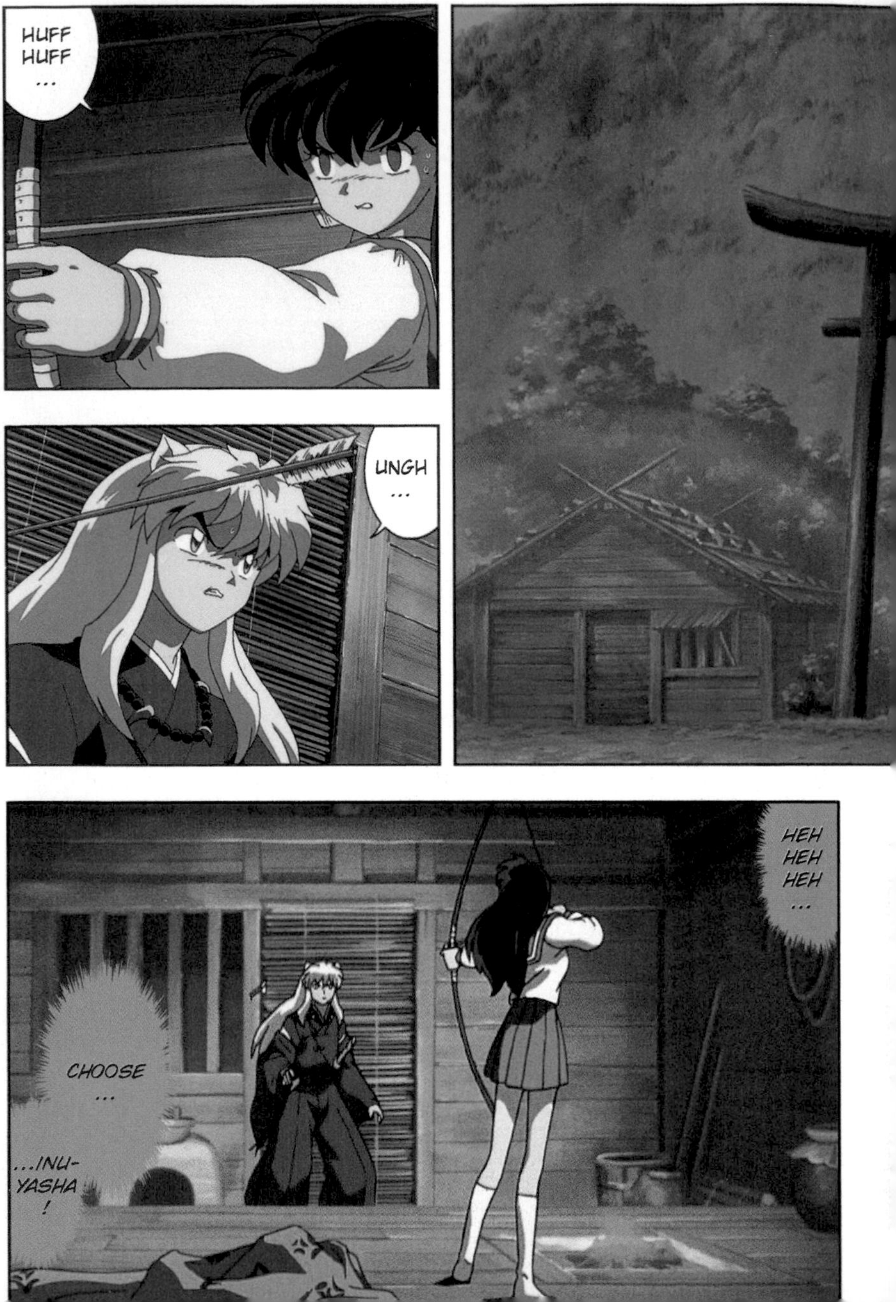
HUFF HUFF ...
UNGH ...
HEH HEH HEH ...
CHOOSE ...
...INU-YASHA!

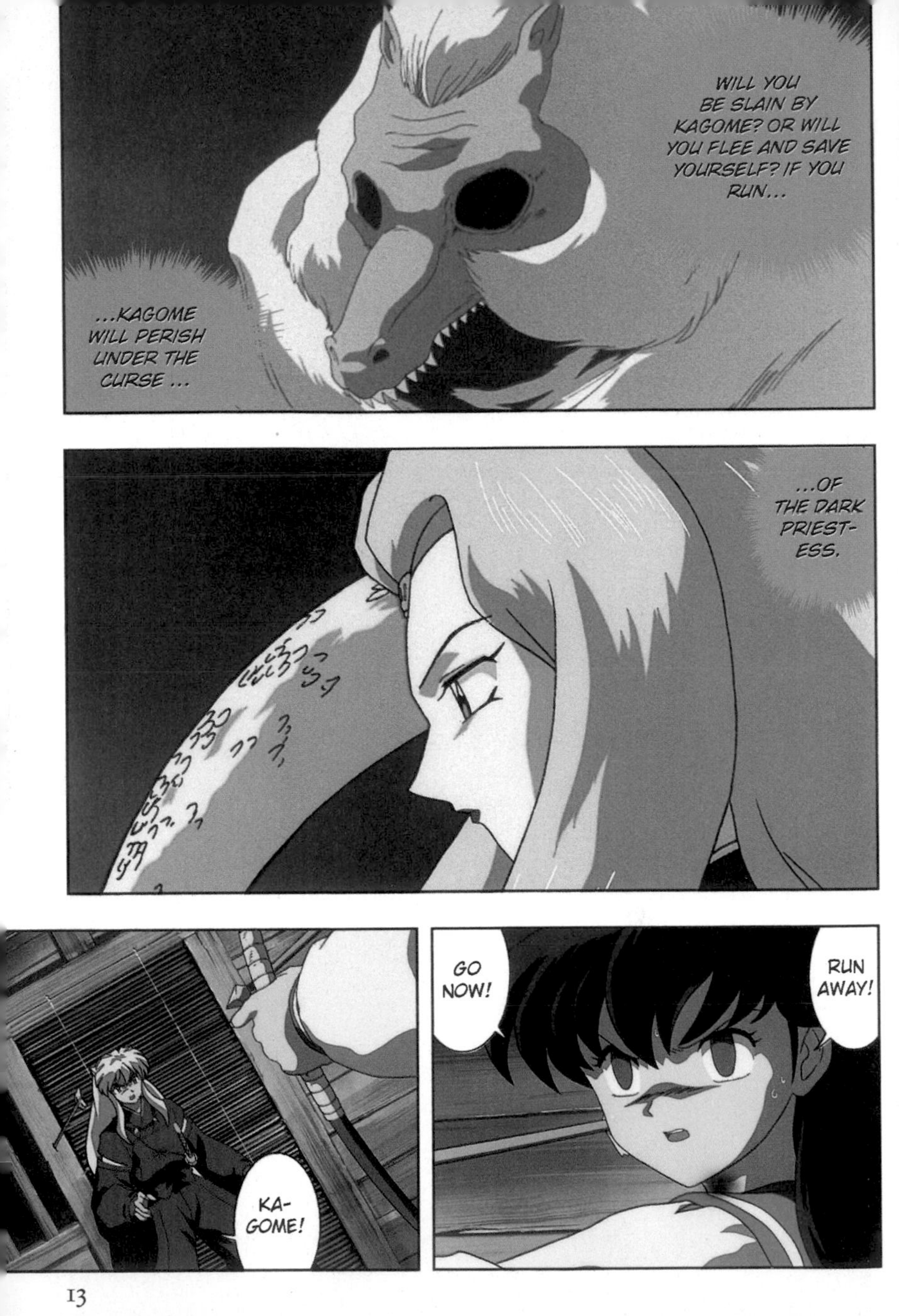
WILL YOU BE SLAIN BY KAGOME? OR WILL YOU FLEE AND SAVE YOURSELF? IF YOU RUN...
...KAGOME WILL PERISH UNDER THE CURSE ...
...OF THE DARK PRIEST-ESS.
RUN AWAY!
GO NOW!
KA-GOME!

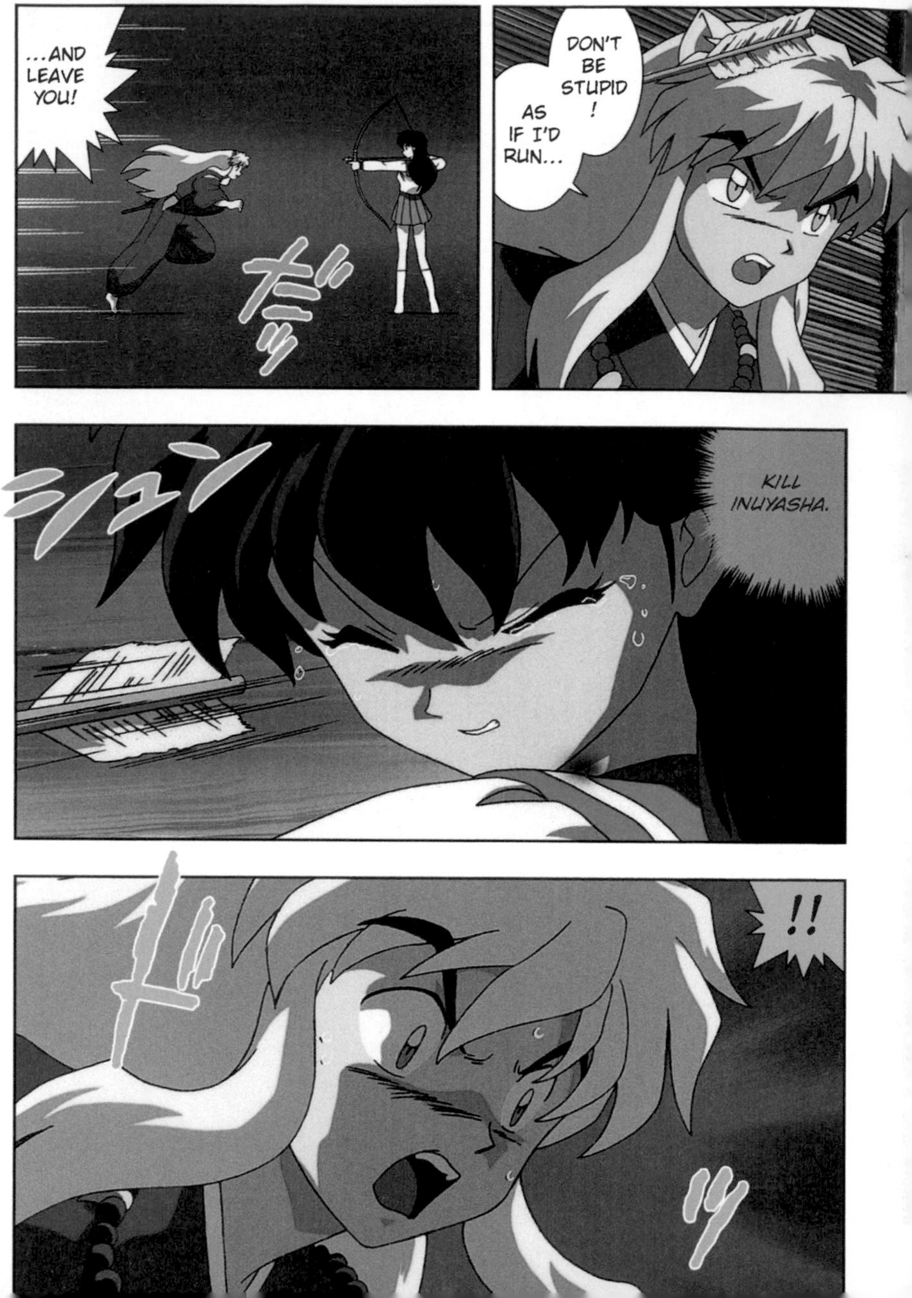
DON'T BE STUPID!
AS IF I'D RUN...
...AND LEAVE YOU!
だッ
シュン
KILL INUYASHA.
!!

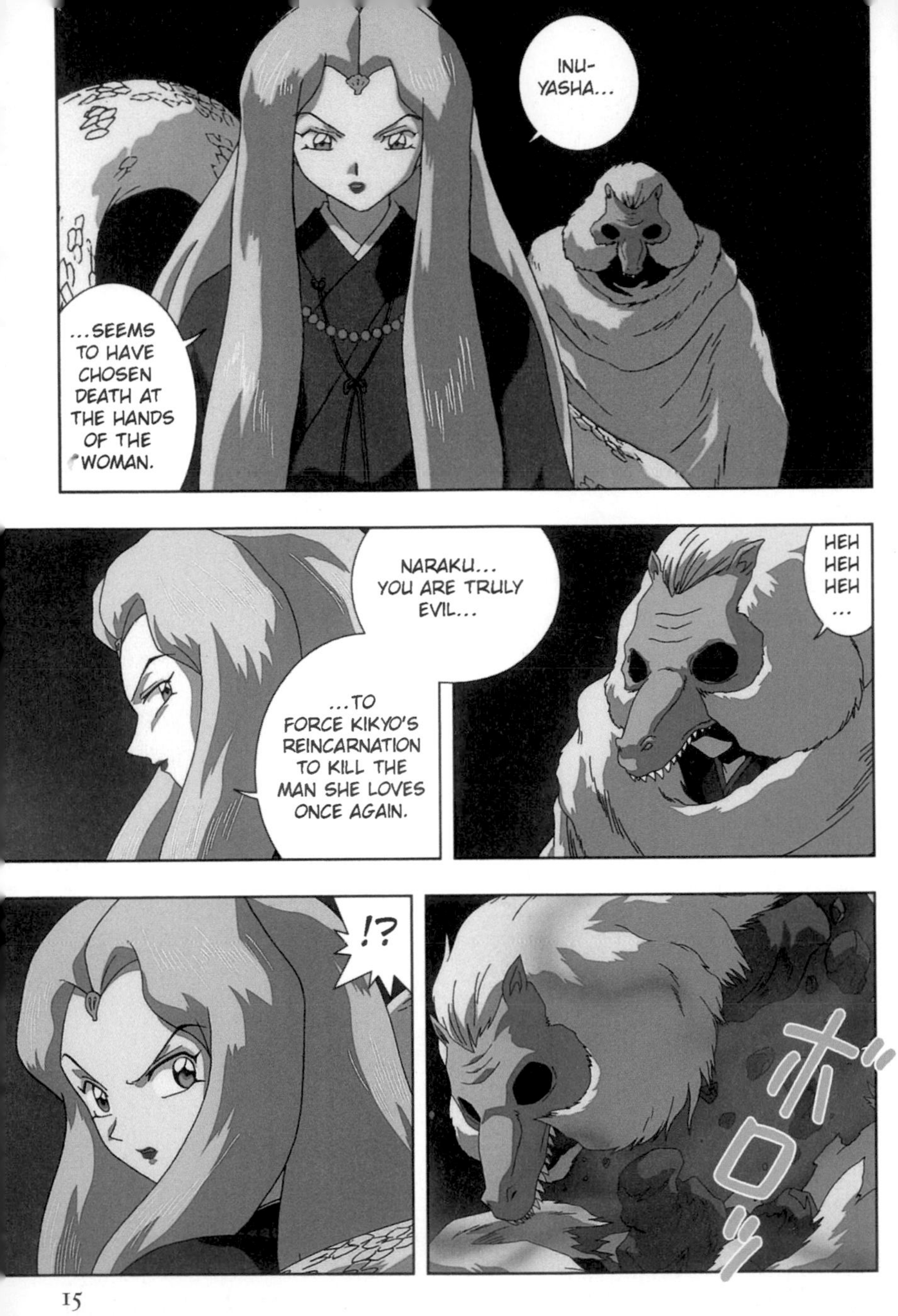
INU-YASHA...
...SEEMS TO HAVE CHOSEN DEATH AT THE HANDS OF THE WOMAN.
HEH HEH HEH ...
NARAKU... YOU ARE TRULY EVIL...
...TO FORCE KIKYO'S REINCARNATION TO KILL THE MAN SHE LOVES ONCE AGAIN.
ボロッ
!?

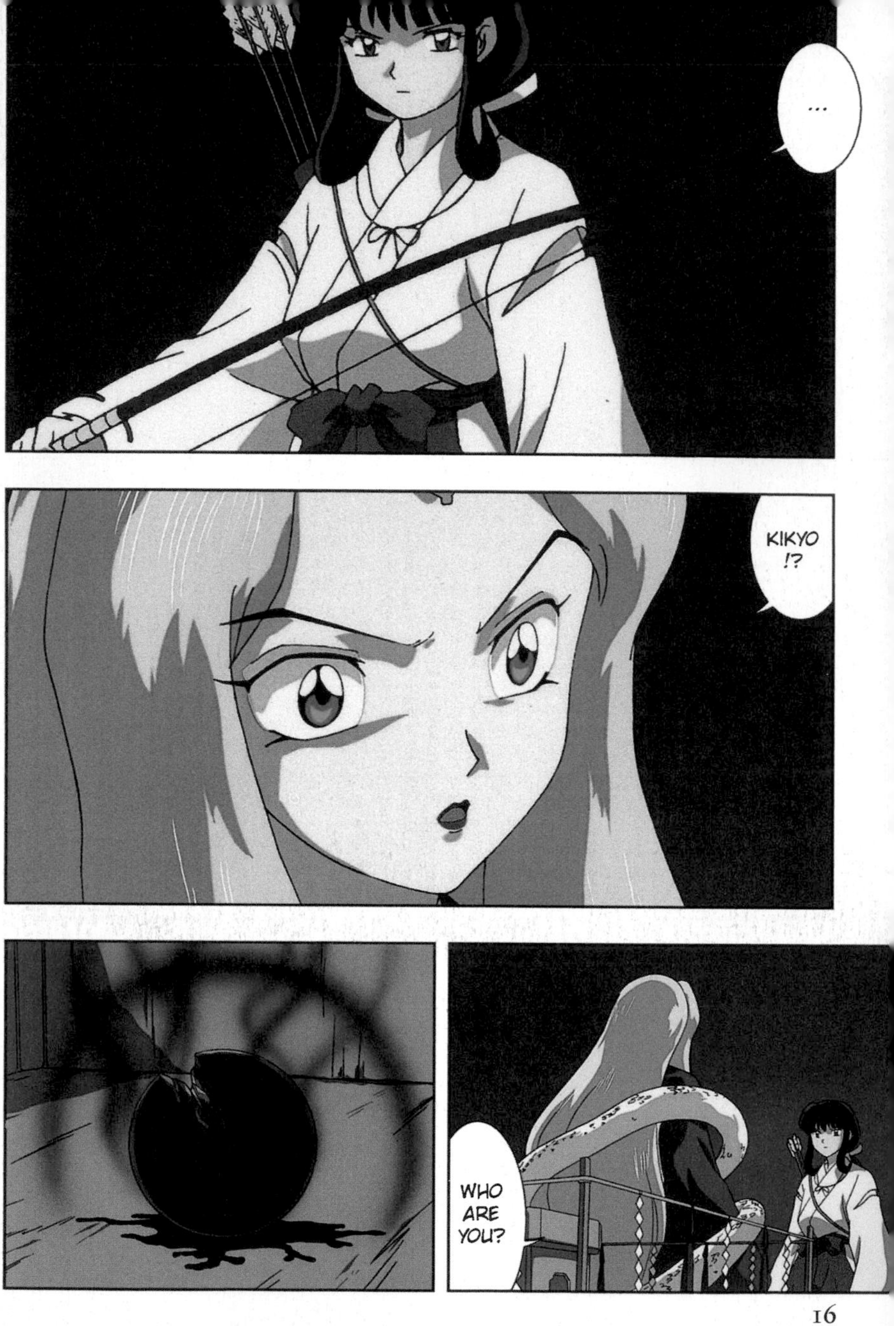
...
KIKYO !?
WHO ARE YOU?

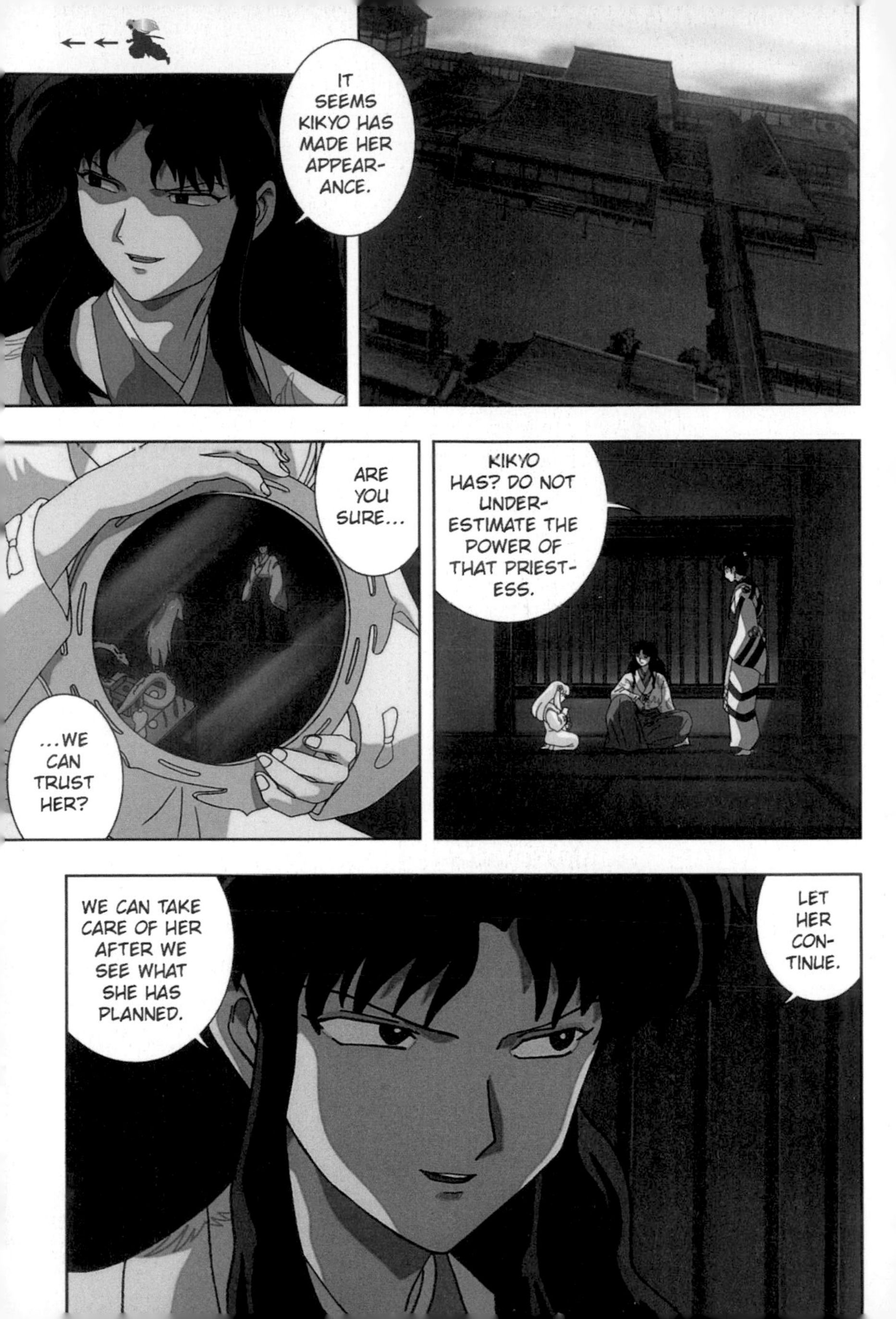
IT SEEMS KIKYO HAS MADE HER APPEARANCE.
KIKYO HAS? DO NOT UNDER-ESTIMATE THE POWER OF THAT PRIEST-ESS.
ARE YOU SURE...
...WE CAN TRUST HER?
LET HER CON-TINUE.
WE CAN TAKE CARE OF HER AFTER WE SEE WHAT SHE HAS PLANNED.

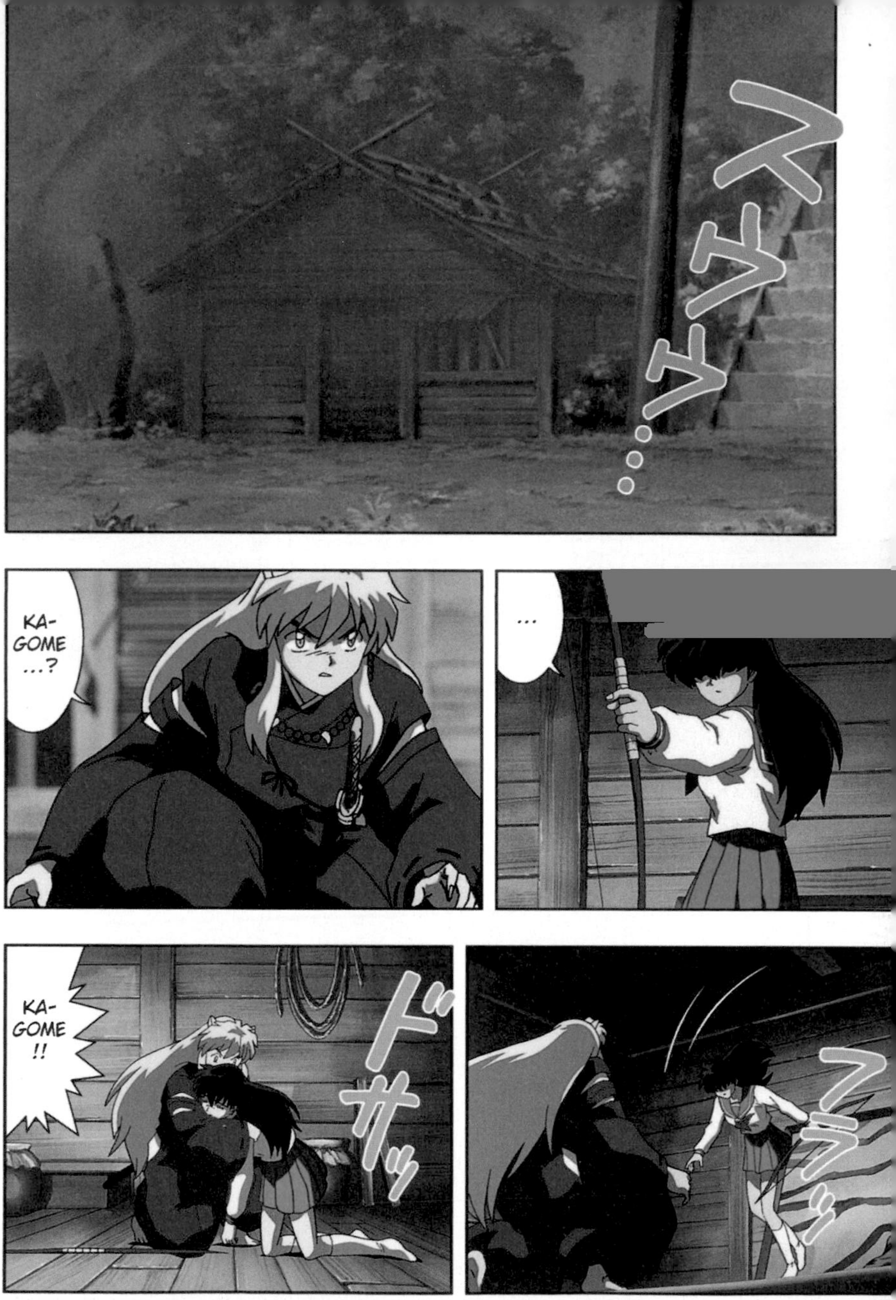
スェェ…
...
KA-GOME ...?
フラッ
ドサッ
KA-GOME !!

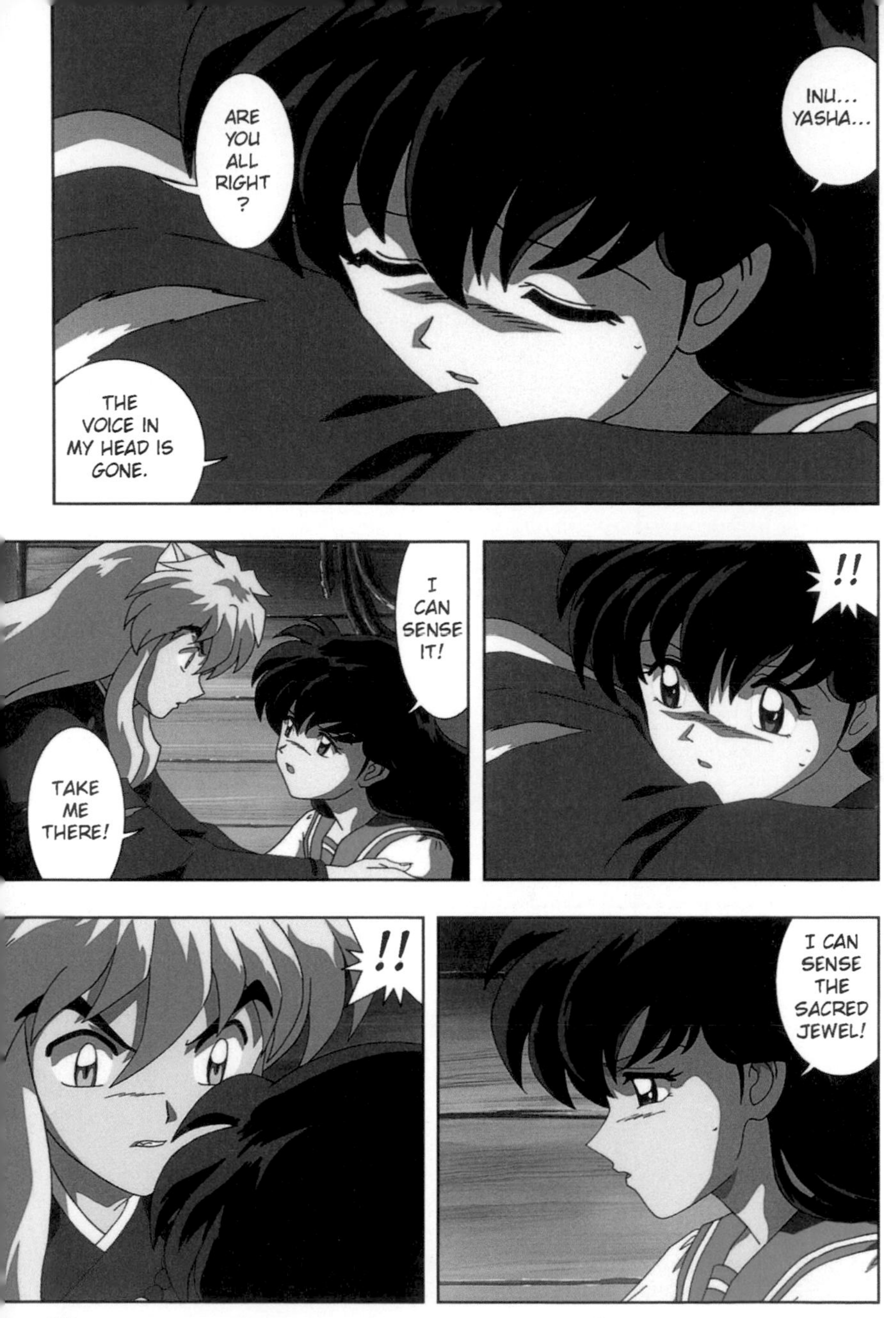
INU... YASHA...
ARE YOU ALL RIGHT?
THE VOICE IN MY HEAD IS GONE.
!!
I CAN SENSE IT!
TAKE ME THERE!
I CAN SENSE THE SACRED JEWEL!
!!

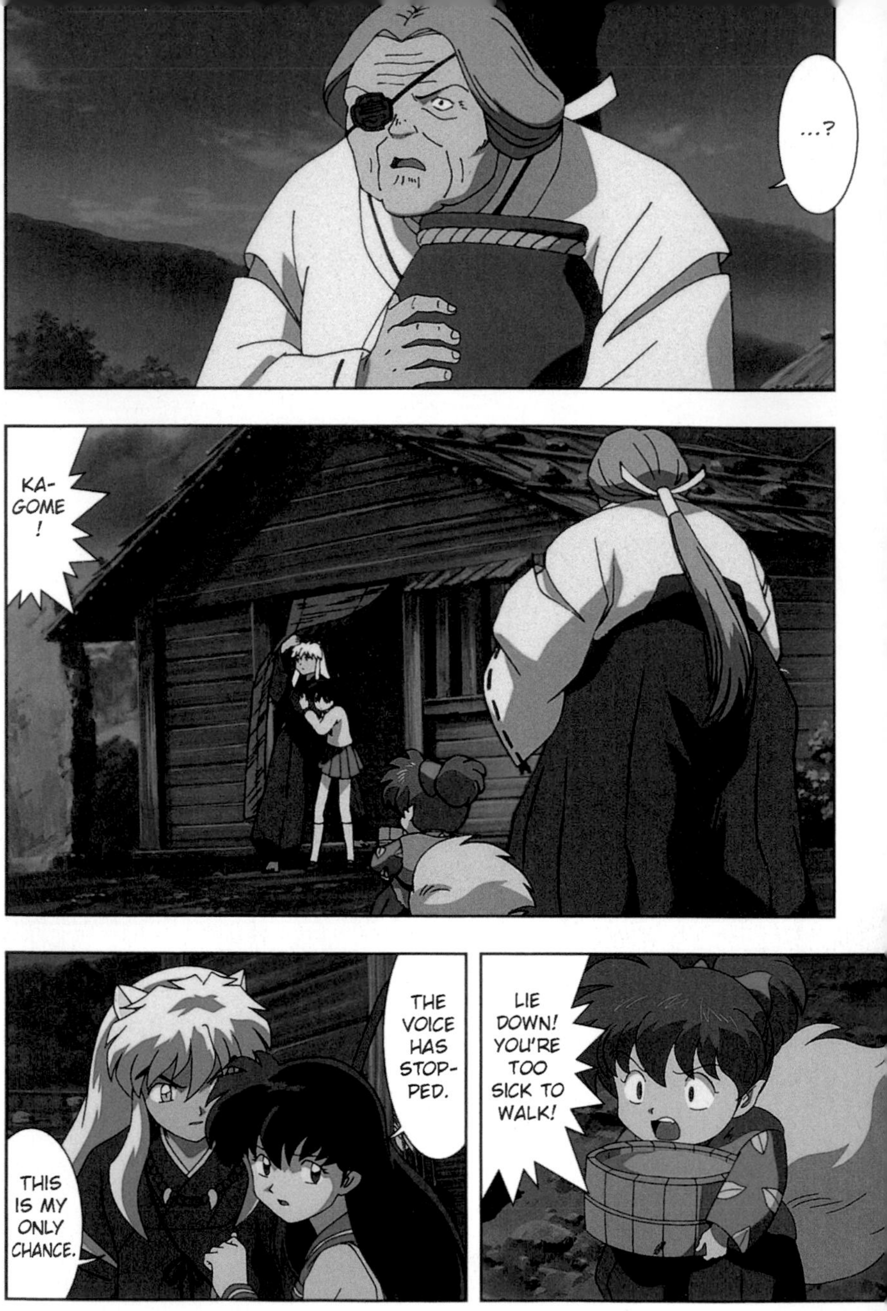
...?
KA-GOME!
LIE DOWN! YOU'RE TOO SICK TO WALK!
THE VOICE HAS STOP-PED.
THIS IS MY ONLY CHANCE.

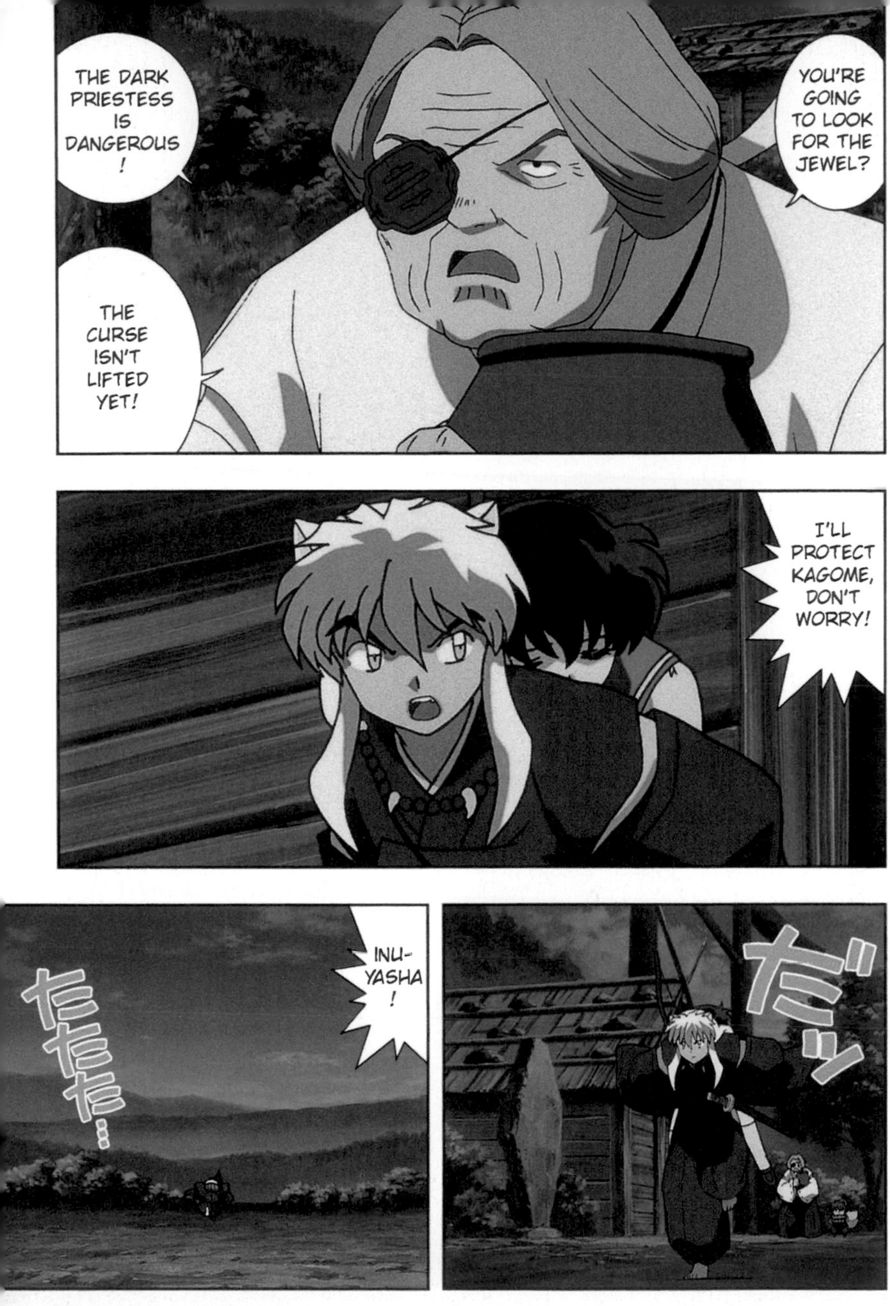
YOU'RE GOING TO LOOK FOR THE JEWEL?
THE DARK PRIESTESS IS DANGEROUS!
THE CURSE ISN'T LIFTED YET!
I'LL PROTECT KAGOME, DON'T WORRY!
だッ
INU-YASHA!
たたた…

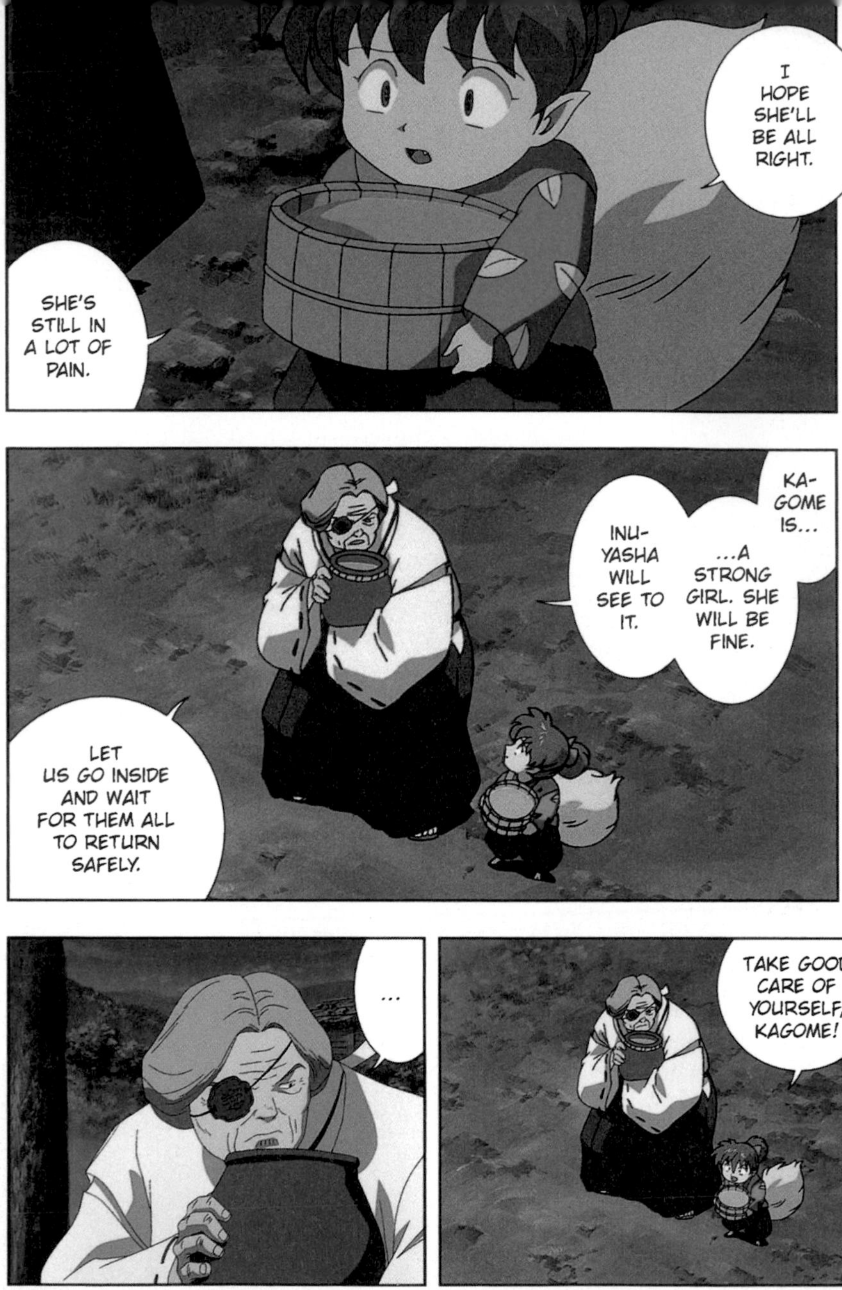
I HOPE SHE'LL BE ALL RIGHT.
SHE'S STILL IN A LOT OF PAIN.
KA-GOME IS...
...A STRONG GIRL. SHE WILL BE FINE.
INU-YASHA WILL SEE TO IT.
LET US GO INSIDE AND WAIT FOR THEM ALL TO RETURN SAFELY.
TAKE GOOD CARE OF YOURSELF, KAGOME!
...

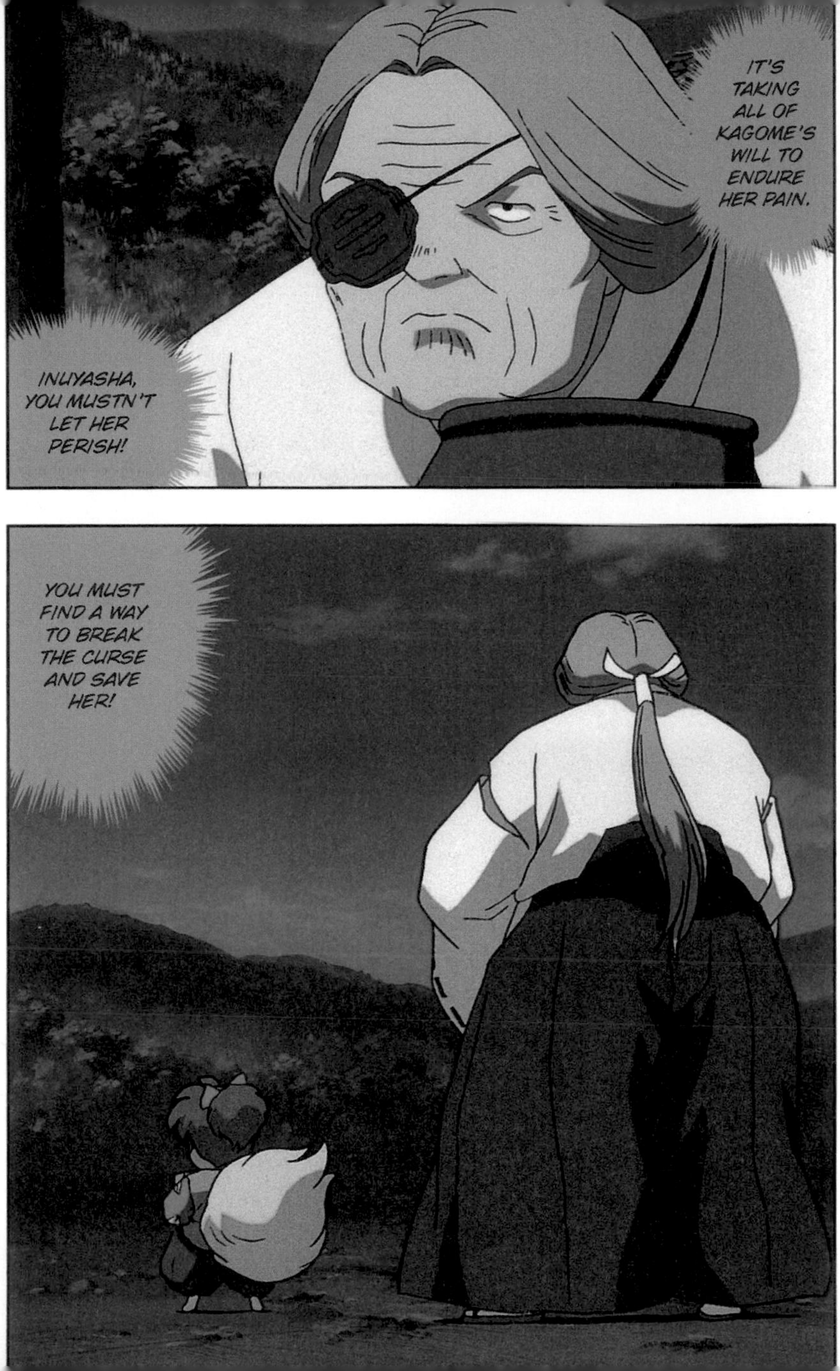
IT'S TAKING ALL OF KAGOME'S WILL TO ENDURE HER PAIN.
INUYASHA, YOU MUSTN'T LET HER PERISH!
YOU MUST FIND A WAY TO BREAK THE CURSE AND SAVE HER!

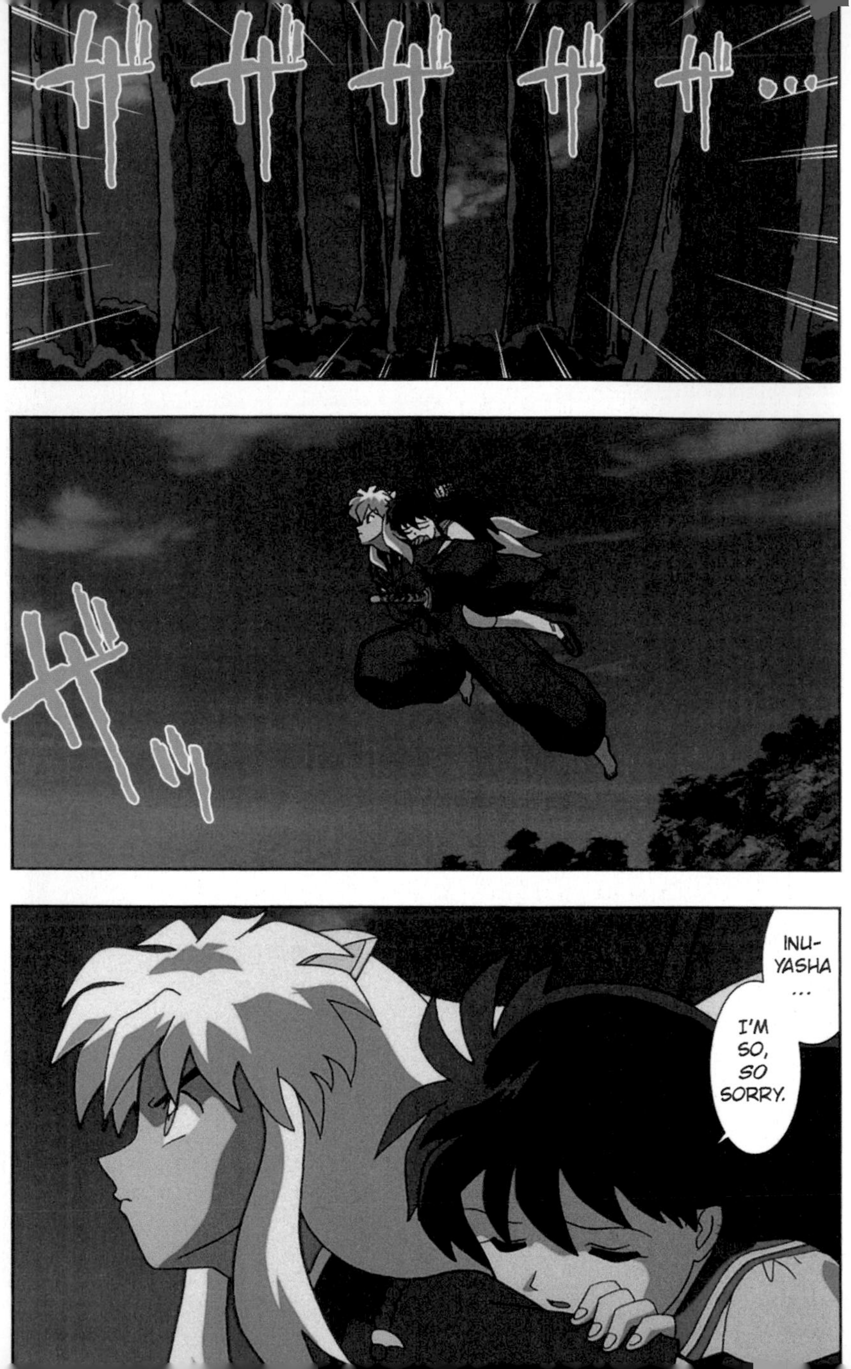
ザザザザザ…
ザッ
INU-YASHA...
I'M SO, SO SORRY.

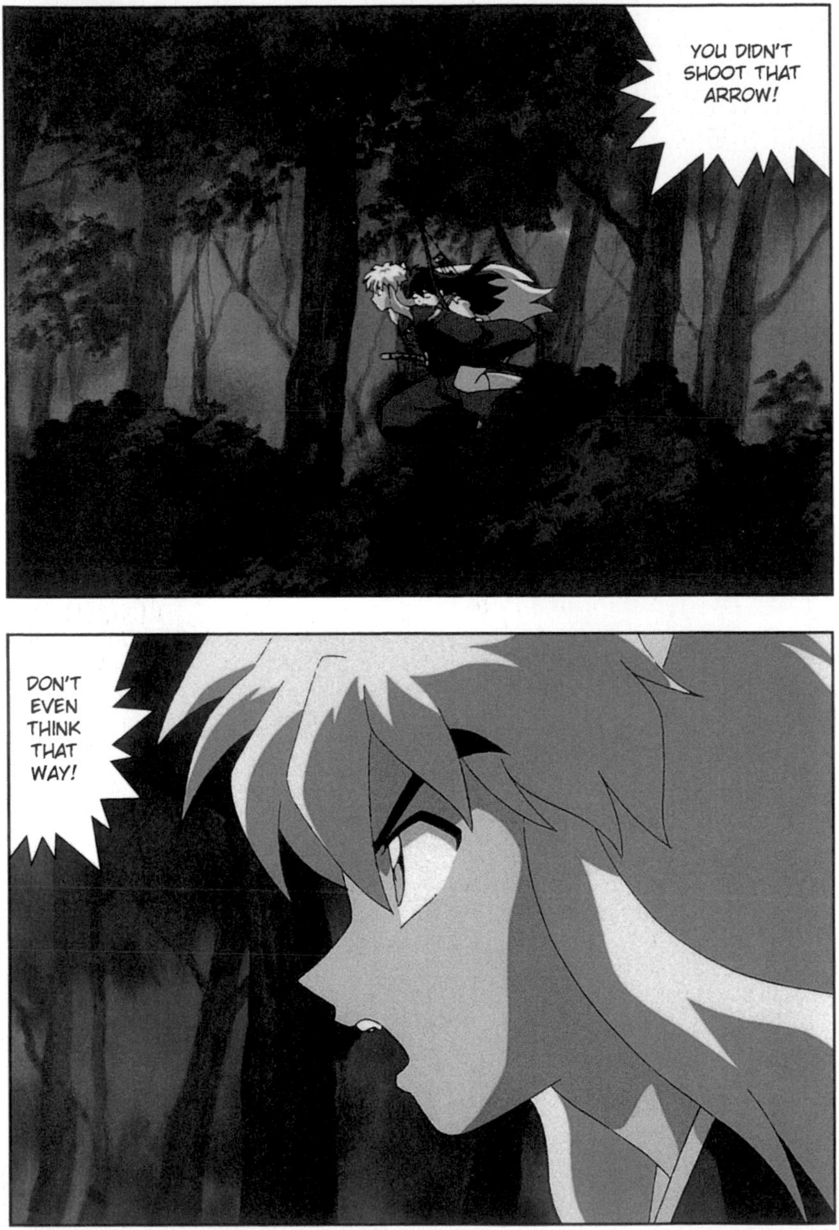
YOU DIDN'T SHOOT THAT ARROW!
DON'T EVEN THINK THAT WAY!

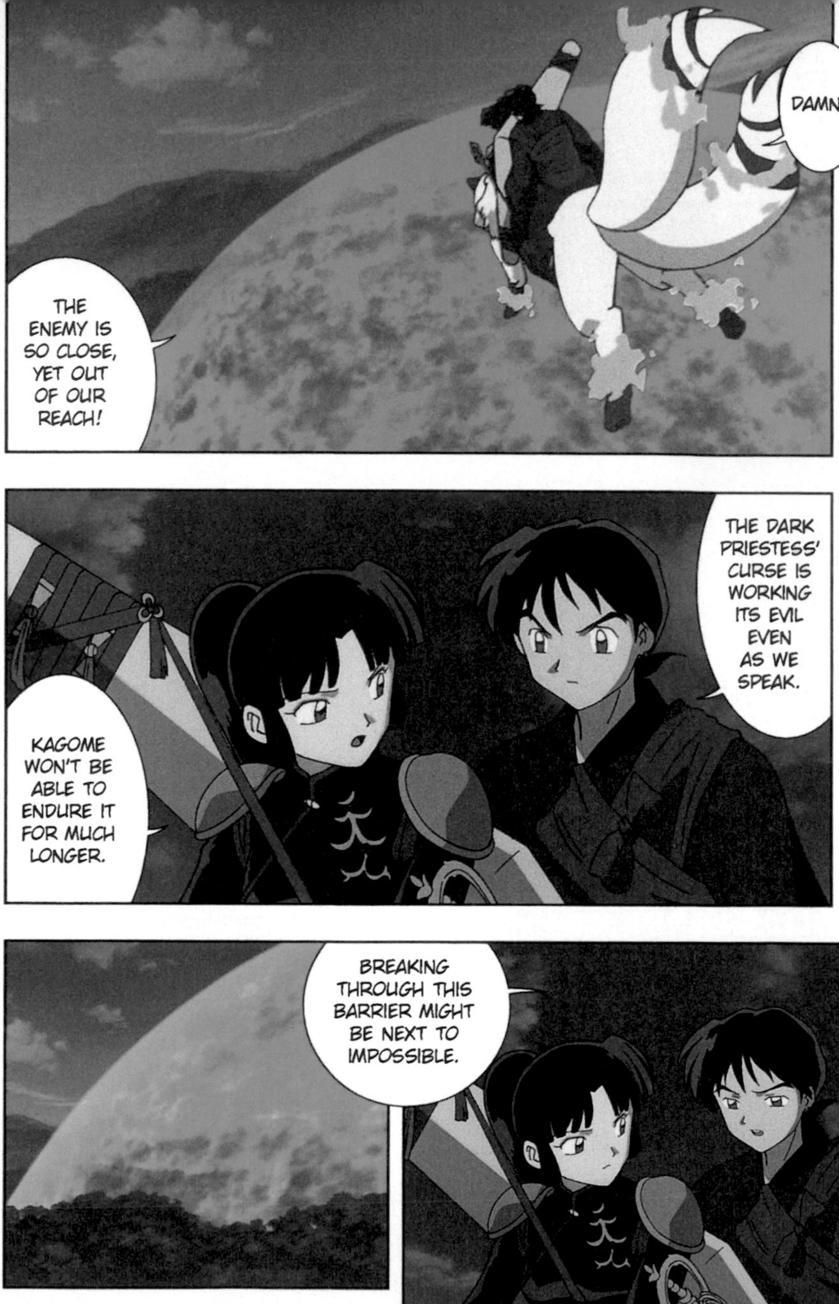
DAMN!
THE ENEMY IS SO CLOSE, YET OUT OF OUR REACH!
THE DARK PRIESTESS' CURSE IS WORKING ITS EVIL EVEN AS WE SPEAK.
KAGOME WON'T BE ABLE TO ENDURE IT FOR MUCH LONGER.
BREAKING THROUGH THIS BARRIER MIGHT BE NEXT TO IMPOSSIBLE.

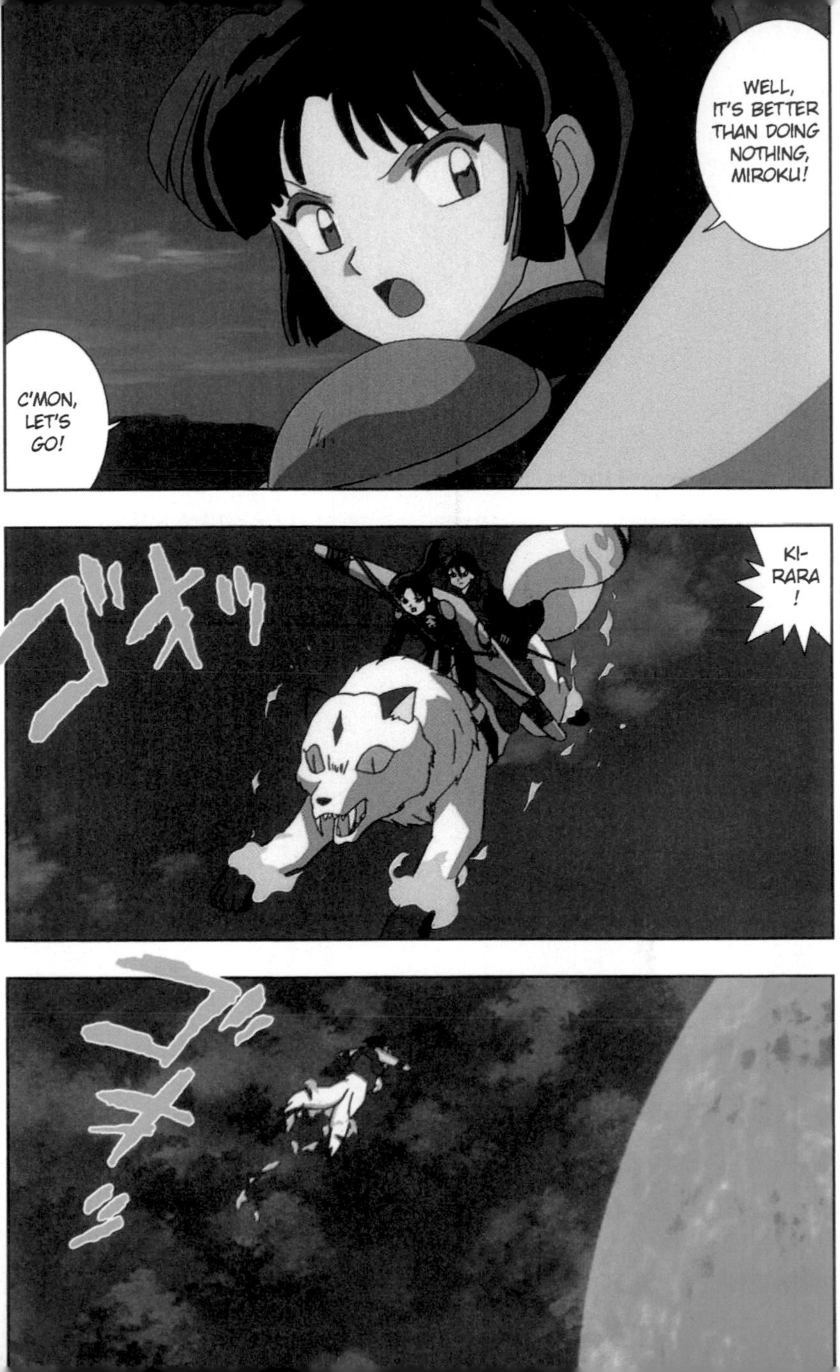
WELL, IT'S BETTER THAN DOING NOTHING, MIROKU!
C'MON, LET'S GO!
KI-RARA!
ゴオッ

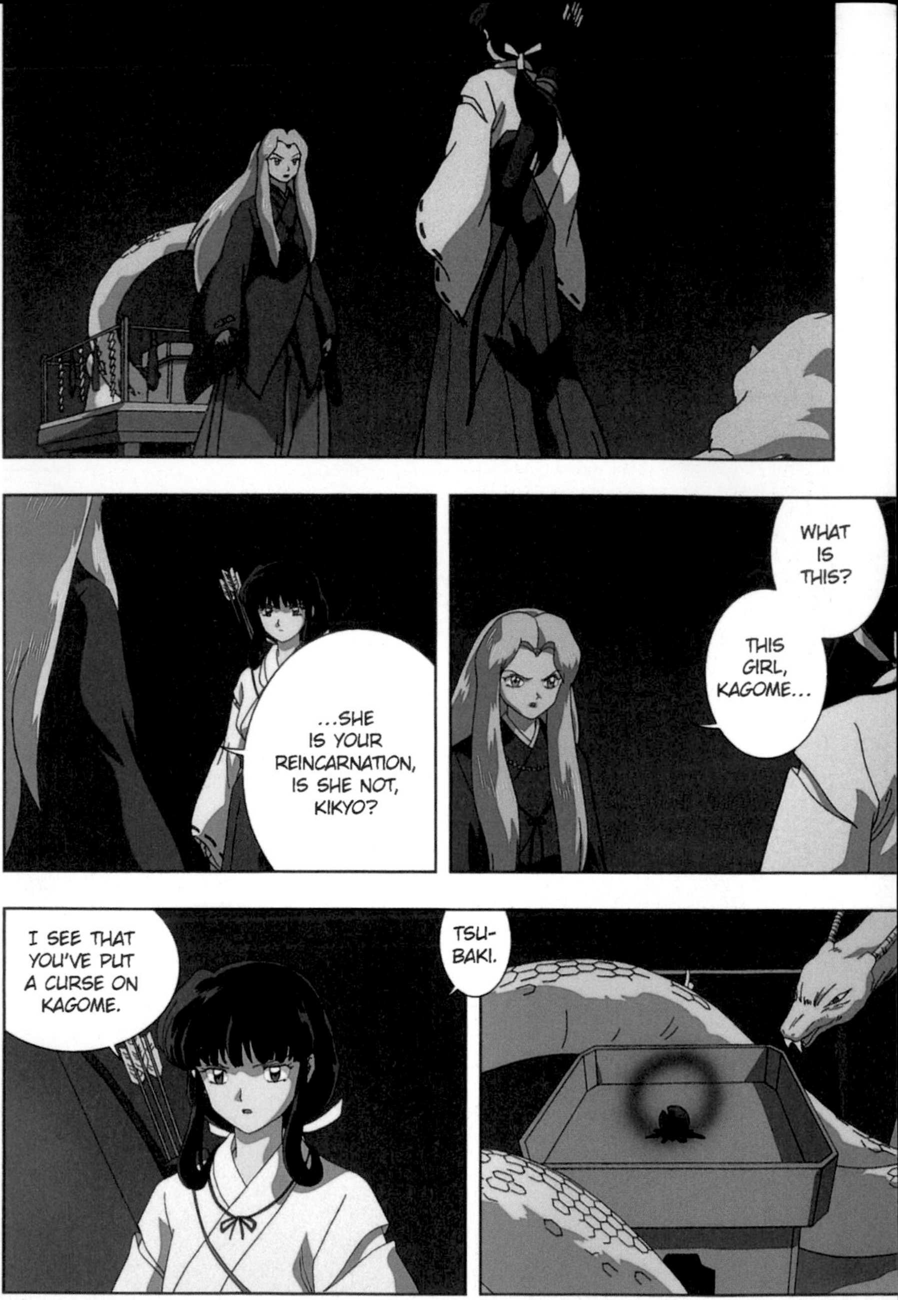
WHAT IS THIS?
THIS GIRL, KAGOME...
...SHE IS YOUR REINCARNATION, IS SHE NOT, KIKYO?
TSU-BAKI.
I SEE THAT YOU'VE PUT A CURSE ON KAGOME.

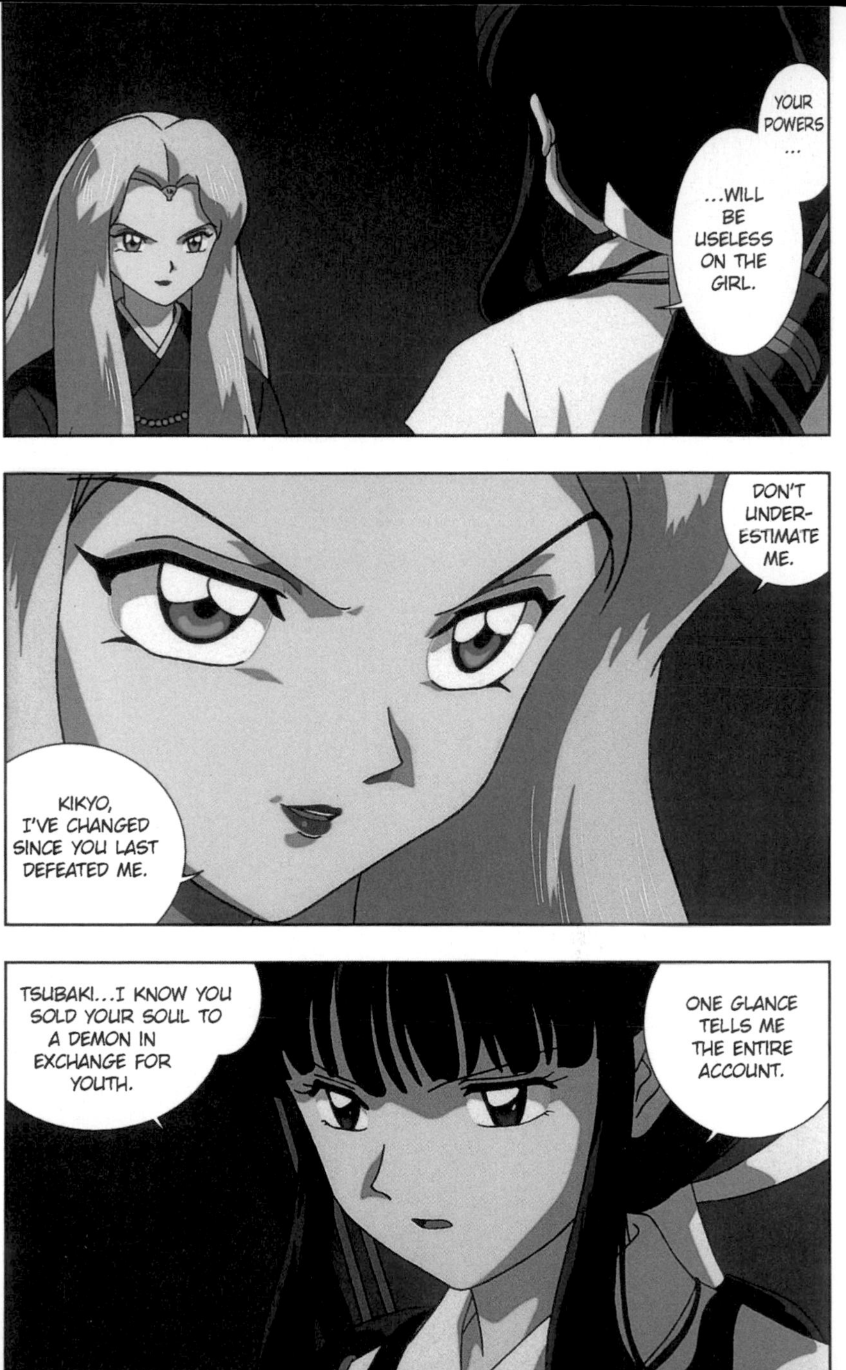
YOUR POWERS ...
...WILL BE USELESS ON THE GIRL.
DON'T UNDER-ESTIMATE ME.
KIKYO, I'VE CHANGED SINCE YOU LAST DEFEATED ME.
ONE GLANCE TELLS ME THE ENTIRE ACCOUNT.
TSUBAKI...I KNOW YOU SOLD YOUR SOUL TO A DEMON IN EXCHANGE FOR YOUTH.

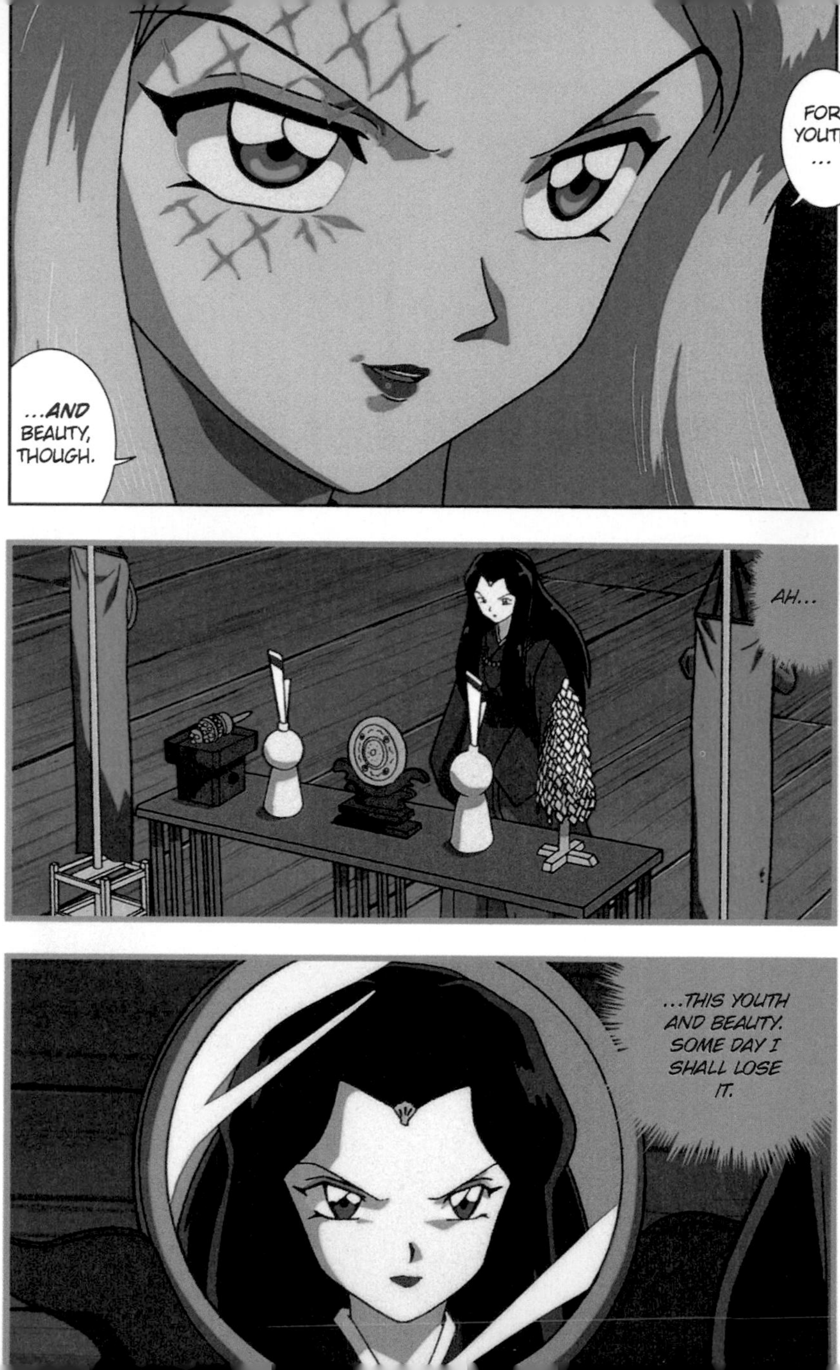
FOR YOUTH ...
...AND BEAUTY, THOUGH.
AH...
...THIS YOUTH AND BEAUTY. SOME DAY I SHALL LOSE IT.

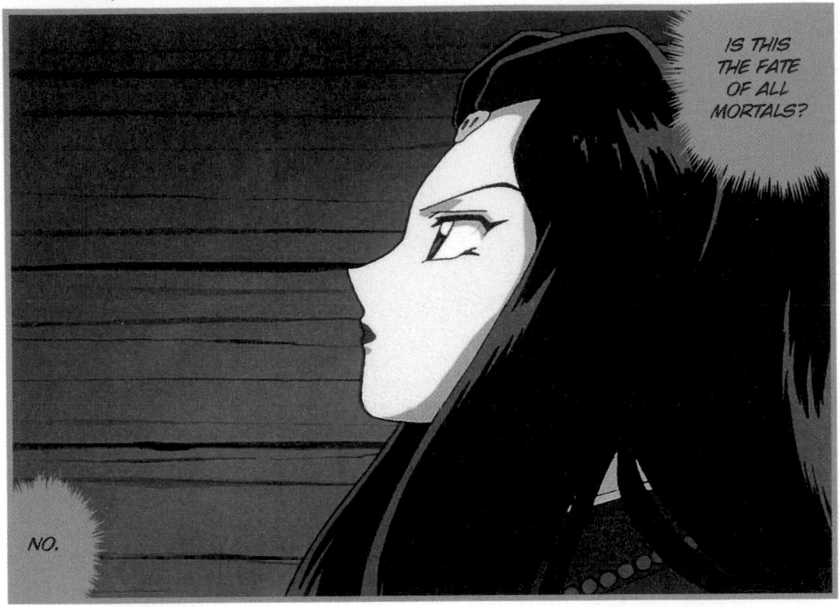
IS THIS THE FATE OF ALL MORTALS?
NO.

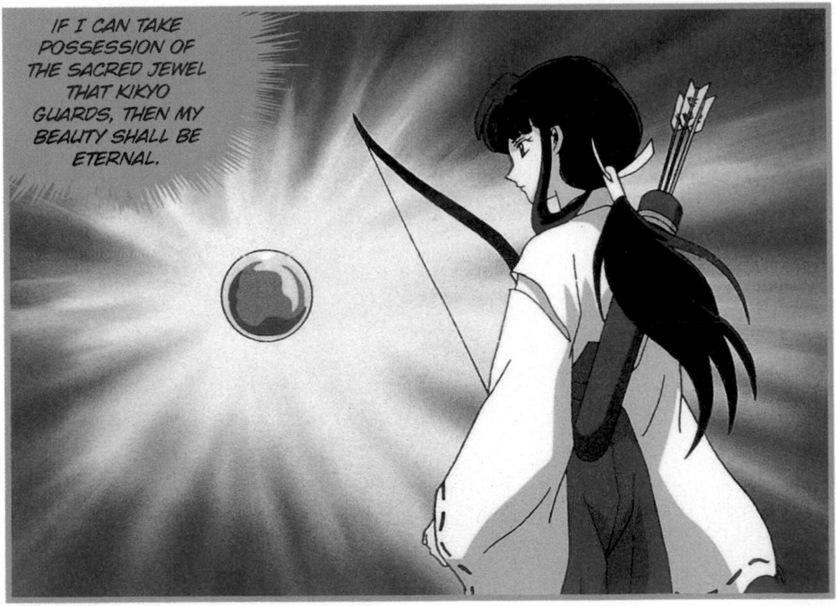
IF I CAN TAKE POSSESSION OF THE SACRED JEWEL THAT KIKYO GUARDS, THEN MY BEAUTY SHALL BE ETERNAL.

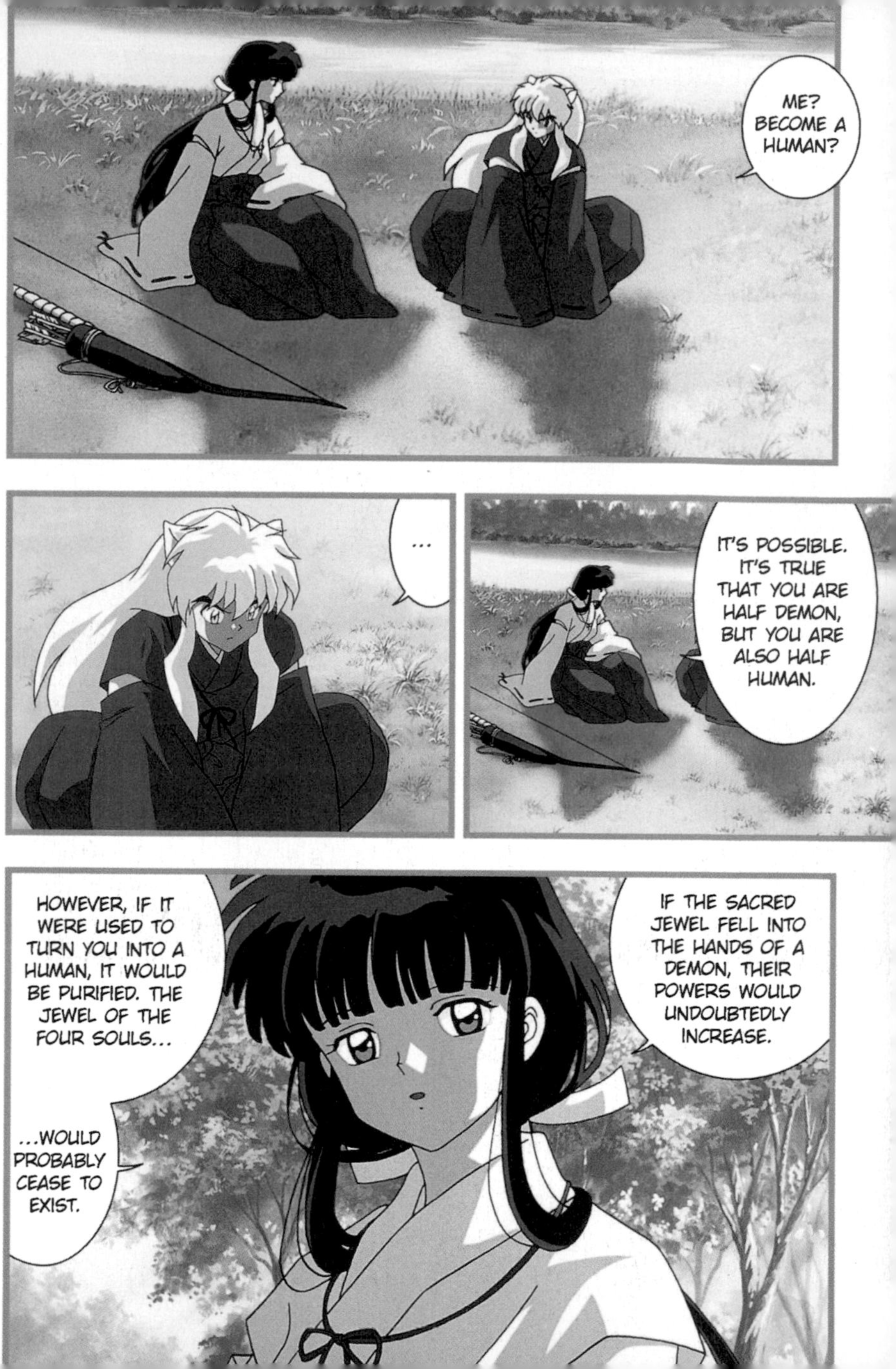
ME? BECOME A HUMAN?
IT'S POSSIBLE. IT'S TRUE THAT YOU ARE HALF DEMON, BUT YOU ARE ALSO HALF HUMAN.
...
IF THE SACRED JEWEL FELL INTO THE HANDS OF A DEMON, THEIR POWERS WOULD UNDOUBTEDLY INCREASE.
HOWEVER, IF IT WERE USED TO TURN YOU INTO A HUMAN, IT WOULD BE PURIFIED. THE JEWEL OF THE FOUR SOULS...
...WOULD PROBABLY CEASE TO EXIST.

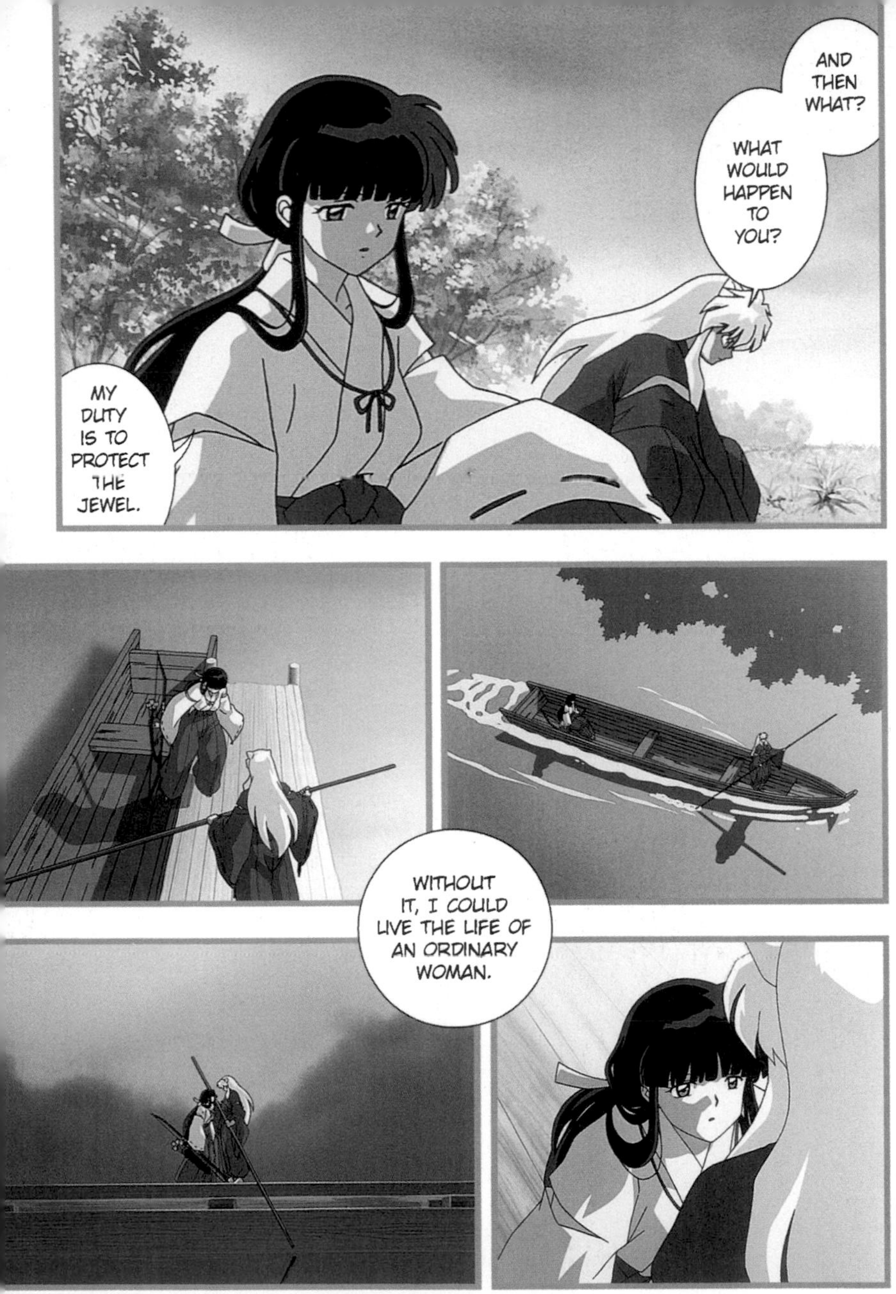
AND THEN WHAT?
WHAT WOULD HAPPEN TO YOU?
MY DUTY IS TO PROTECT THE JEWEL.
WITHOUT IT, I COULD LIVE THE LIFE OF AN ORDINARY WOMAN.

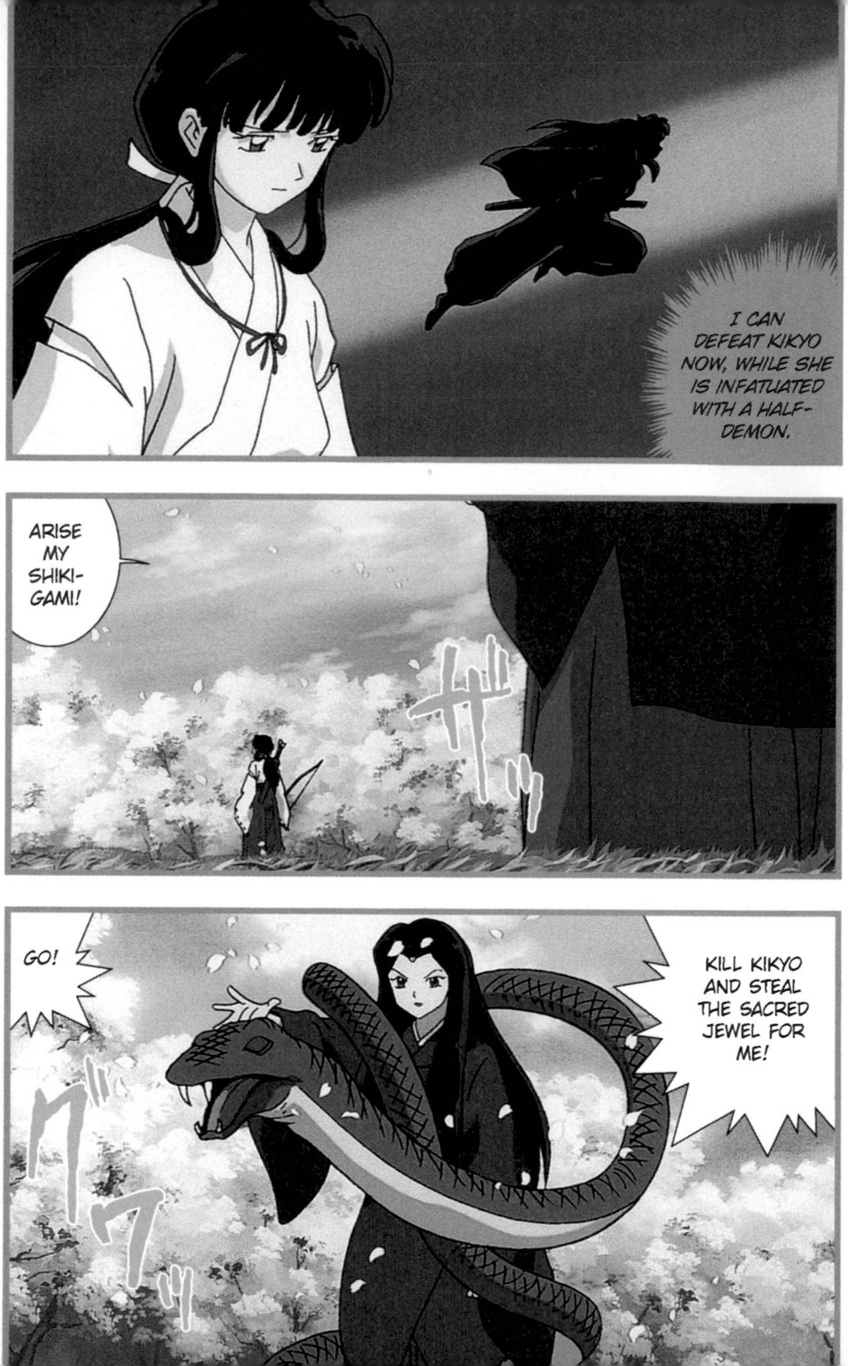
I CAN DEFEAT KIKYO NOW, WHILE SHE IS INFATUATED WITH A HALF-DEMON.
ARISE MY SHIKI-GAMI!
KILL KIKYO AND STEAL THE SACRED JEWEL FOR ME!
GO!

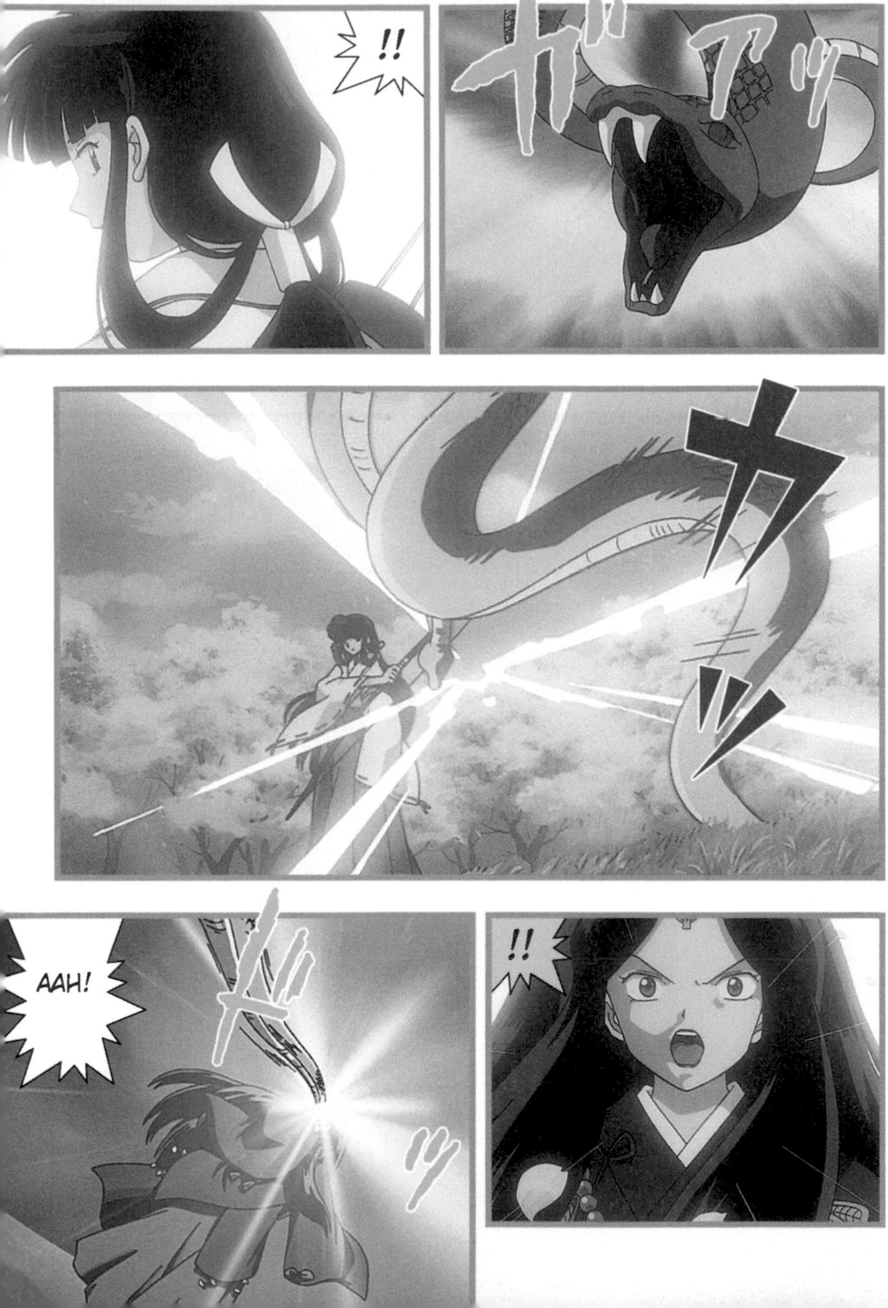
ガアッ
!!
カッ
!!
AAH!

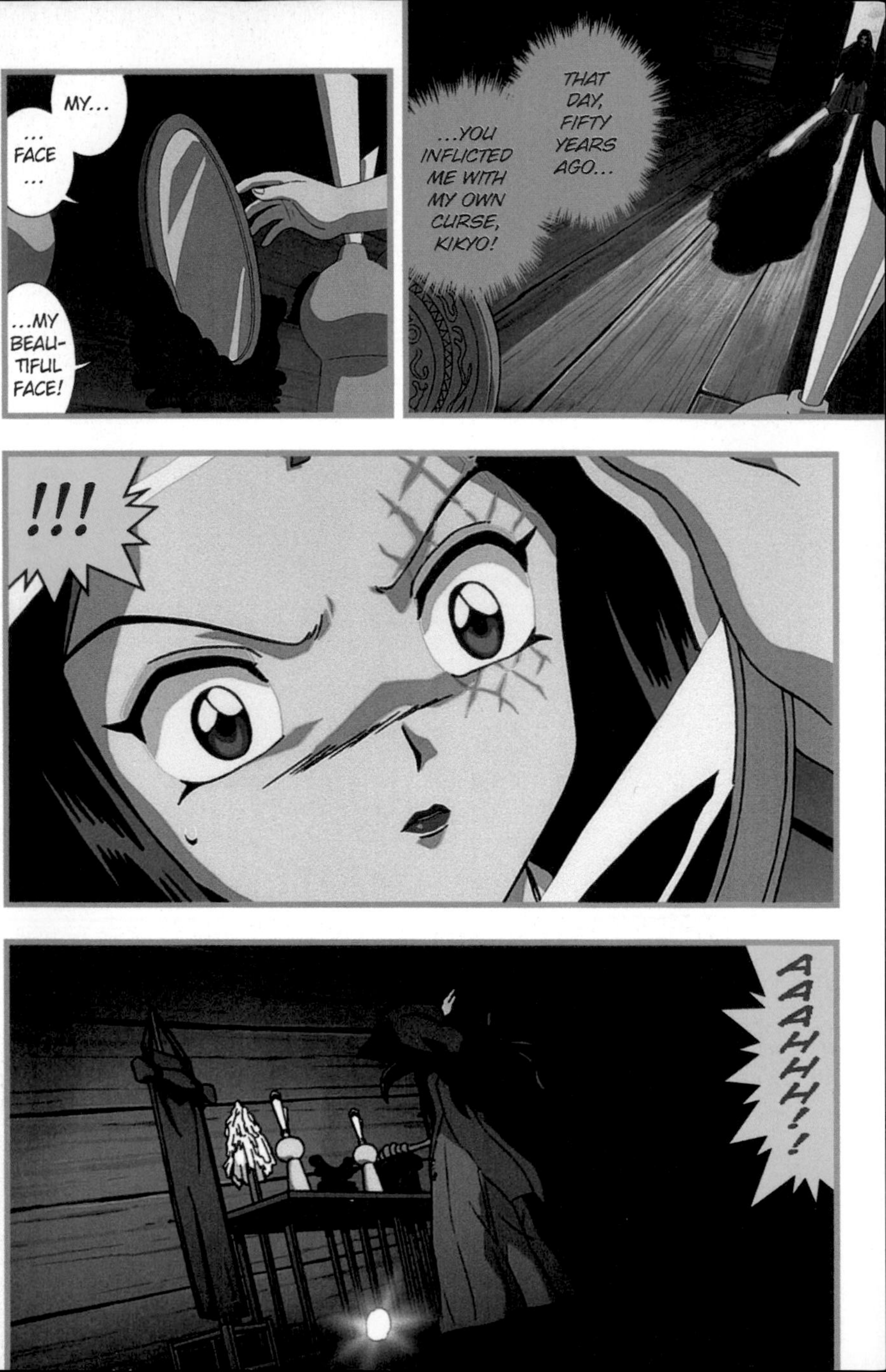
THAT DAY, FIFTY YEARS AGO...
...YOU INFLICTED ME WITH MY OWN CURSE, KIKYO!
MY...
...FACE...
...MY BEAUTIFUL FACE!
!!!
AAAHHH!!

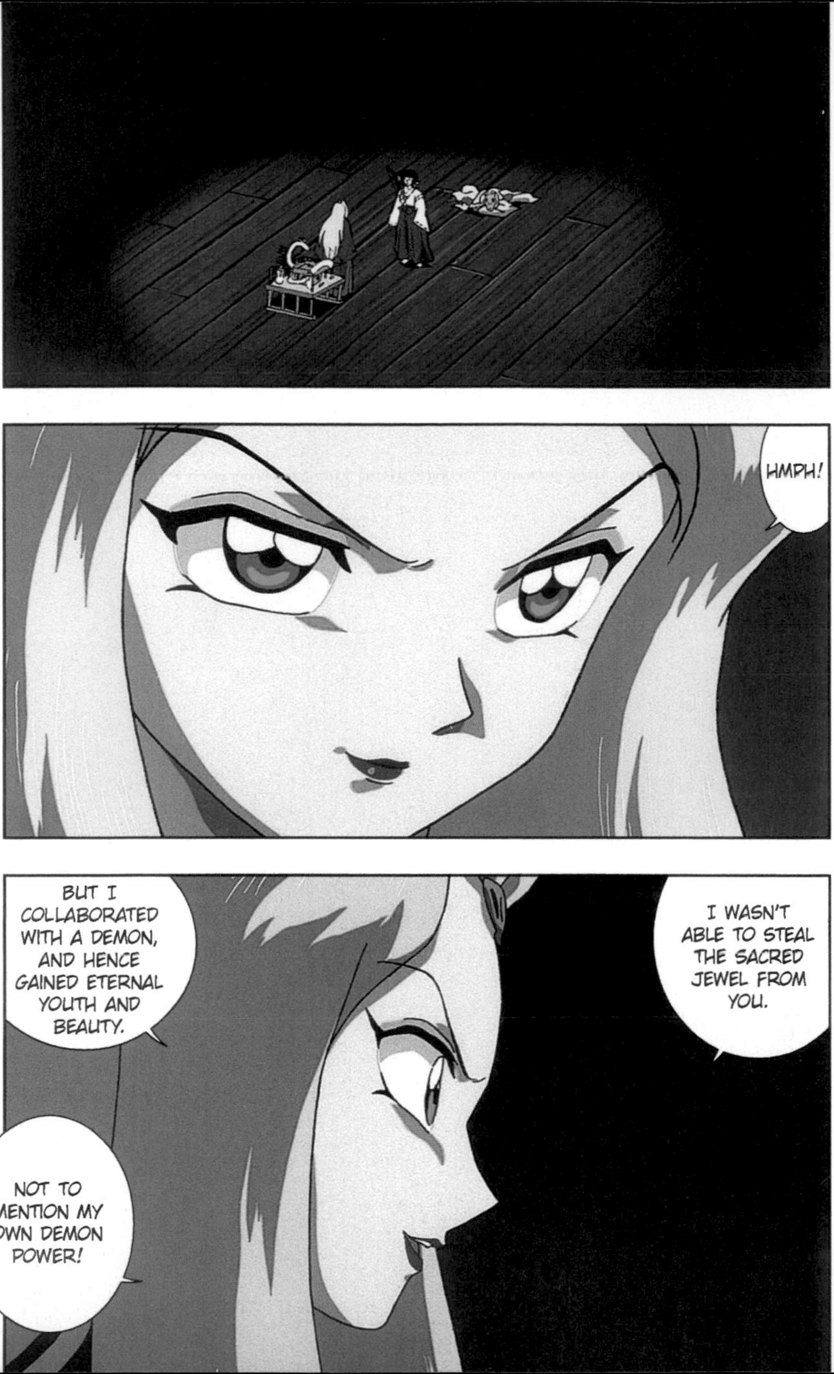
HMPH!
I WASN'T ABLE TO STEAL THE SACRED JEWEL FROM YOU.
BUT I COLLABORATED WITH A DEMON, AND HENCE GAINED ETERNAL YOUTH AND BEAUTY.
NOT TO MENTION MY OWN DEMON POWER!

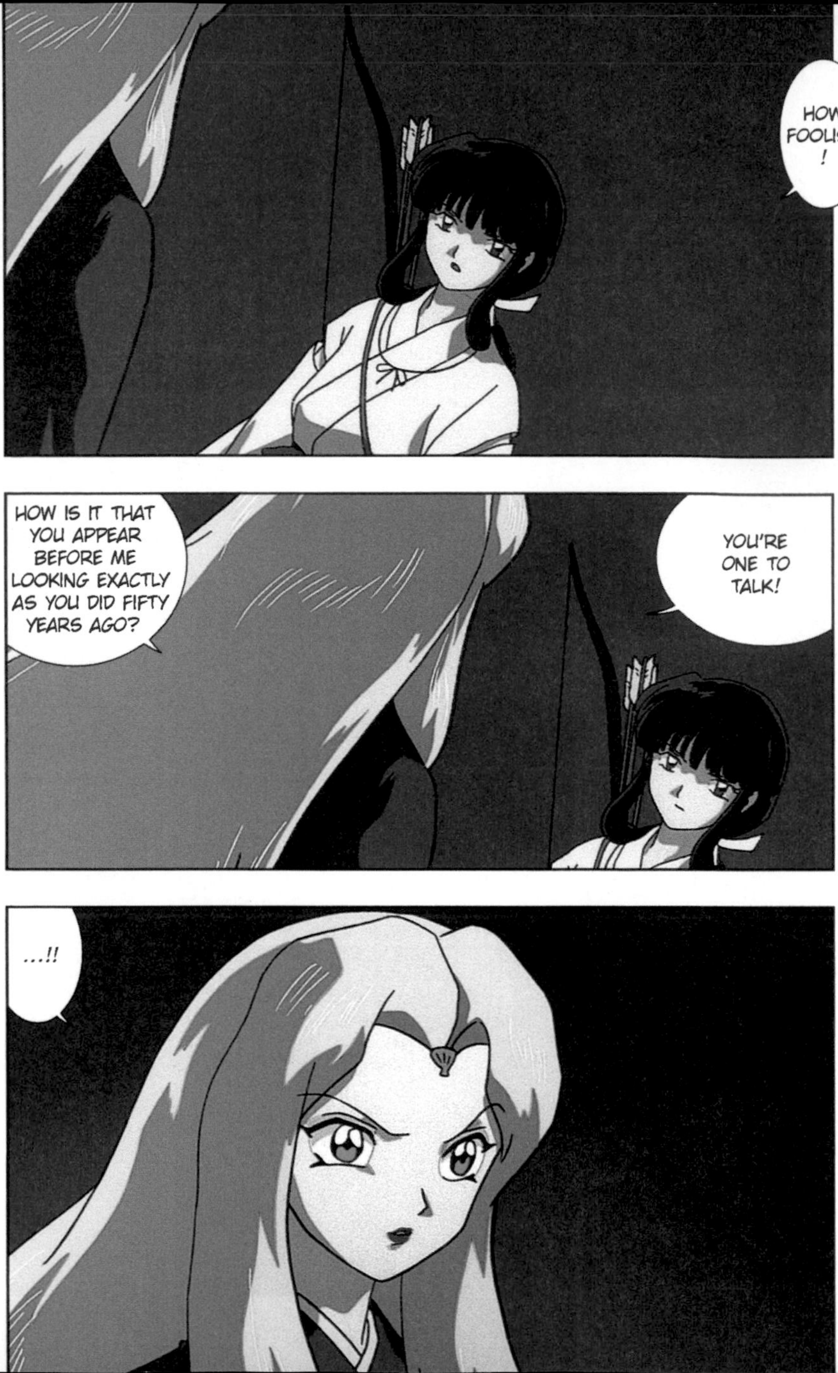
HOW FOOLISH!
HOW IS IT THAT YOU APPEAR BEFORE ME LOOKING EXACTLY AS YOU DID FIFTY YEARS AGO?
YOU'RE ONE TO TALK!
...!!

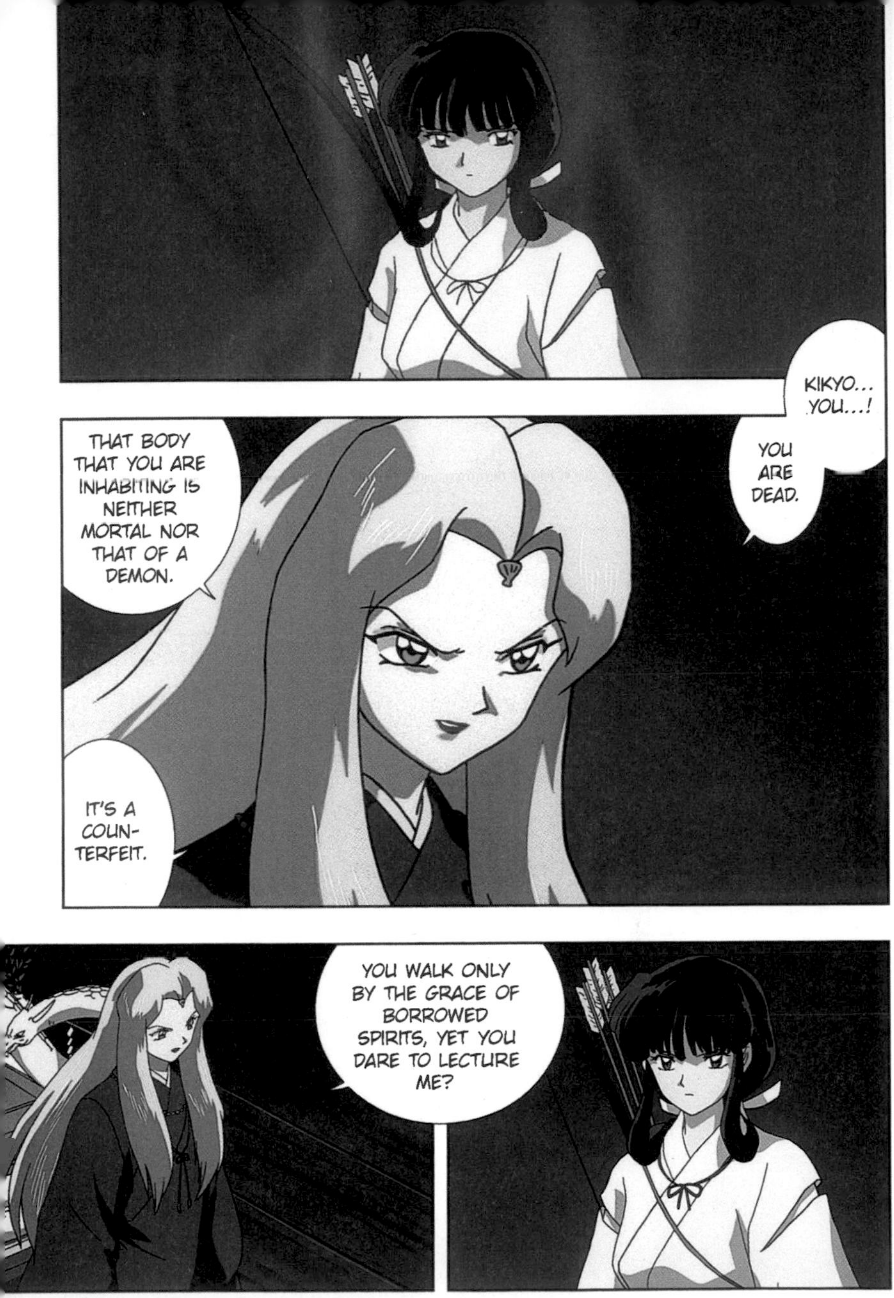
KIKYO... YOU...!
YOU ARE DEAD.
THAT BODY THAT YOU ARE INHABITING IS NEITHER MORTAL NOR THAT OF A DEMON.
IT'S A COUNTERFEIT.
YOU WALK ONLY BY THE GRACE OF BORROWED SPIRITS, YET YOU DARE TO LECTURE ME?

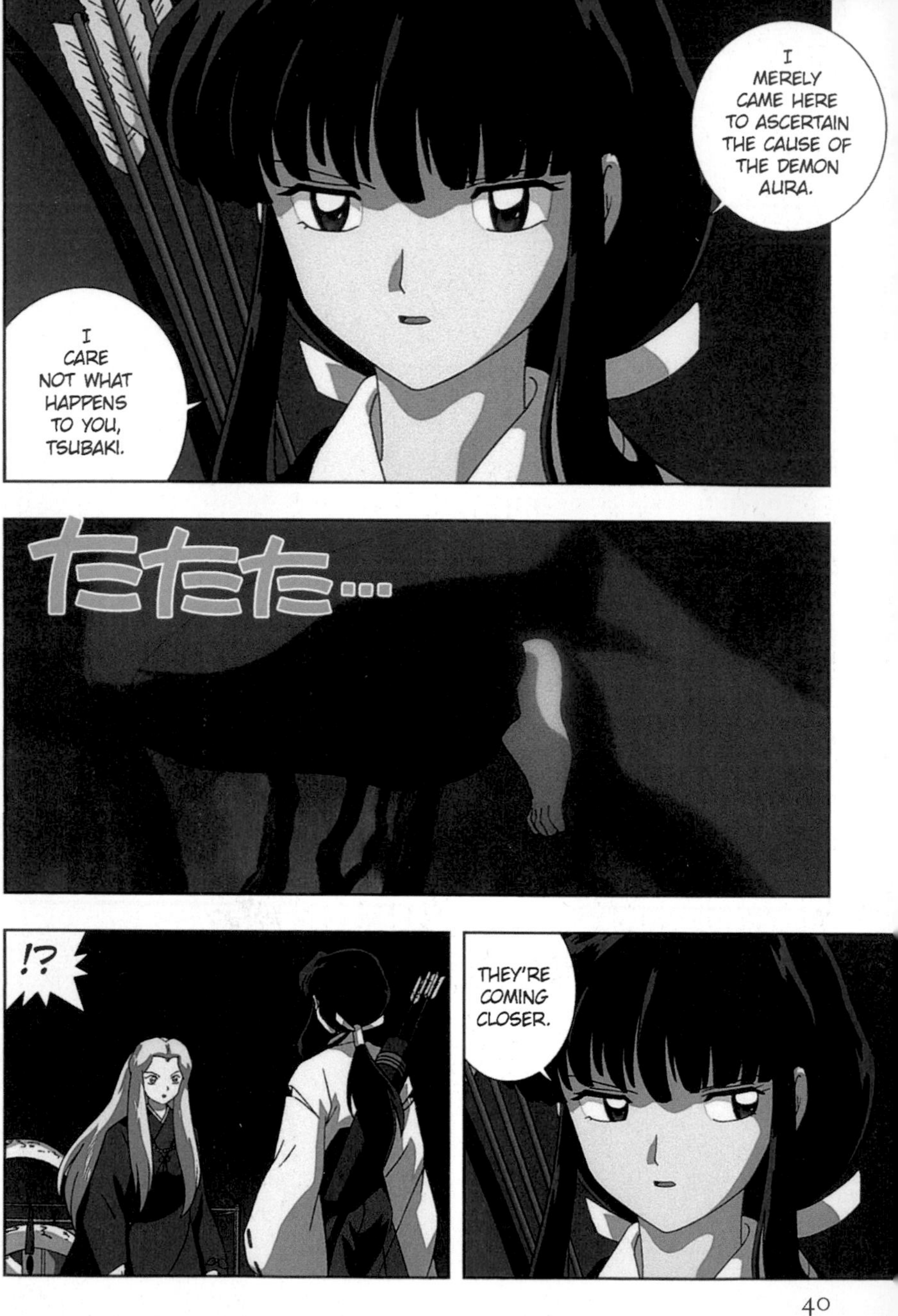
I MERELY CAME HERE TO ASCERTAIN THE CAUSE OF THE DEMON AURA.
I CARE NOT WHAT HAPPENS TO YOU, TSUBAKI.
たたたた...
THEY'RE COMING CLOSER.
!?

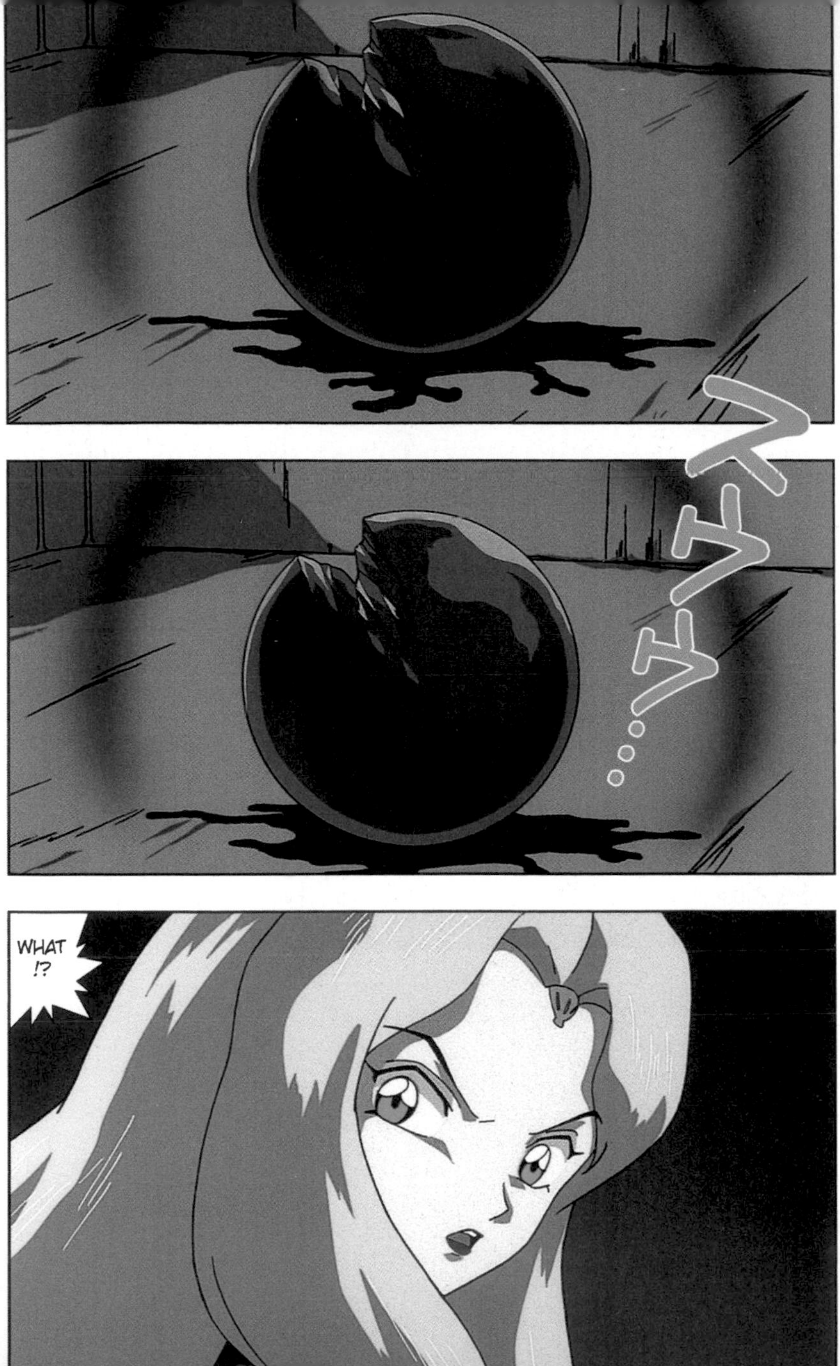
WHAT !?

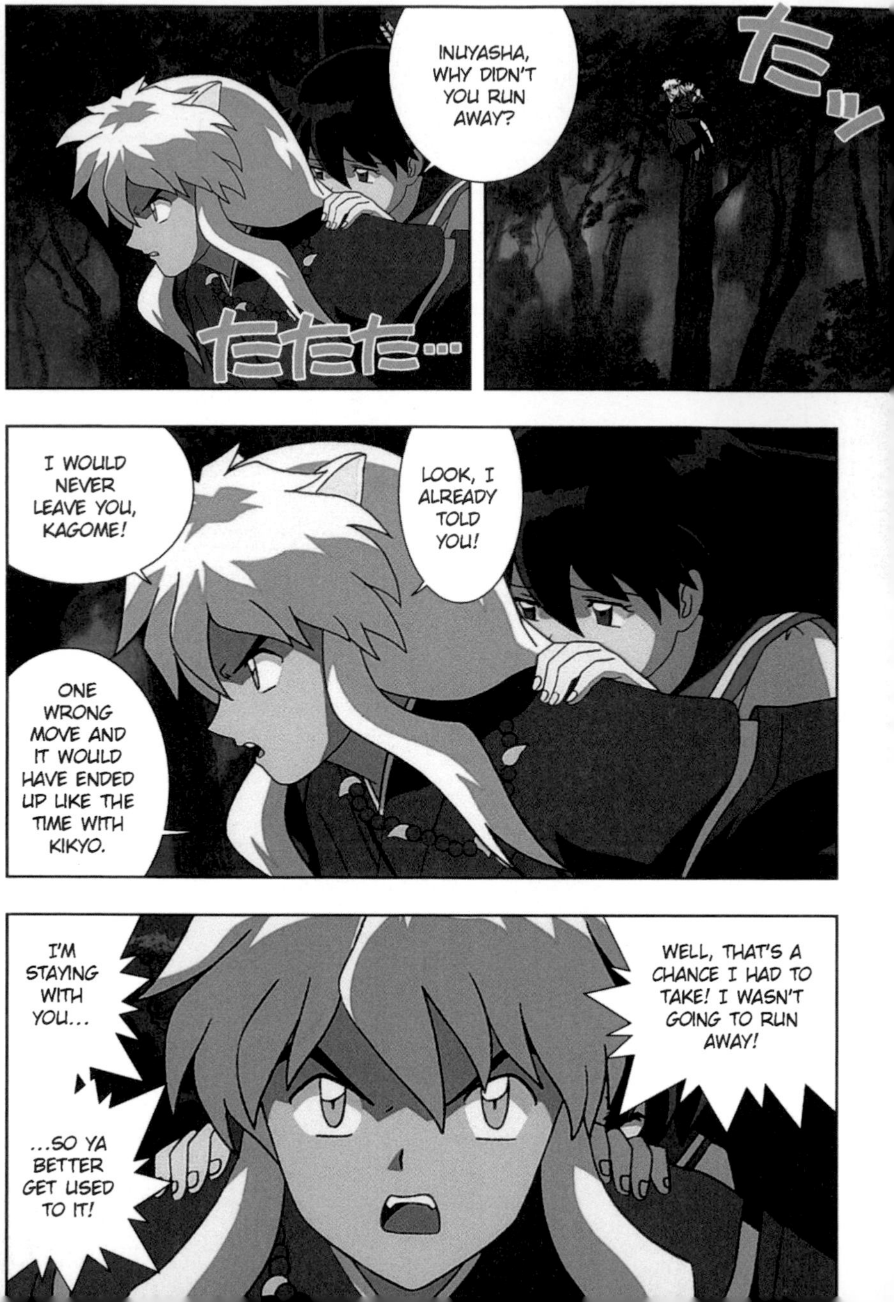
タッ
INUYASHA, WHY DIDN'T YOU RUN AWAY?
たたた…
LOOK, I ALREADY TOLD YOU!
I WOULD NEVER LEAVE YOU, KAGOME!
ONE WRONG MOVE AND IT WOULD HAVE ENDED UP LIKE THE TIME WITH KIKYO.
WELL, THAT'S A CHANCE I HAD TO TAKE! I WASN'T GOING TO RUN AWAY!
I'M STAYING WITH YOU…
…SO YA BETTER GET USED TO IT!

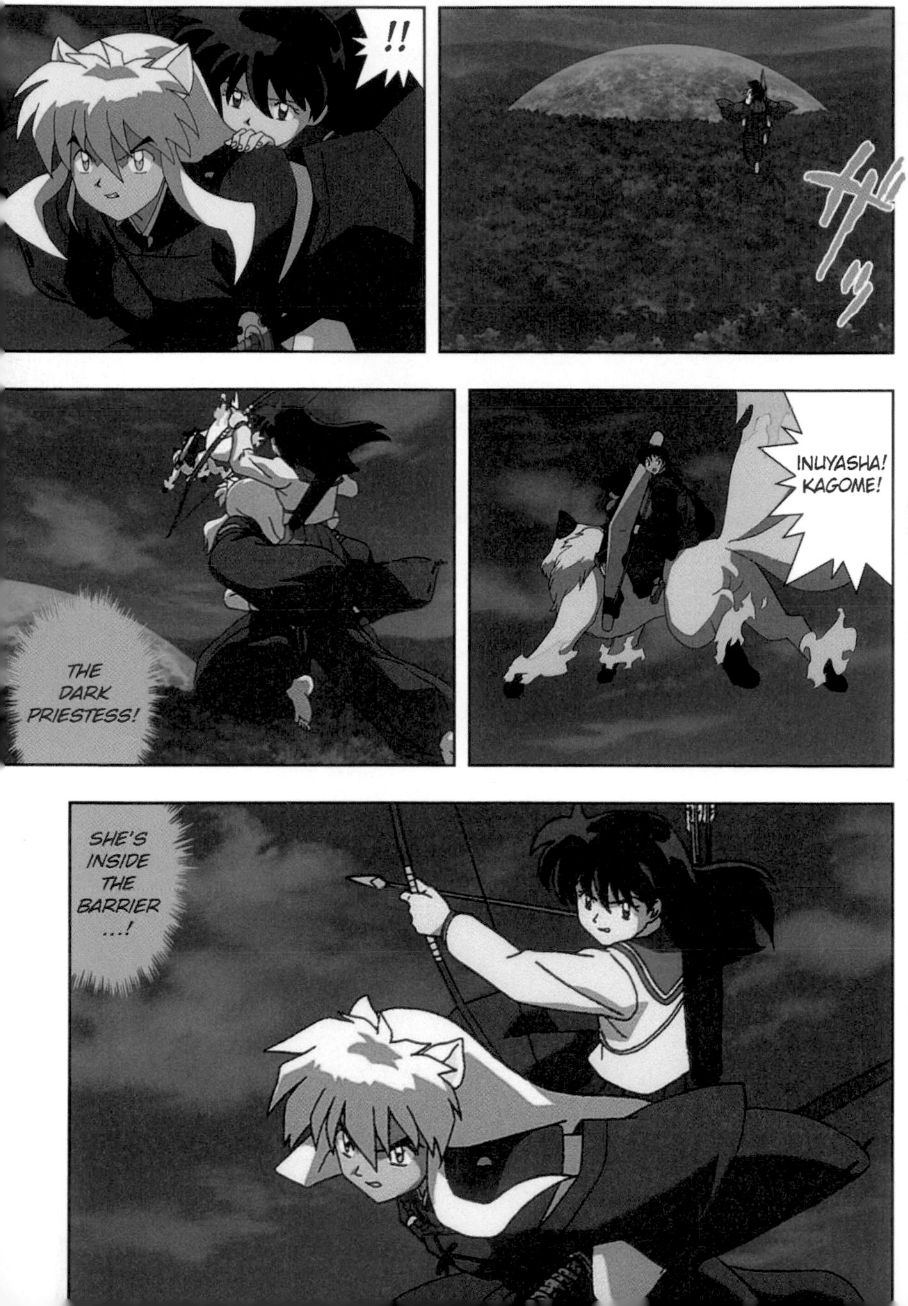
ザッ
!!
INUYASHA! KAGOME!
THE DARK PRIESTESS!
SHE'S INSIDE THE BARRIER ...!

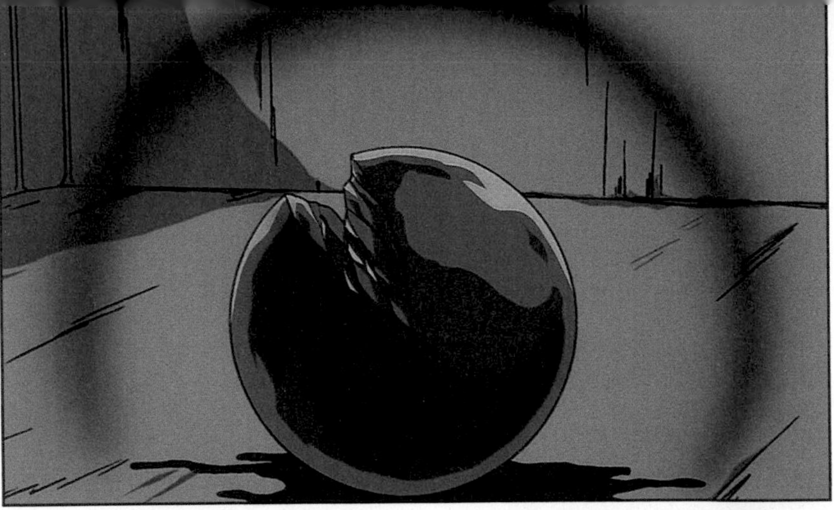

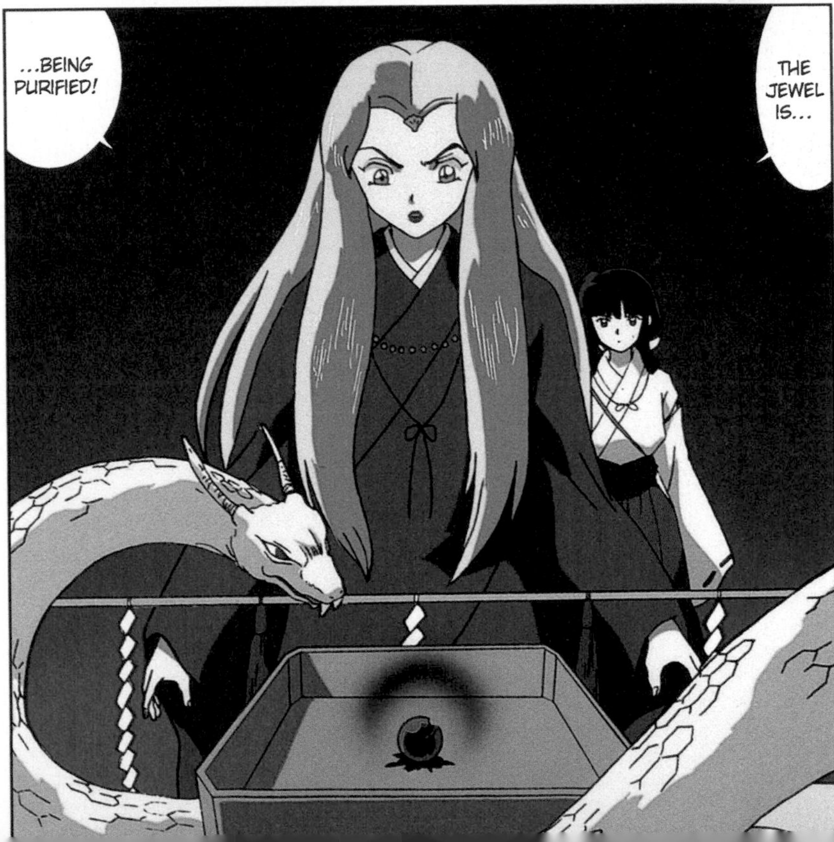
THE JEWEL IS...
...BEING PURIFIED!

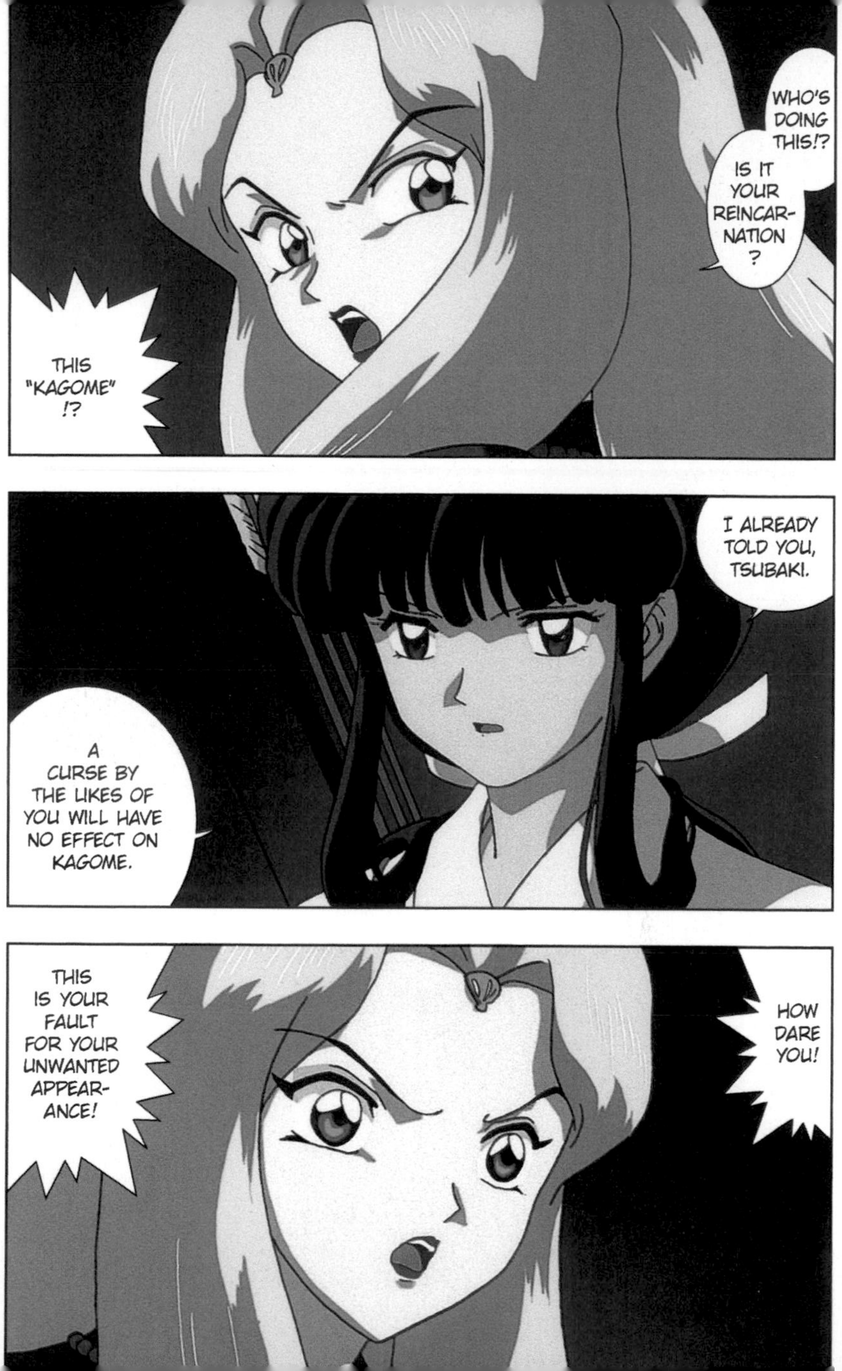
WHO'S DOING THIS!?
IS IT YOUR REINCARNATION?
THIS "KAGOME" !?
I ALREADY TOLD YOU, TSUBAKI.
A CURSE BY THE LIKES OF YOU WILL HAVE NO EFFECT ON KAGOME.
HOW DARE YOU!
THIS IS YOUR FAULT FOR YOUR UNWANTED APPEARANCE!

THIS BARRIER'S COMIN' DOWN...!

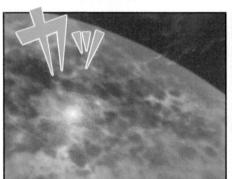

KAGOME BROKE THROUGH IT!

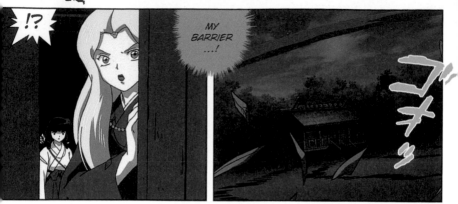

!?

MY BARRIER ...!

THAT'S HIM...!

INU- YASHA !

!!

...MISSED HIM.

OH NO, KAGOME ...

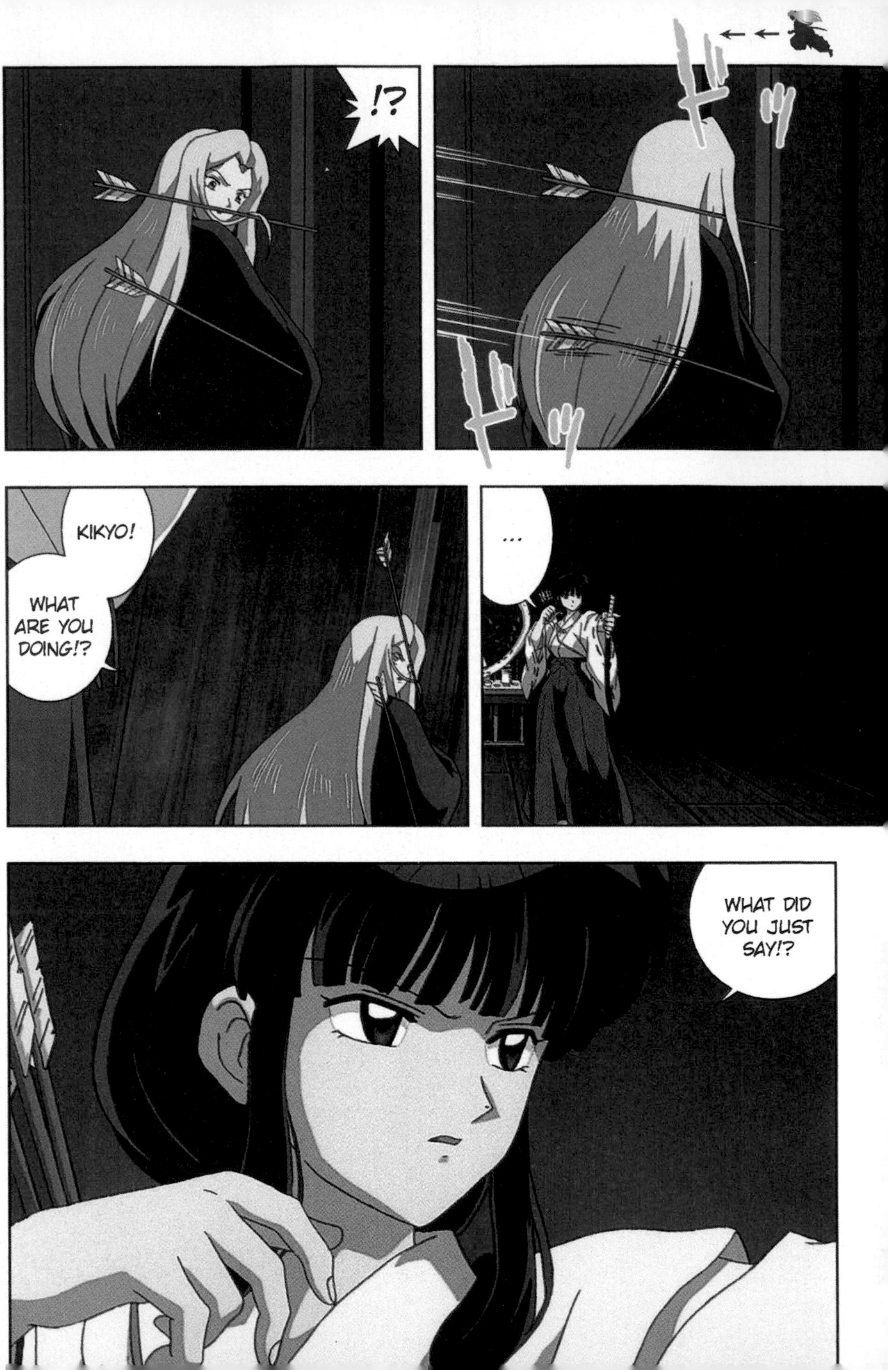
!?
...
KIKYO!
WHAT ARE YOU DOING!?
WHAT DID YOU JUST SAY!?

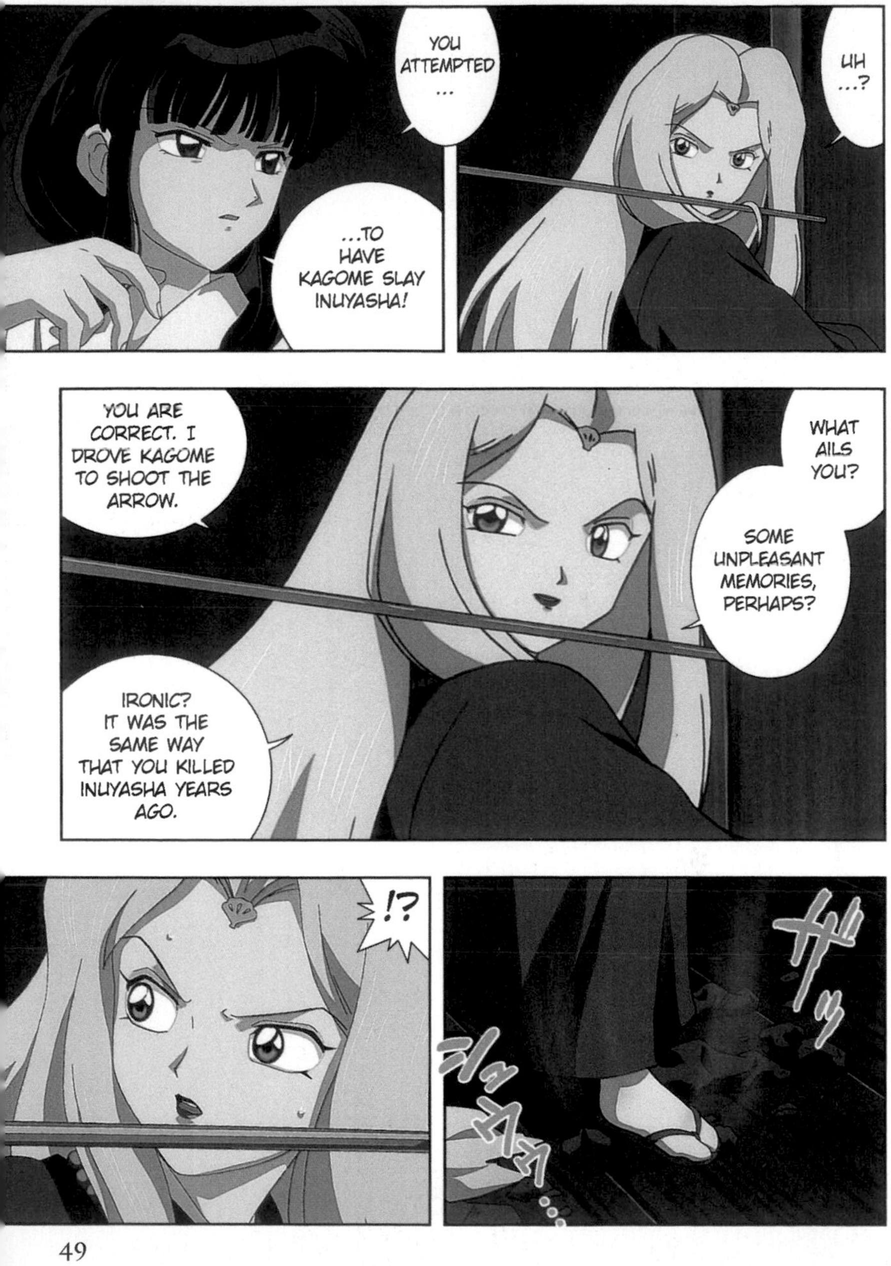
UH ...?
YOU ATTEMPTED ...
...TO HAVE KAGOME SLAY INUYASHA!
WHAT AILS YOU?
SOME UNPLEASANT MEMORIES, PERHAPS?
YOU ARE CORRECT. I DROVE KAGOME TO SHOOT THE ARROW.
IRONIC? IT WAS THE SAME WAY THAT YOU KILLED INUYASHA YEARS AGO.
!?

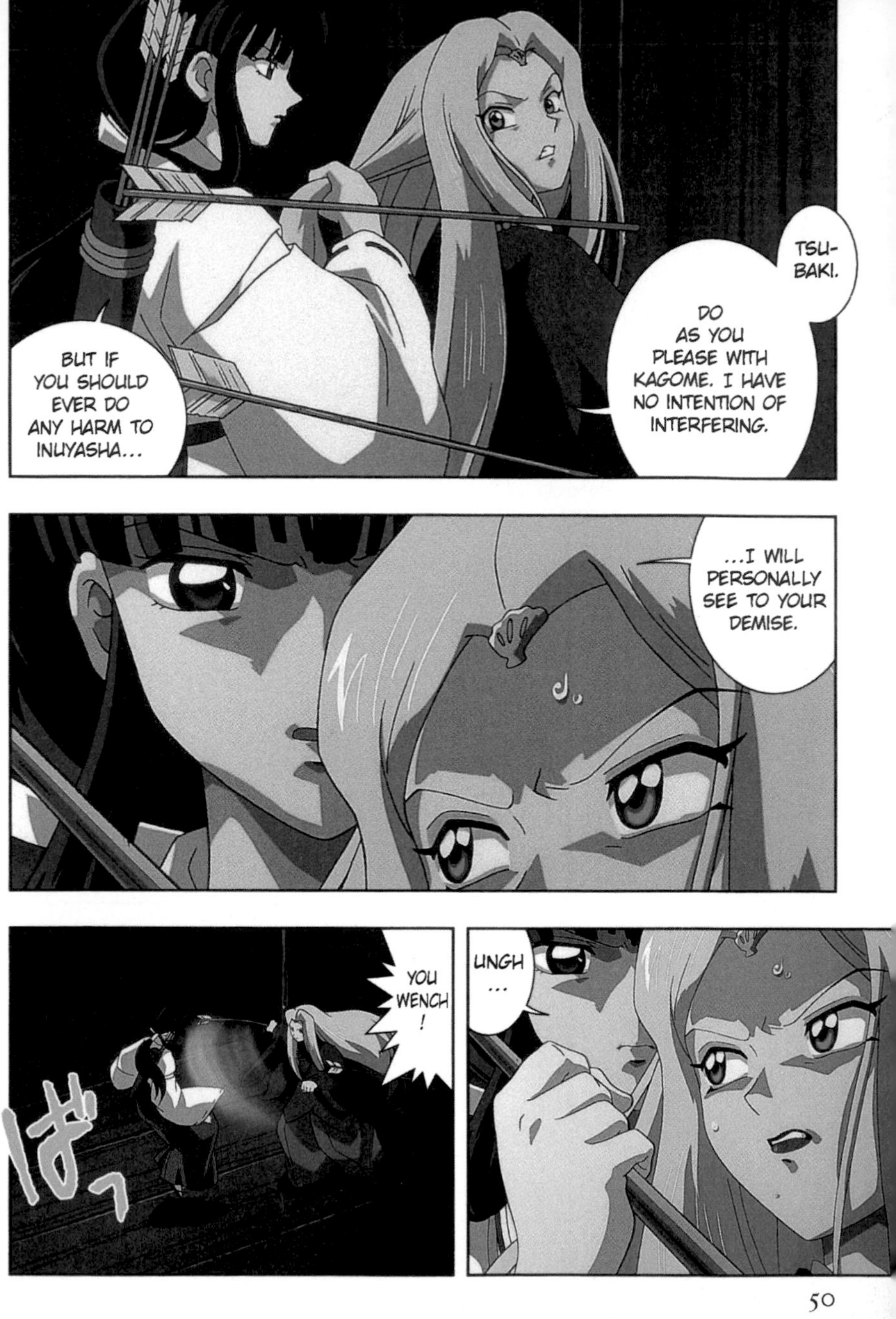
TSU-BAKI.
DO AS YOU PLEASE WITH KAGOME. I HAVE NO INTENTION OF INTERFERING.
BUT IF YOU SHOULD EVER DO ANY HARM TO INUYASHA...
...I WILL PERSONALLY SEE TO YOUR DEMISE.
UNGH ...
YOU WENCH!
ぱっ

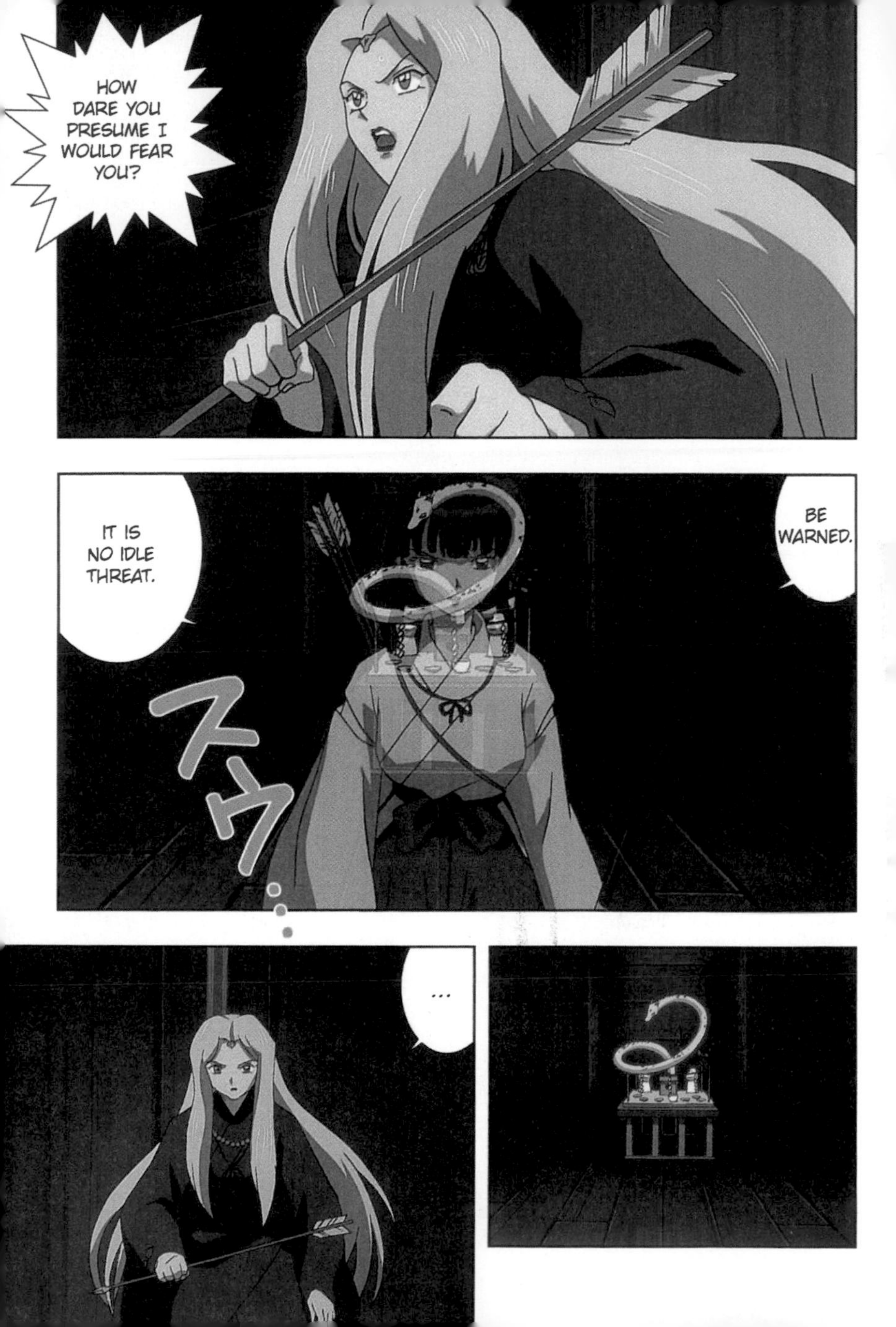
HOW DARE YOU PRESUME I WOULD FEAR YOU?
BE WARNED.
IT IS NO IDLE THREAT.
スゥ
...

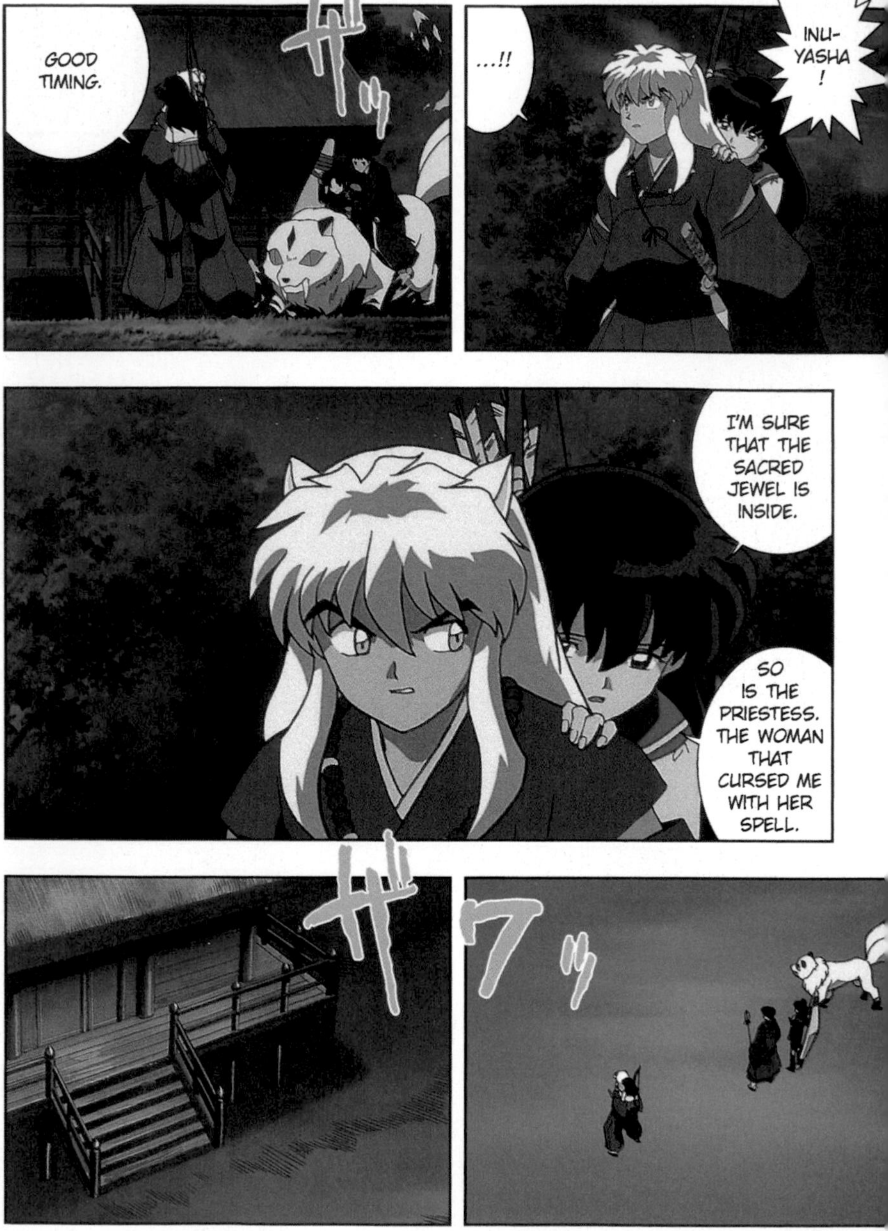
INU-YASHA !
...!!
GOOD TIMING.
ザッ
I'M SURE THAT THE SACRED JEWEL IS INSIDE.
SO IS THE PRIESTESS. THE WOMAN THAT CURSED ME WITH HER SPELL.
ザワッ

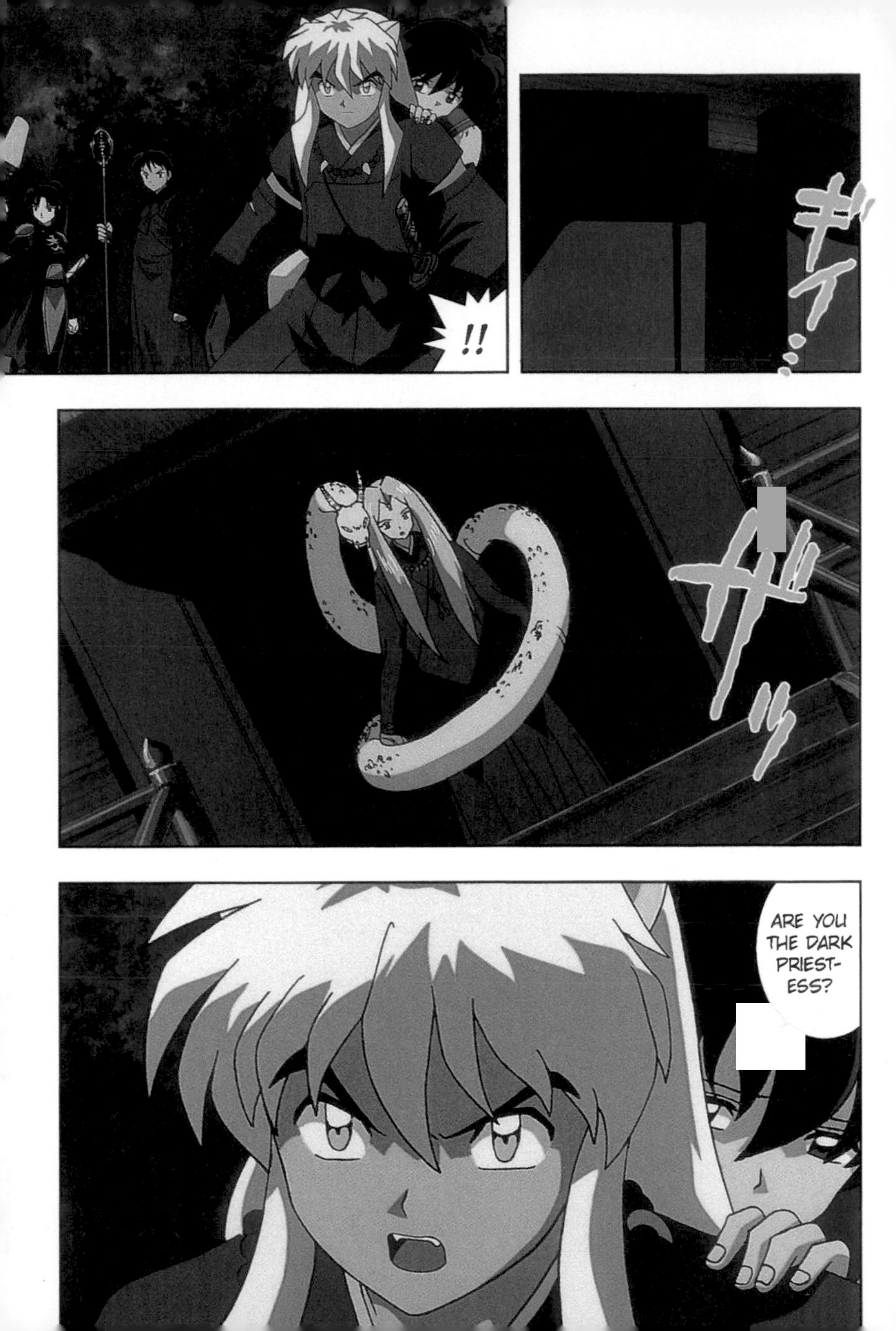
ギイ…
!!
ザッ
ARE YOU THE DARK PRIEST-ESS?

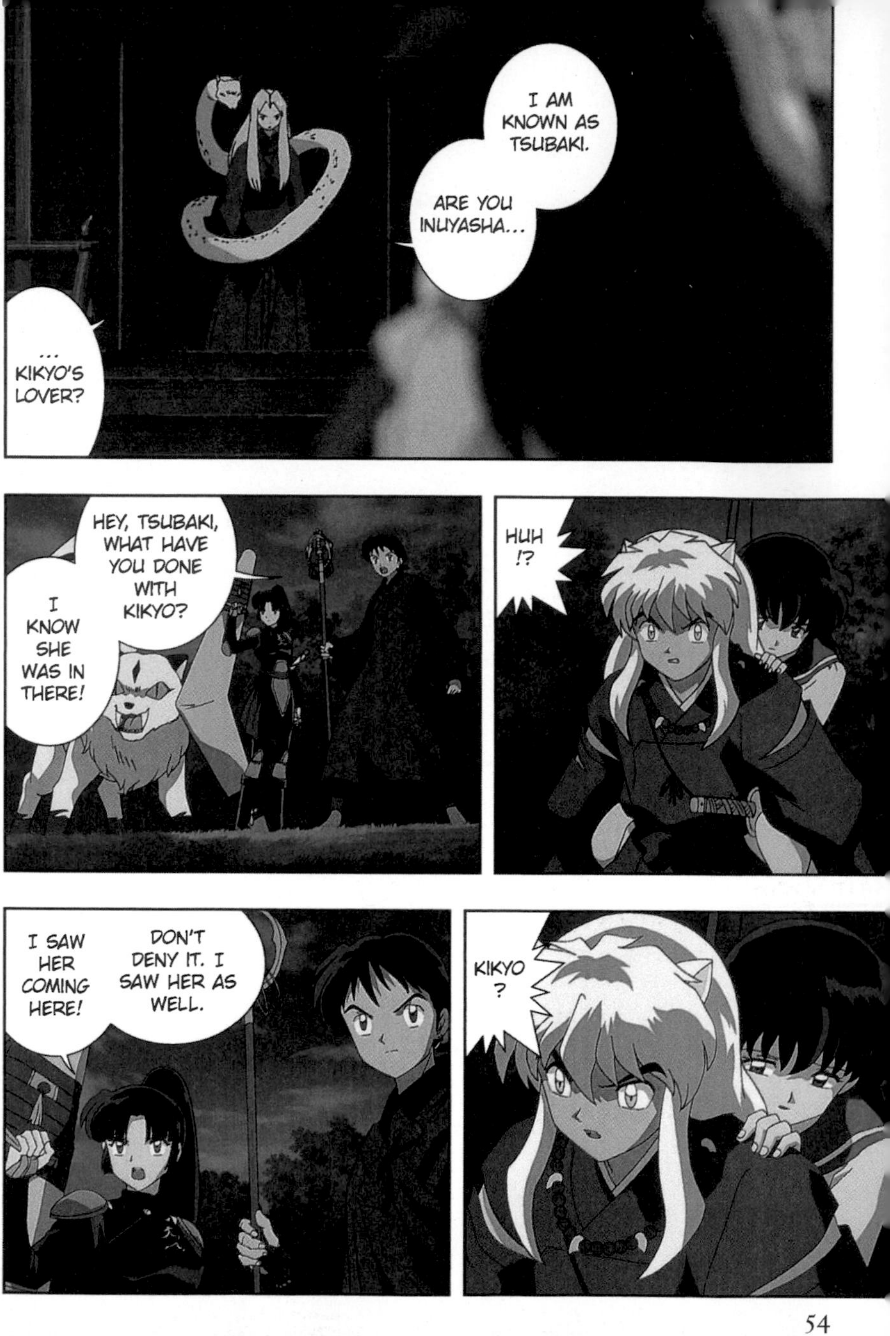
I AM KNOWN AS TSUBAKI.
ARE YOU INUYASHA...
... KIKYO'S LOVER?
HUH!?
HEY, TSUBAKI, WHAT HAVE YOU DONE WITH KIKYO?
I KNOW SHE WAS IN THERE!
KIKYO?
DON'T DENY IT. I SAW HER AS WELL.
I SAW HER COMING HERE!

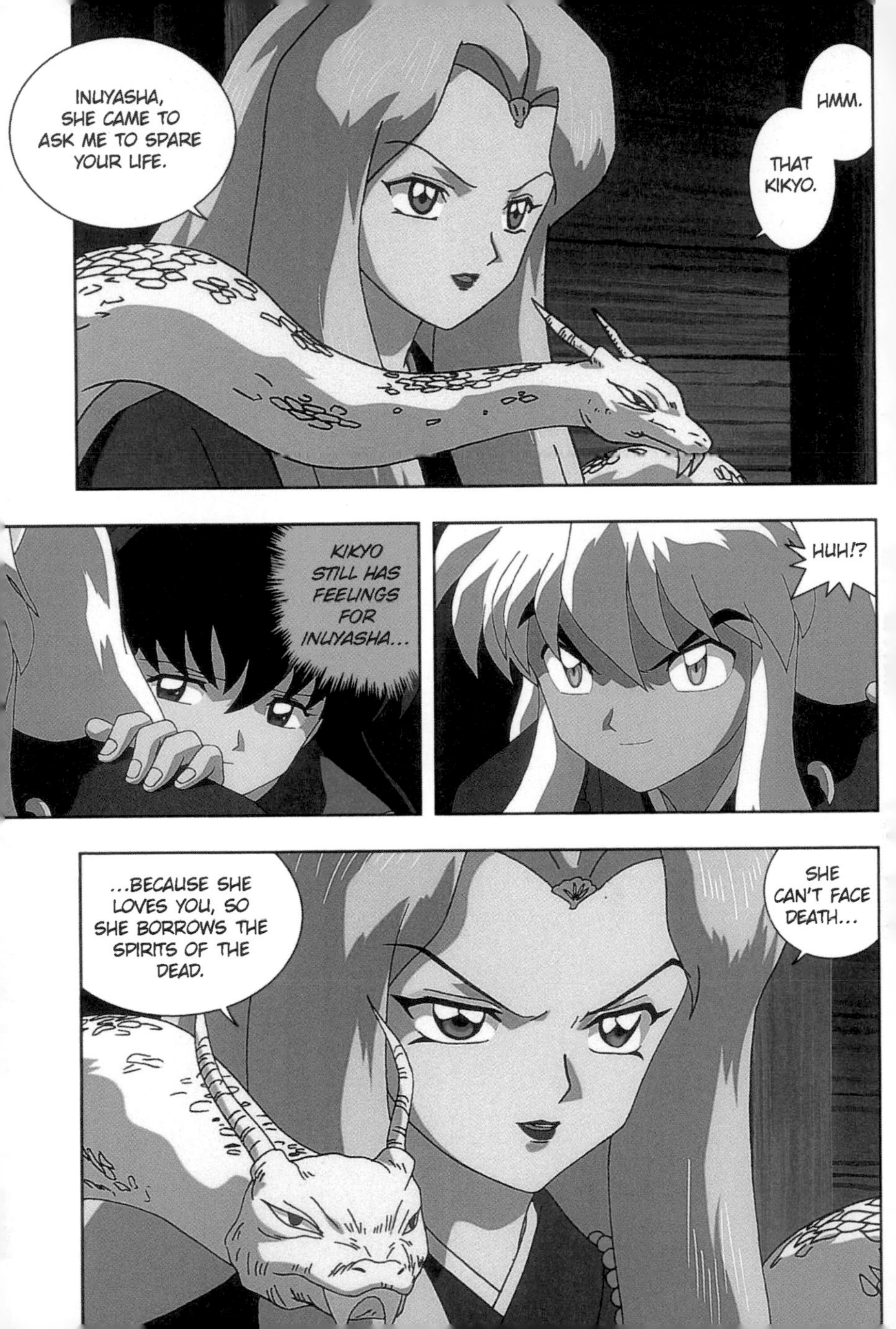
HMM.
THAT KIKYO.
INUYASHA, SHE CAME TO ASK ME TO SPARE YOUR LIFE.
HUH!?
KIKYO STILL HAS FEELINGS FOR INUYASHA...
SHE CAN'T FACE DEATH...
...BECAUSE SHE LOVES YOU, SO SHE BORROWS THE SPIRITS OF THE DEAD.

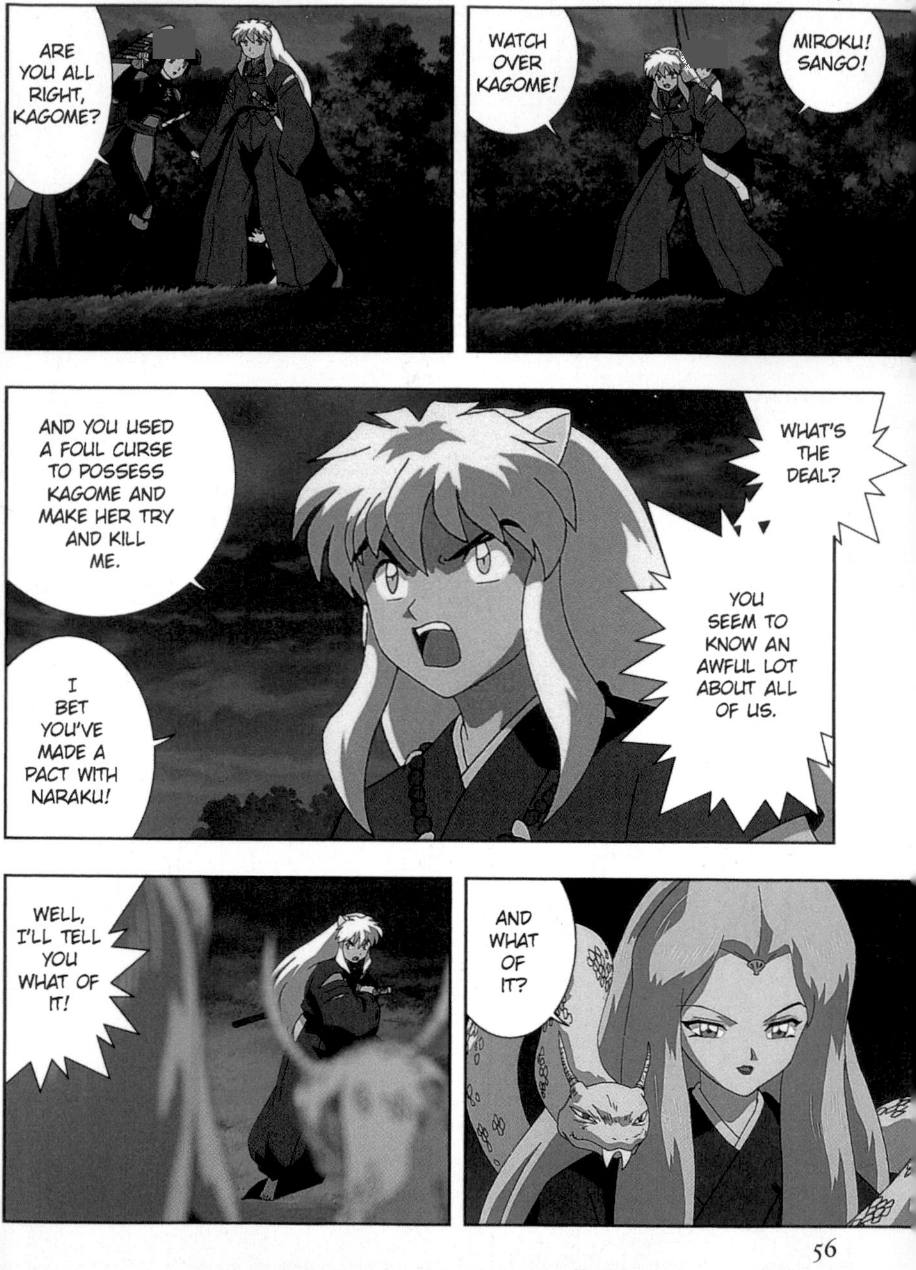
MIROKU! SANGO!
WATCH OVER KAGOME!
ARE YOU ALL RIGHT, KAGOME?
WHAT'S THE DEAL?
YOU SEEM TO KNOW AN AWFUL LOT ABOUT ALL OF US.
AND YOU USED A FOUL CURSE TO POSSESS KAGOME AND MAKE HER TRY AND KILL ME.
I BET YOU'VE MADE A PACT WITH NARAKU!
AND WHAT OF IT?
WELL, I'LL TELL YOU WHAT OF IT!

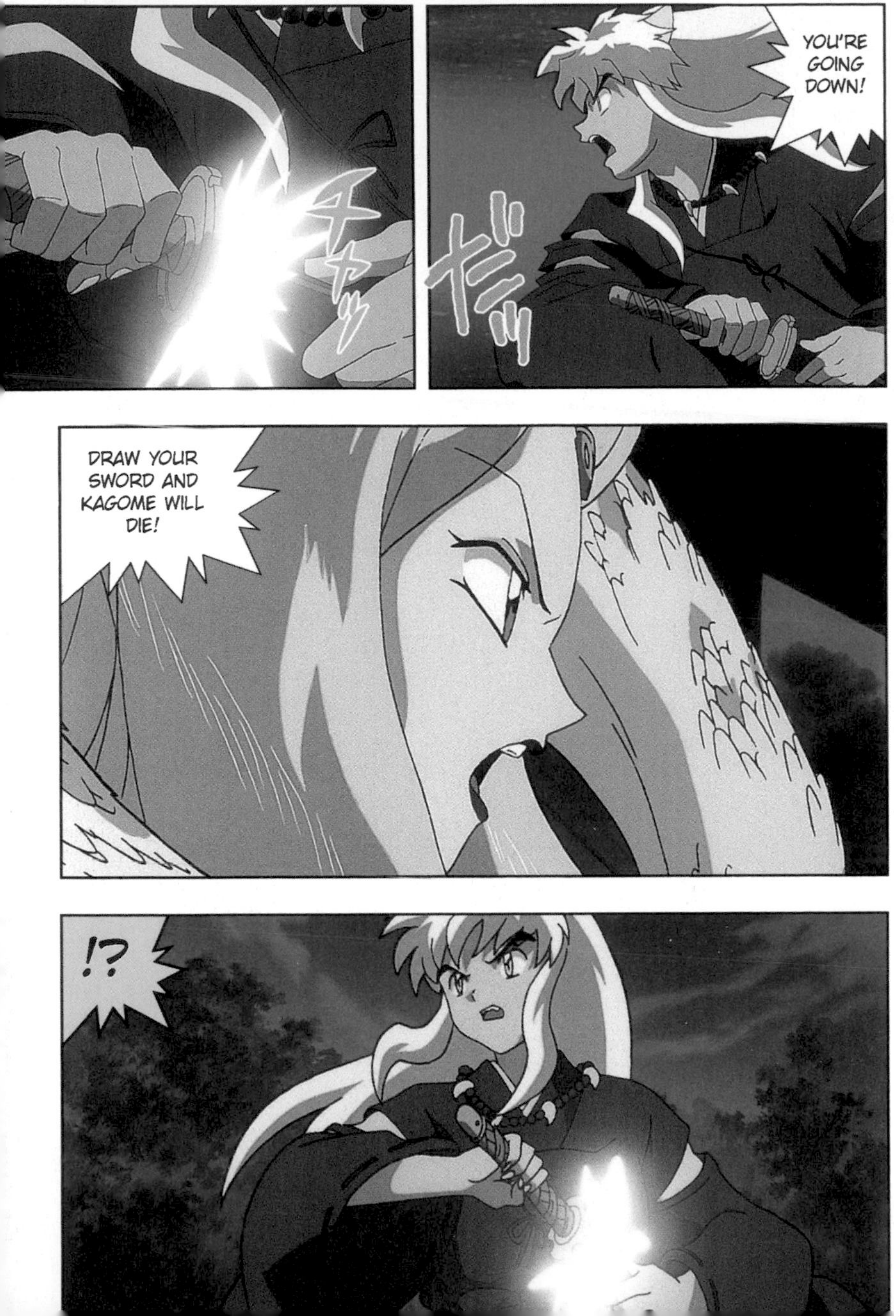
YOU'RE GOING DOWN!
ザッ
チャッ
DRAW YOUR SWORD AND KAGOME WILL DIE!
!?

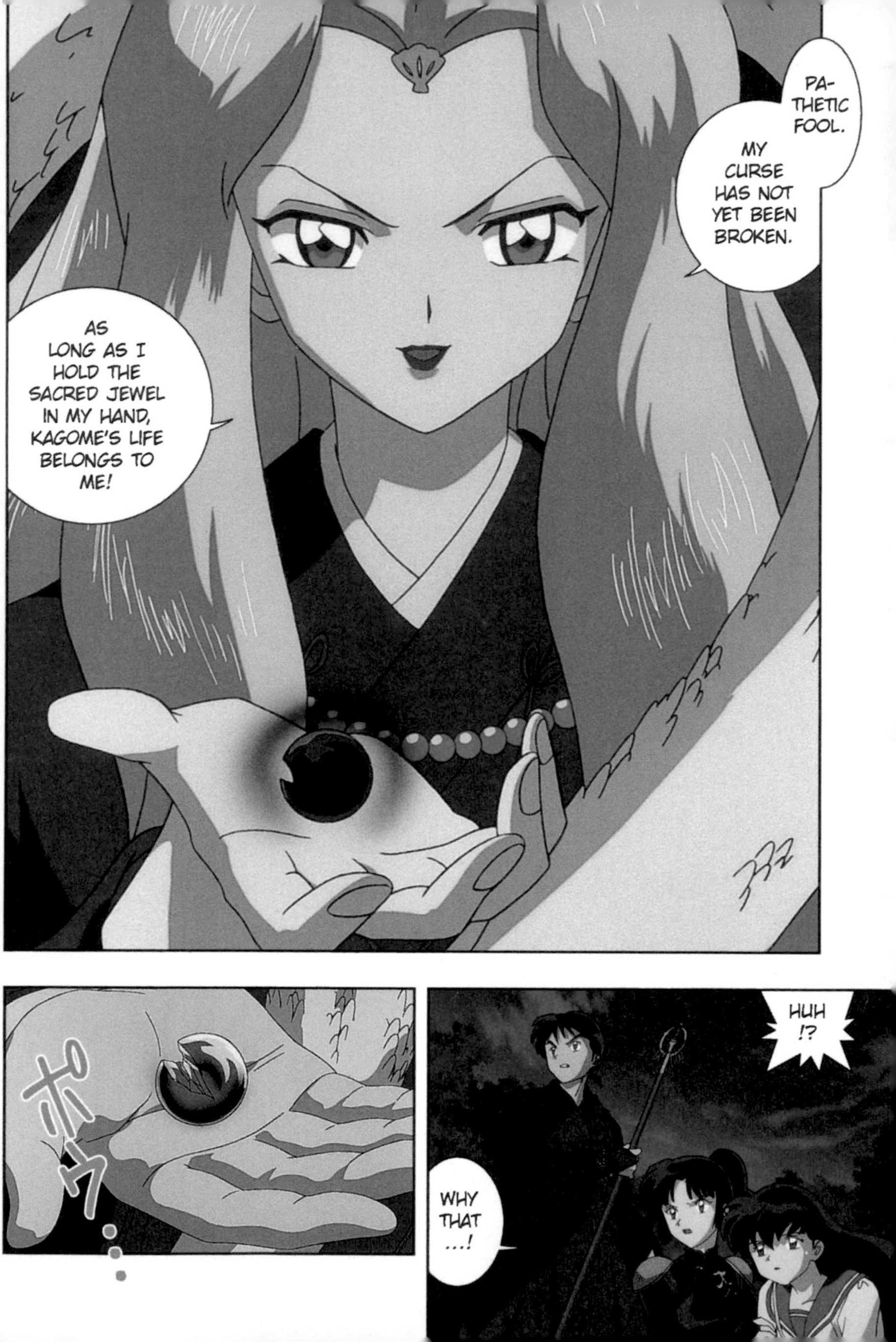
PATHETIC FOOL.
MY CURSE HAS NOT YET BEEN BROKEN.
AS LONG AS I HOLD THE SACRED JEWEL IN MY HAND, KAGOME'S LIFE BELONGS TO ME!
HUH !?
WHY THAT ...!
ポゥ…

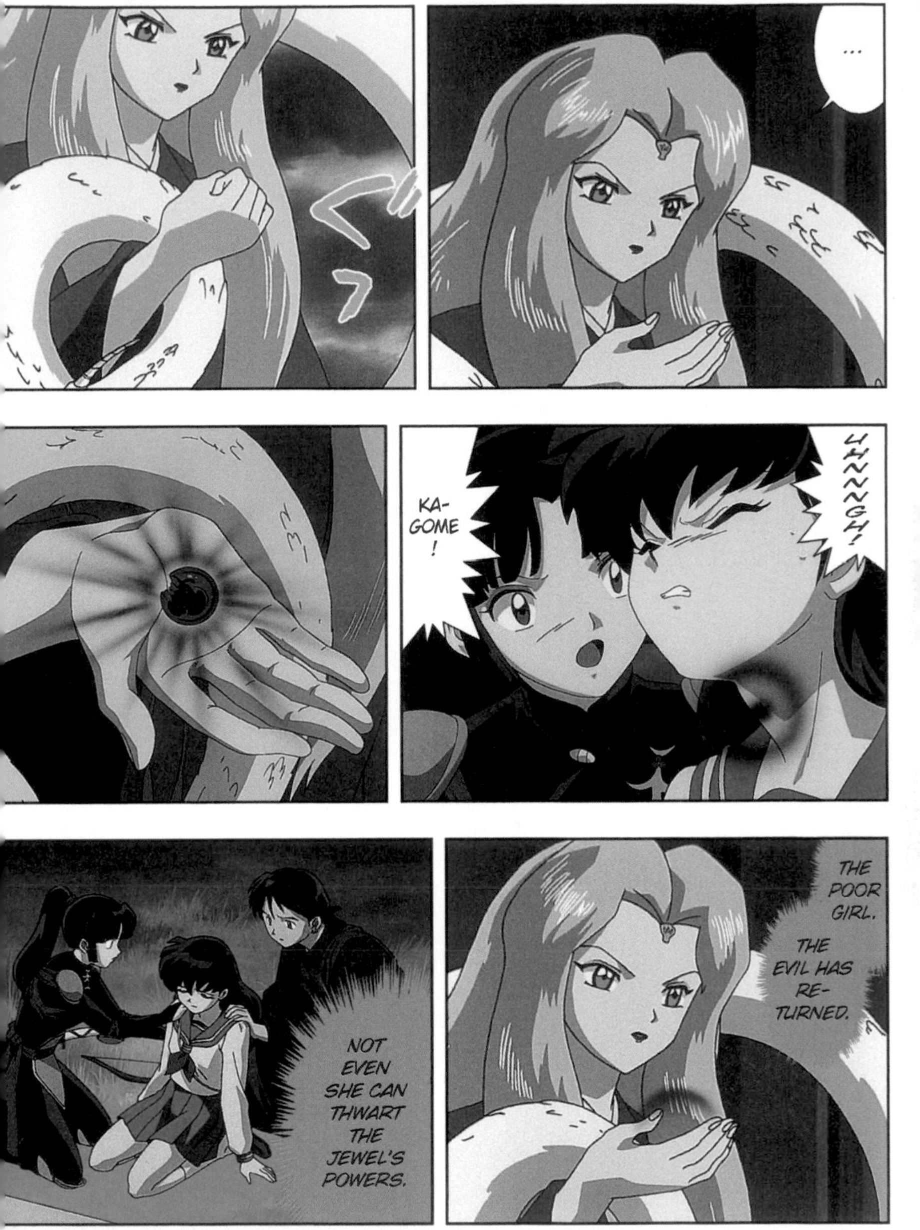
...
UHNNNGH!
KA-GOME!
THE POOR GIRL.
THE EVIL HAS RE-TURNED.
NOT EVEN SHE CAN THWART THE JEWEL'S POWERS.

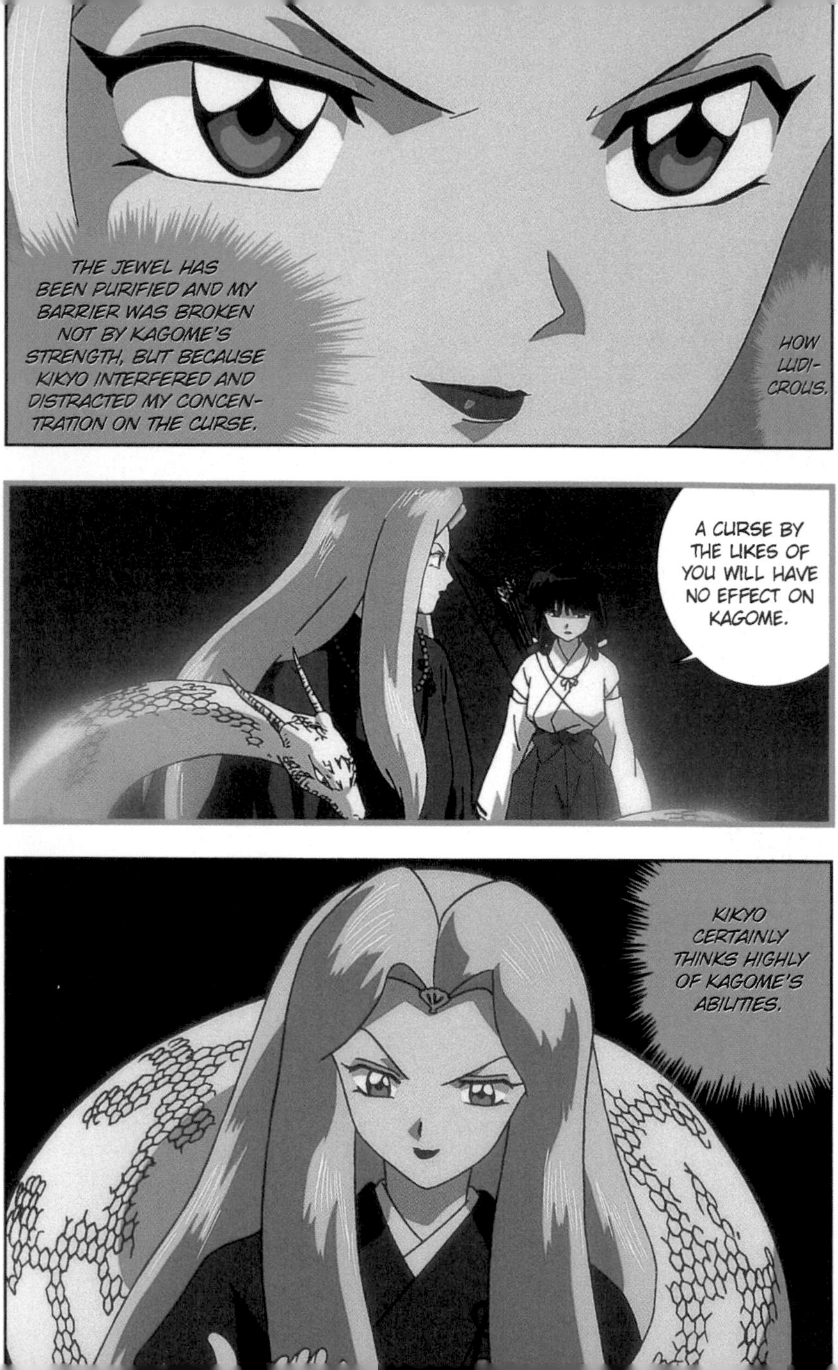
THE JEWEL HAS BEEN PURIFIED AND MY BARRIER WAS BROKEN NOT BY KAGOME'S STRENGTH, BUT BECAUSE KIKYO INTERFERED AND DISTRACTED MY CONCENTRATION ON THE CURSE.
HOW LUDICROUS.
A CURSE BY THE LIKES OF YOU WILL HAVE NO EFFECT ON KAGOME.
KIKYO CERTAINLY THINKS HIGHLY OF KAGOME'S ABILITIES.

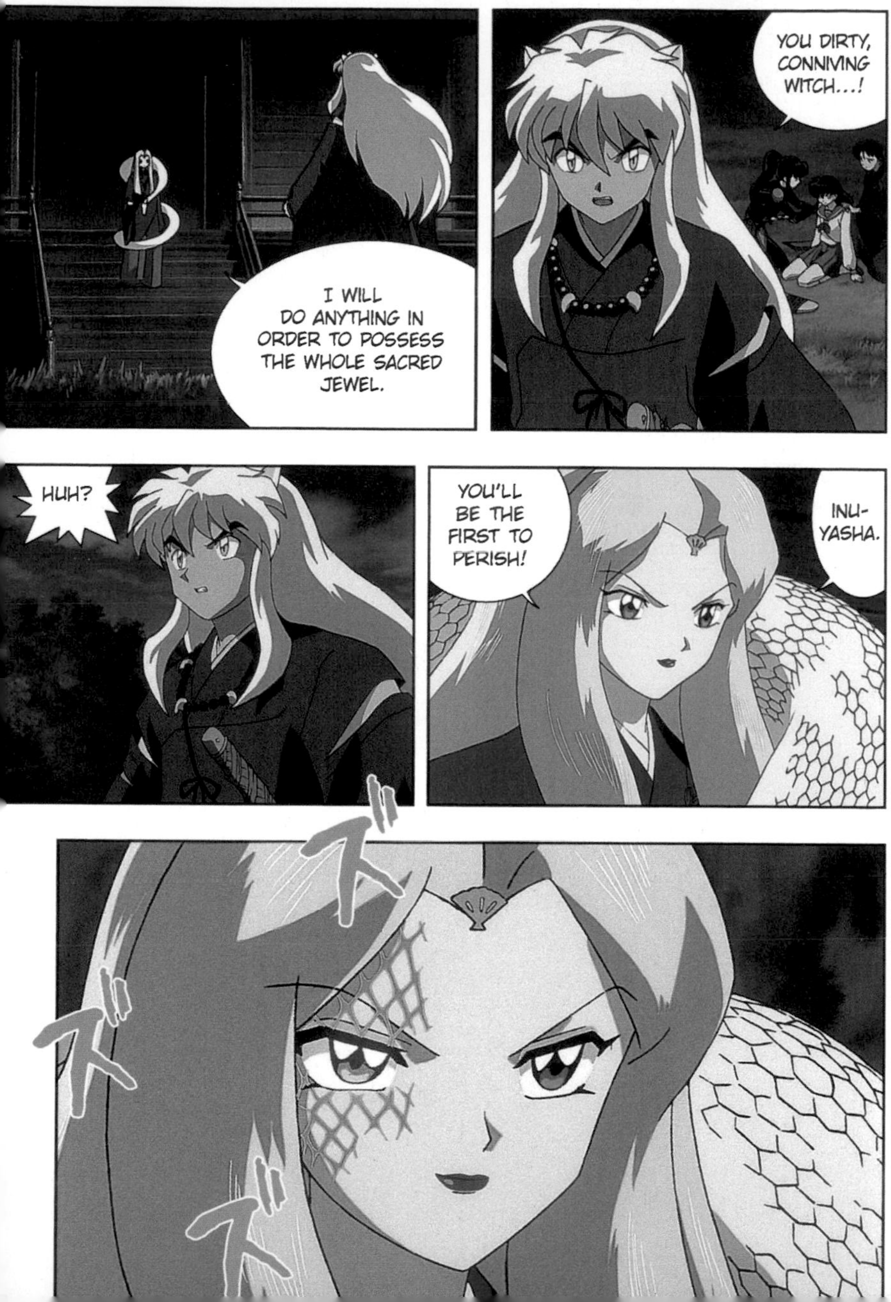
YOU DIRTY, CONNIVING WITCH...!
I WILL DO ANYTHING IN ORDER TO POSSESS THE WHOLE SACRED JEWEL.
INU-YASHA.
YOU'LL BE THE FIRST TO PERISH!
HUH?
ズ
ズ
ズ

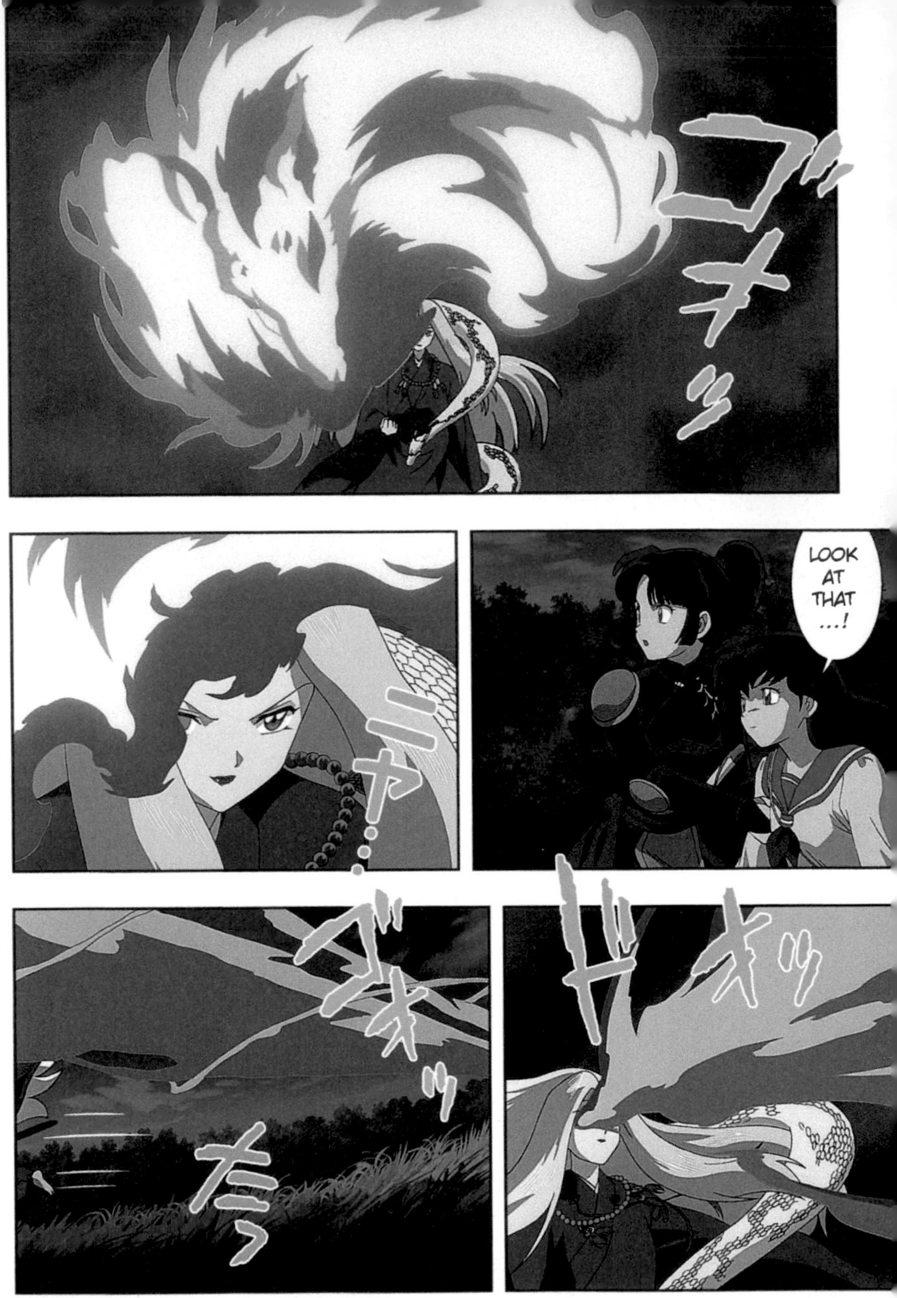
ゴオッ
LOOK AT THAT ...!
ニヤ…
ドオッ
ゴオッ
たっ

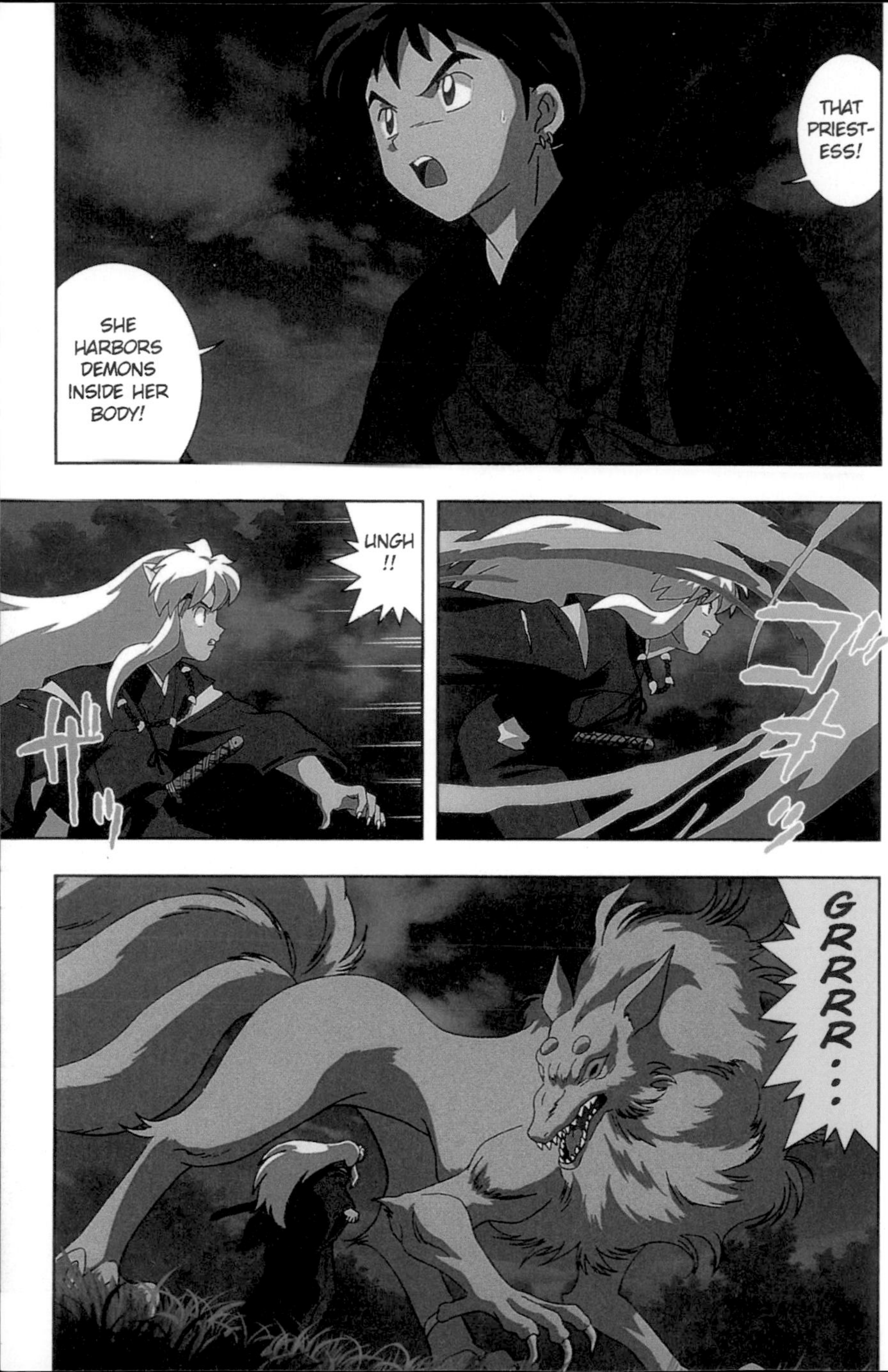
THAT PRIEST-ESS!
SHE HARBORS DEMONS INSIDE HER BODY!
UNGH !!
GRRRR...

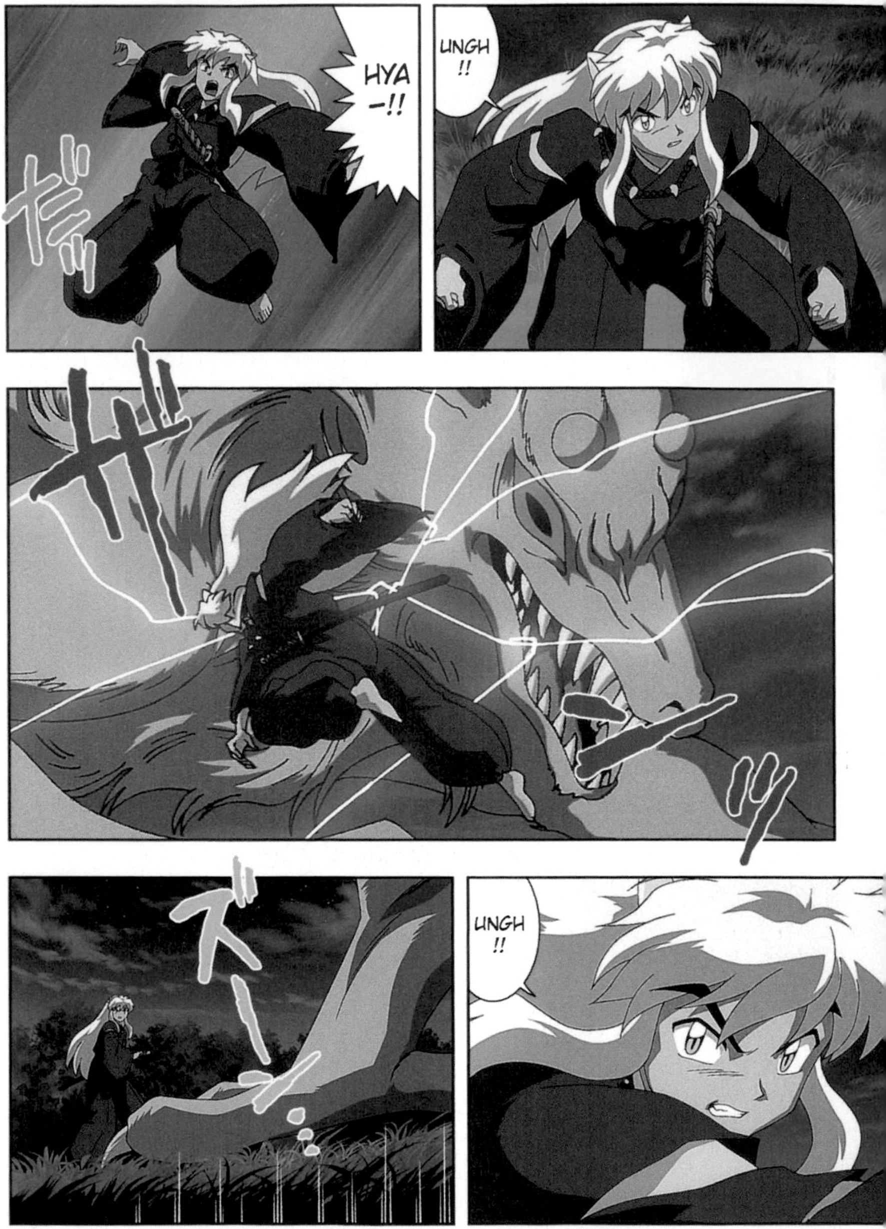
UNGH !!
HYA-!!
UNGH !!

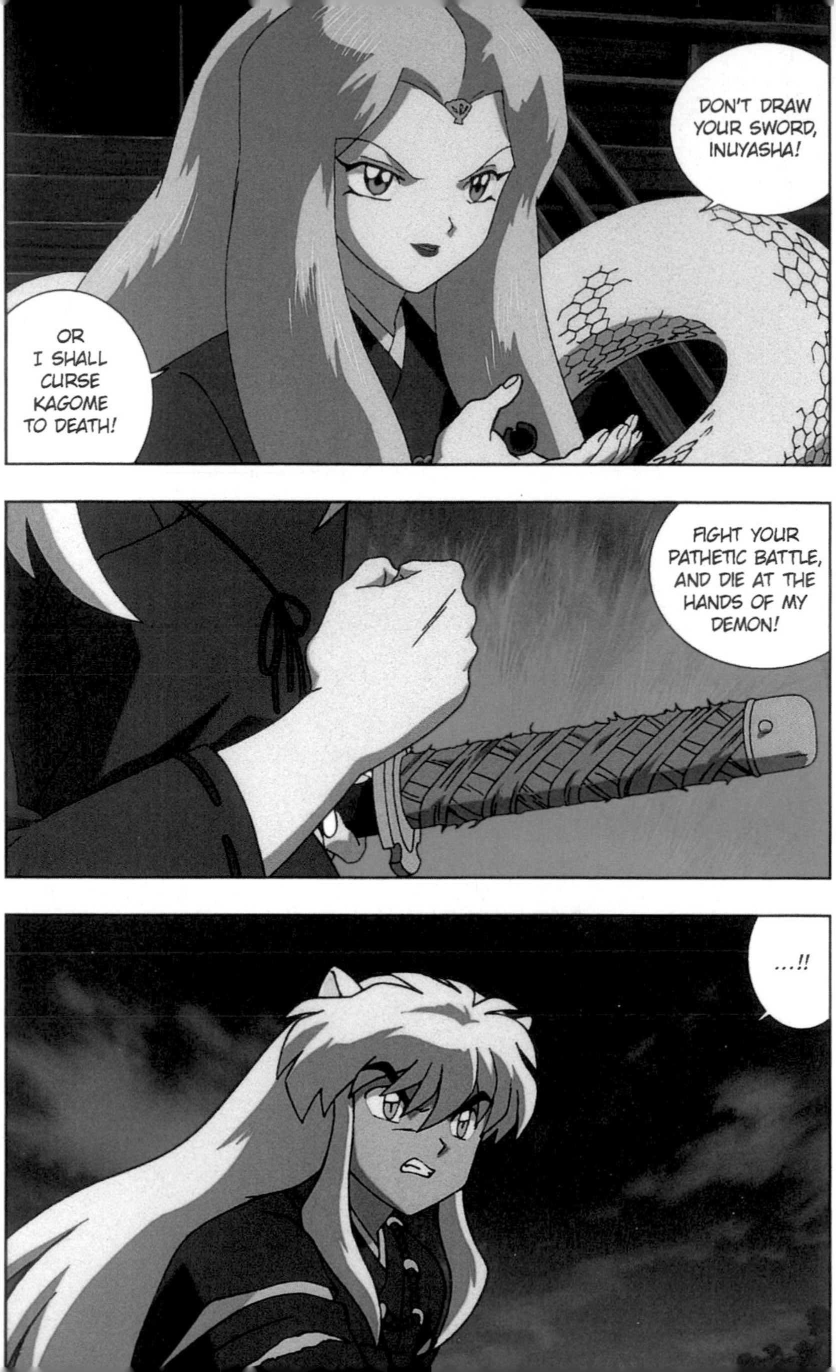
DON'T DRAW YOUR SWORD, INUYASHA!
OR I SHALL CURSE KAGOME TO DEATH!
FIGHT YOUR PATHETIC BATTLE, AND DIE AT THE HANDS OF MY DEMON!
...!!

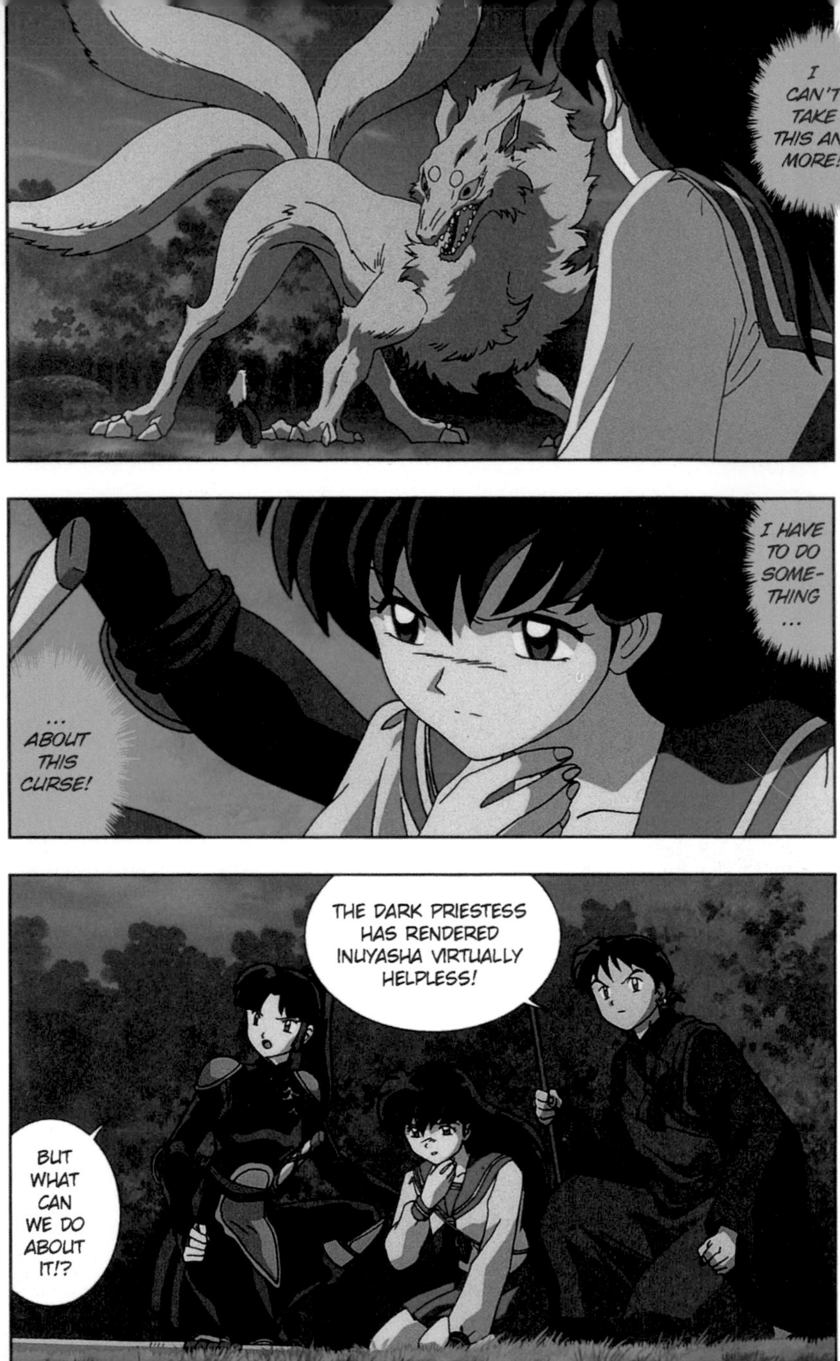
I CAN'T TAKE THIS ANY MORE!
I HAVE TO DO SOMETHING ...
... ABOUT THIS CURSE!
THE DARK PRIESTESS HAS RENDERED INUYASHA VIRTUALLY HELPLESS!
BUT WHAT CAN WE DO ABOUT IT!?

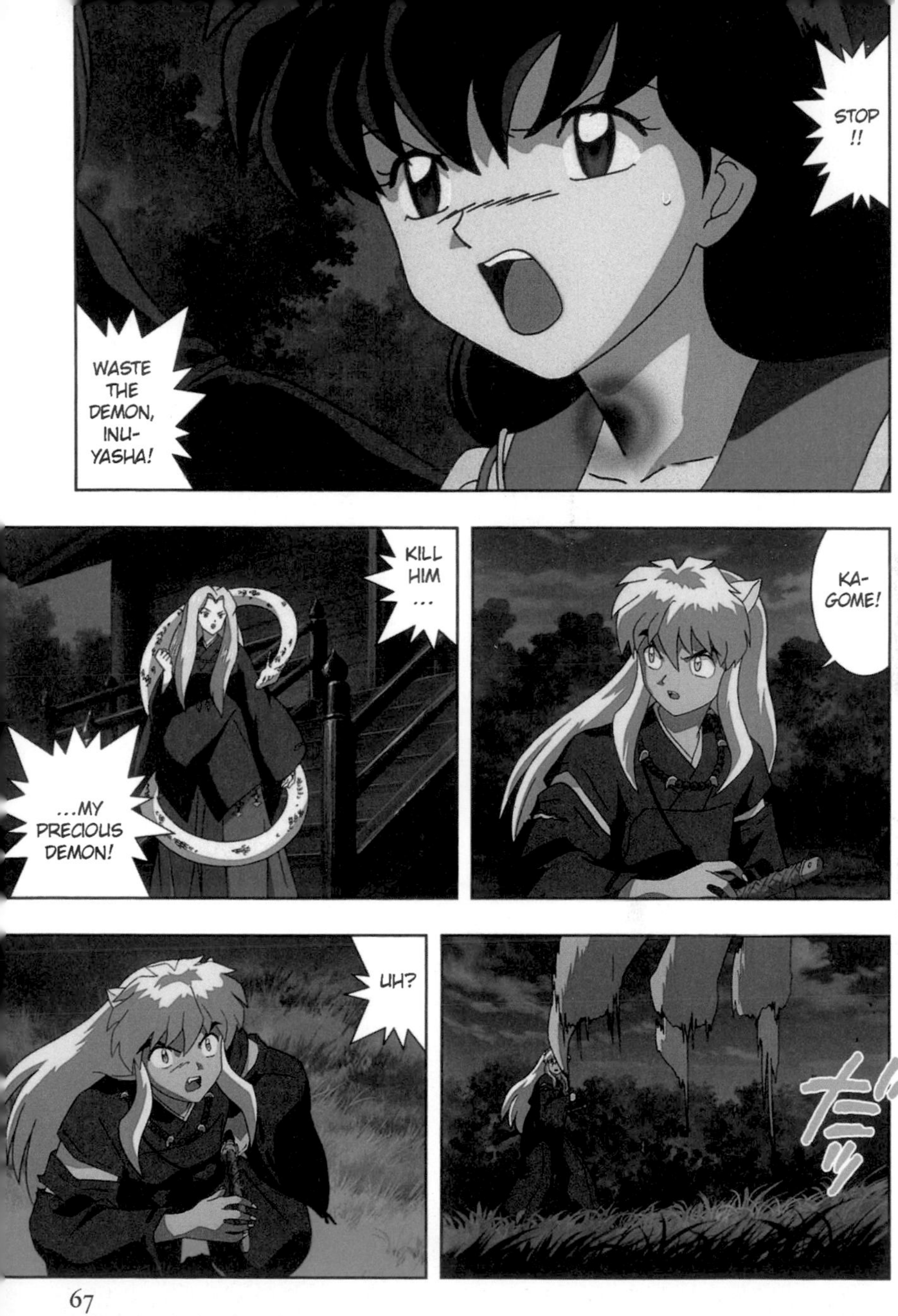
STOP !!
WASTE THE DEMON, INU-YASHA!
KA-GOME!
KILL HIM ...
...MY PRECIOUS DEMON!
だッ
UH?

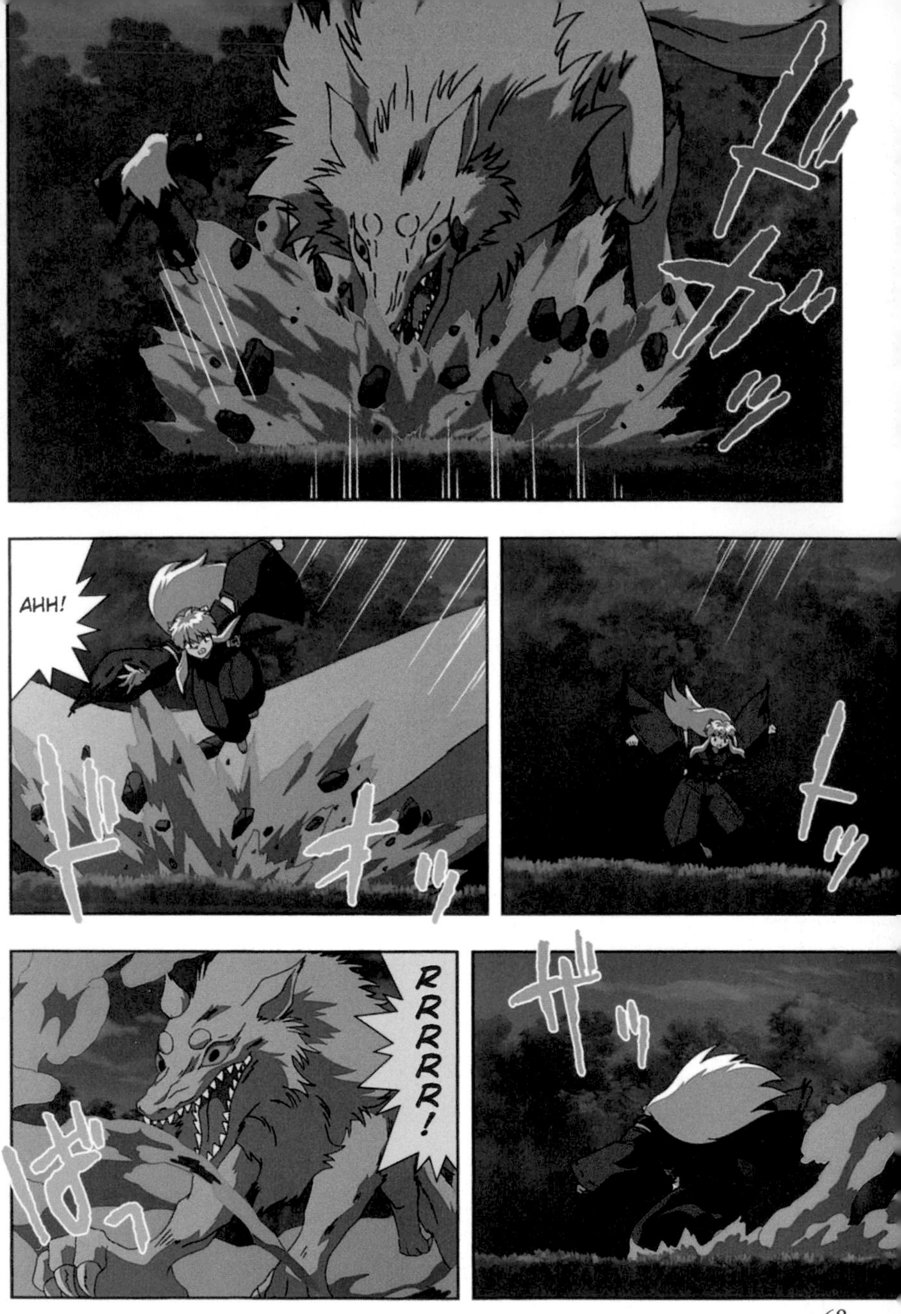
ドガッ
トッ
AHH!
ドオッ
ザッ
RRRRR!
ばっ

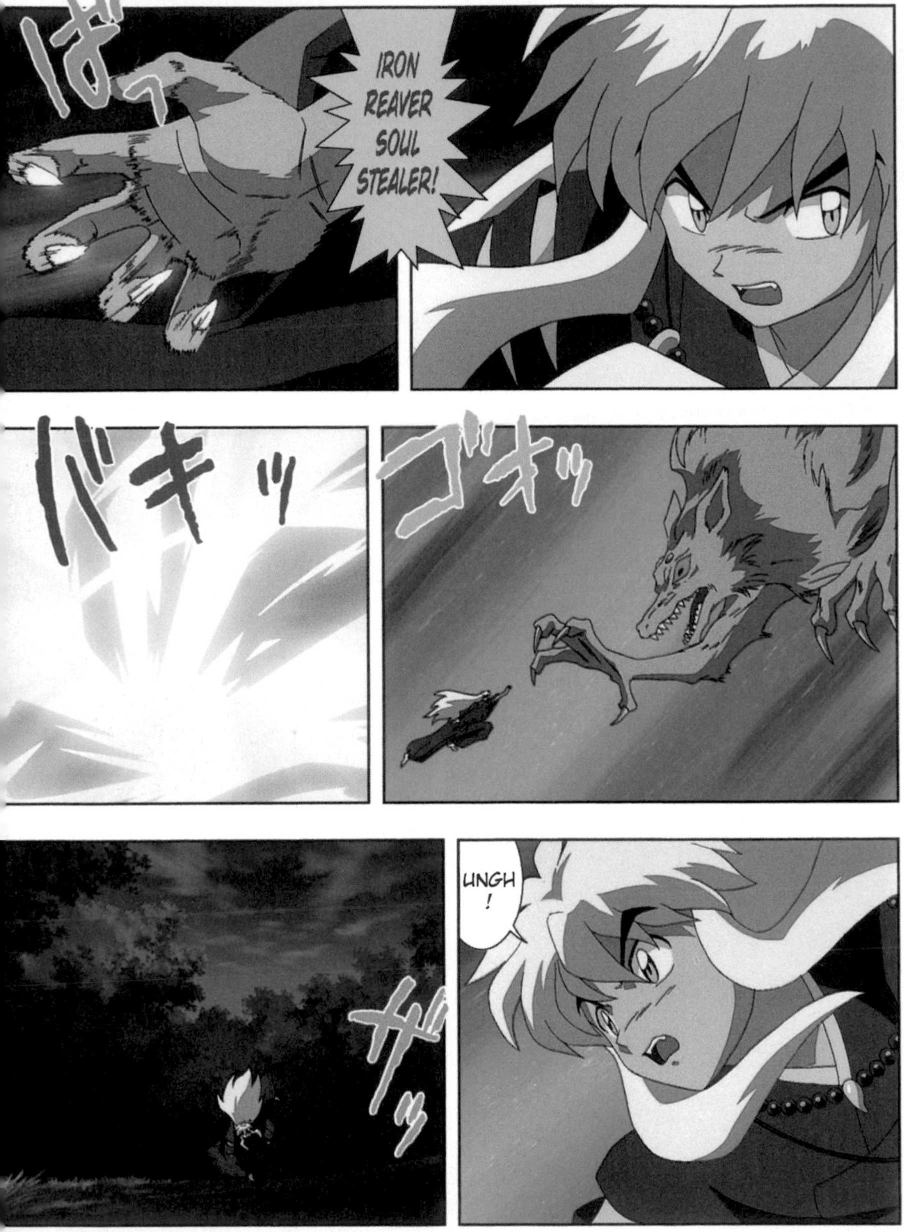
IRON REAVER SOUL STEALER!
ばっ
ゴォッ
バキッ
UNGH!
ザッ

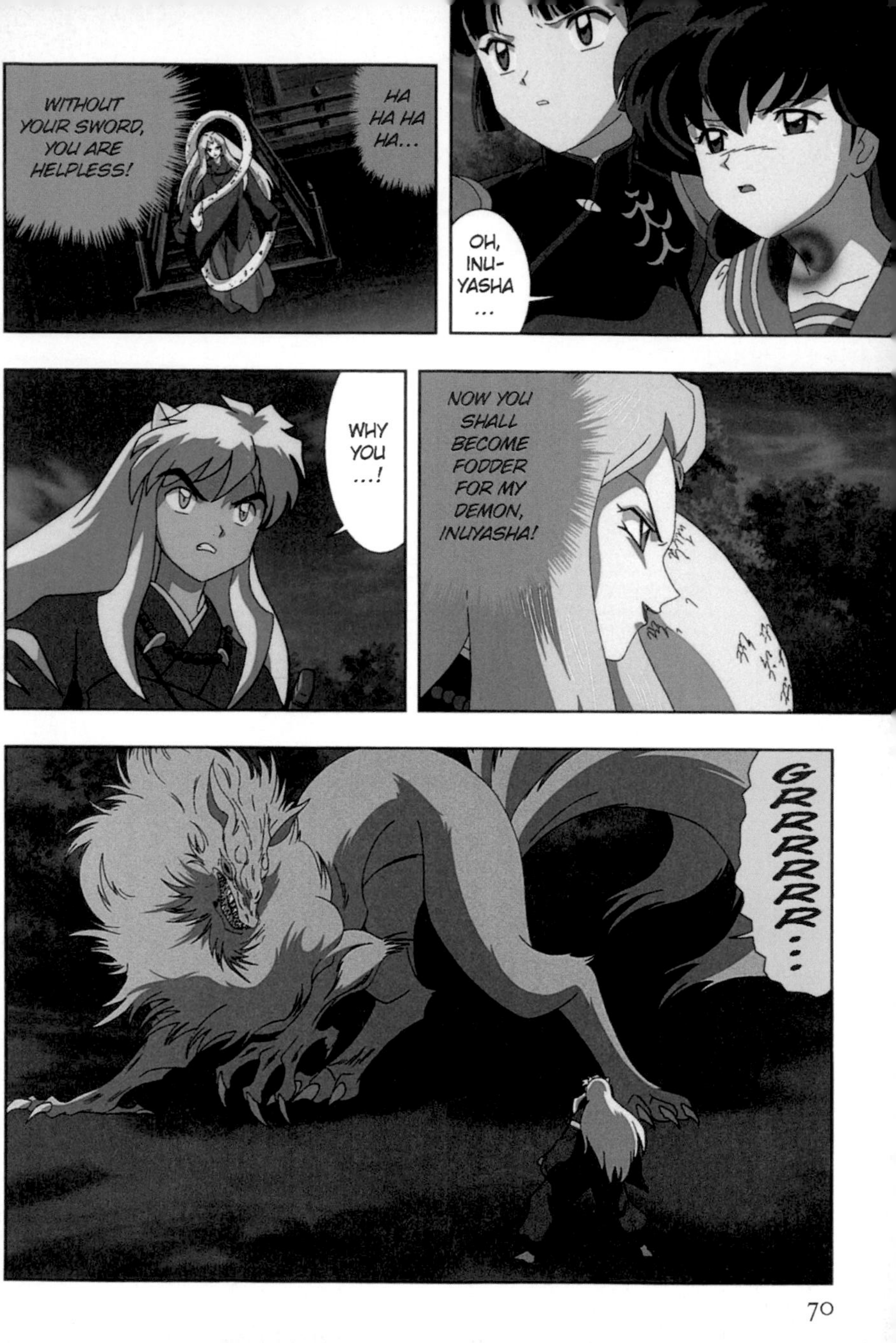
WITHOUT YOUR SWORD, YOU ARE HELPLESS!
HA HA HA HA...
OH, INU-YASHA ...
WHY YOU ...!
NOW YOU SHALL BECOME FODDER FOR MY DEMON, INUYASHA!
GRRRRRR...

62
Tsubaki's Unrelenting Evil Spell

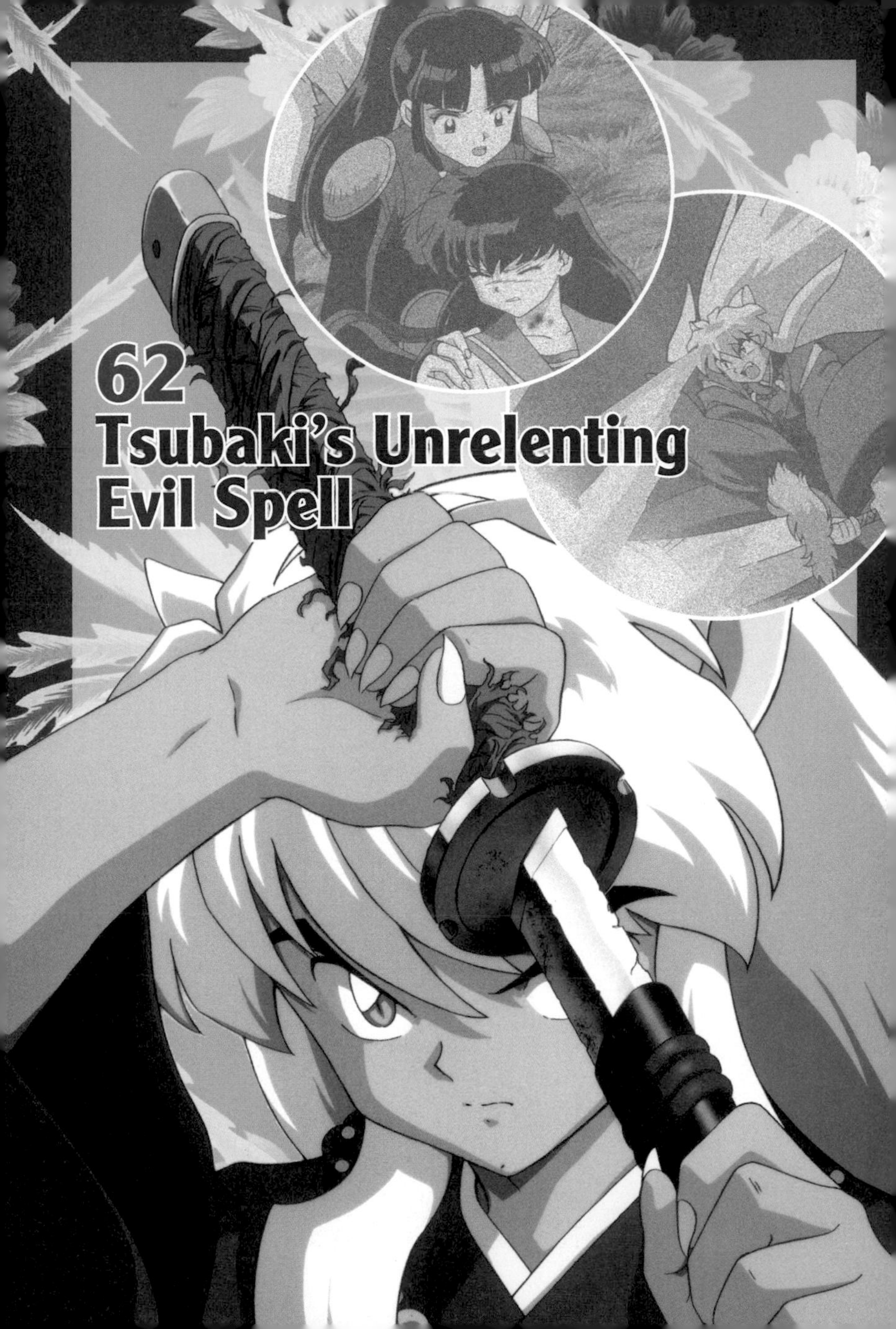

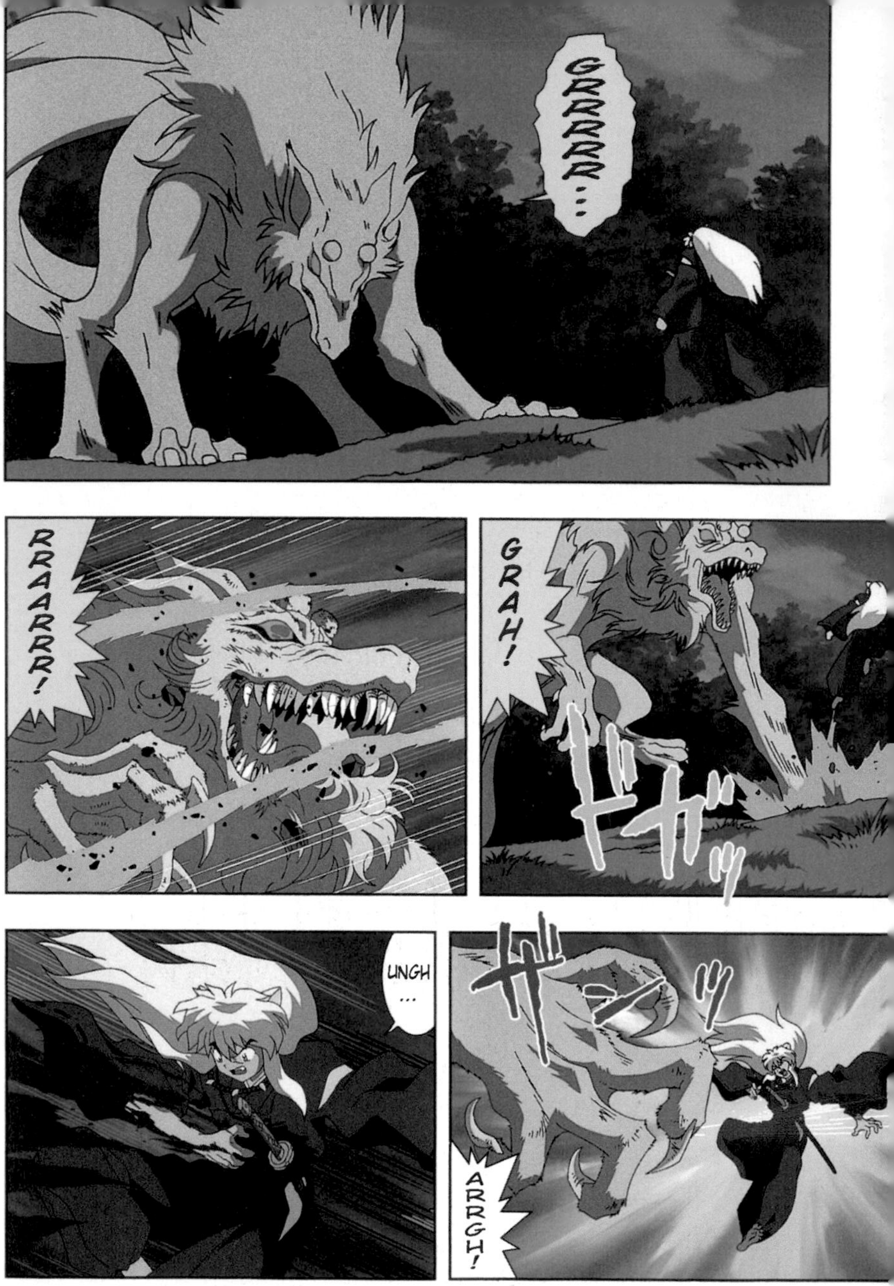
GRRRRR...
GRAH!
ドガッ
RRAARRR!
ザンッ
ARRGH!
UNGH ...

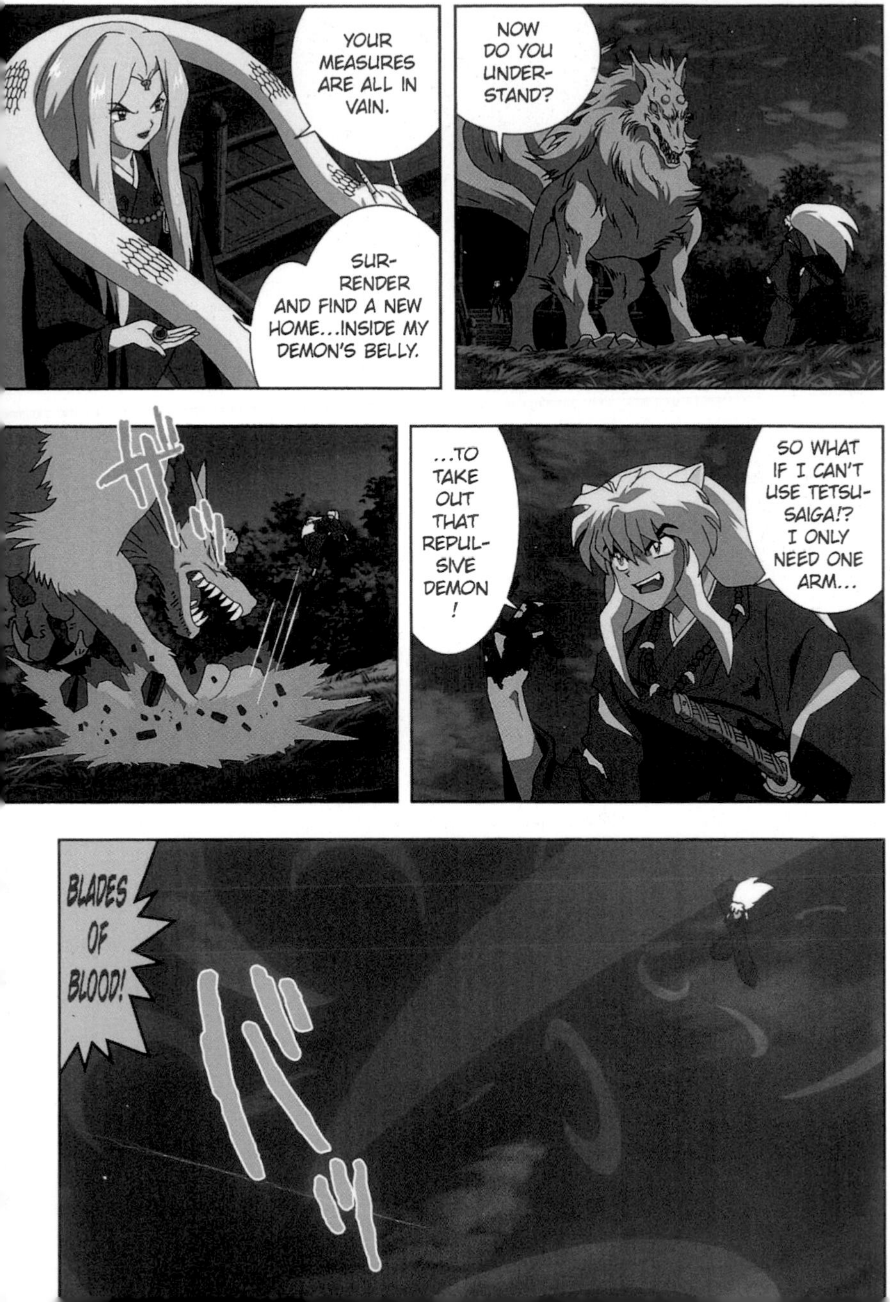
NOW DO YOU UNDER-STAND?
YOUR MEASURES ARE ALL IN VAIN.
SUR-RENDER AND FIND A NEW HOME...INSIDE MY DEMON'S BELLY.
SO WHAT IF I CAN'T USE TETSU-SAIGA!? I ONLY NEED ONE ARM...
...TO TAKE OUT THAT REPUL-SIVE DEMON!
BLADES OF BLOOD!

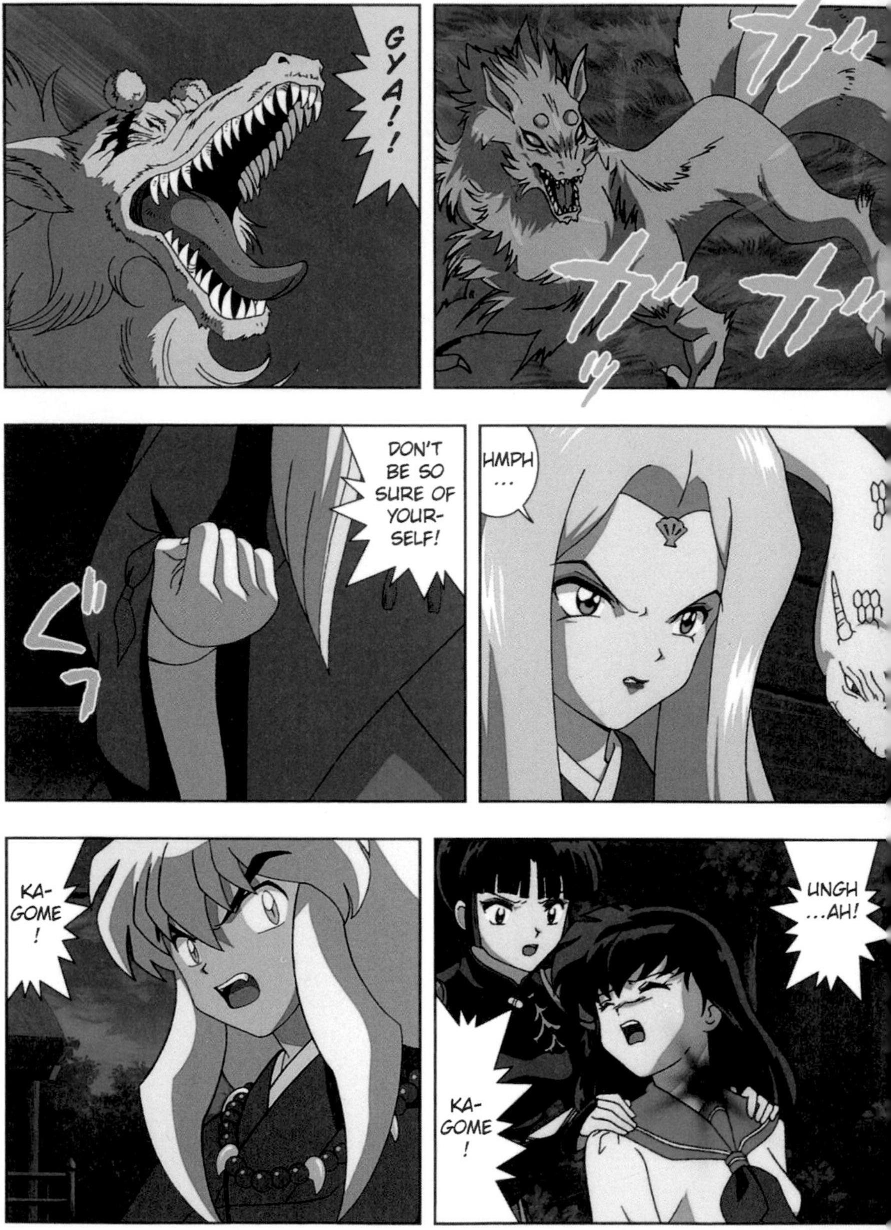
GYA!!
HMPH ...
DON'T BE SO SURE OF YOUR-SELF!
UNGH ...AH!
KA-GOME!
KA-GOME!

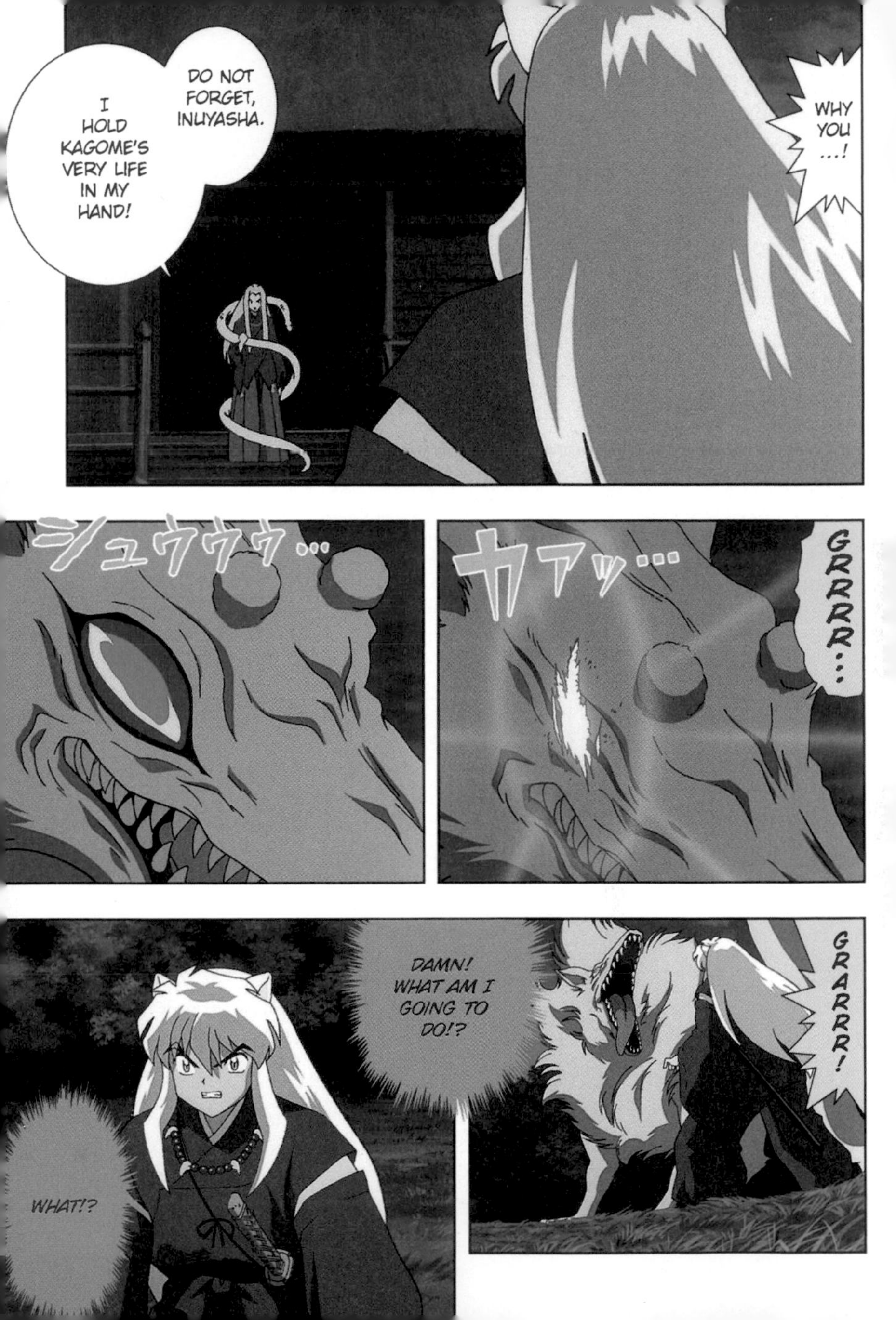
WHY YOU ...!
DO NOT FORGET, INUYASHA.
I HOLD KAGOME'S VERY LIFE IN MY HAND!
カァッ...
GRRRR..
シュウウウ...
GRARRR!
DAMN! WHAT AM I GOING TO DO!?
WHAT!?

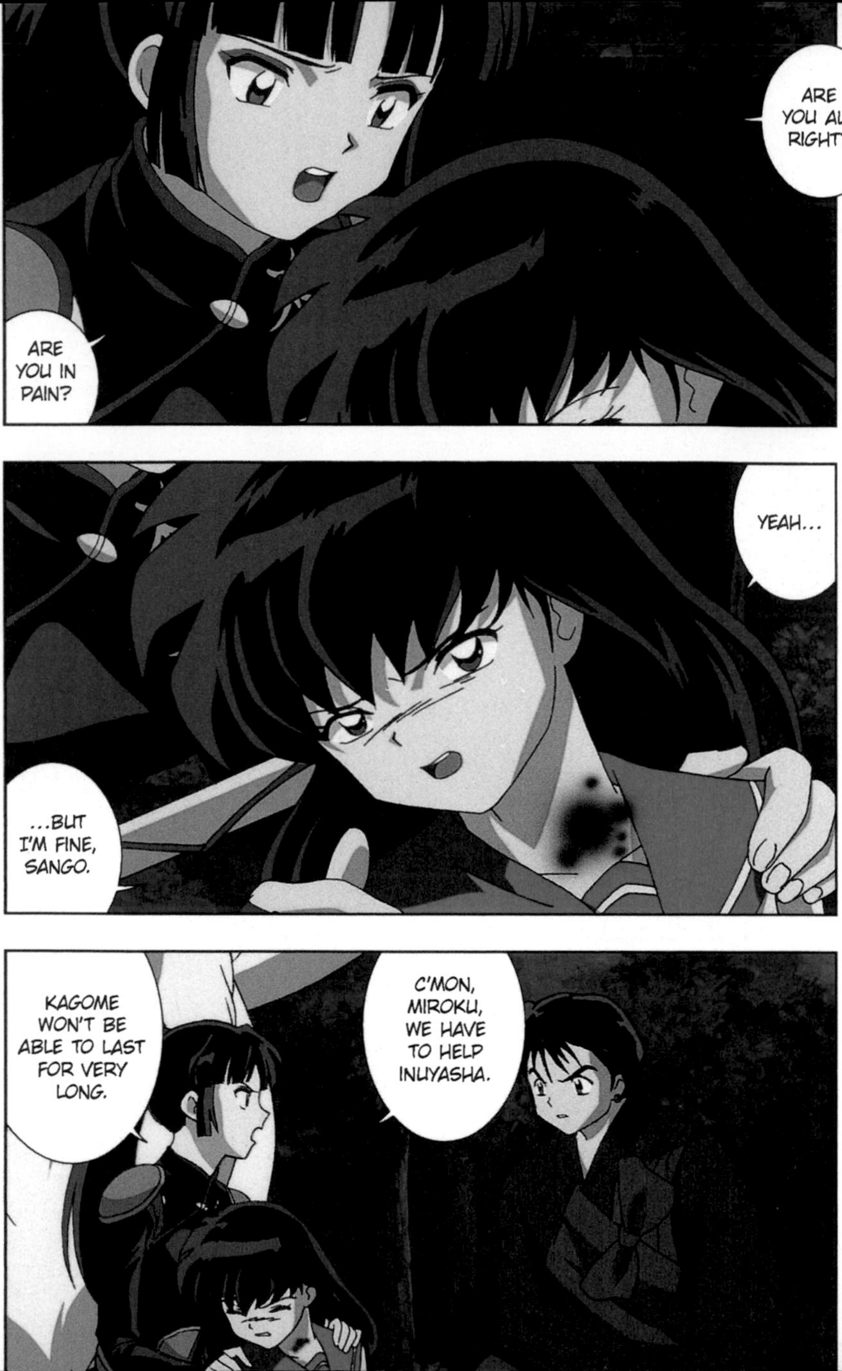
ARE YOU ALL RIGHT?
ARE YOU IN PAIN?
YEAH...
...BUT I'M FINE, SANGO.
C'MON, MIROKU, WE HAVE TO HELP INUYASHA.
KAGOME WON'T BE ABLE TO LAST FOR VERY LONG.

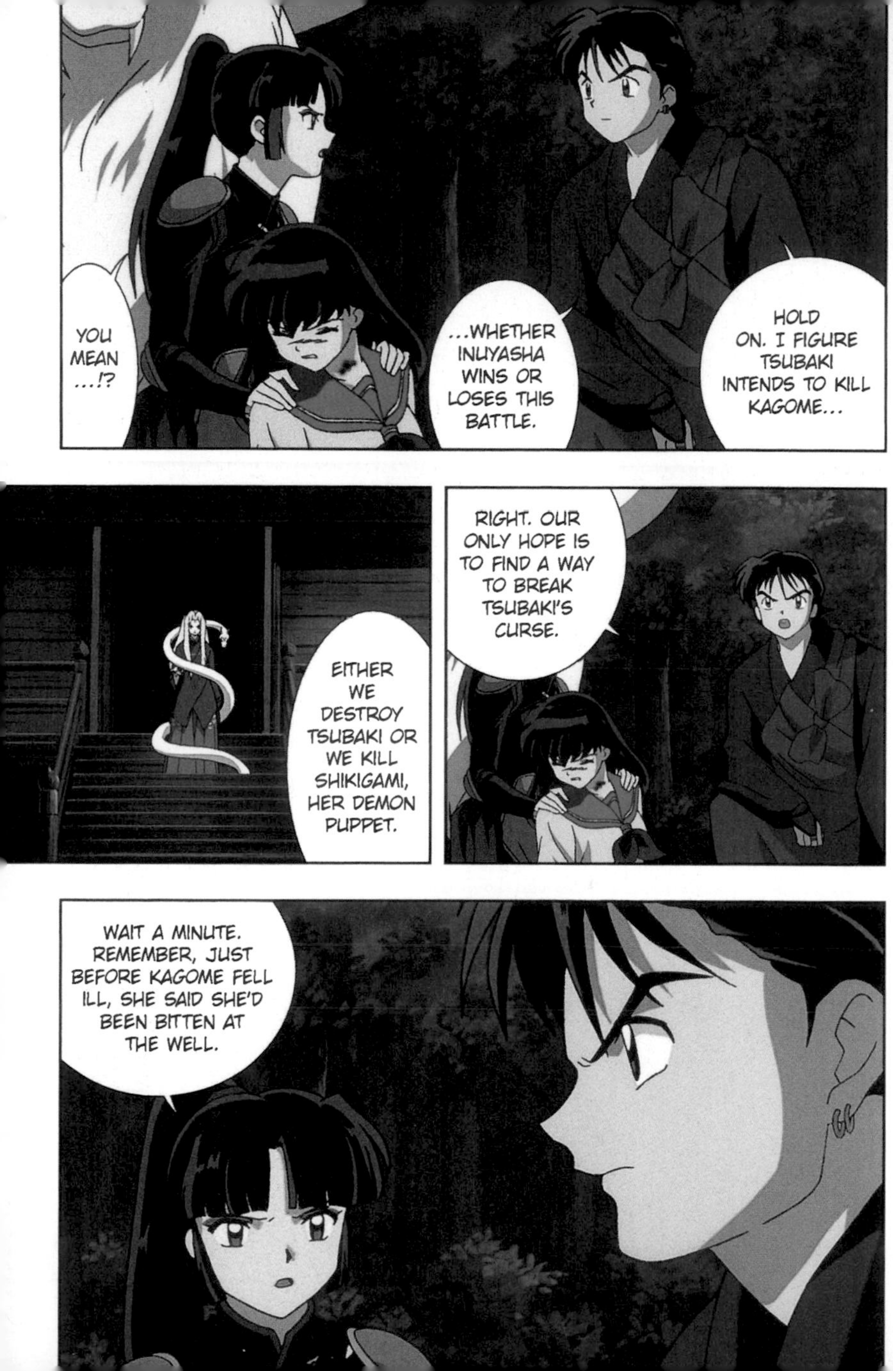
HOLD ON. I FIGURE TSUBAKI INTENDS TO KILL KAGOME...
...WHETHER INUYASHA WINS OR LOSES THIS BATTLE.
YOU MEAN ...!?
RIGHT. OUR ONLY HOPE IS TO FIND A WAY TO BREAK TSUBAKI'S CURSE.
EITHER WE DESTROY TSUBAKI OR WE KILL SHIKIGAMI, HER DEMON PUPPET.
WAIT A MINUTE. REMEMBER, JUST BEFORE KAGOME FELL ILL, SHE SAID SHE'D BEEN BITTEN AT THE WELL.

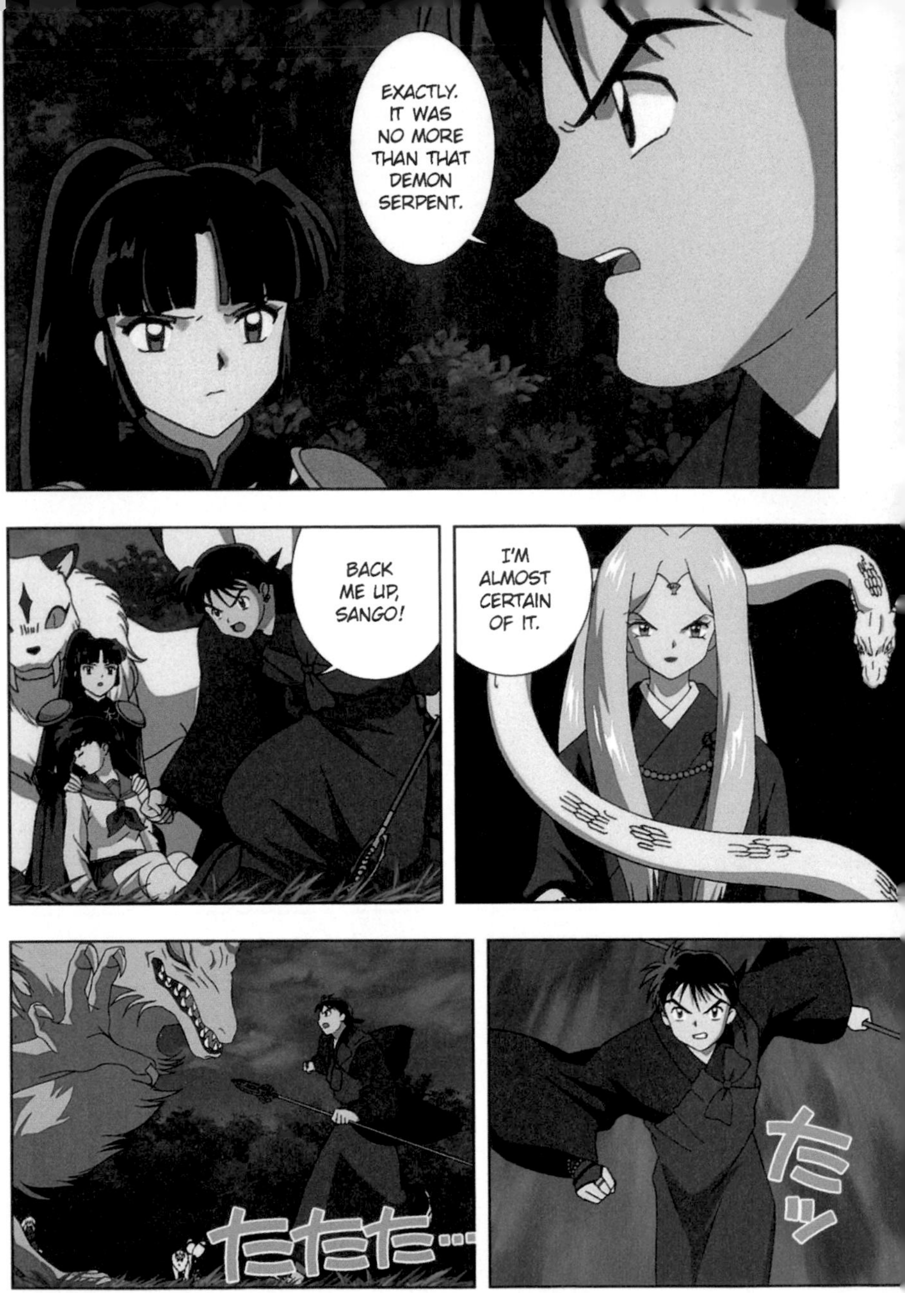
EXACTLY. IT WAS NO MORE THAN THAT DEMON SERPENT.
I'M ALMOST CERTAIN OF IT.
BACK ME UP, SANGO!
たッ
たたたた…

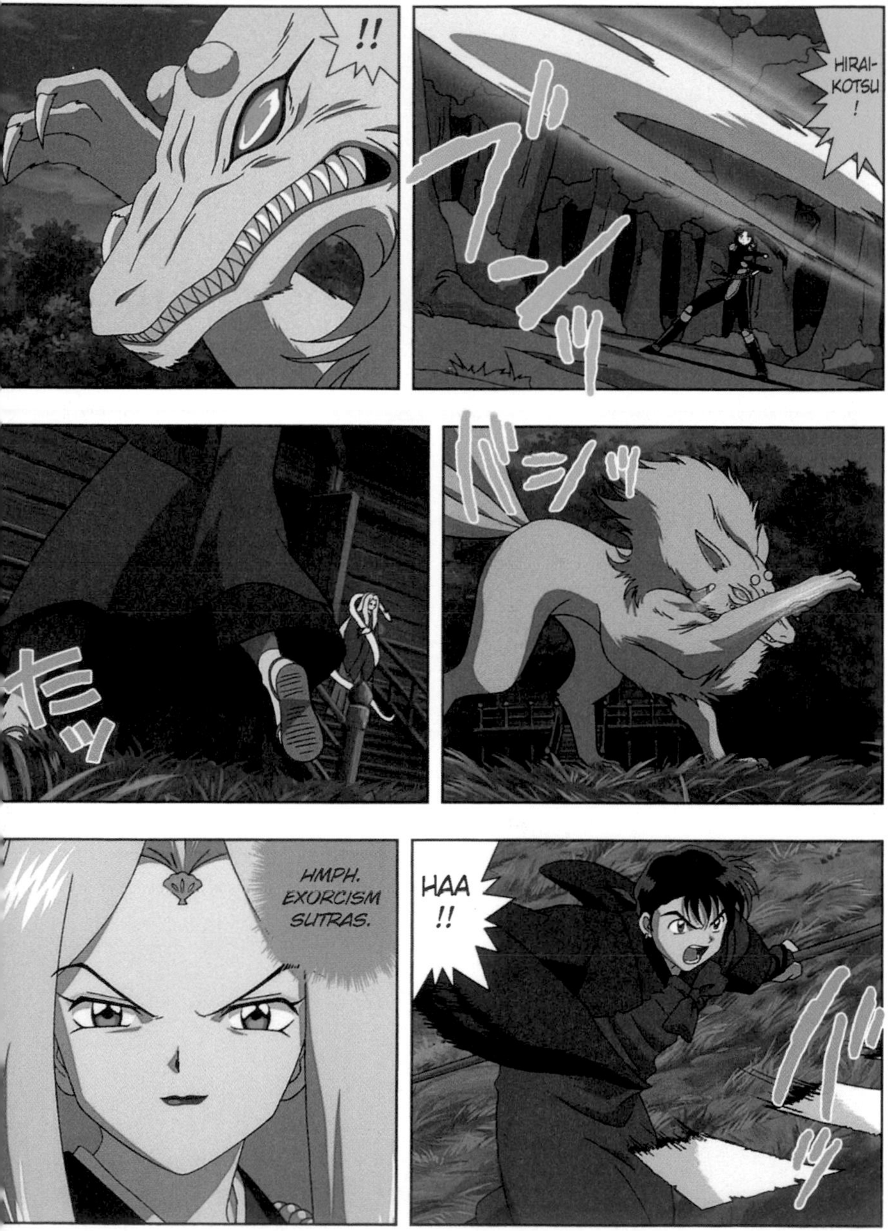
HIRAI-KOTSU!
!!
HAA!!
HMPH. EXORCISM SUTRAS.

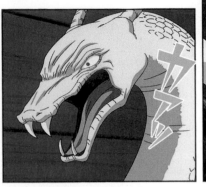

THEY'RE
USELESS
ON ME!

FOOL!
MY CURSE
CANNOT BE
BROKEN!

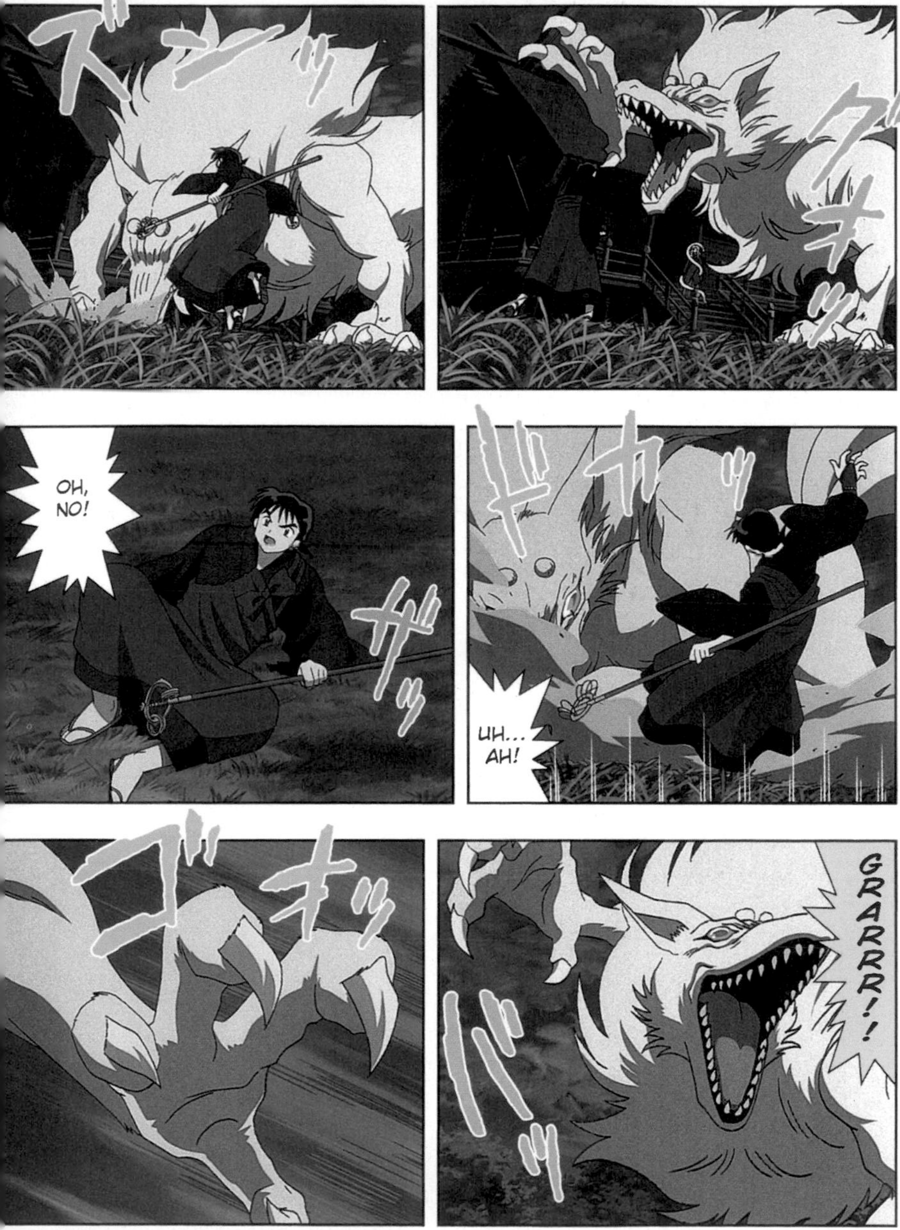
グキッ
ズンッ
ドカッ
UH... AH!
OH, NO!
ザッ
GRARRR!!
バッ
ゴオッ

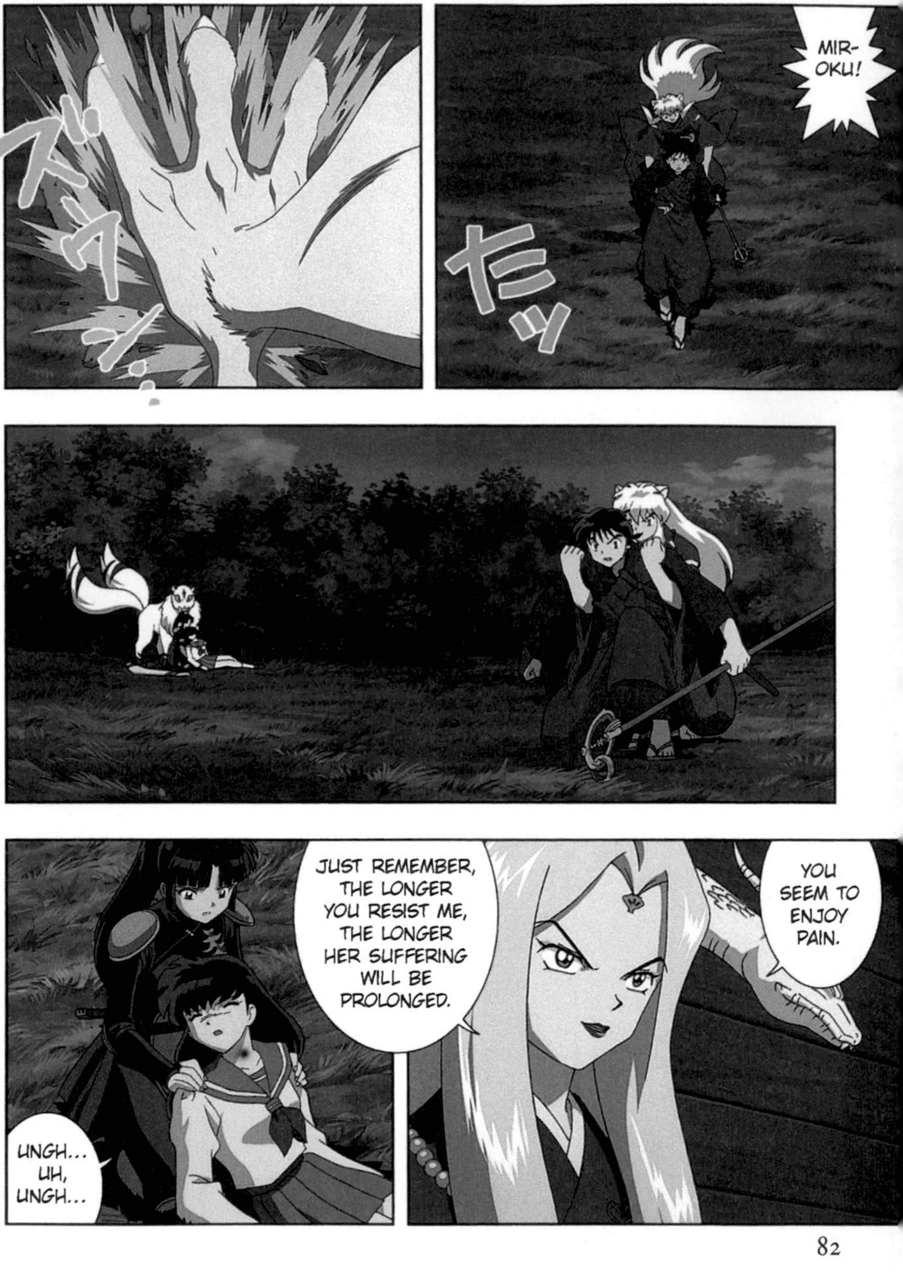
MIR-OKU!
タッ
YOU SEEM TO ENJOY PAIN.
JUST REMEMBER, THE LONGER YOU RESIST ME, THE LONGER HER SUFFERING WILL BE PROLONGED.
UNGH... UH, UNGH...

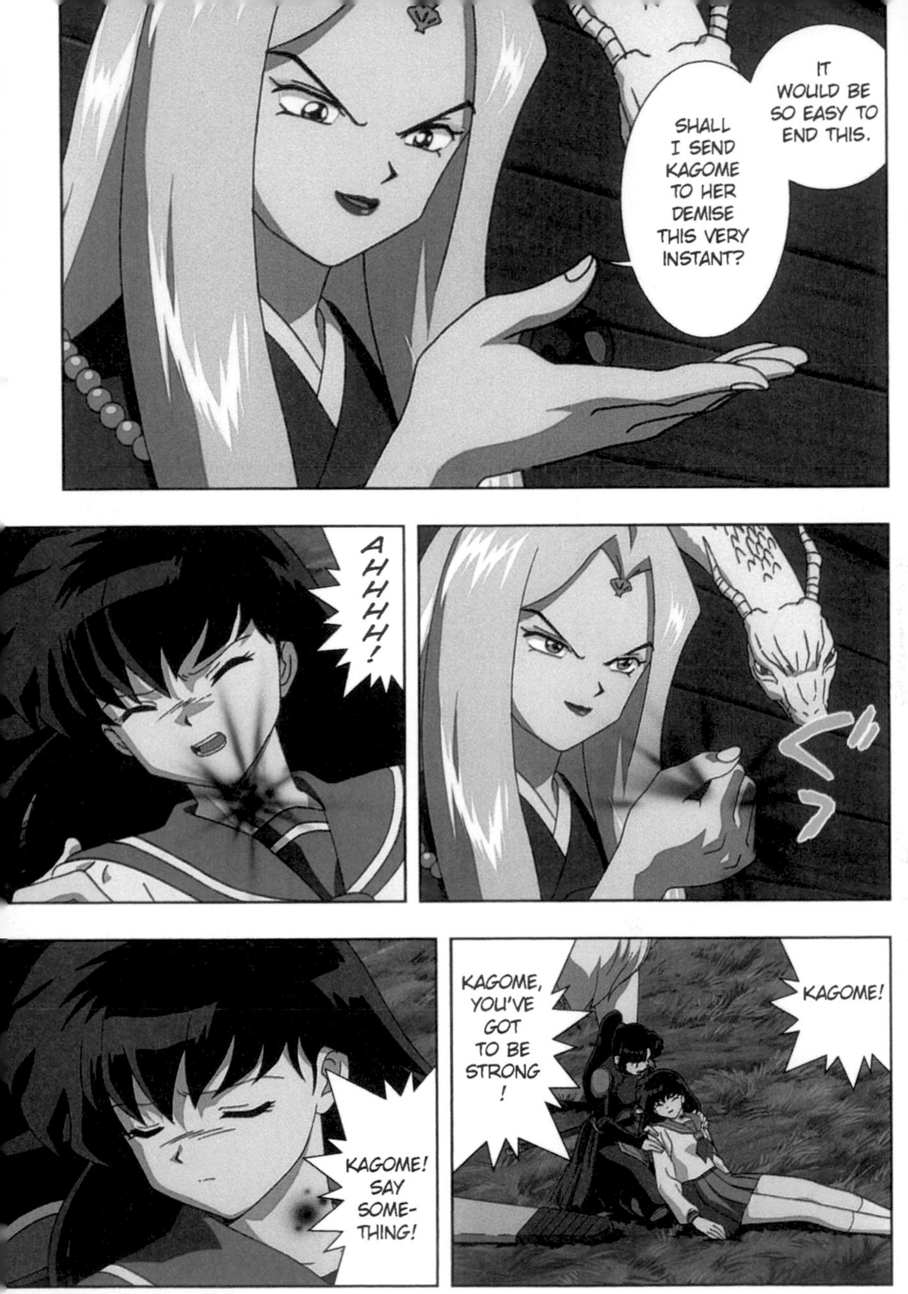
IT WOULD BE SO EASY TO END THIS.
SHALL I SEND KAGOME TO HER DEMISE THIS VERY INSTANT?
ぐっ
AHHHHH!
KAGOME!
KAGOME, YOU'VE GOT TO BE STRONG!
KAGOME! SAY SOME-THING!

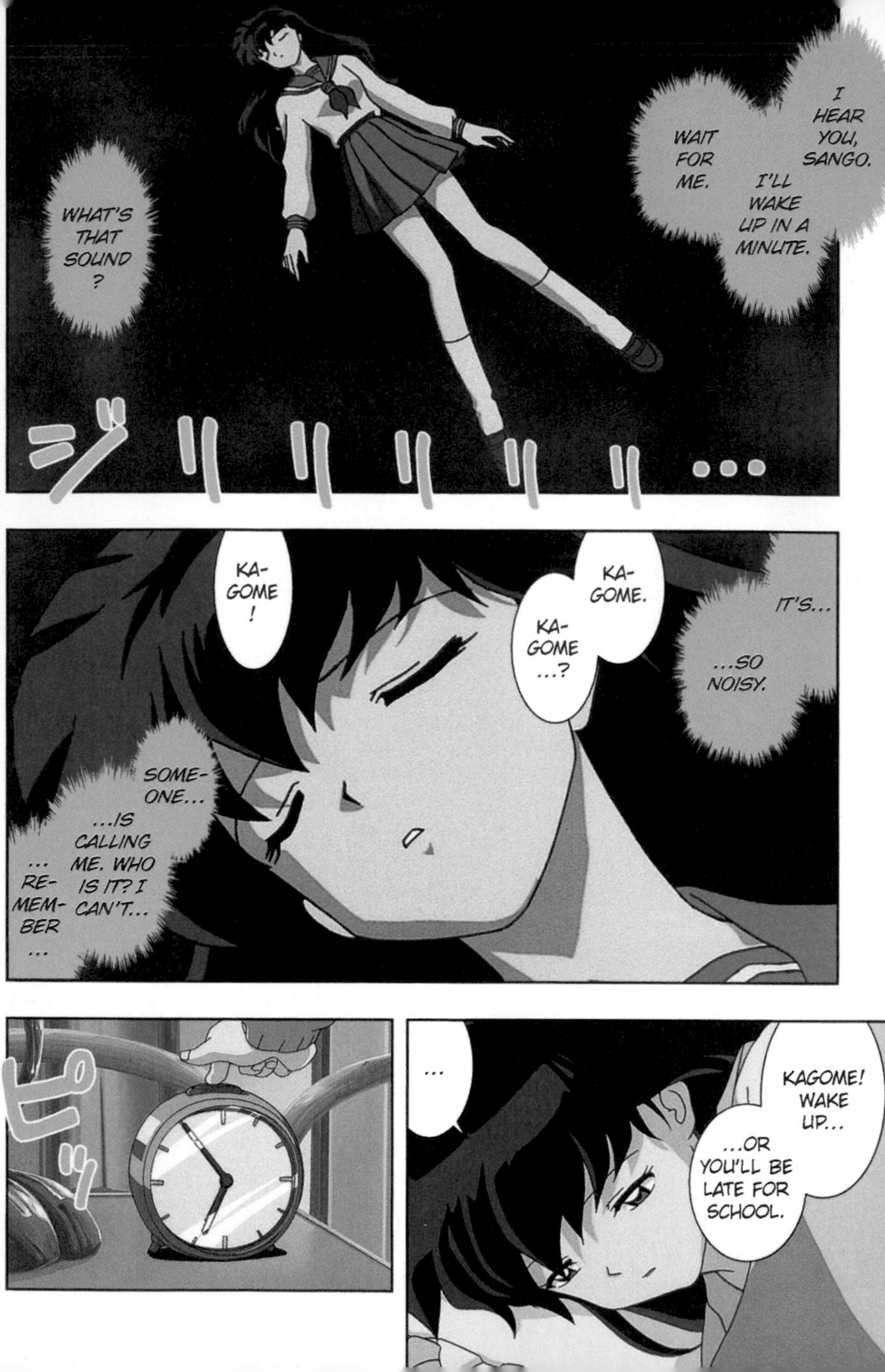

I HEAR YOU, SANGO.
I'LL WAKE UP IN A MINUTE.
WAIT FOR ME.
WHAT'S THAT SOUND?
ジリリリリリ…
IT'S...
...SO NOISY.
KA-GOME.
KA-GOME...?
KA-GOME!
SOME-ONE...
...IS CALLING ME. WHO IS IT? I CAN'T...
...RE-MEM-BER...
KAGOME! WAKE UP...
...OR YOU'LL BE LATE FOR SCHOOL.
...
ピッ

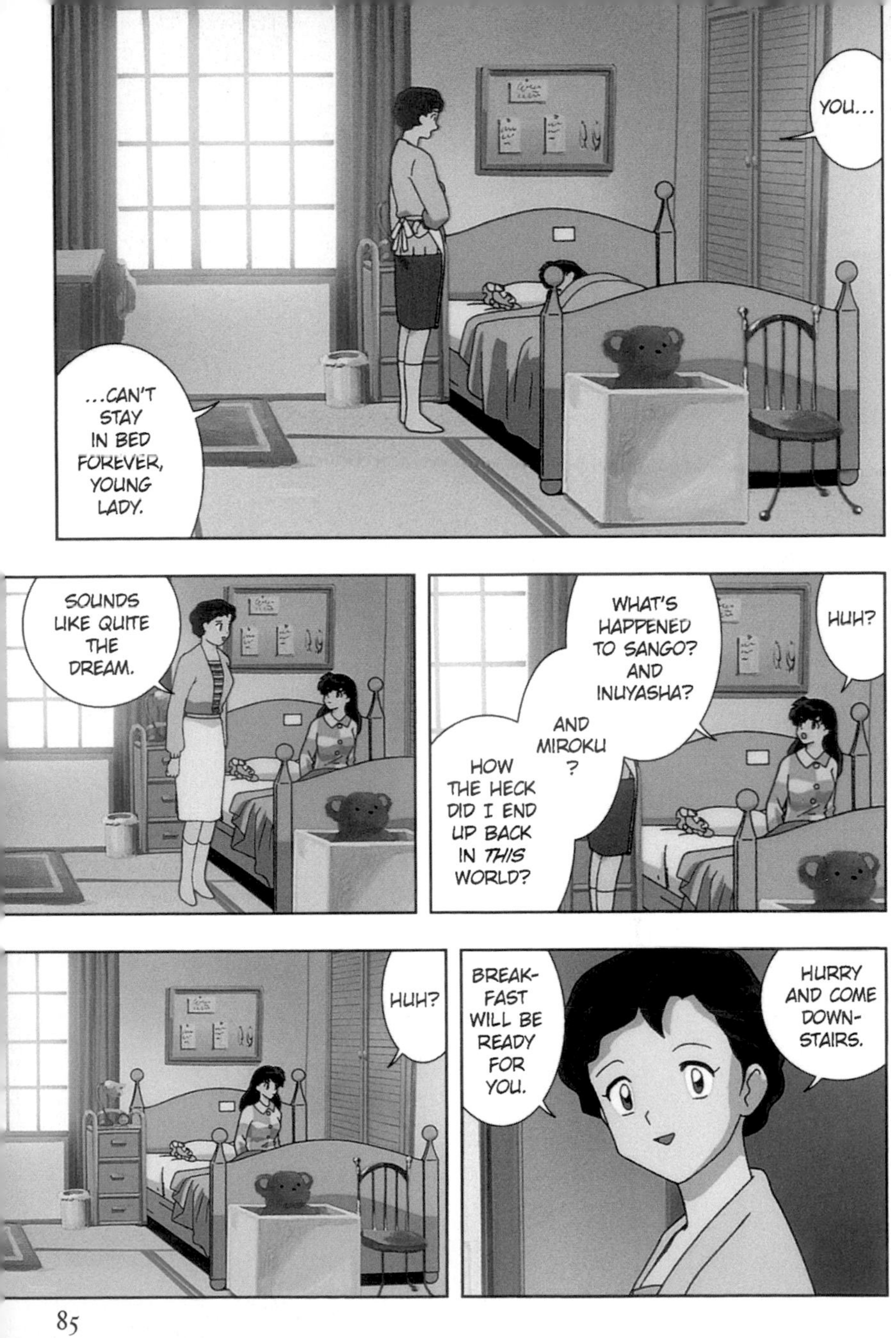
YOU...
...CAN'T STAY IN BED FOREVER, YOUNG LADY.
HUH?
WHAT'S HAPPENED TO SANGO? AND INUYASHA?
AND MIROKU?
HOW THE HECK DID I END UP BACK IN *THIS* WORLD?
SOUNDS LIKE QUITE THE DREAM.
HURRY AND COME DOWNSTAIRS.
BREAKFAST WILL BE READY FOR YOU.
HUH?

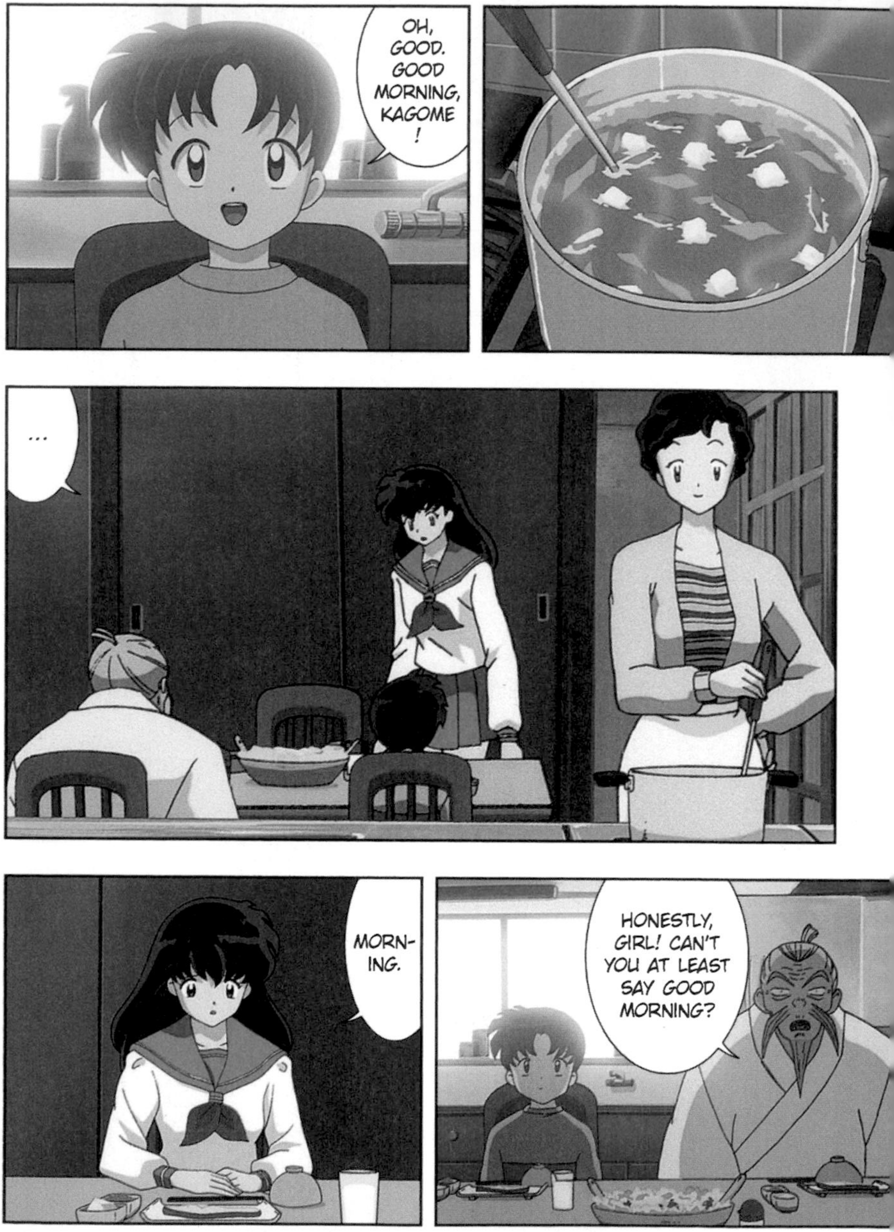
OH, GOOD. GOOD MORNING, KAGOME!
...
HONESTLY, GIRL! CAN'T YOU AT LEAST SAY GOOD MORNING?
MORN-ING.

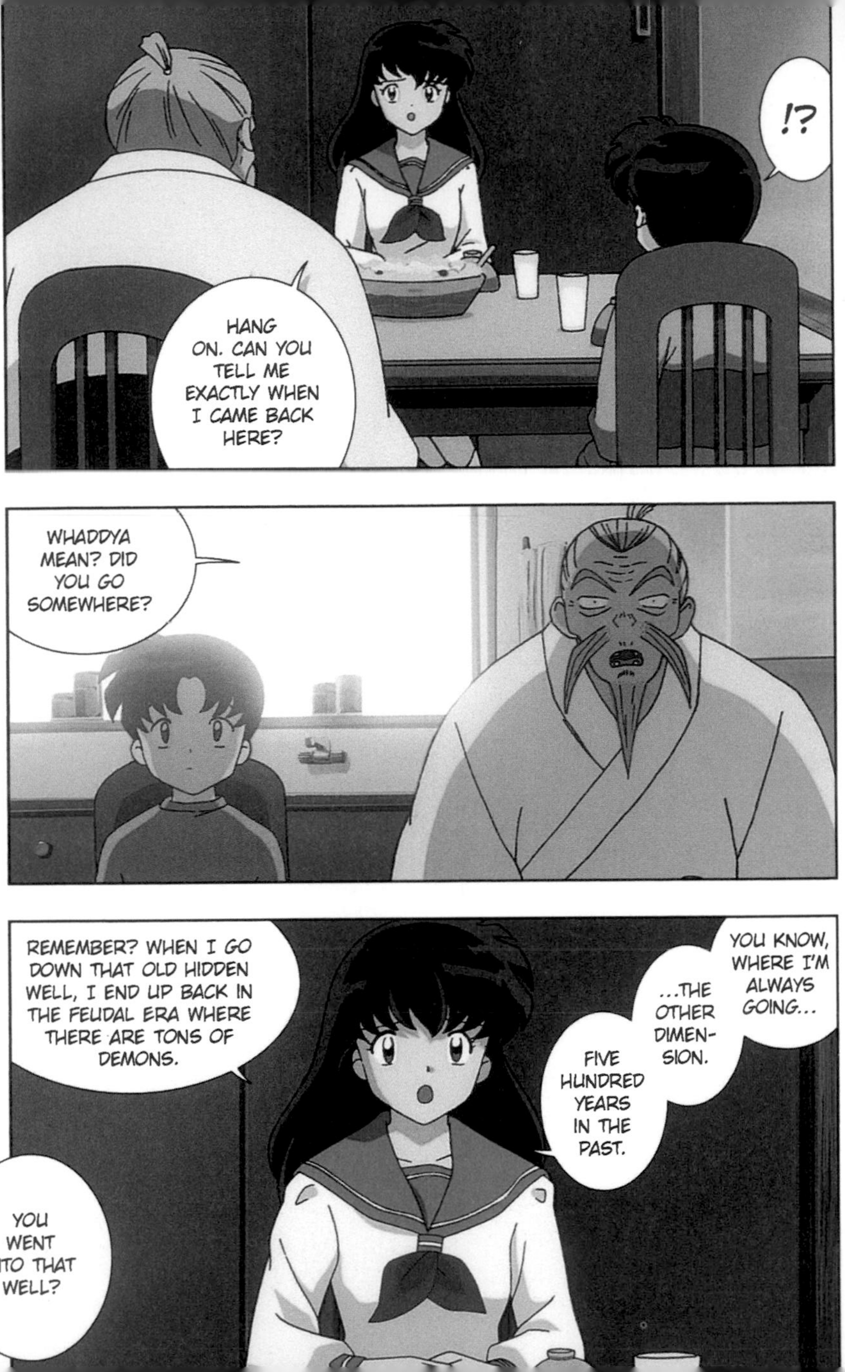
!?
HANG ON. CAN YOU TELL ME EXACTLY WHEN I CAME BACK HERE?
WHADDYA MEAN? DID YOU GO SOMEWHERE?
YOU KNOW, WHERE I'M ALWAYS GOING...
...THE OTHER DIMEN-SION.
FIVE HUNDRED YEARS IN THE PAST.
REMEMBER? WHEN I GO DOWN THAT OLD HIDDEN WELL, I END UP BACK IN THE FEUDAL ERA WHERE THERE ARE TONS OF DEMONS.
YOU WENT INTO THAT WELL?

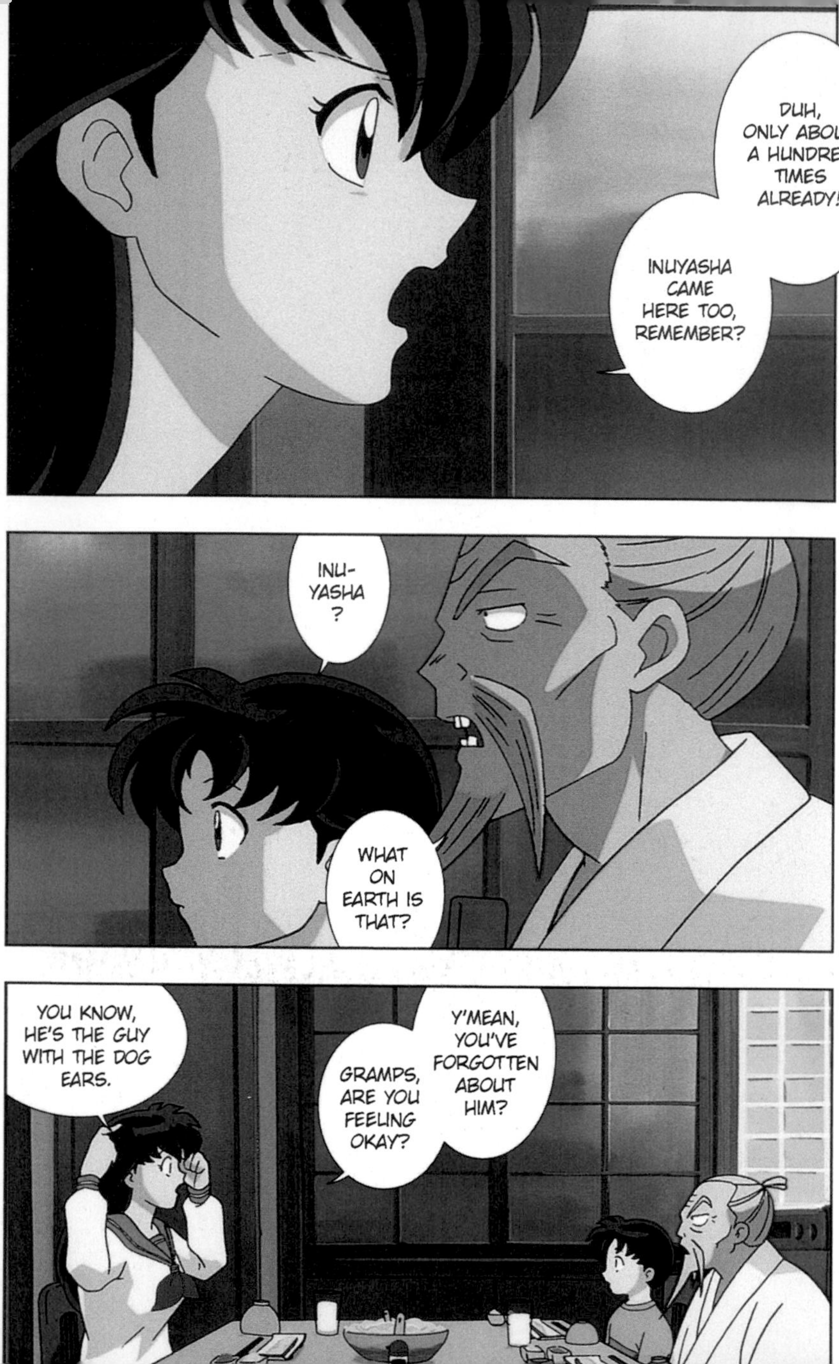
DUH, ONLY ABOUT A HUNDRED TIMES ALREADY!
INUYASHA CAME HERE TOO, REMEMBER?
INU-YASHA?
WHAT ON EARTH IS THAT?
Y'MEAN, YOU'VE FORGOTTEN ABOUT HIM?
GRAMPS, ARE YOU FEELING OKAY?
YOU KNOW, HE'S THE GUY WITH THE DOG EARS.

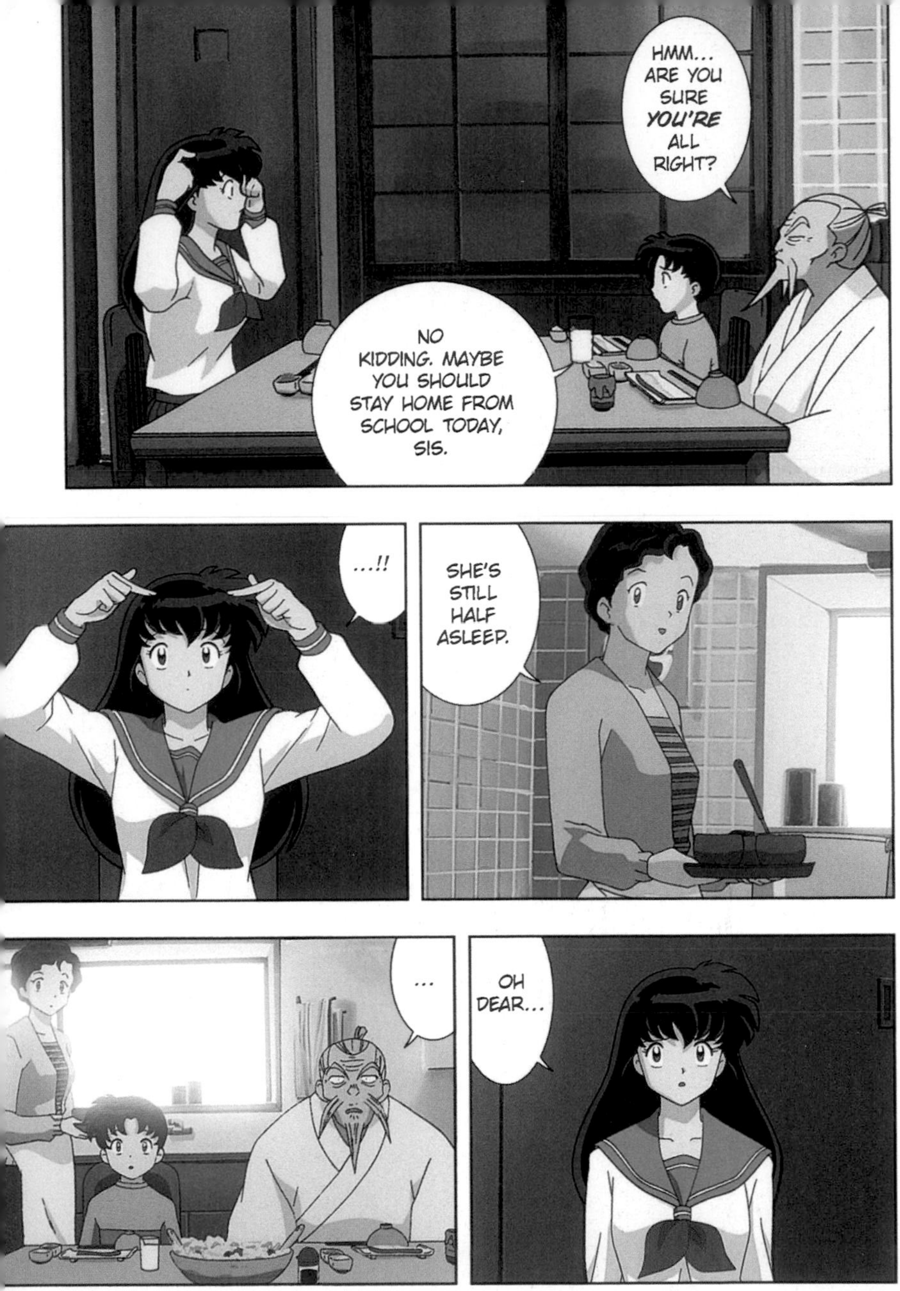
HMM... ARE YOU SURE YOU'RE ALL RIGHT?
NO KIDDING. MAYBE YOU SHOULD STAY HOME FROM SCHOOL TODAY, SIS.
SHE'S STILL HALF ASLEEP.
...!!
OH DEAR...
...

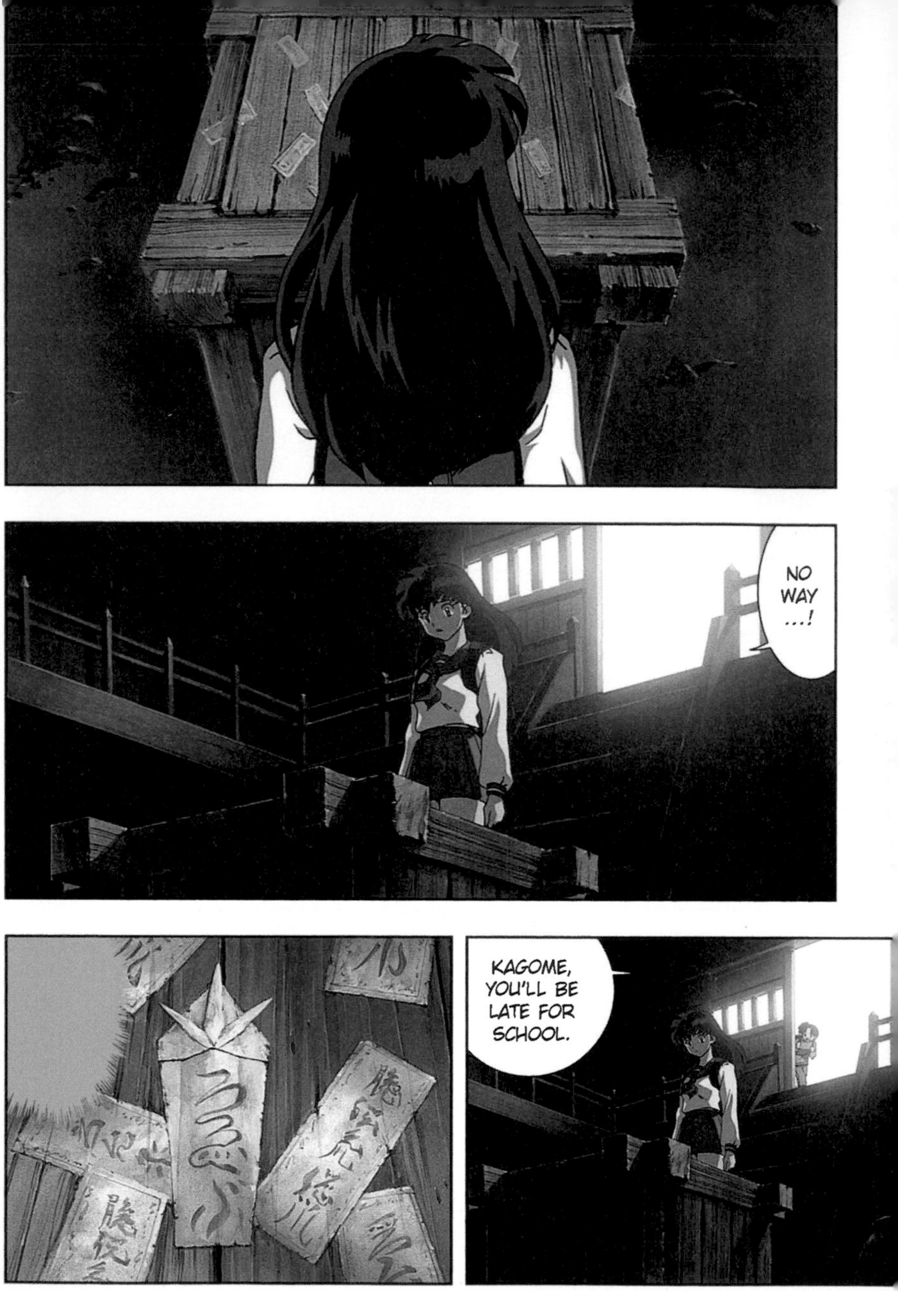
NO WAY ...!
KAGOME, YOU'LL BE LATE FOR SCHOOL.

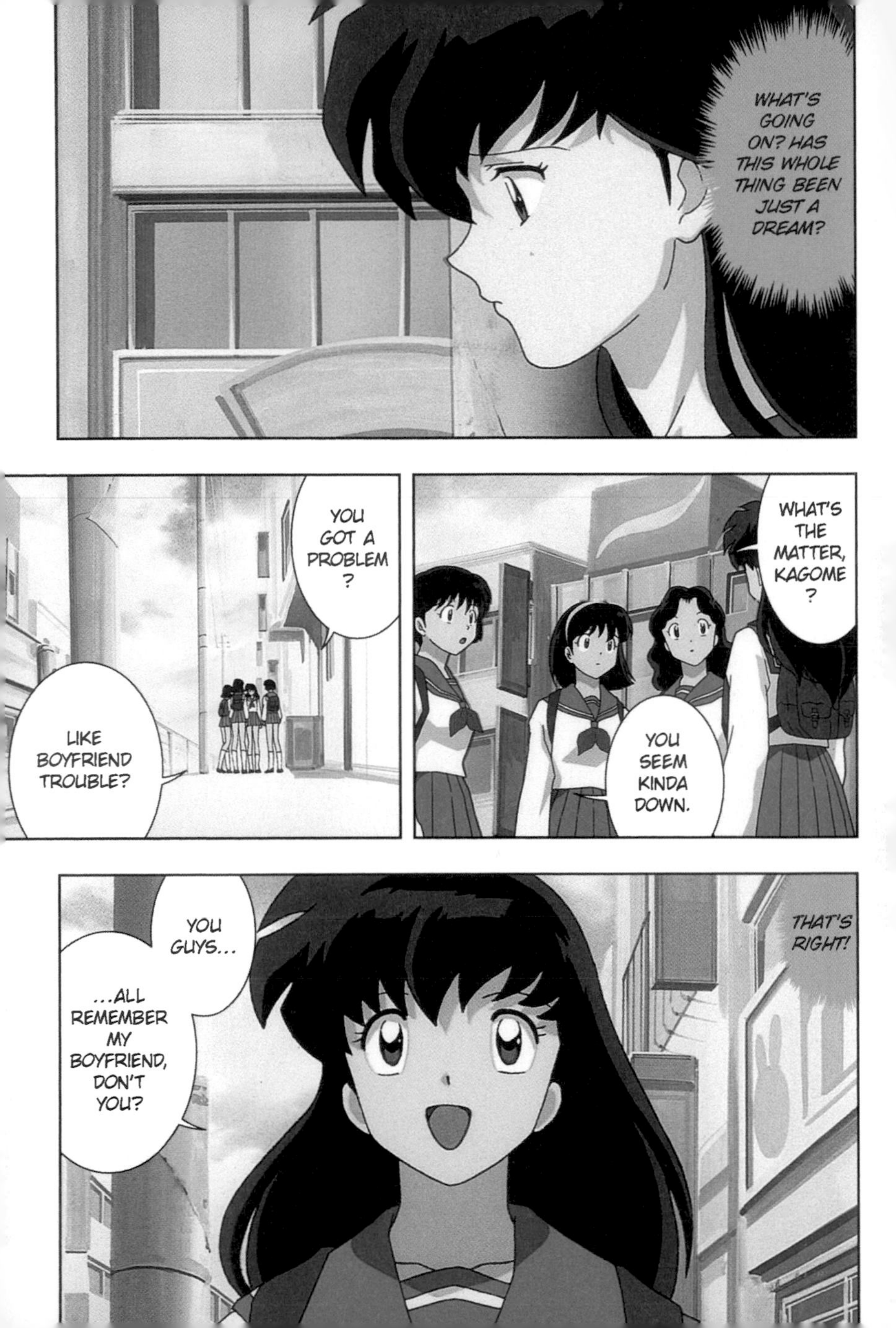
WHAT'S GOING ON? HAS THIS WHOLE THING BEEN JUST A DREAM?
WHAT'S THE MATTER, KAGOME?
YOU SEEM KINDA DOWN.
YOU GOT A PROBLEM?
LIKE BOYFRIEND TROUBLE?
THAT'S RIGHT!
YOU GUYS...
...ALL REMEMBER MY BOYFRIEND, DON'T YOU?

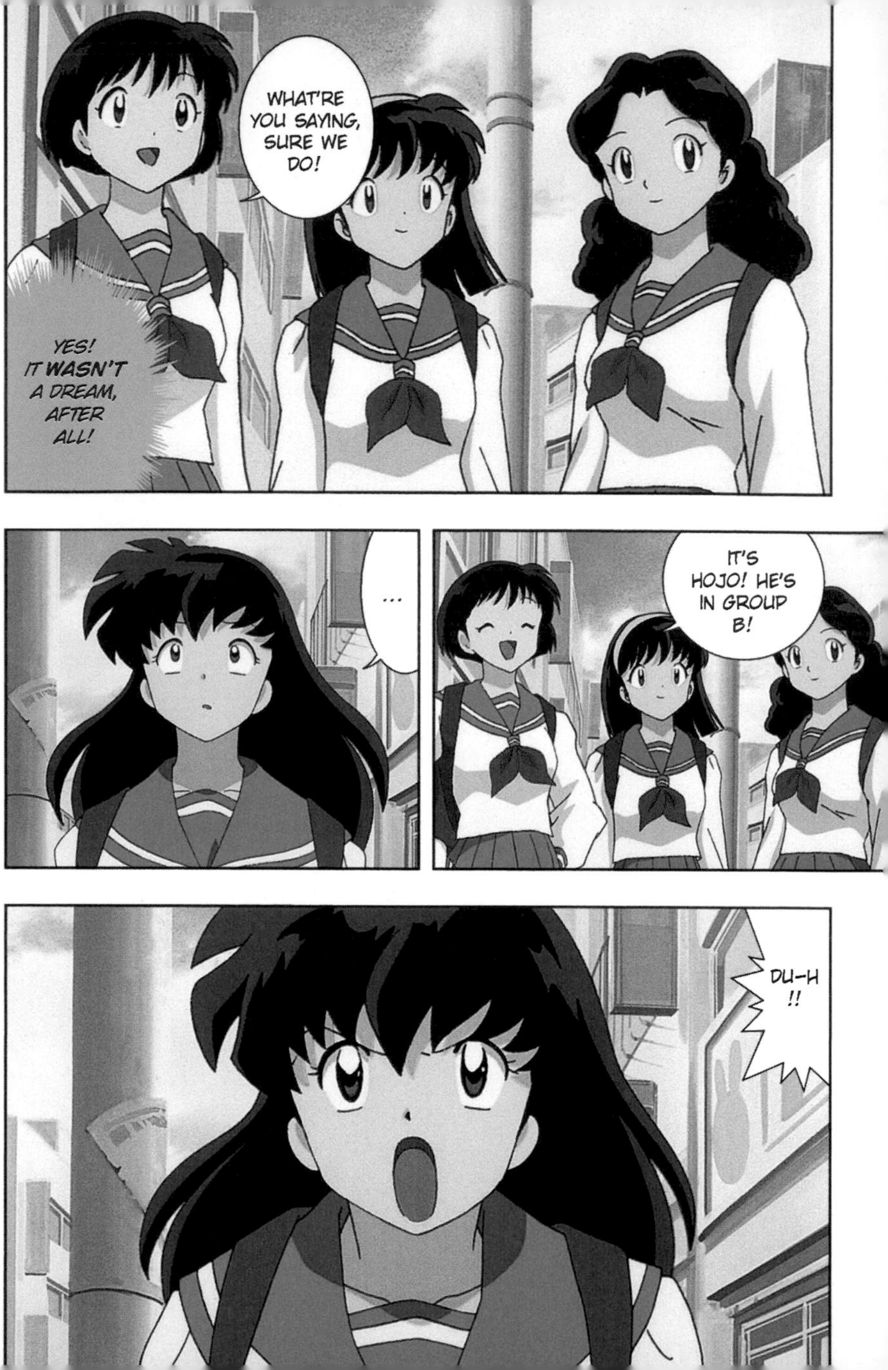
WHAT'RE YOU SAYING, SURE WE DO!
YES! IT WASN'T A DREAM, AFTER ALL!
IT'S HOJO! HE'S IN GROUP B!
...
DU-H !!

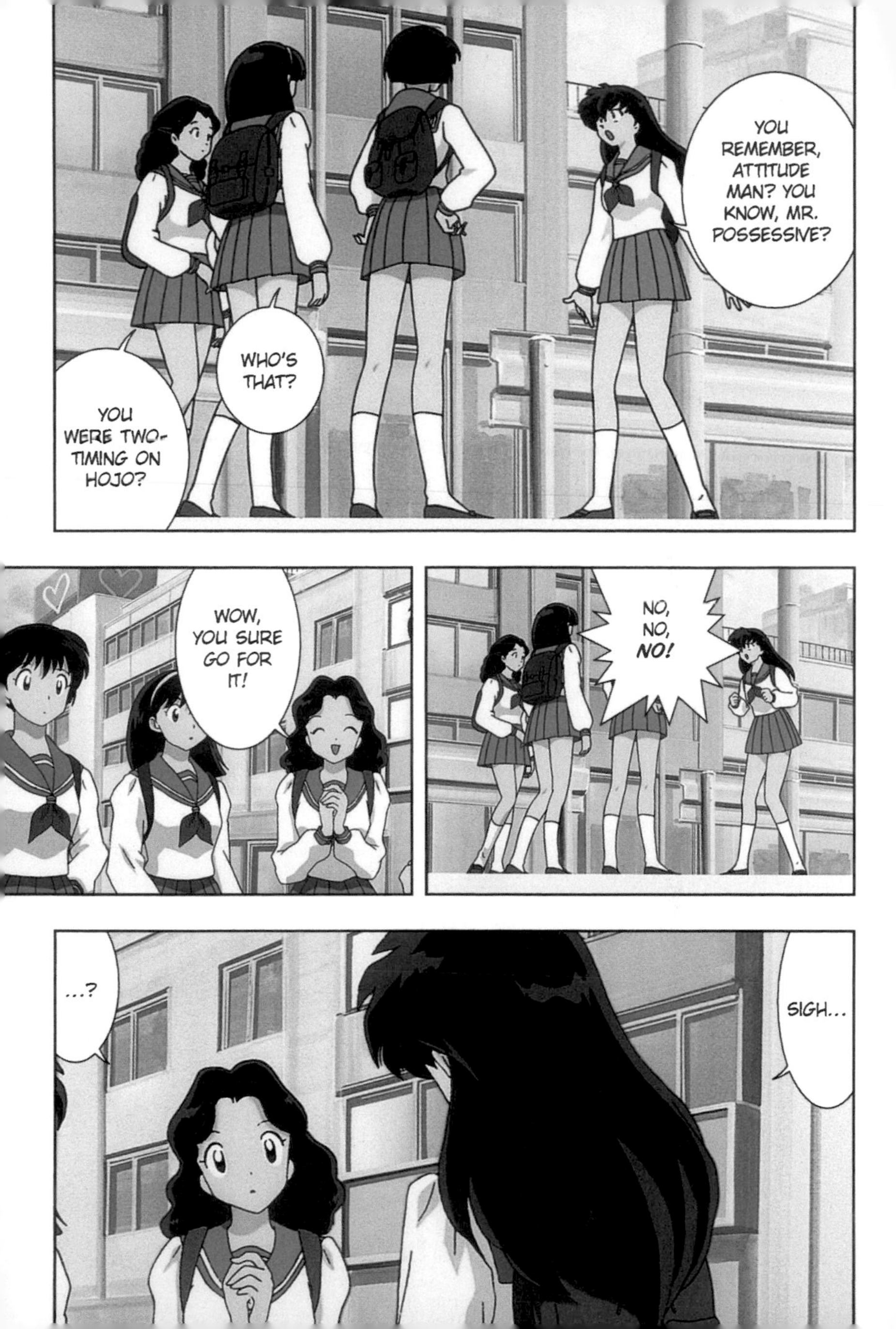
YOU REMEMBER, ATTITUDE MAN? YOU KNOW, MR. POSSESSIVE?
WHO'S THAT?
YOU WERE TWO-TIMING ON HOJO?
NO, NO, *NO!*
WOW, YOU SURE GO FOR IT!
SIGH...
...?

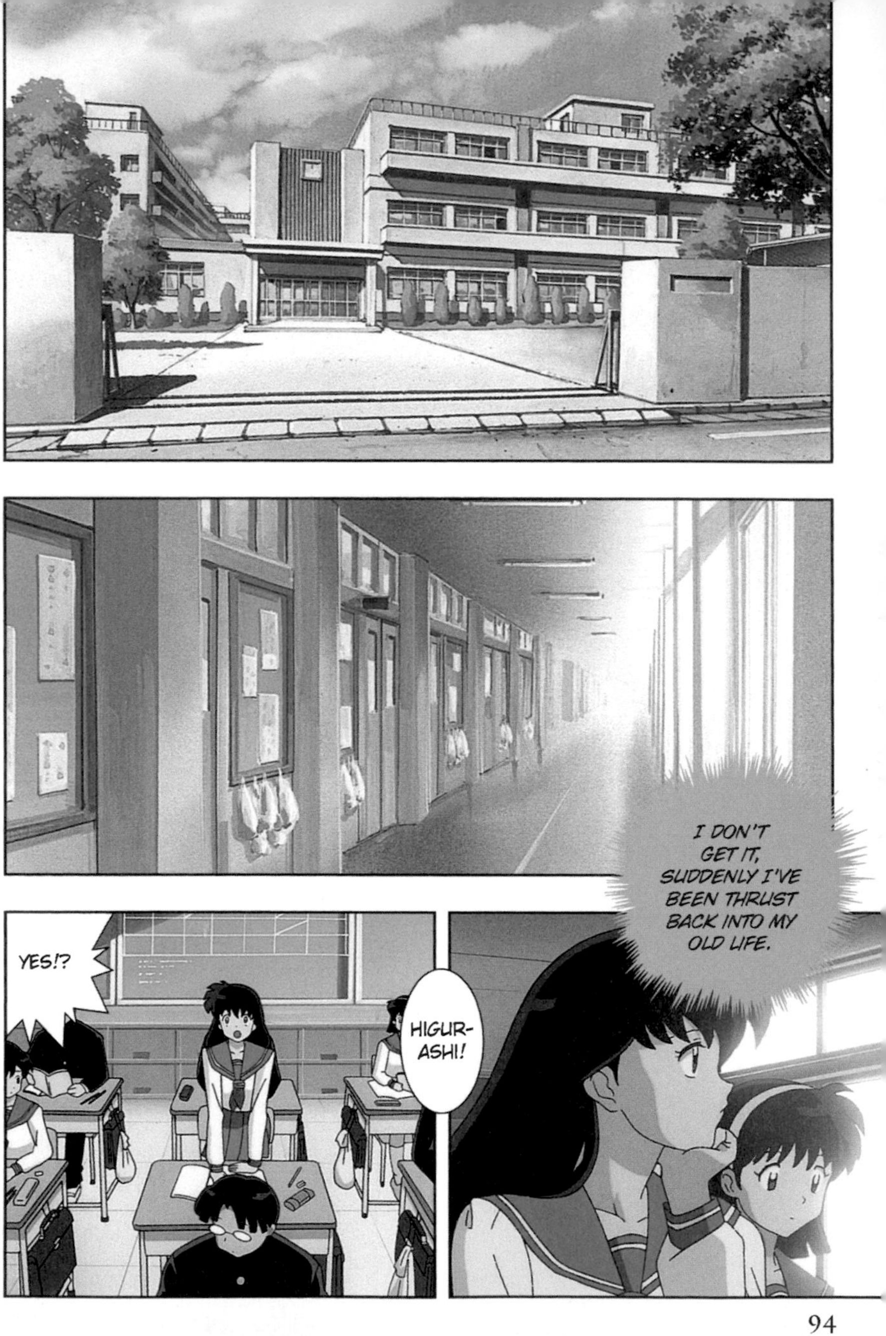
I DON'T GET IT, SUDDENLY I'VE BEEN THRUST BACK INTO MY OLD LIFE.
HIGUR-ASHI!
YES!?

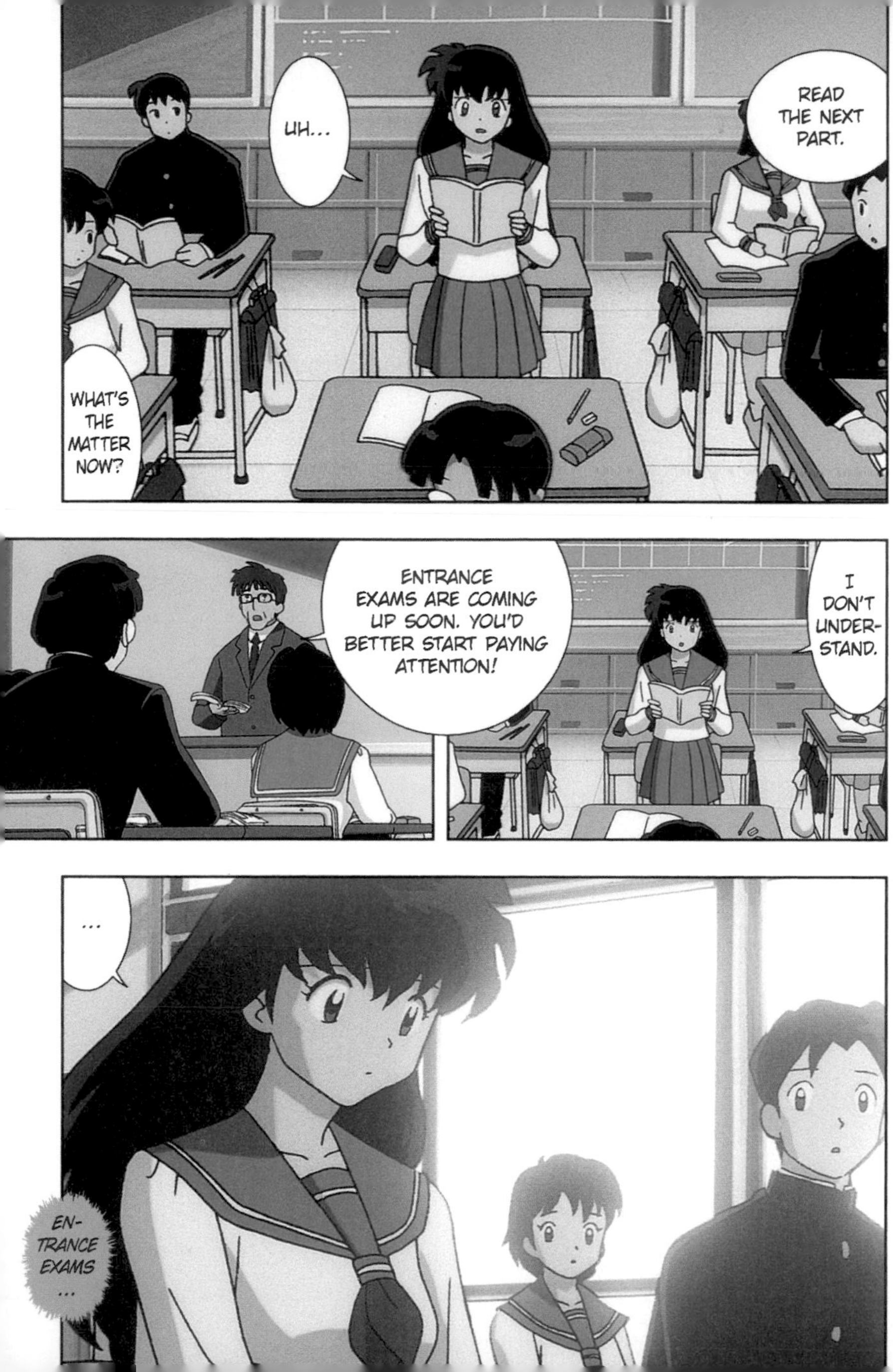
READ THE NEXT PART.
UH...
WHAT'S THE MATTER NOW?
I DON'T UNDER-STAND.
ENTRANCE EXAMS ARE COMING UP SOON. YOU'D BETTER START PAYING ATTENTION!
...
EN-TRANCE EXAMS ...

...I'M SUPPOSED TO STUDY FOR EXAMS.

YEAH...

THAT'S MY REAL LIFE.

THAT WAS HOW I WANTED...

HUH?

...MY LIFE TO BE.

KAGOME...!

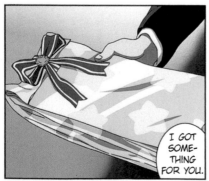

I GOT SOMETHING FOR YOU.

HEY, YOU.

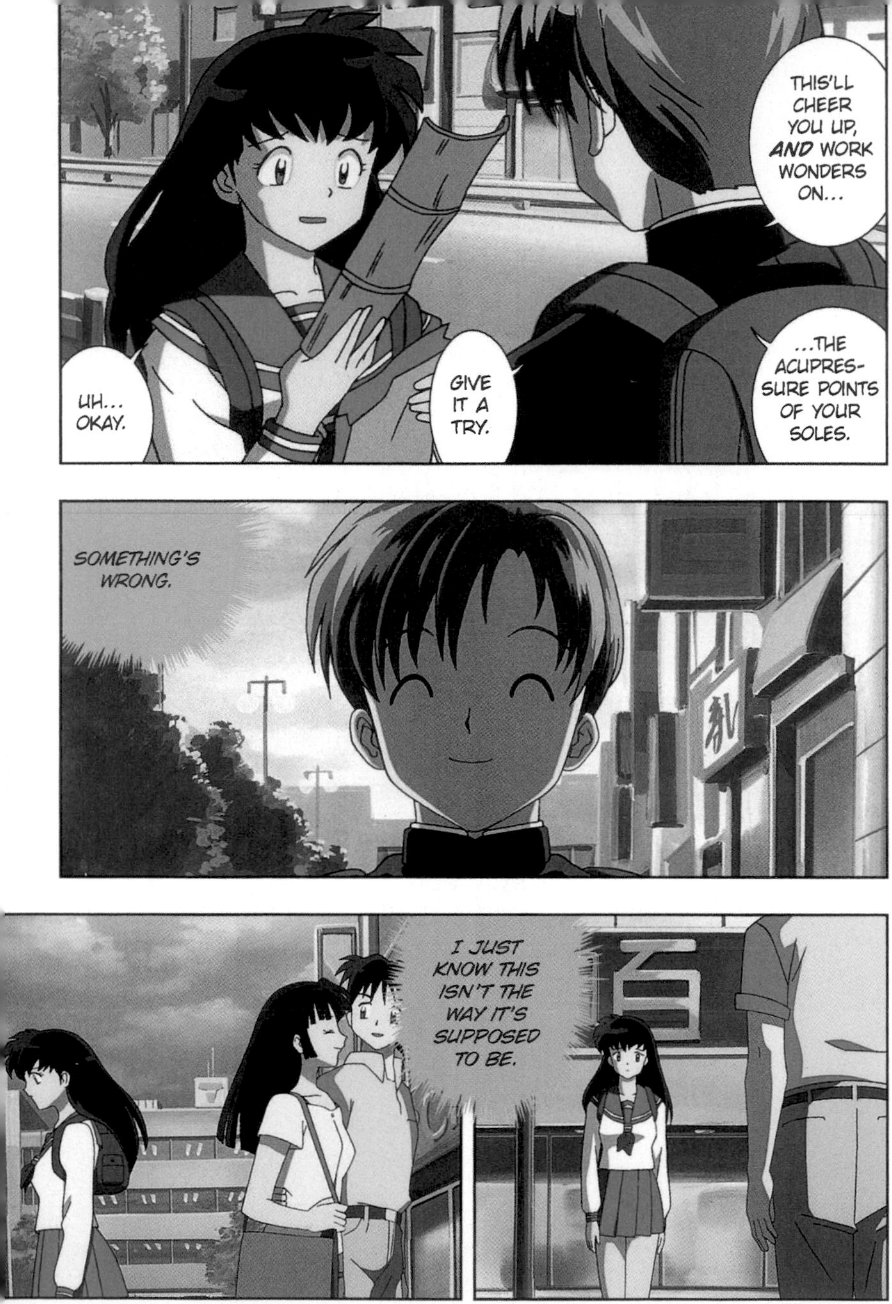
THIS'LL CHEER YOU UP, AND WORK WONDERS ON...
...THE ACUPRES-SURE POINTS OF YOUR SOLES.
GIVE IT A TRY.
UH... OKAY.
SOMETHING'S WRONG.
I JUST KNOW THIS ISN'T THE WAY IT'S SUPPOSED TO BE.

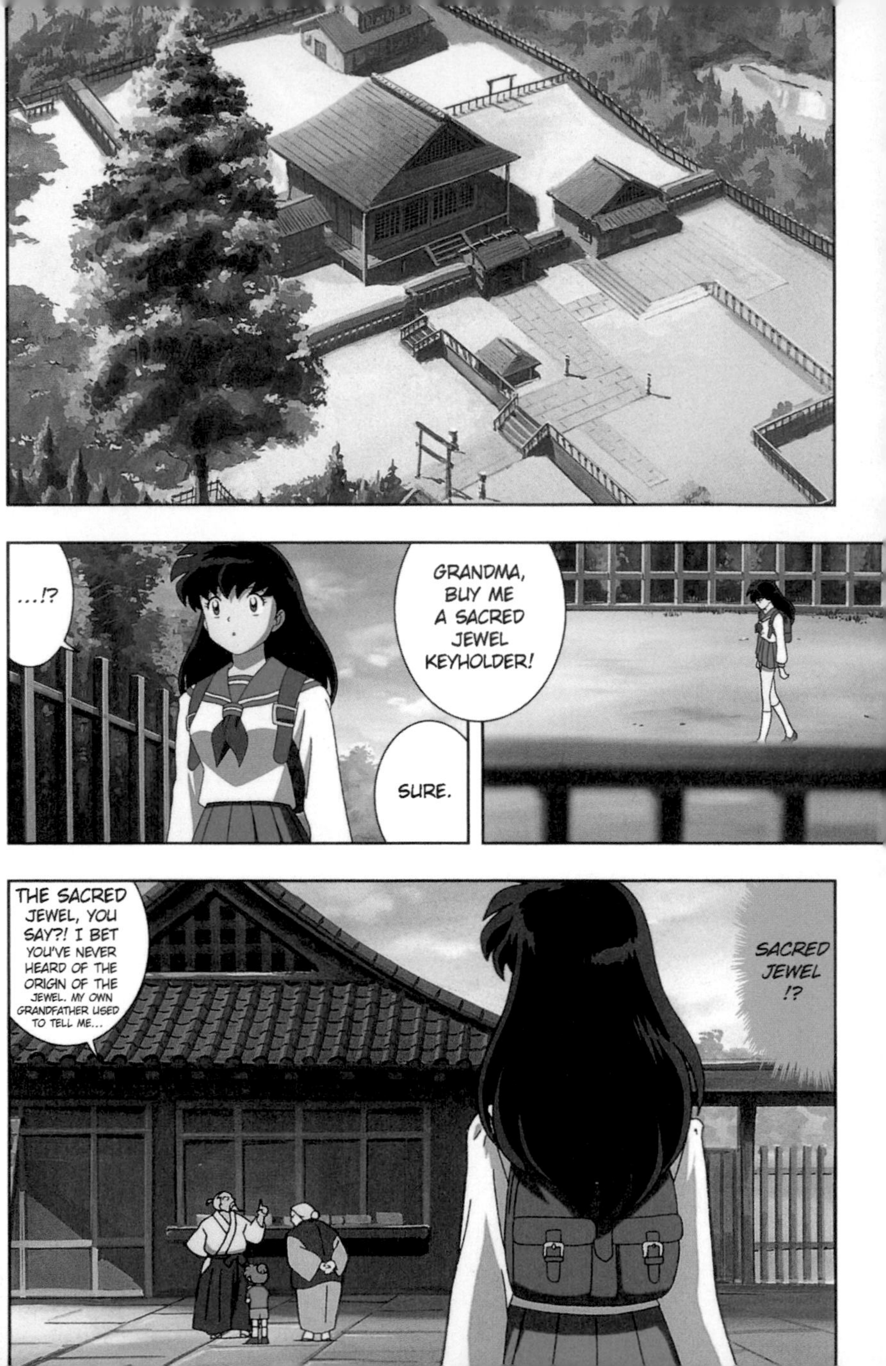
GRANDMA, BUY ME A SACRED JEWEL KEYHOLDER!
SURE.
...!?
SACRED JEWEL !?
THE SACRED JEWEL, YOU SAY?! I BET YOU'VE NEVER HEARD OF THE ORIGIN OF THE JEWEL. MY OWN GRANDFATHER USED TO TELL ME...

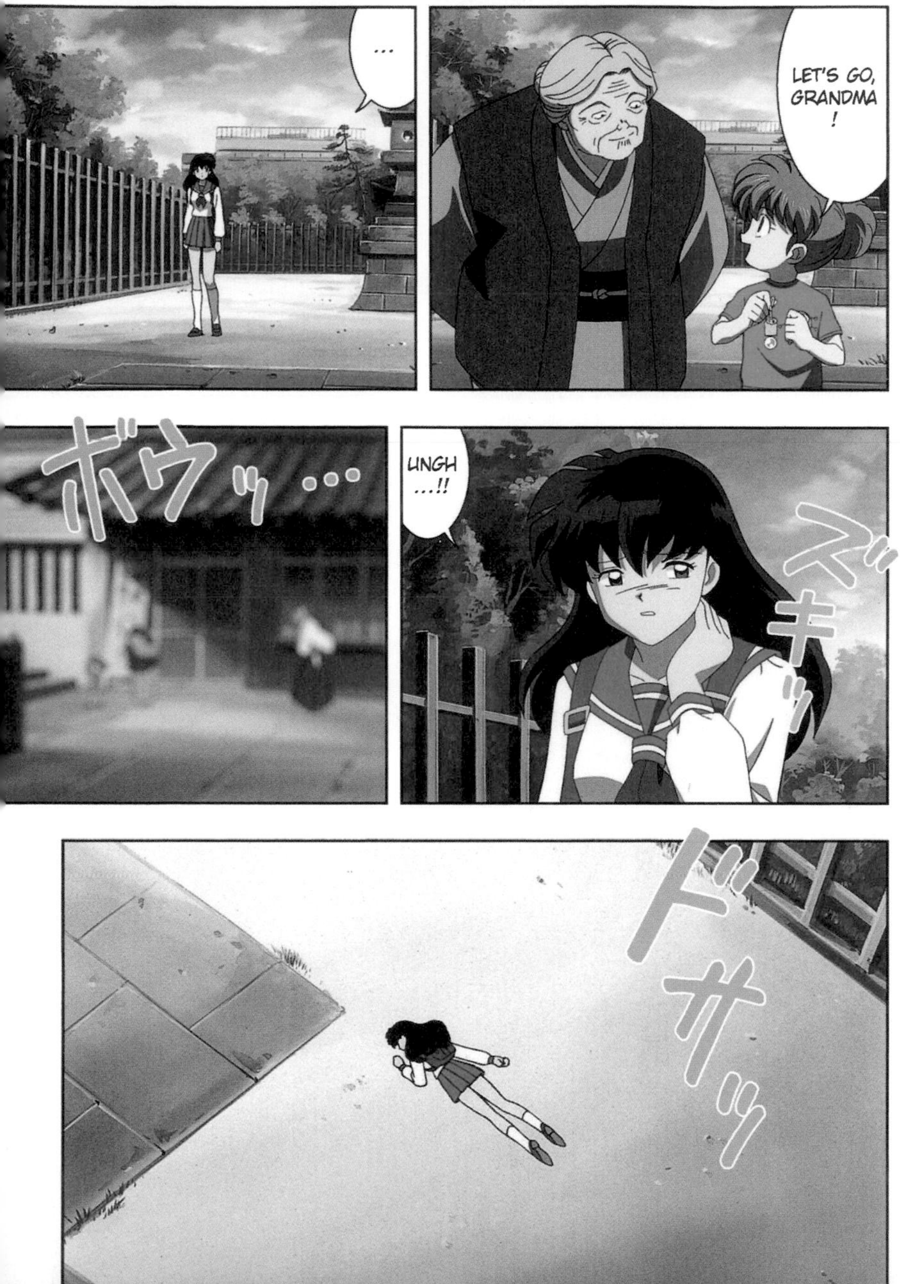
LET'S GO, GRANDMA!
...
UNGH ...!!
ズキッ
ボウッ...
ドサッ

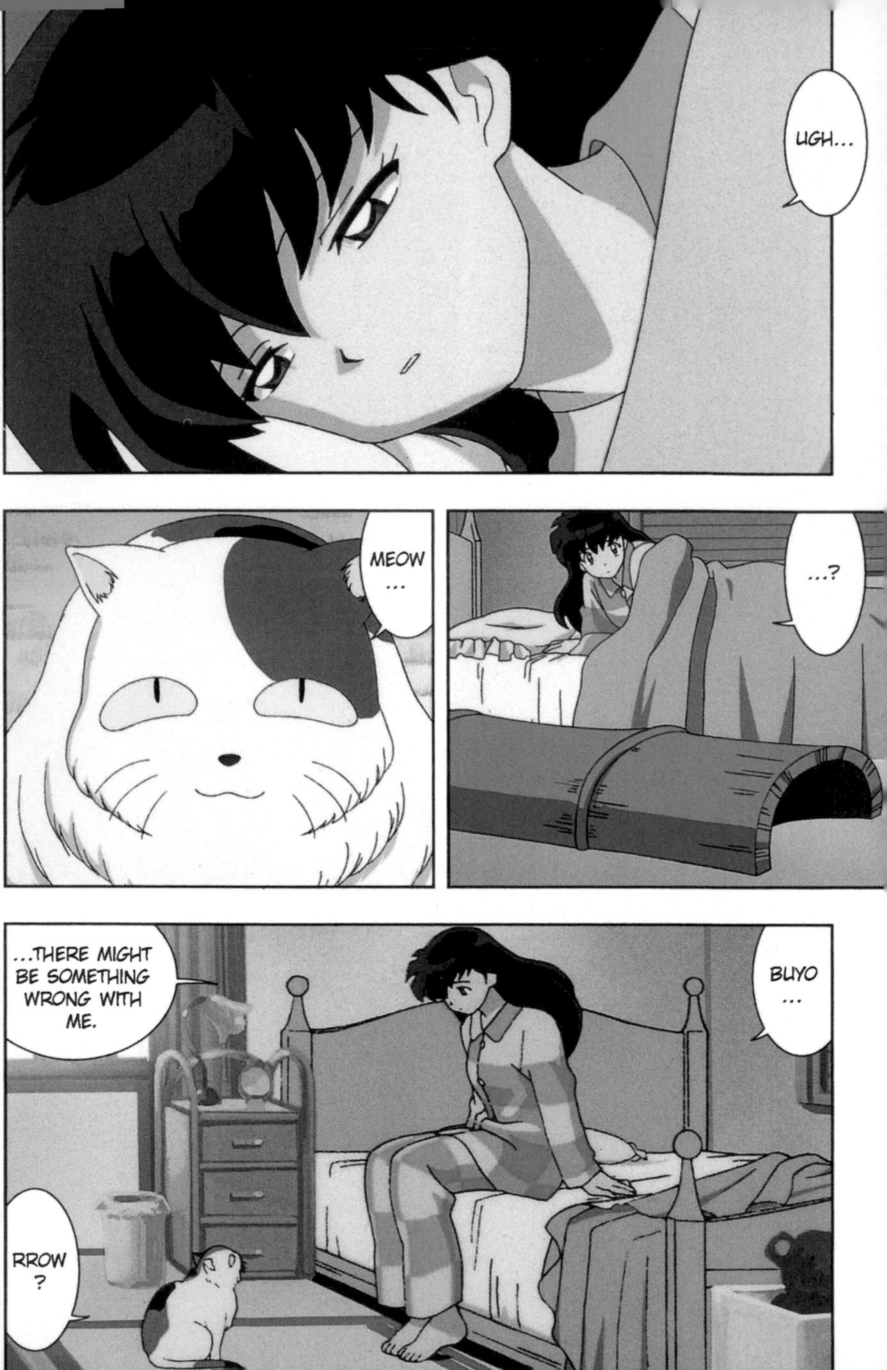
UGH...
...?
MEOW ...
BUYO ...
...THERE MIGHT BE SOMETHING WRONG WITH ME.
RROW ?

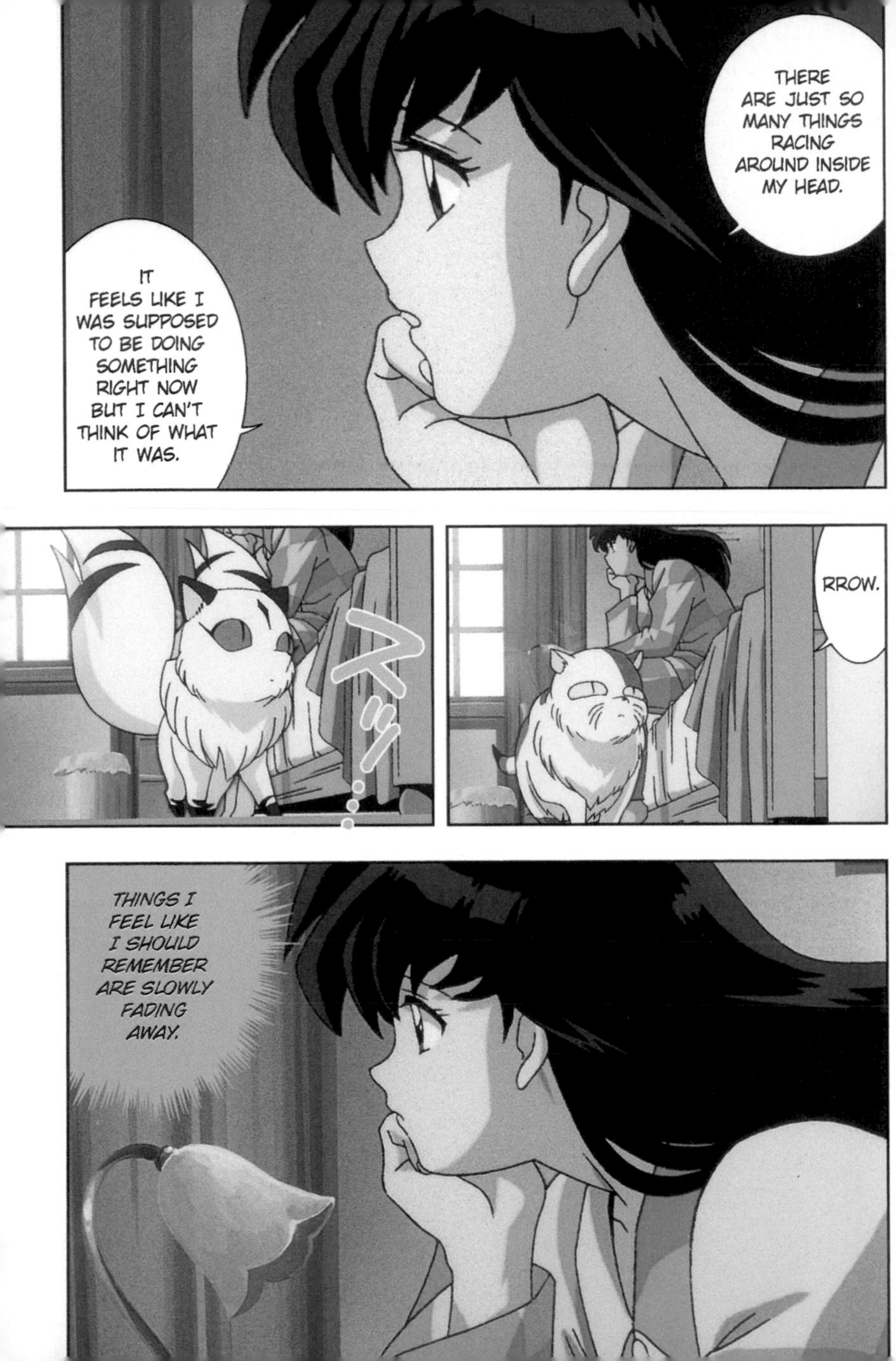
THERE ARE JUST SO MANY THINGS RACING AROUND INSIDE MY HEAD.
IT FEELS LIKE I WAS SUPPOSED TO BE DOING SOMETHING RIGHT NOW BUT I CAN'T THINK OF WHAT IT WAS.
RROW.
スッ
THINGS I FEEL LIKE I SHOULD REMEMBER ARE SLOWLY FADING AWAY.

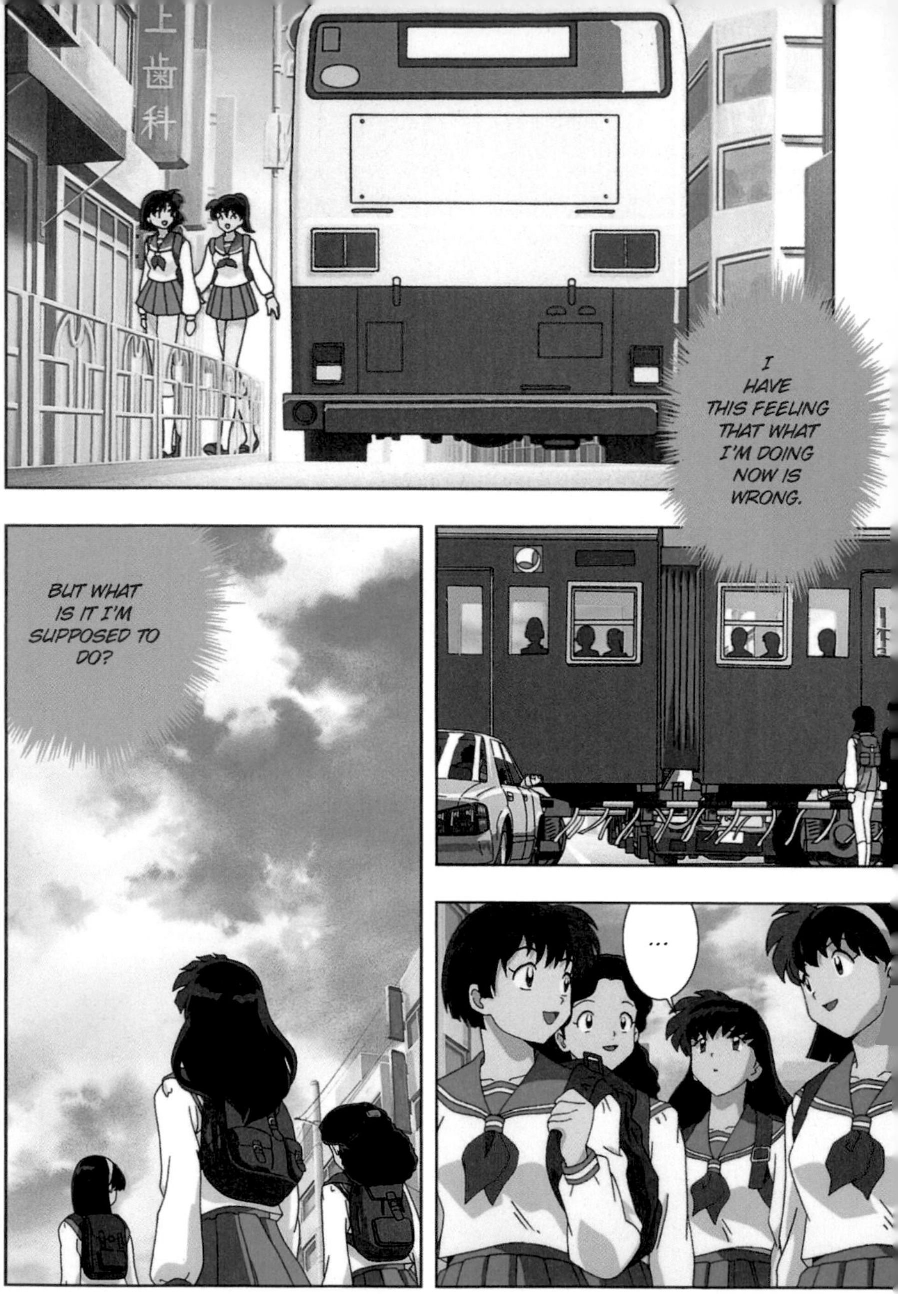
I HAVE THIS FEELING THAT WHAT I'M DOING NOW IS WRONG.
上歯科
...
BUT WHAT IS IT I'M SUPPOSED TO DO?

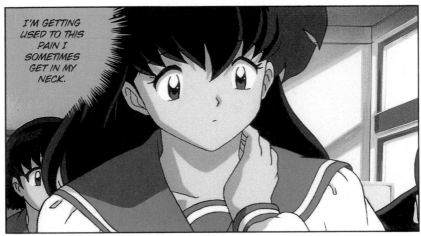

I'M GETTING USED TO THIS PAIN I SOMETIMES GET IN MY NECK.

AND NOW I HARDLY EVEN WORRY ABOUT IT.

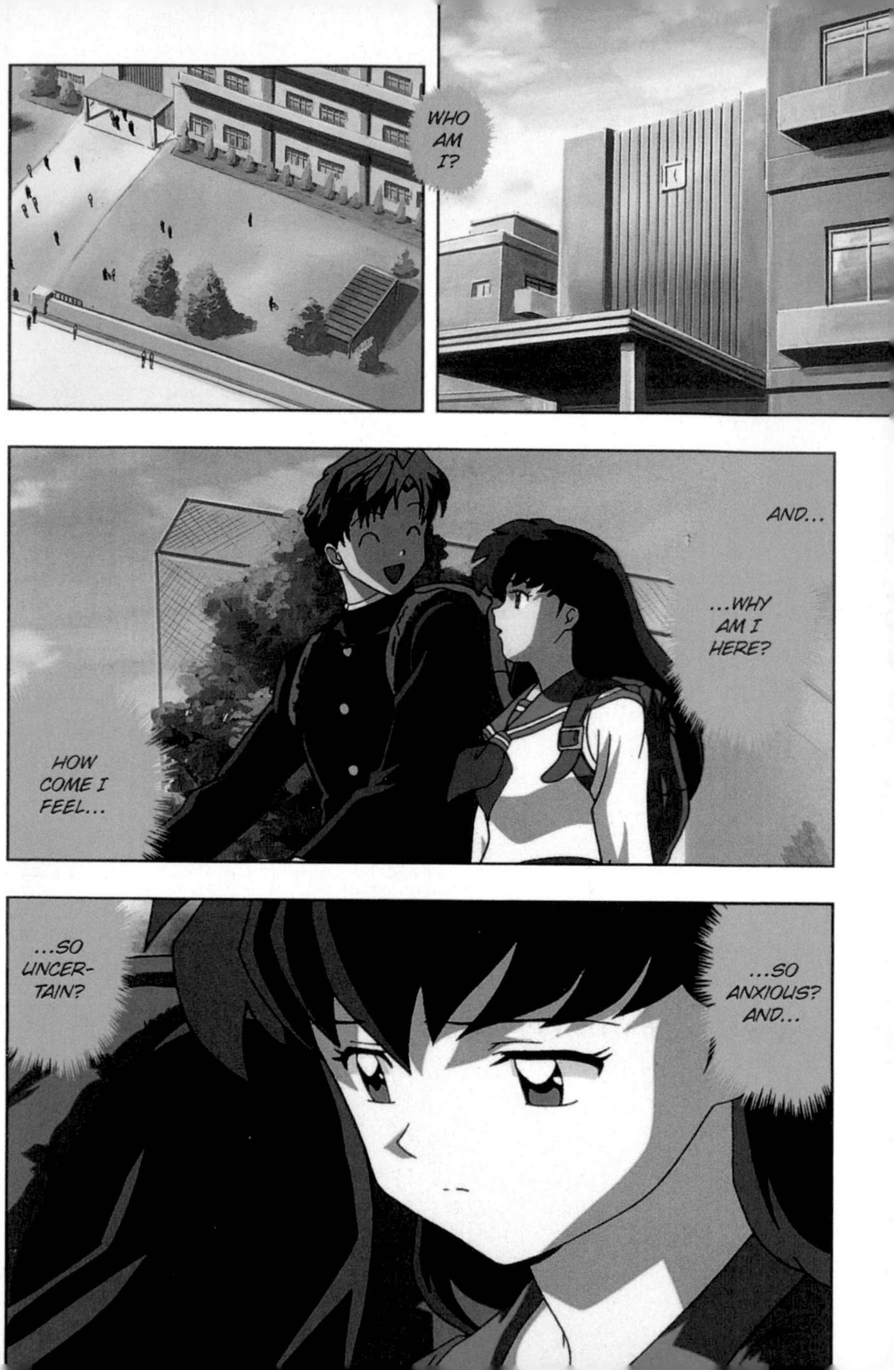
WHO AM I?
AND...
...WHY AM I HERE?
HOW COME I FEEL...
...SO ANXIOUS? AND...
...SO UNCER-TAIN?

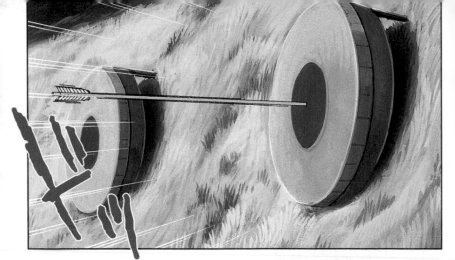

WHAT'S WRONG, KAGOME?

...!!

KA-GOME...?

I'M SORRY.

I'VE GOTTA GO, HOJO.

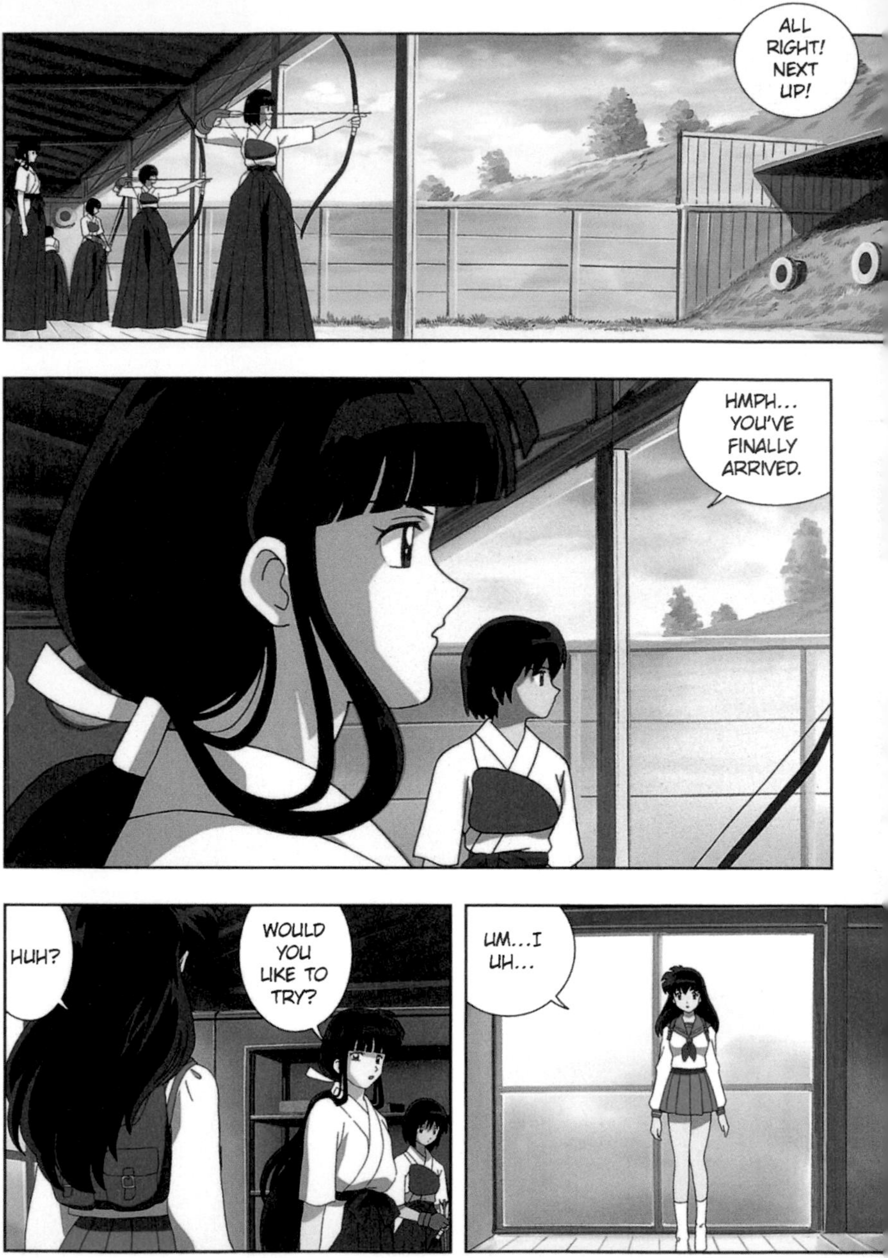
ALL RIGHT! NEXT UP!
HMPH... YOU'VE FINALLY ARRIVED.
UM...I UH...
WOULD YOU LIKE TO TRY?
HUH?

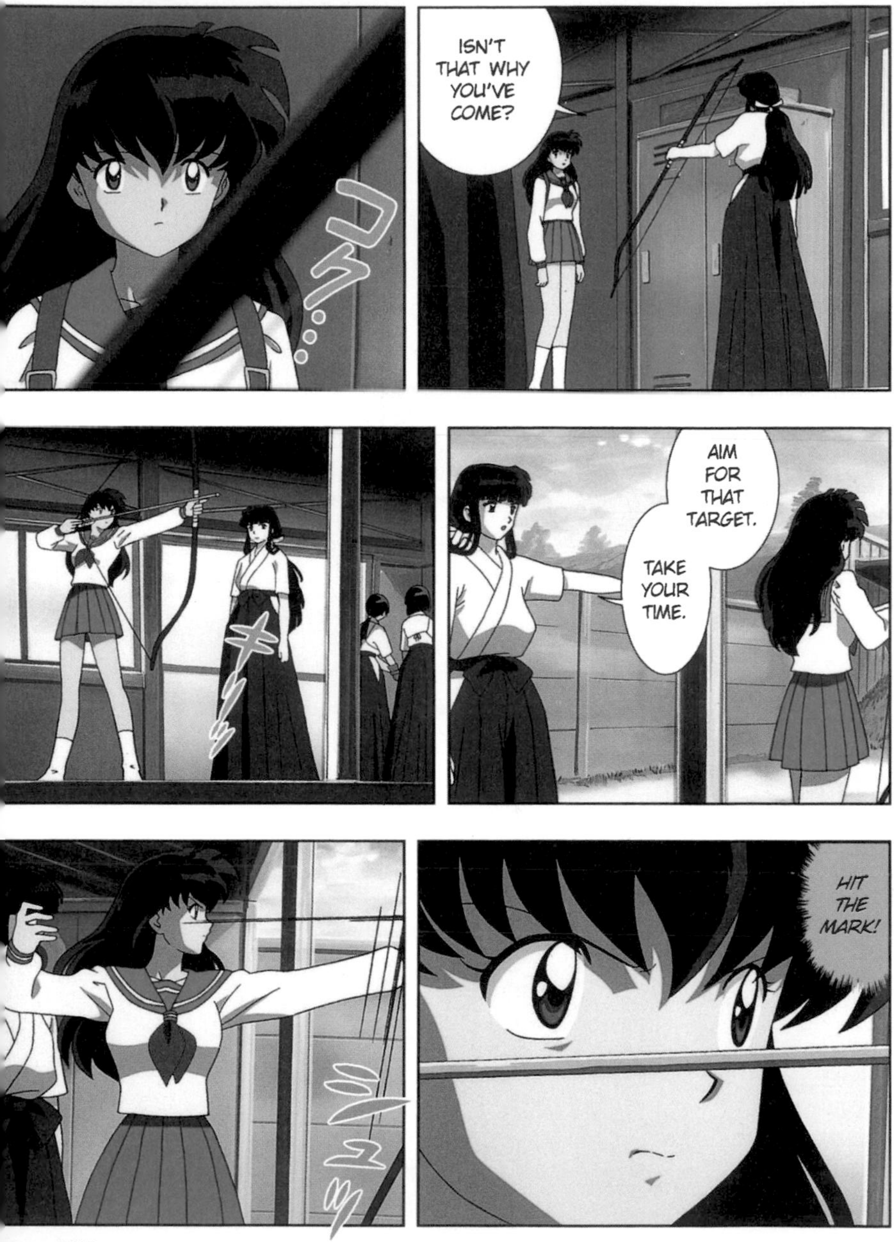
ISN'T THAT WHY YOU'VE COME?
AIM FOR THAT TARGET.
TAKE YOUR TIME.
HIT THE MARK!

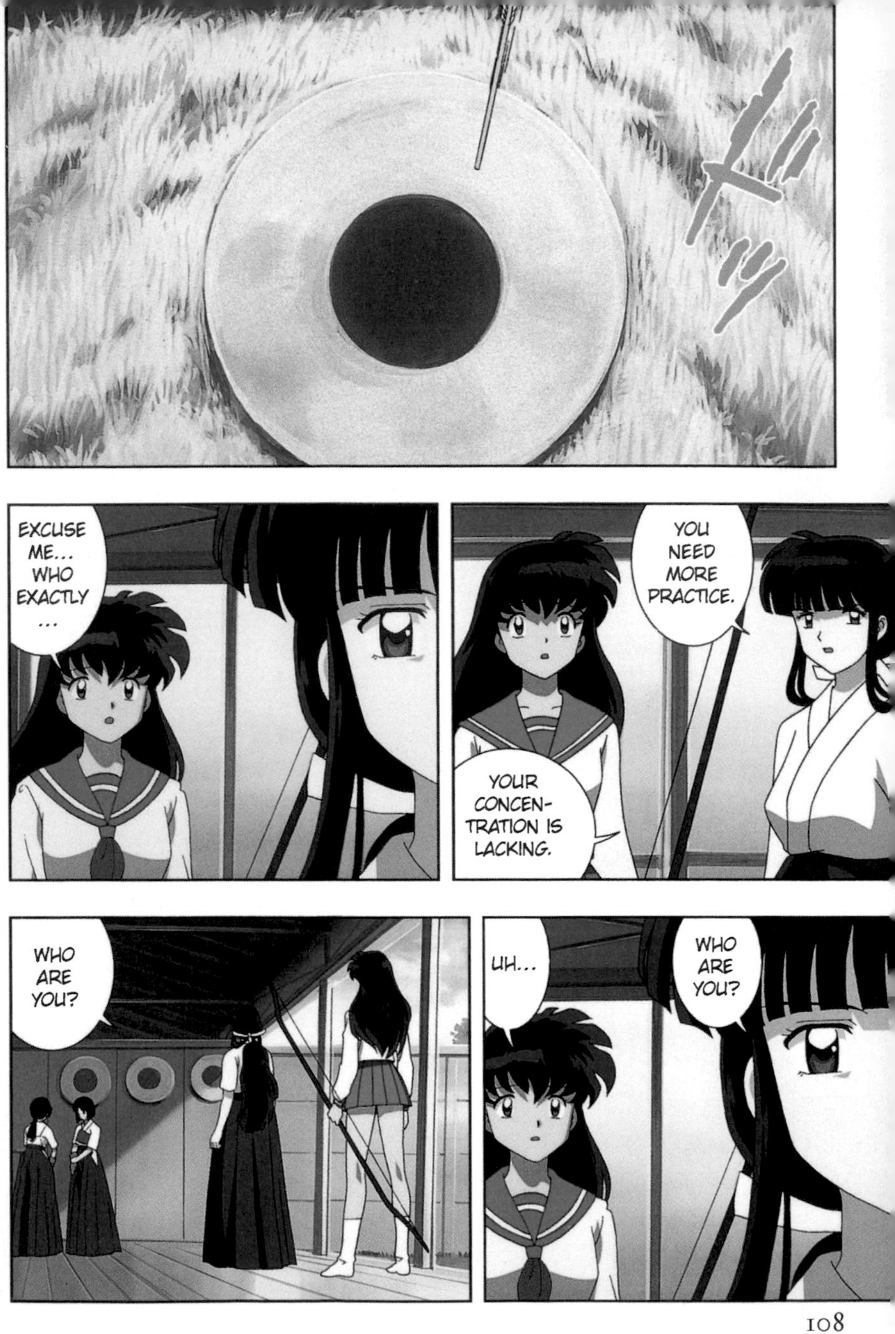
ドッ
YOU NEED MORE PRACTICE.
YOUR CONCEN-TRATION IS LACKING.
EXCUSE ME... WHO EXACTLY ...
WHO ARE YOU?
UH...
WHO ARE YOU?

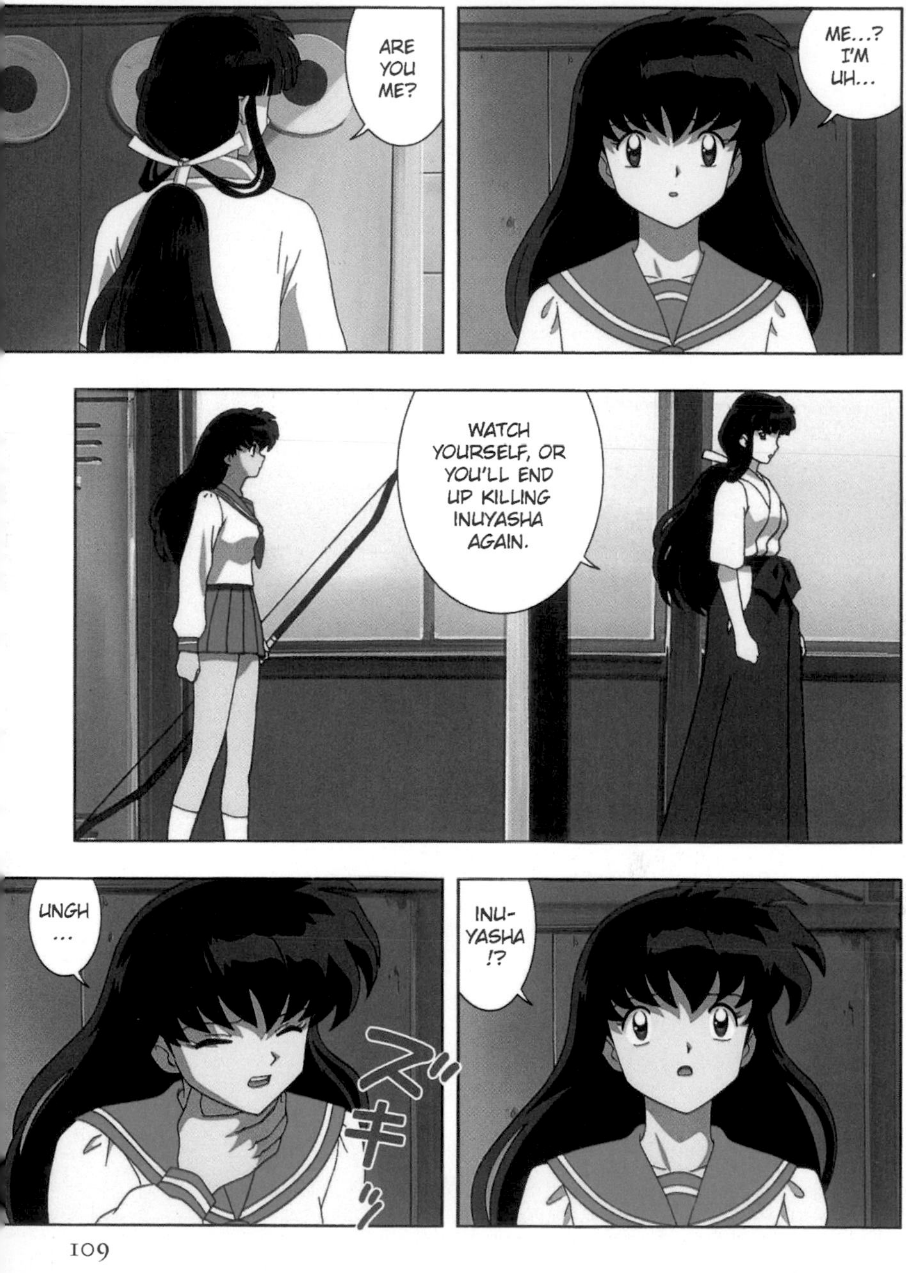
ME...? I'M UH...
ARE YOU ME?
WATCH YOURSELF, OR YOU'LL END UP KILLING INUYASHA AGAIN.
INU-YASHA !?
UNGH ...
ズキッ

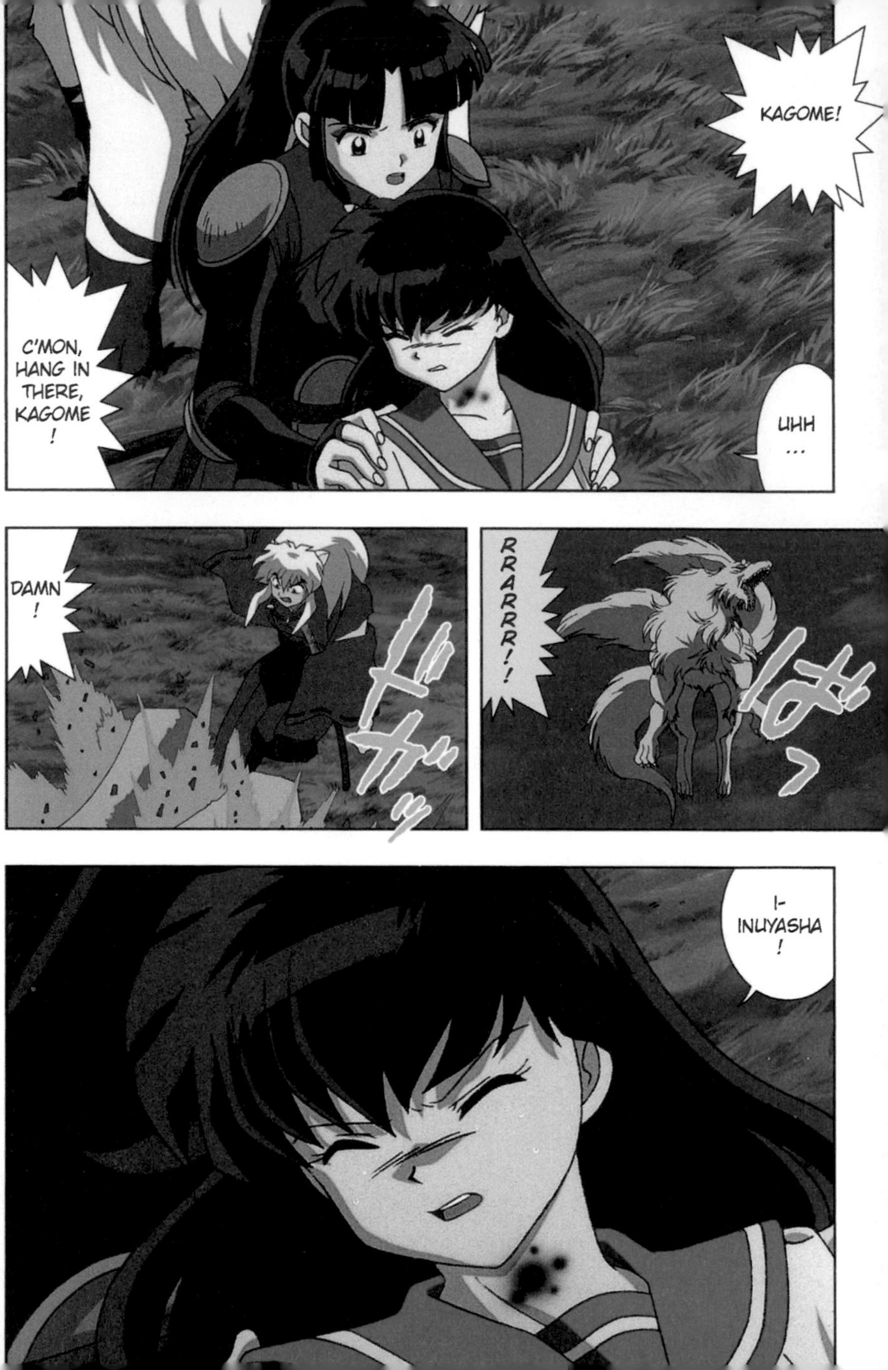
KAGOME!
UHH ...
C'MON, HANG IN THERE, KAGOME !
RRARRRR!!
ばっ
DAMN !
ドガッ
I- INUYASHA !

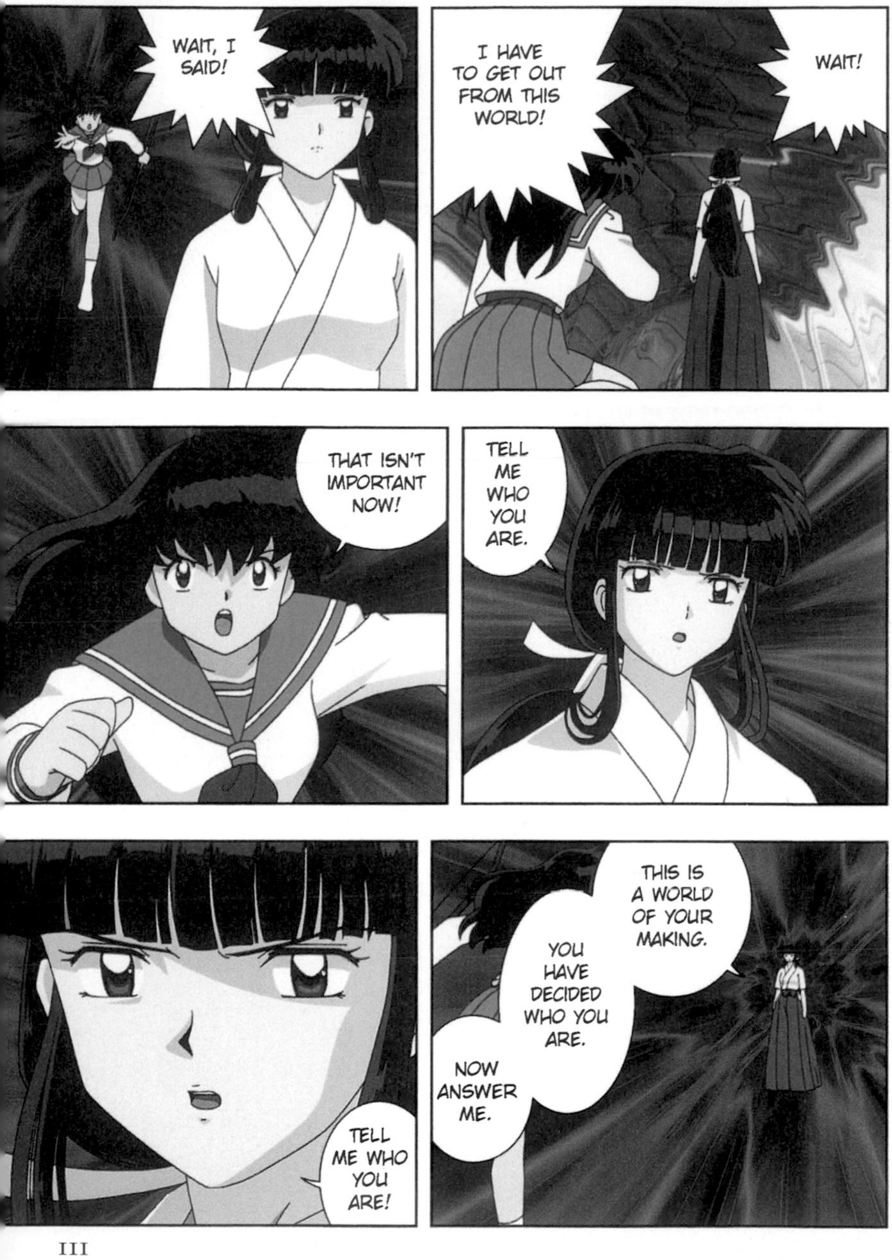
WAIT!
I HAVE TO GET OUT FROM THIS WORLD!
WAIT, I SAID!
TELL ME WHO YOU ARE.
THAT ISN'T IMPORTANT NOW!
THIS IS A WORLD OF YOUR MAKING.
YOU HAVE DECIDED WHO YOU ARE.
NOW ANSWER ME.
TELL ME WHO YOU ARE!

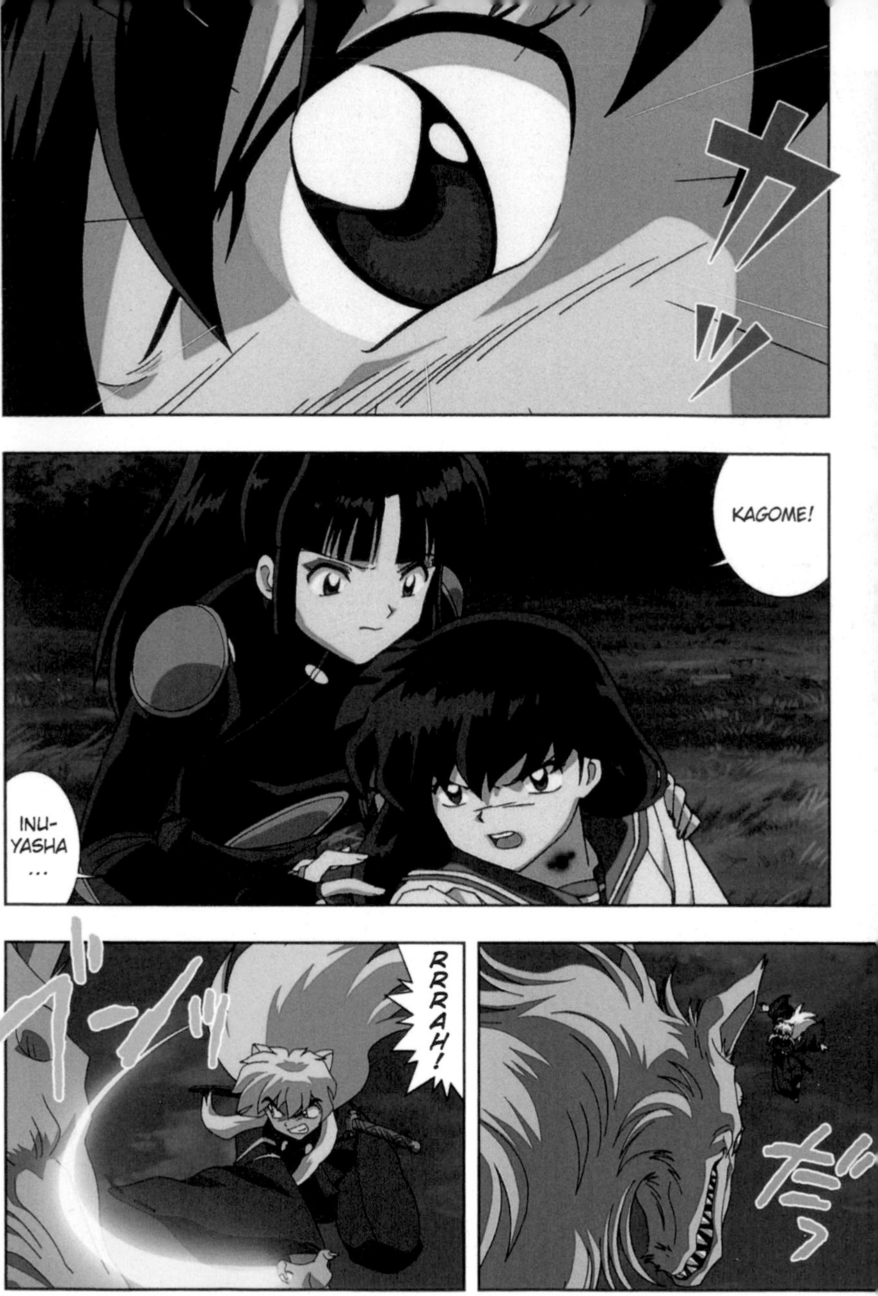
カッ
KAGOME!
INU-YASHA ...
だっ
RRRAH!
ヴーンッ

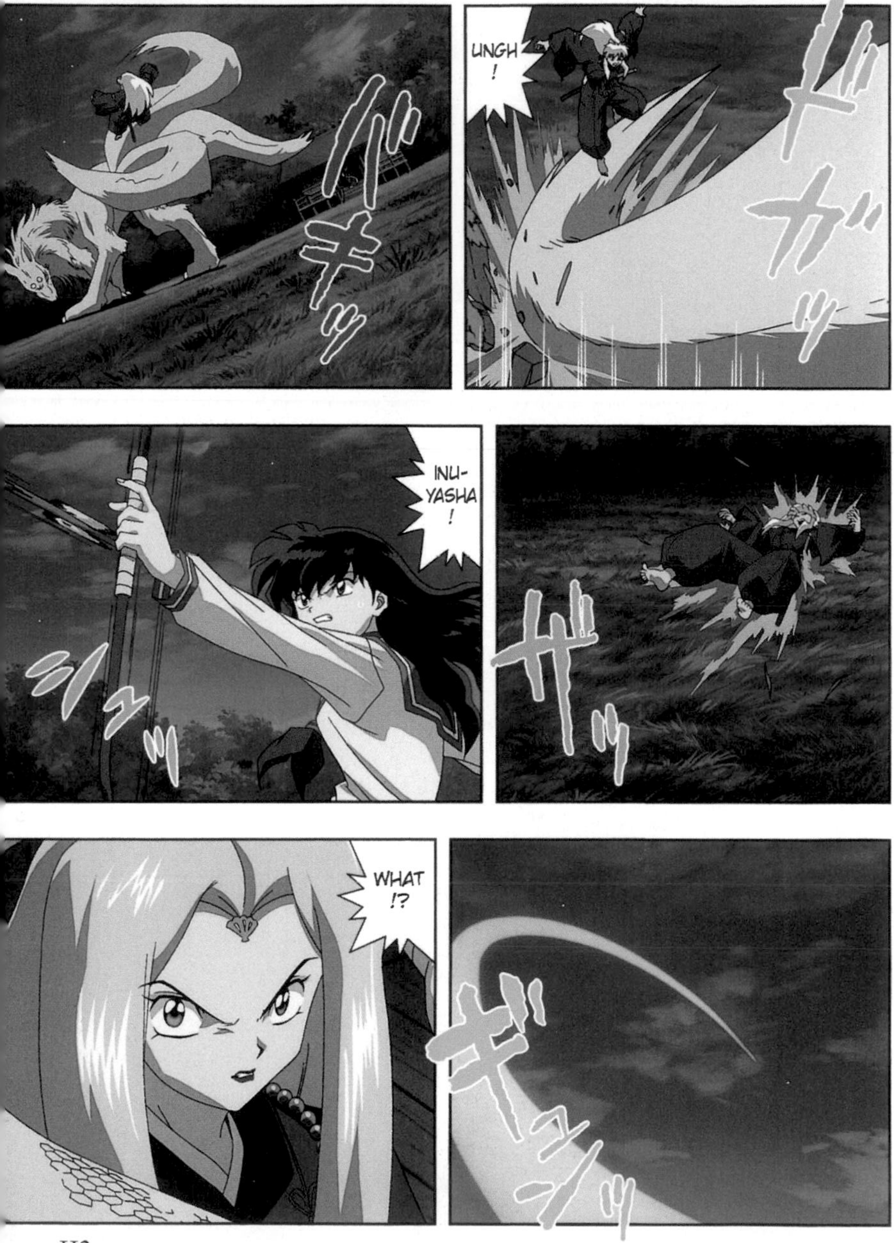
UNGH!
ドガッ
グキッ
ザッ
INU-YASHA!
シュッ
ギュンッ
WHAT!?

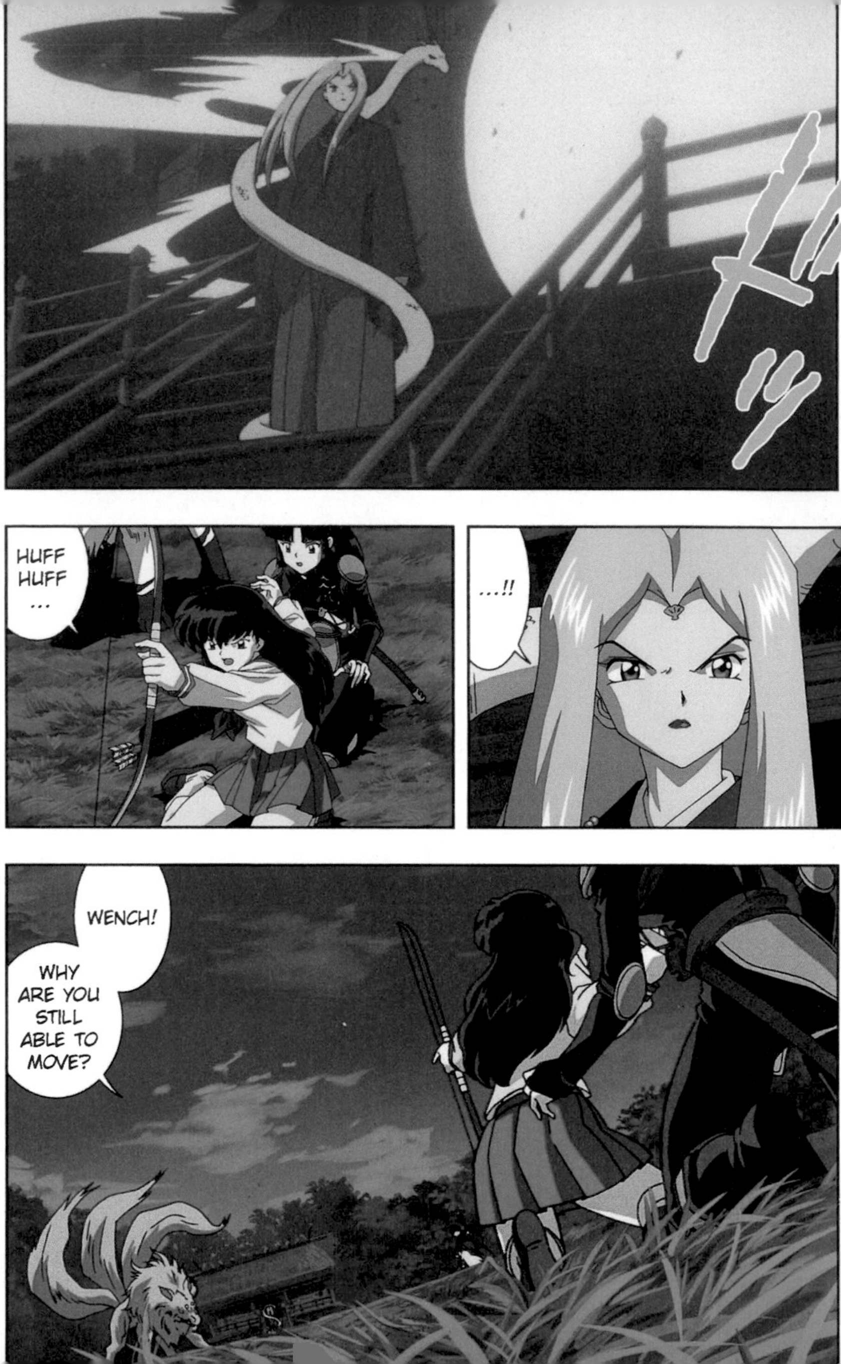
...!!
HUFF HUFF ...
WENCH!
WHY ARE YOU STILL ABLE TO MOVE?

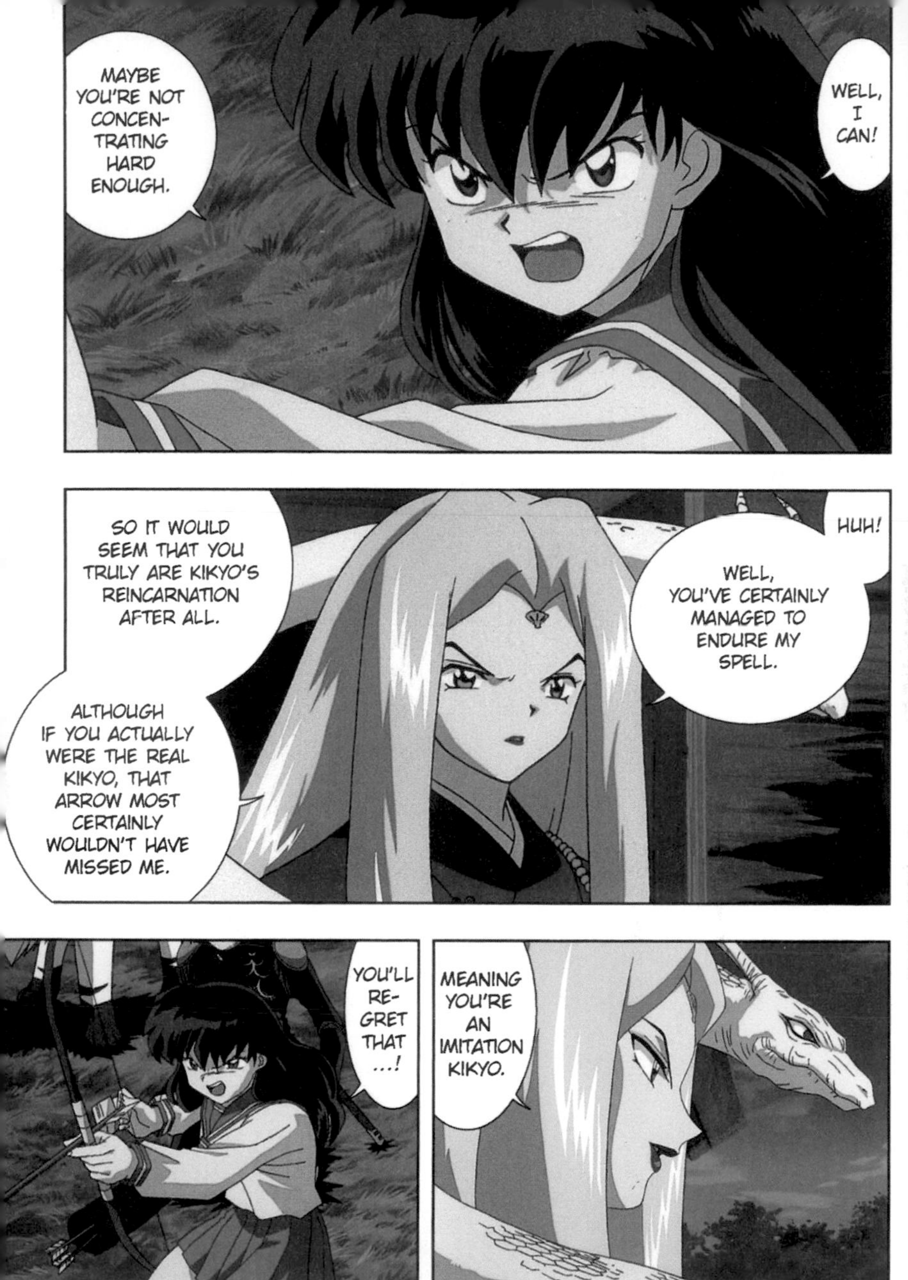
WELL, I CAN!
MAYBE YOU'RE NOT CONCEN-TRATING HARD ENOUGH.
HUH!
WELL, YOU'VE CERTAINLY MANAGED TO ENDURE MY SPELL.
SO IT WOULD SEEM THAT YOU TRULY ARE KIKYO'S REINCARNATION AFTER ALL.
ALTHOUGH IF YOU ACTUALLY WERE THE REAL KIKYO, THAT ARROW MOST CERTAINLY WOULDN'T HAVE MISSED ME.
MEANING YOU'RE AN IMITATION KIKYO.
YOU'LL RE-GRET THAT ...!

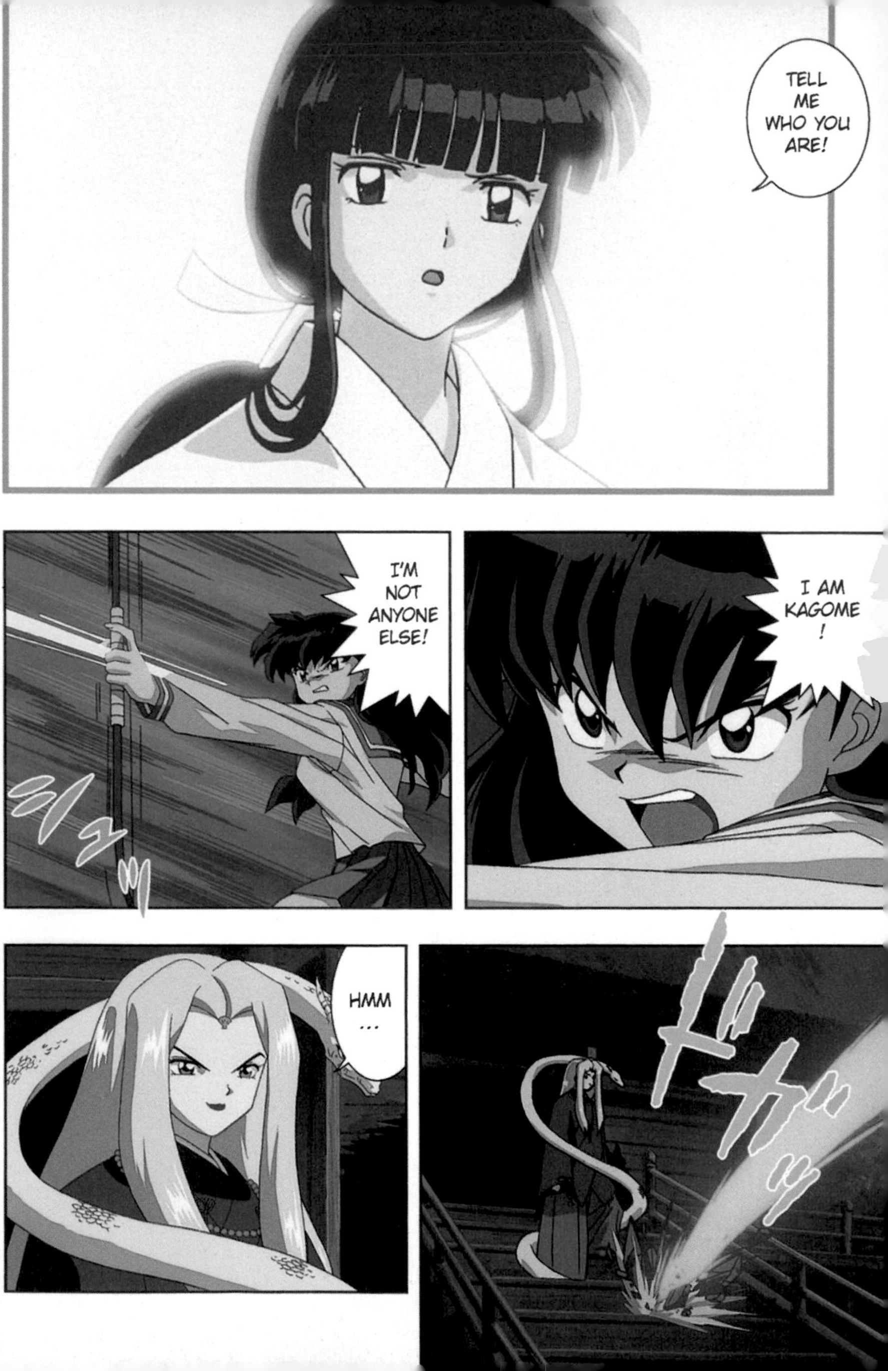
TELL ME WHO YOU ARE!
I AM KAGOME!
I'M NOT ANYONE ELSE!
HMM ...

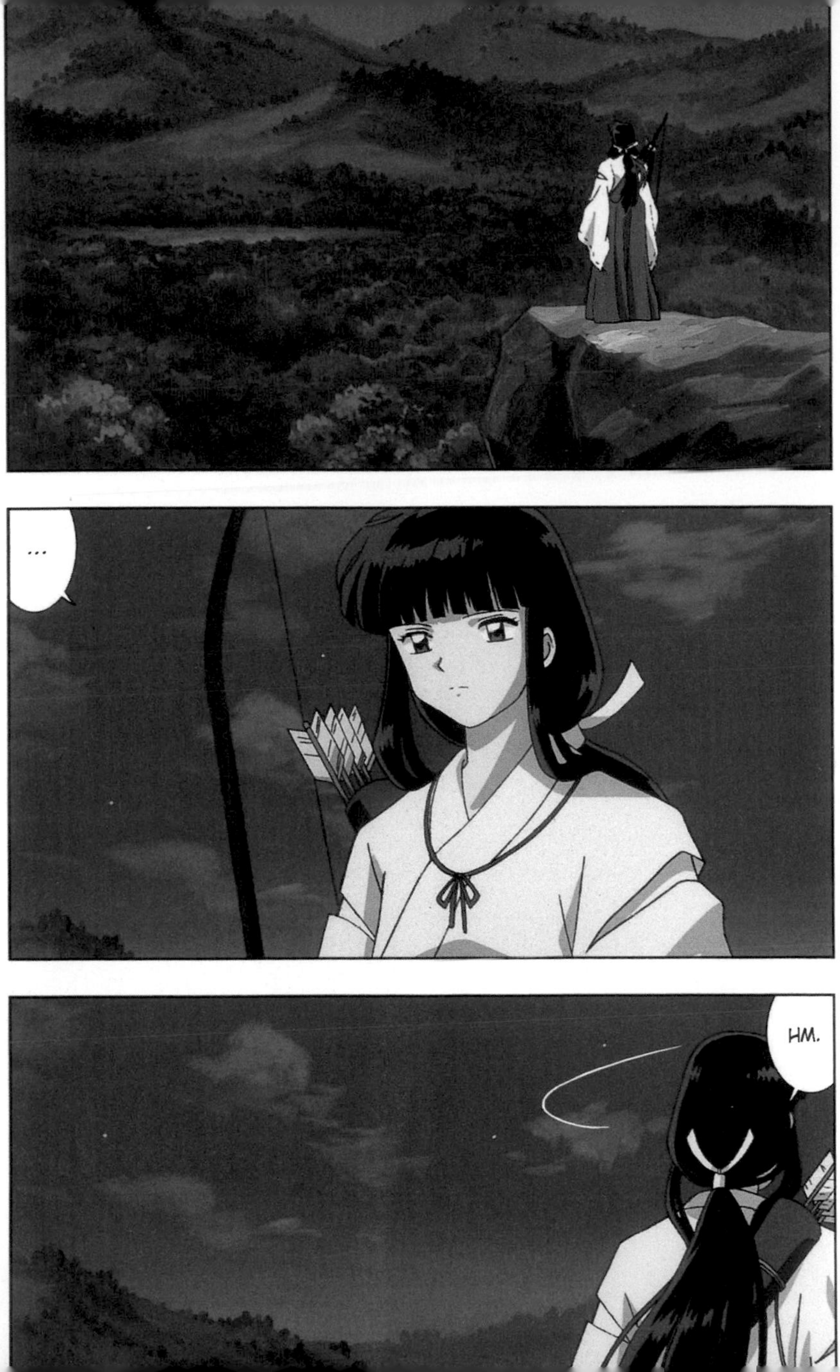
...
HM.

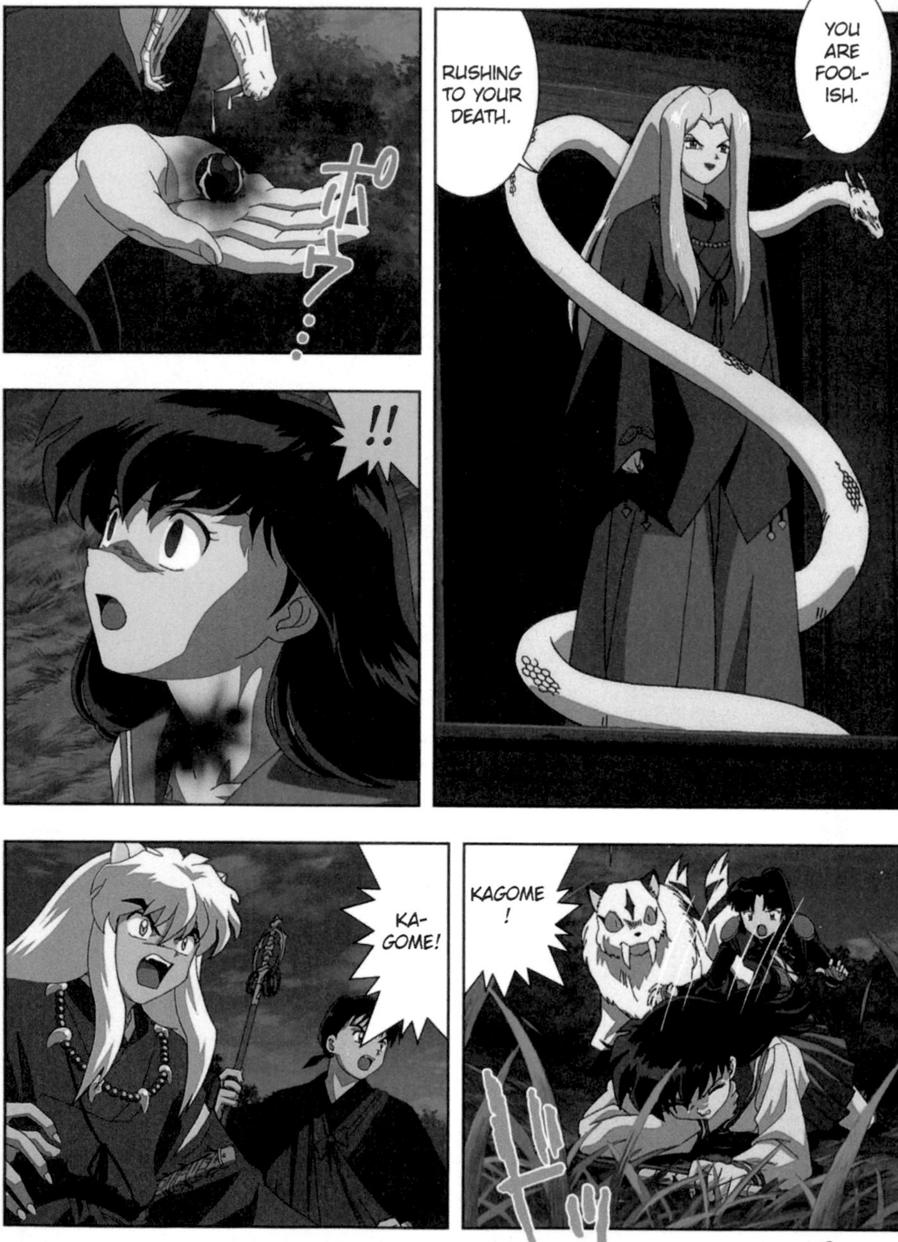
YOU ARE FOOL-ISH.
RUSHING TO YOUR DEATH.
ポゥ…
!!
KAGOME !
ドッ
KA-GOME!

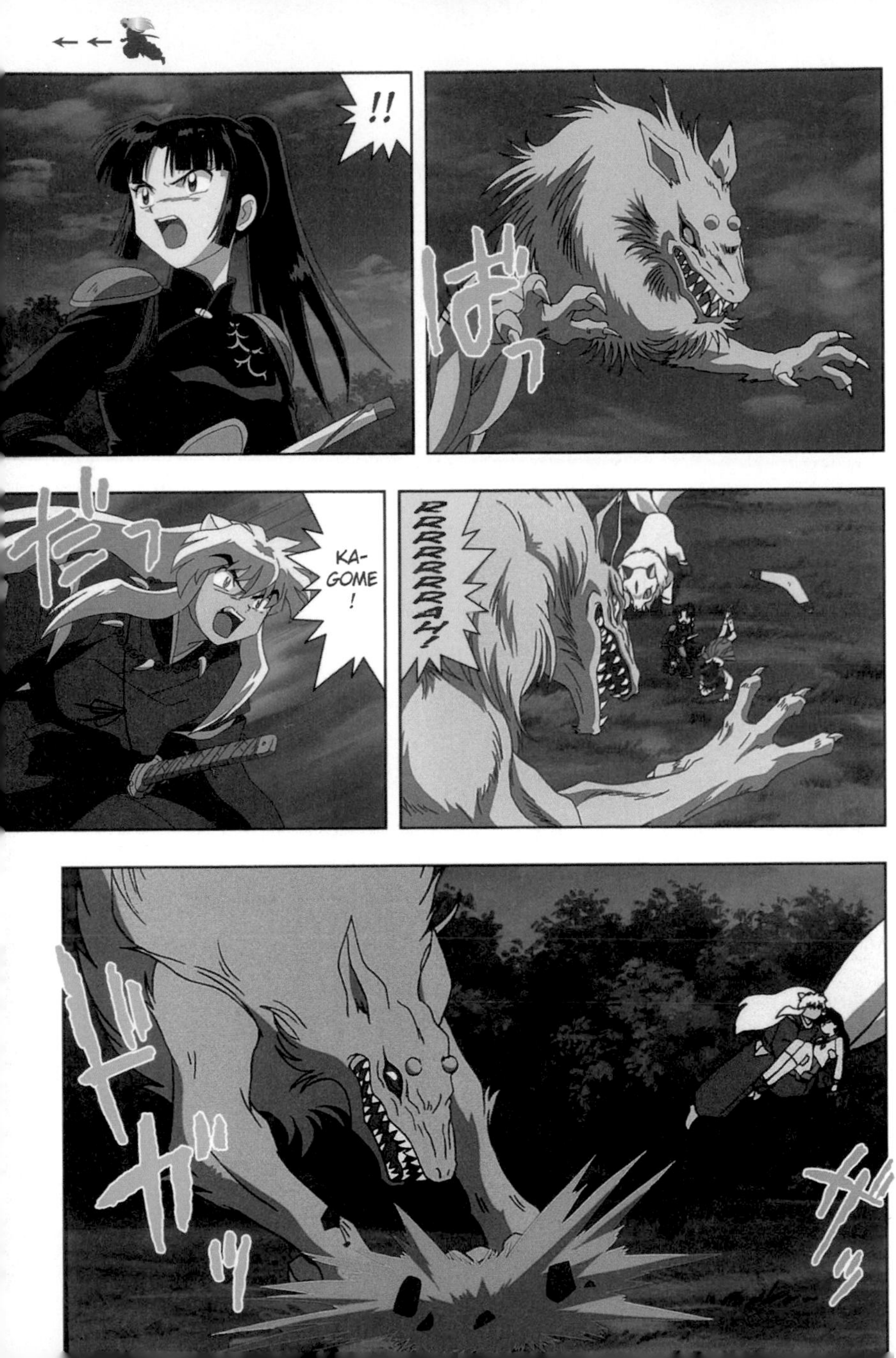

ぼっ
!!
RRRRRRRAH!
ダッ
KA-GOME!
ザッ
ドガッ

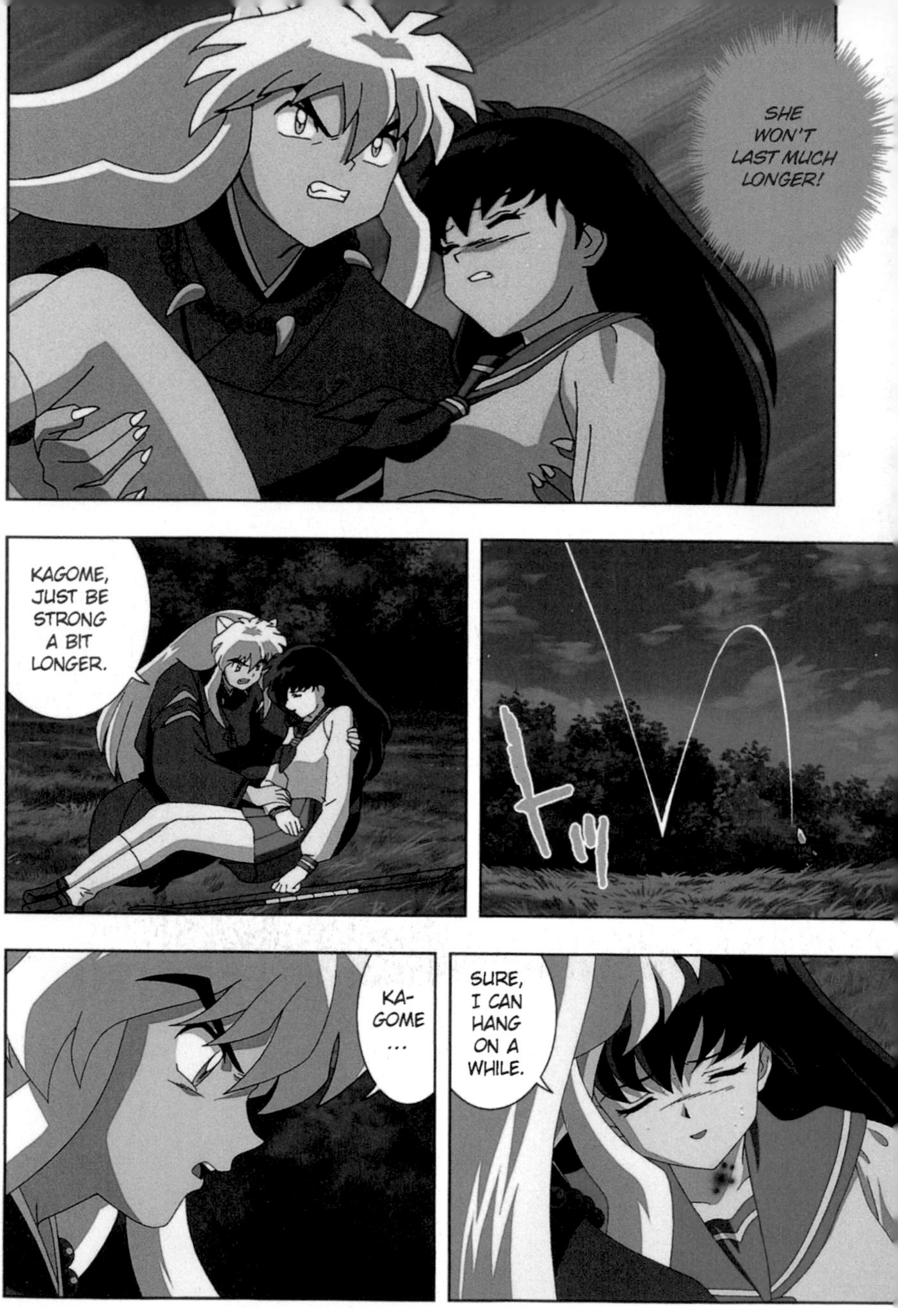
SHE WON'T LAST MUCH LONGER!
KAGOME, JUST BE STRONG A BIT LONGER.
SURE, I CAN HANG ON A WHILE.
KA-GOME ...

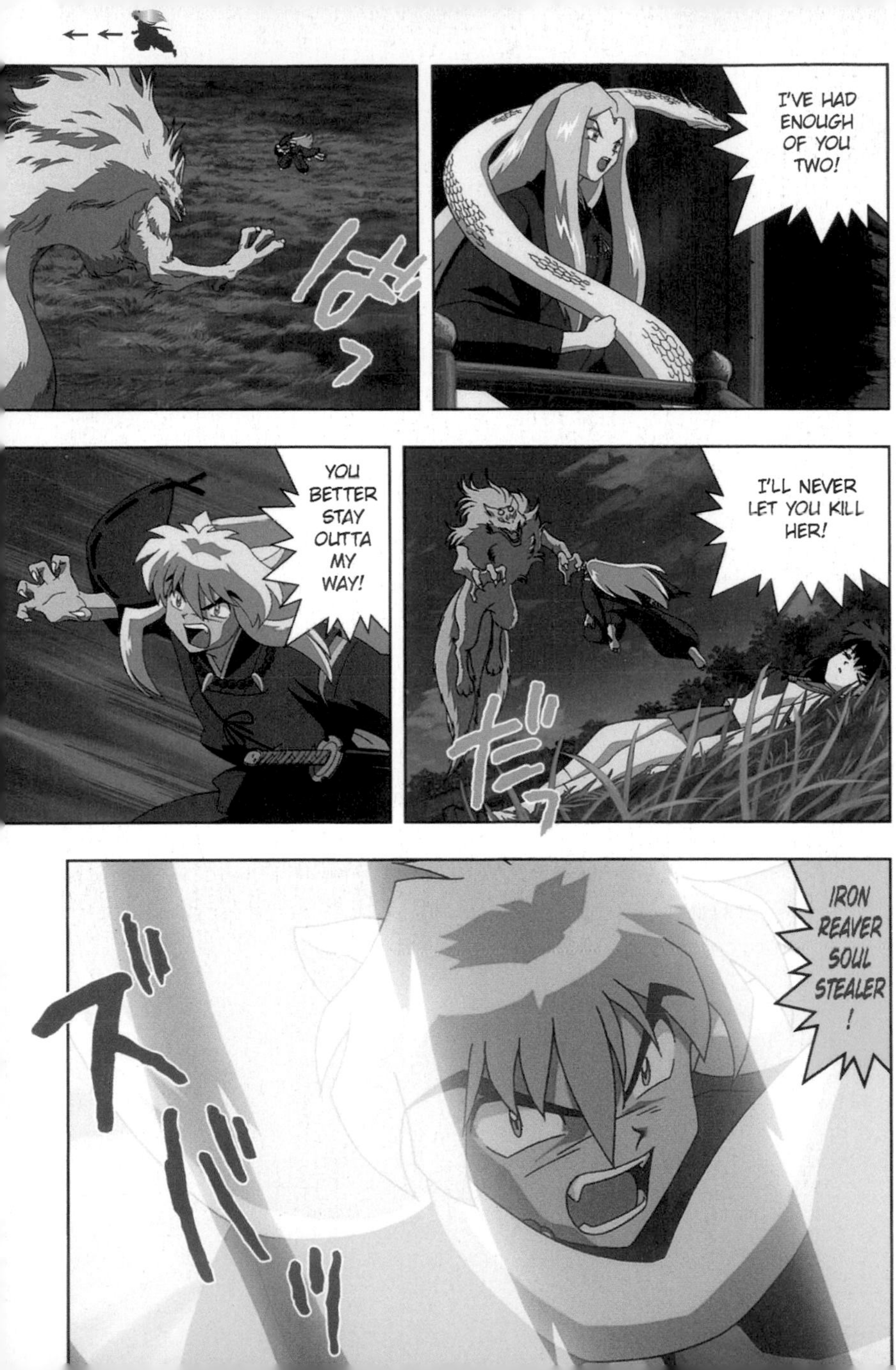
I'VE HAD ENOUGH OF YOU TWO!
ばっ
I'LL NEVER LET YOU KILL HER!
ダッ
YOU BETTER STAY OUTTA MY WAY!
IRON REAVER SOUL STEALER!
ズバッ

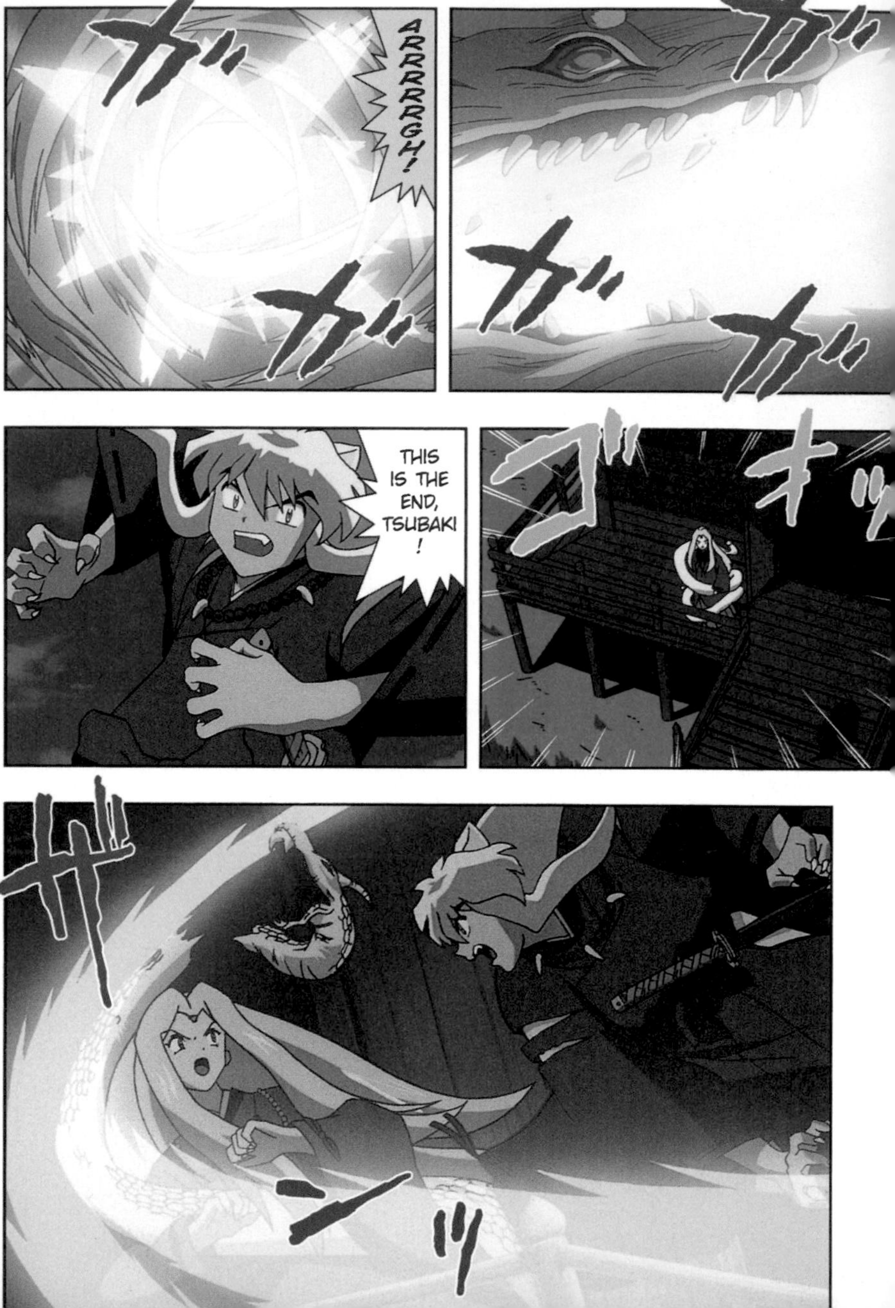
ARRRRRGH!
THIS IS THE END, TSUBAKI!

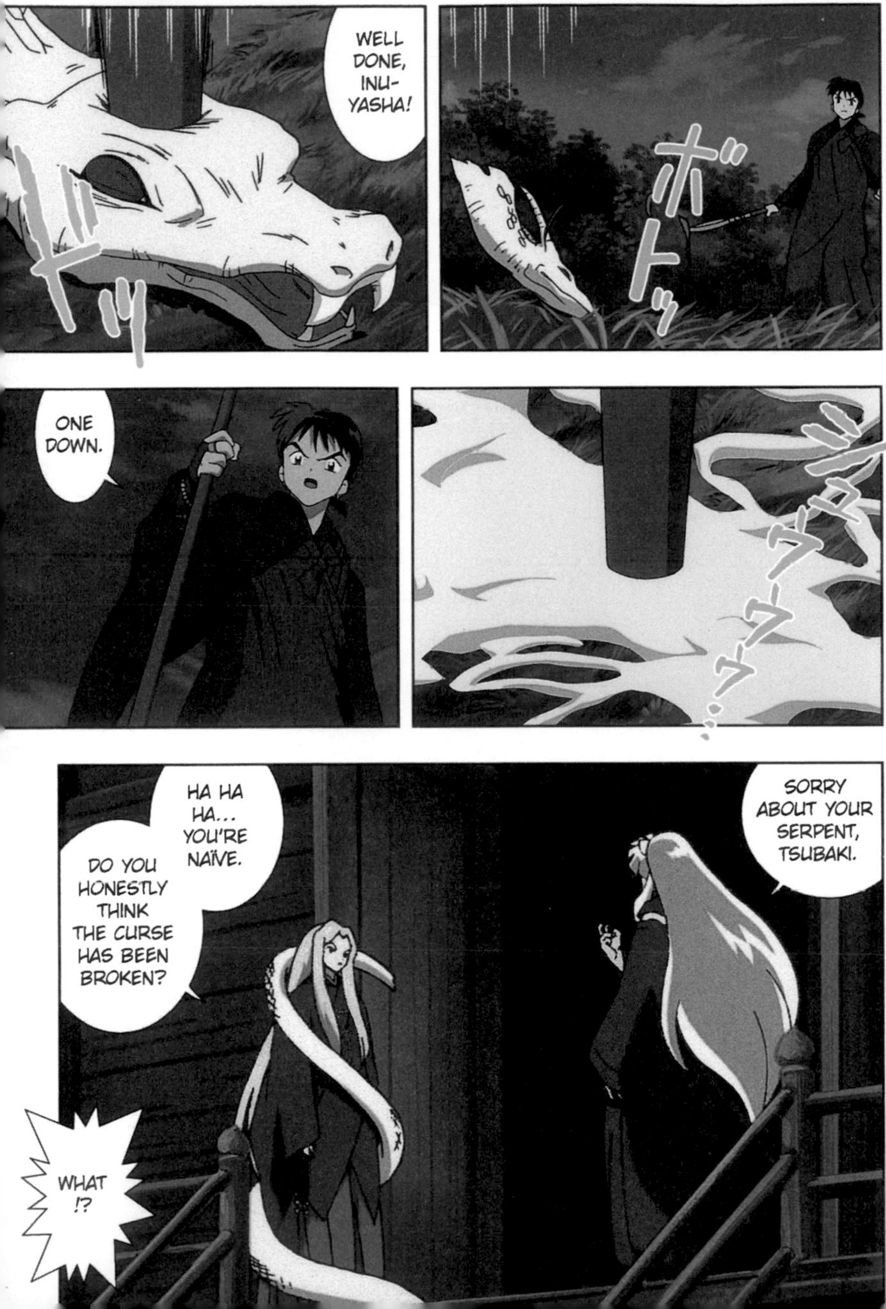
ボトッ
WELL DONE, INU-YASHA!
シュウウウ…
ONE DOWN.
SORRY ABOUT YOUR SERPENT, TSUBAKI.
HA HA HA... YOU'RE NAÏVE.
DO YOU HONESTLY THINK THE CURSE HAS BEEN BROKEN?
WHAT!?

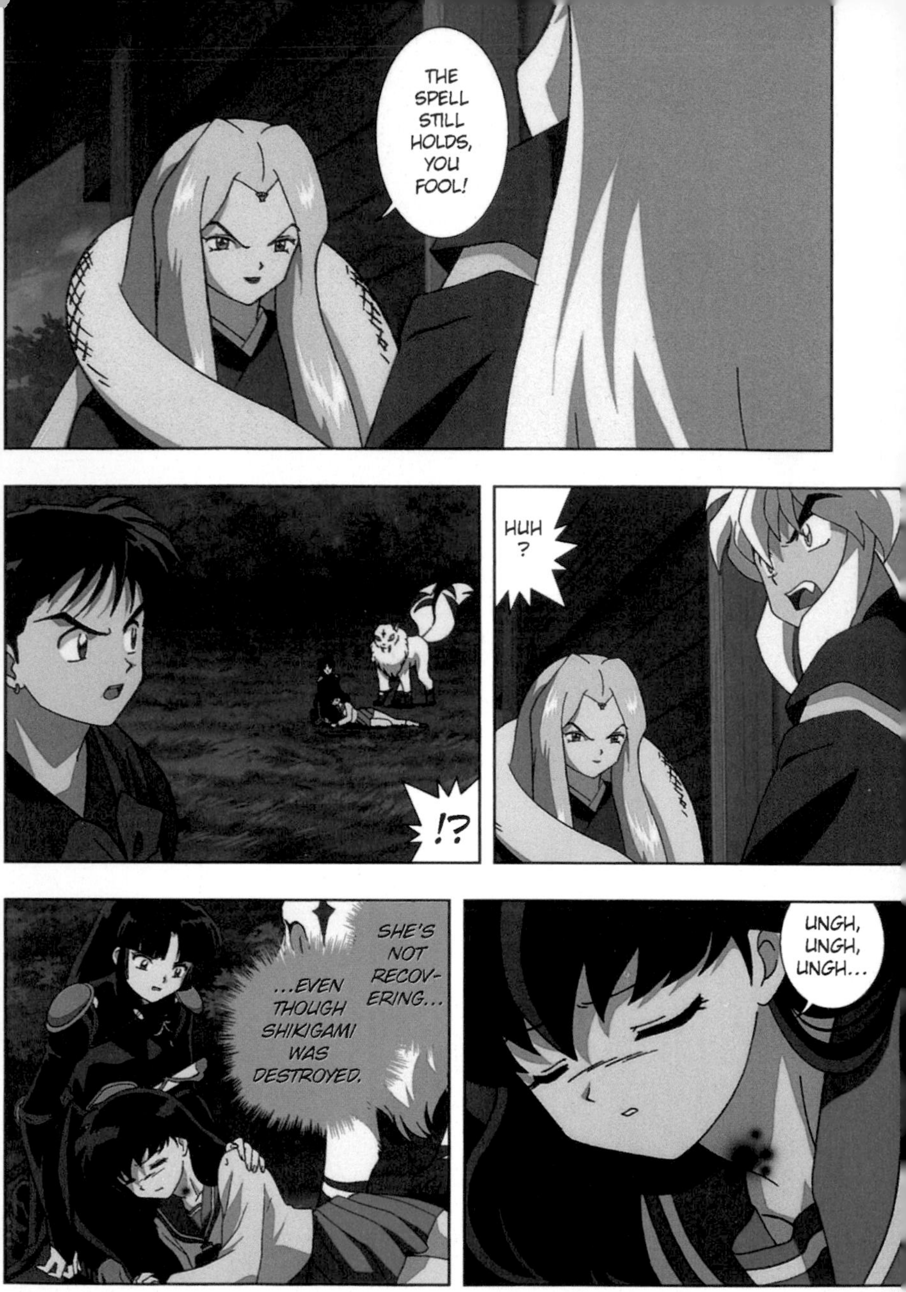
THE SPELL STILL HOLDS, YOU FOOL!
HUH?
!?
UNGH, UNGH, UNGH...
SHE'S NOT RECOV-ERING...
...EVEN THOUGH SHIKIGAMI WAS DESTROYED.

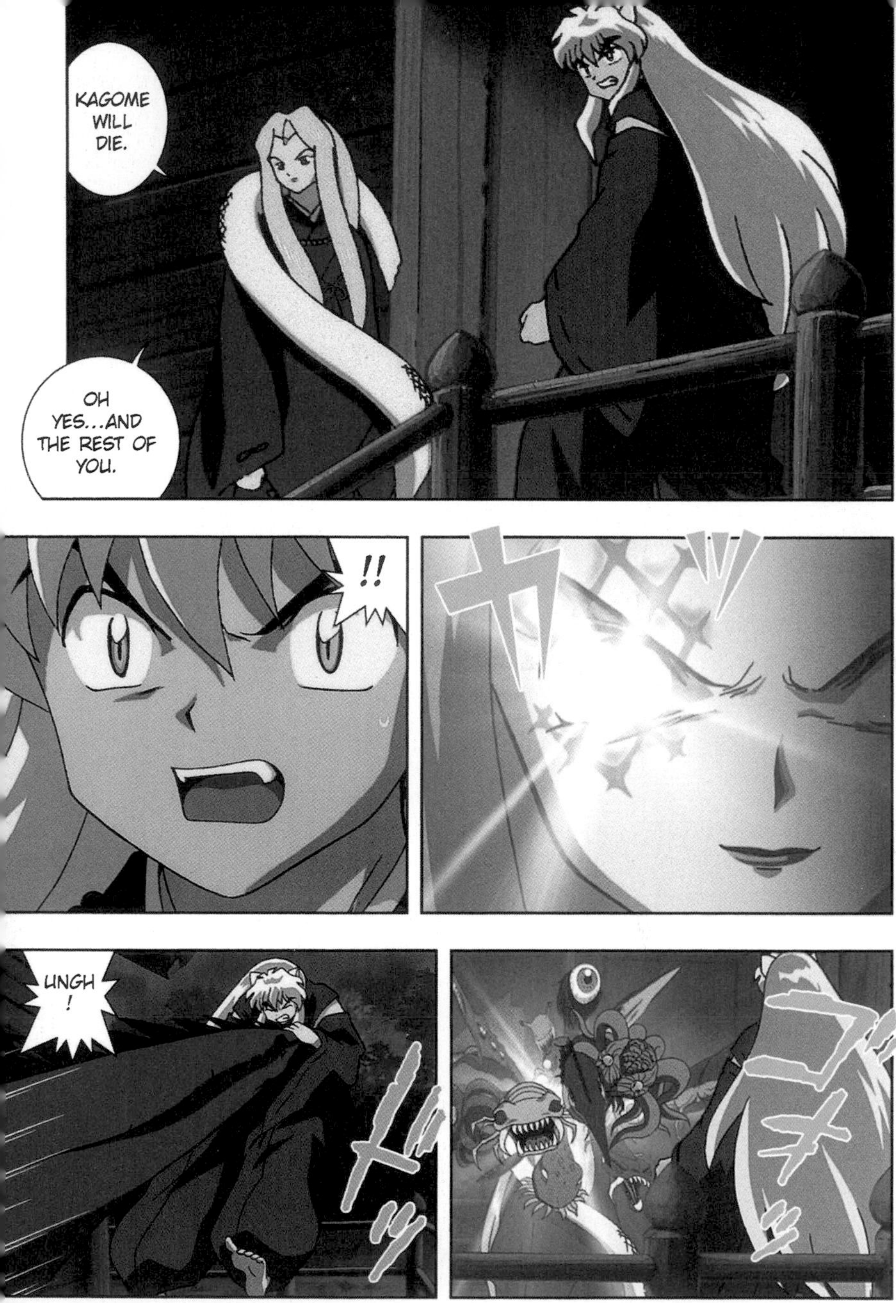
KAGOME WILL DIE.
OH YES...AND THE REST OF YOU.
!!
UNGH!

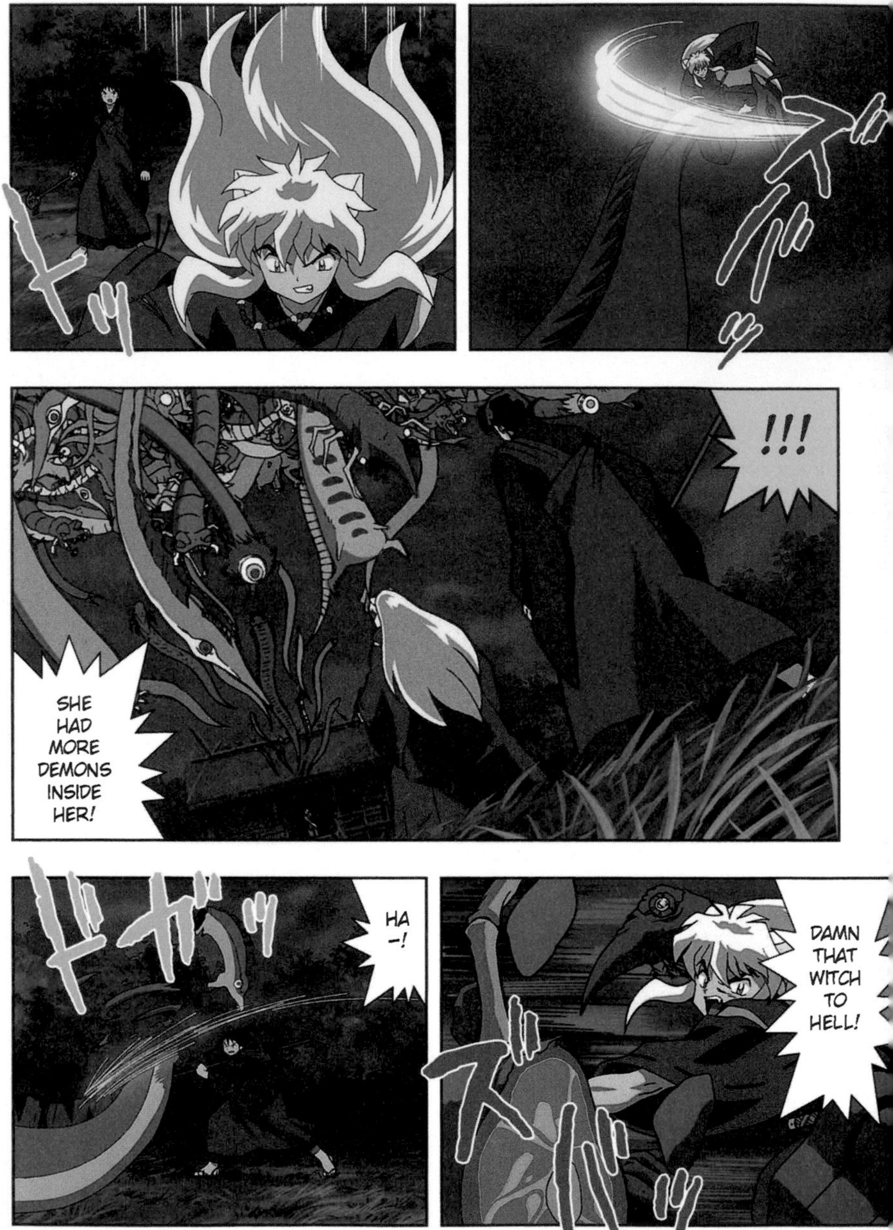
!!!
SHE HAD MORE DEMONS INSIDE HER!
DAMN THAT WITCH TO HELL!
HA—!

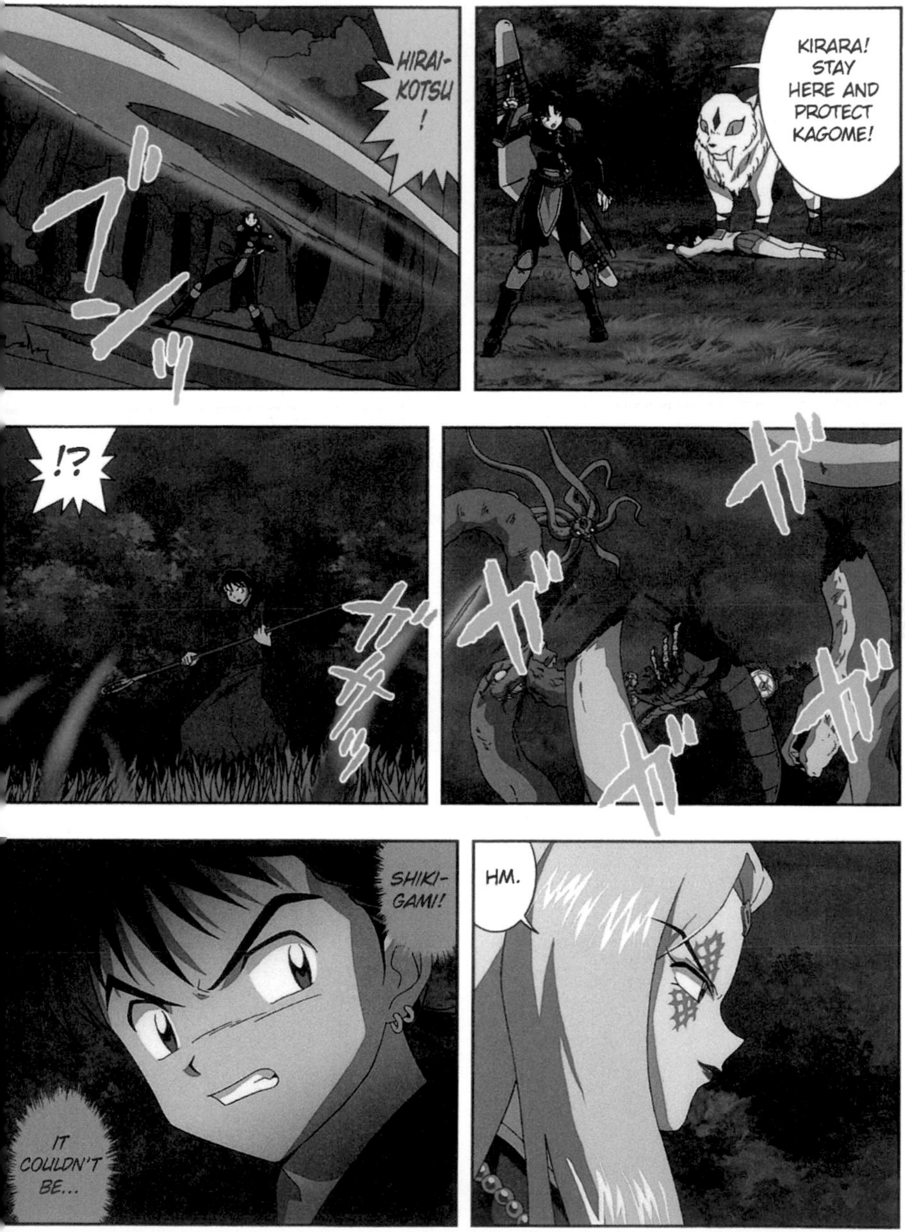
KIRARA! STAY HERE AND PROTECT KAGOME!
HIRAI-KOTSU!
!?
HM.
SHIKI-GAMI!
IT COULDN'T BE...

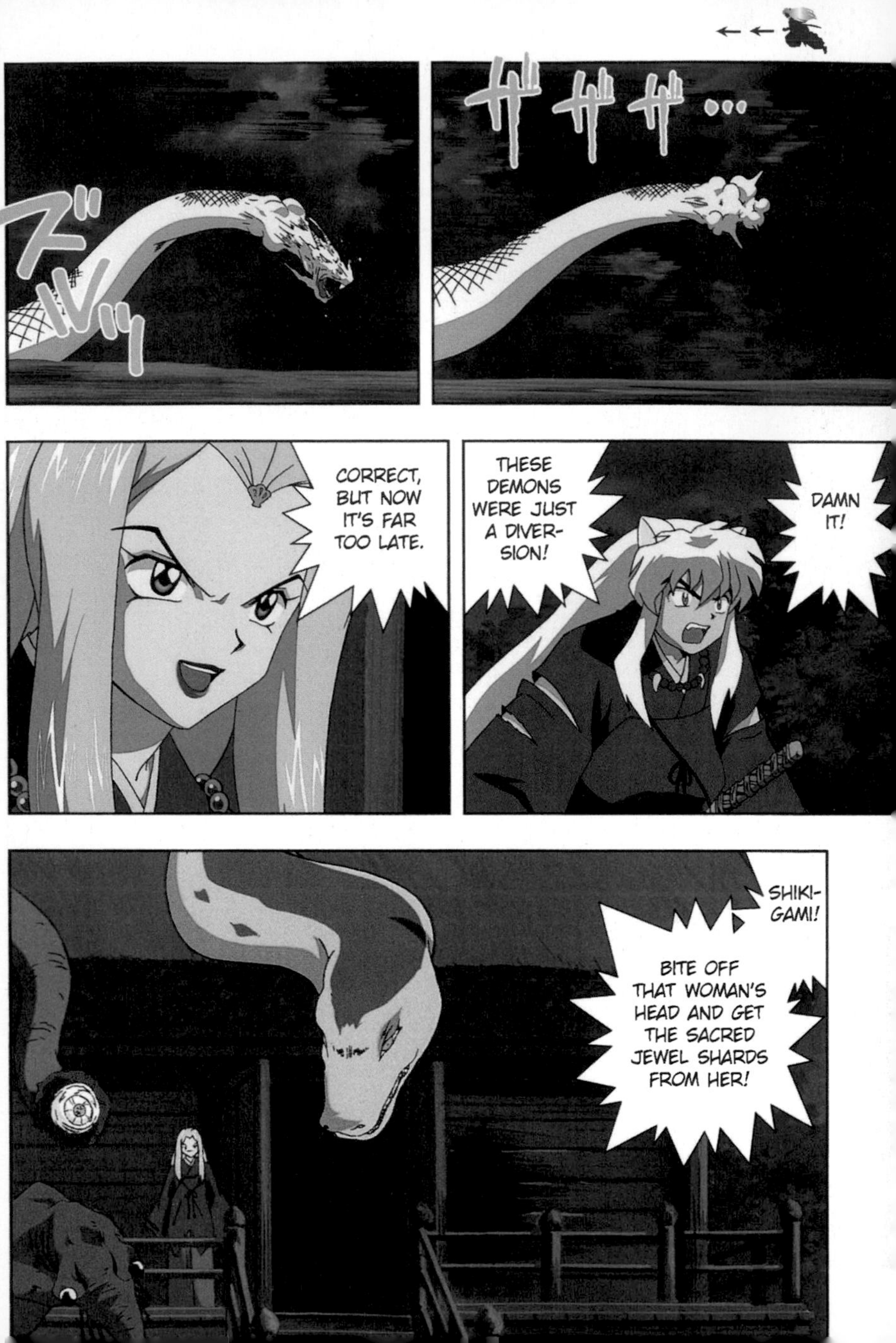
ザザザ…
ズルッ
DAMN IT!
THESE DEMONS WERE JUST A DIVER-SION!
CORRECT, BUT NOW IT'S FAR TOO LATE.
SHIKI-GAMI!
BITE OFF THAT WOMAN'S HEAD AND GET THE SACRED JEWEL SHARDS FROM HER!

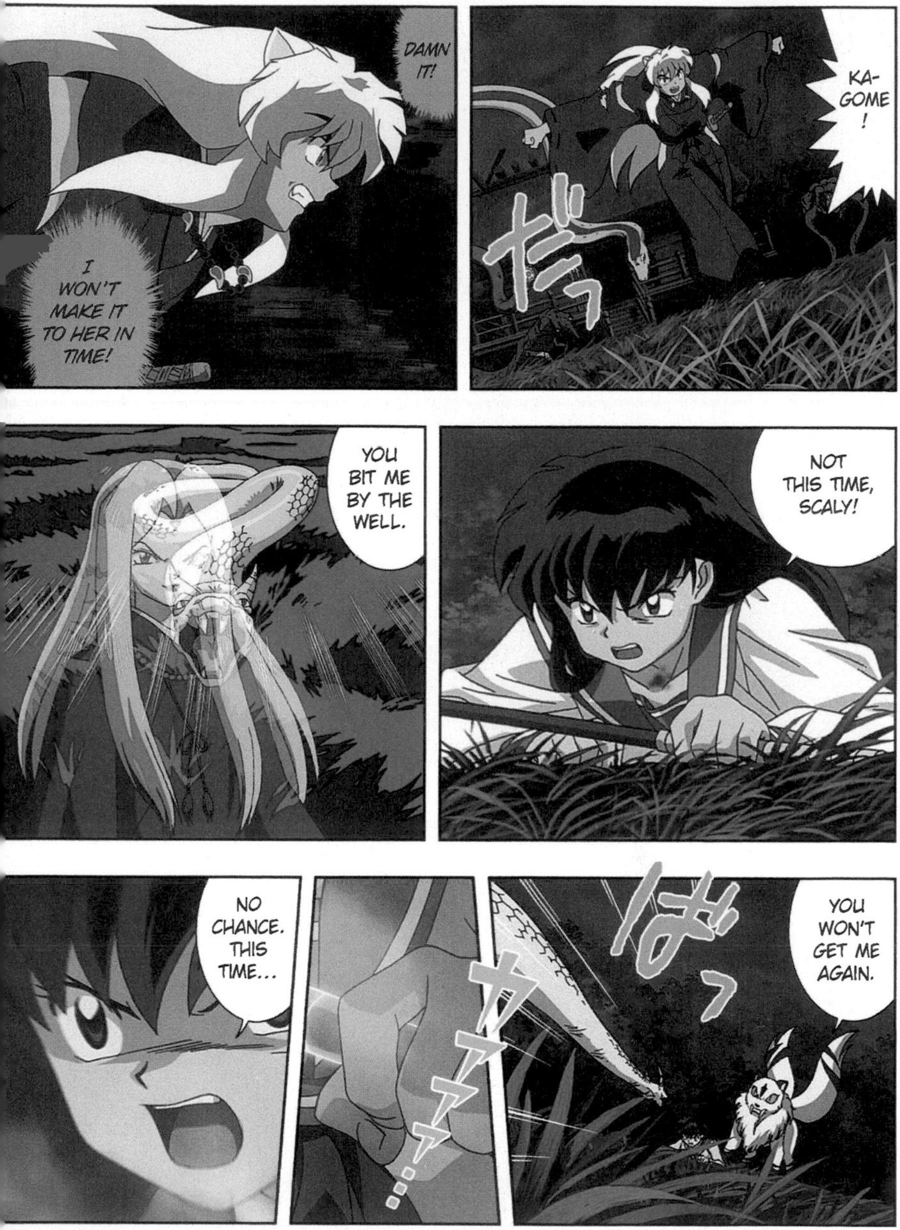
KA-GOME!
ダッ
DAMN IT!
I WON'T MAKE IT TO HER IN TIME!
NOT THIS TIME, SCALY!
YOU BIT ME BY THE WELL.
ばっ
YOU WON'T GET ME AGAIN.
サァァァ…
NO CHANCE. THIS TIME...

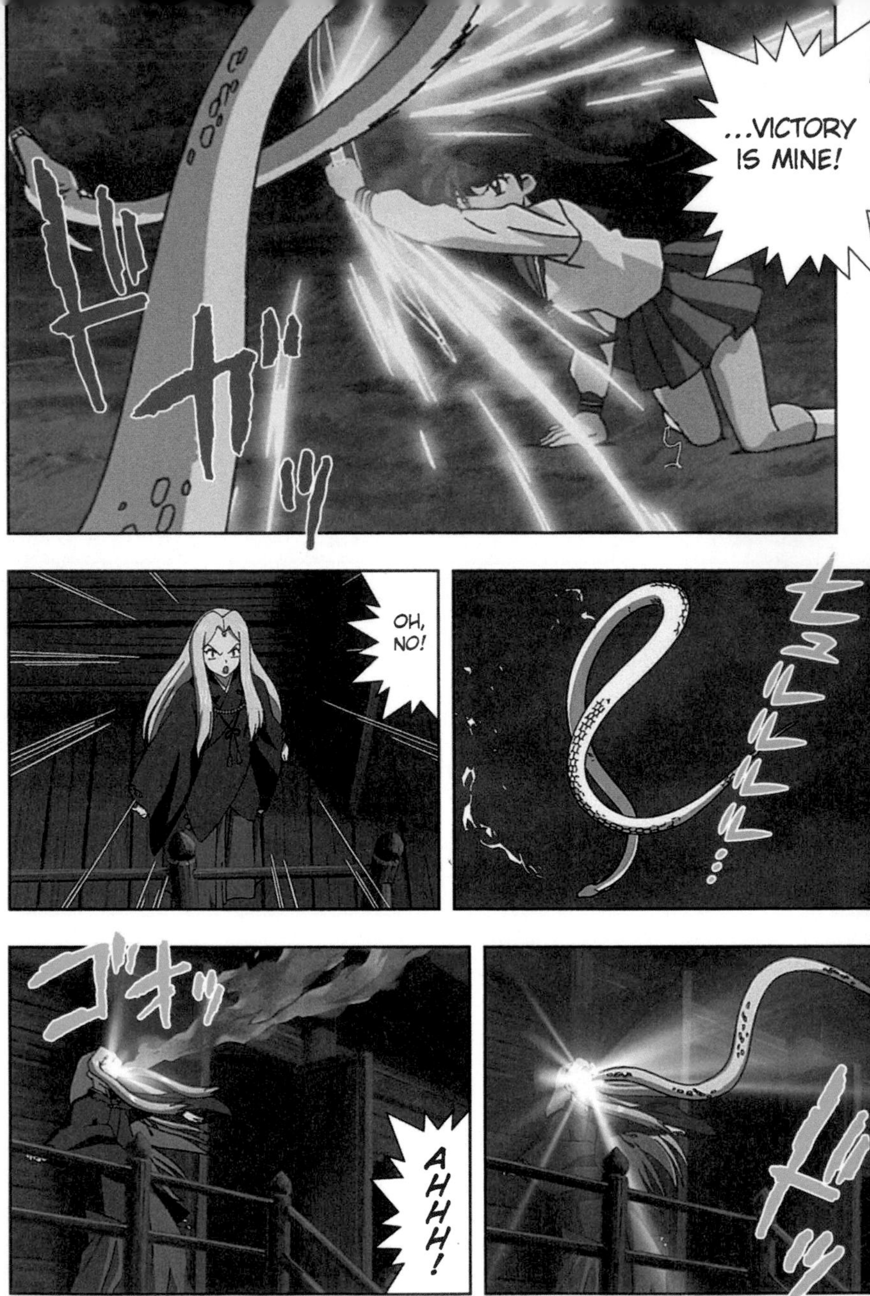

ドガッ
...VICTORY IS MINE!
ヒュルルルル…
OH, NO!
ドッ
ゴォッ
AHHHH!

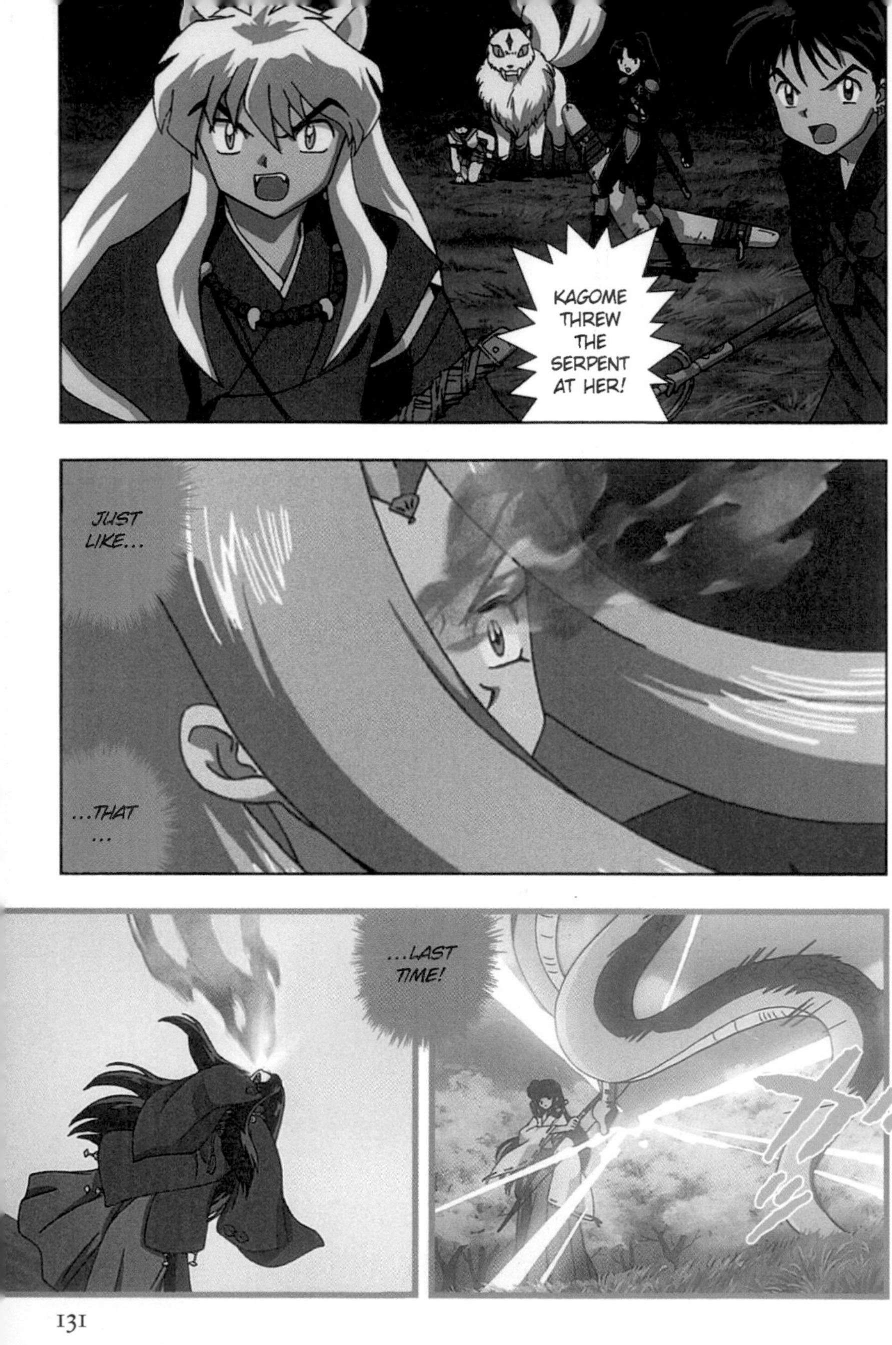
KAGOME THREW THE SERPENT AT HER!
JUST LIKE...
...THAT ...
...LAST TIME!
ガッ

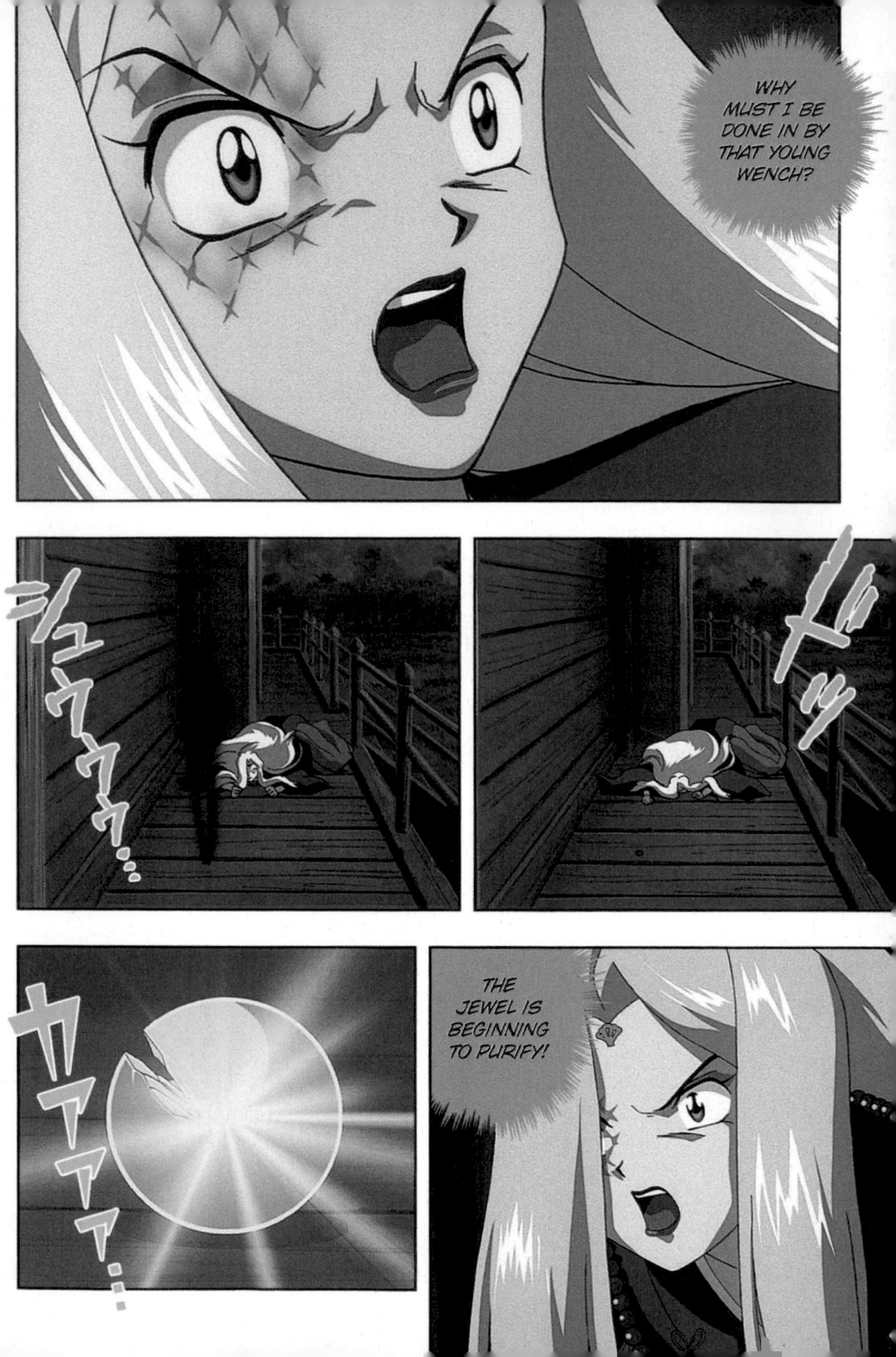
WHY MUST I BE DONE IN BY THAT YOUNG WENCH?
ドッ
シュウウウウ…
THE JEWEL IS BEGINNING TO PURIFY!
カァァァ…

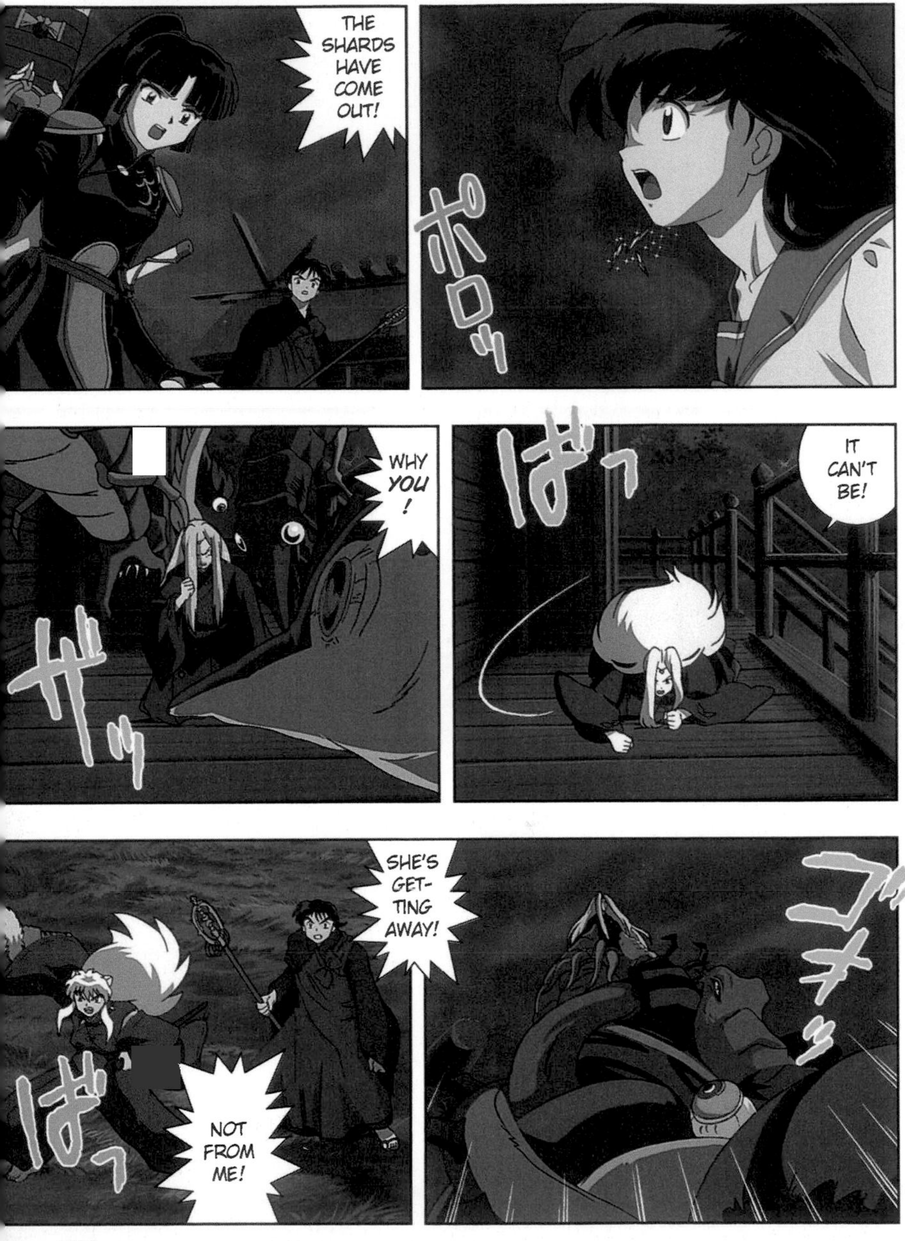
ポロッ
THE SHARDS HAVE COME OUT!
ばっ
IT CAN'T BE!
WHY *YOU*!
ザッ
SHE'S GET-TING AWAY!
ばっ
NOT FROM ME!

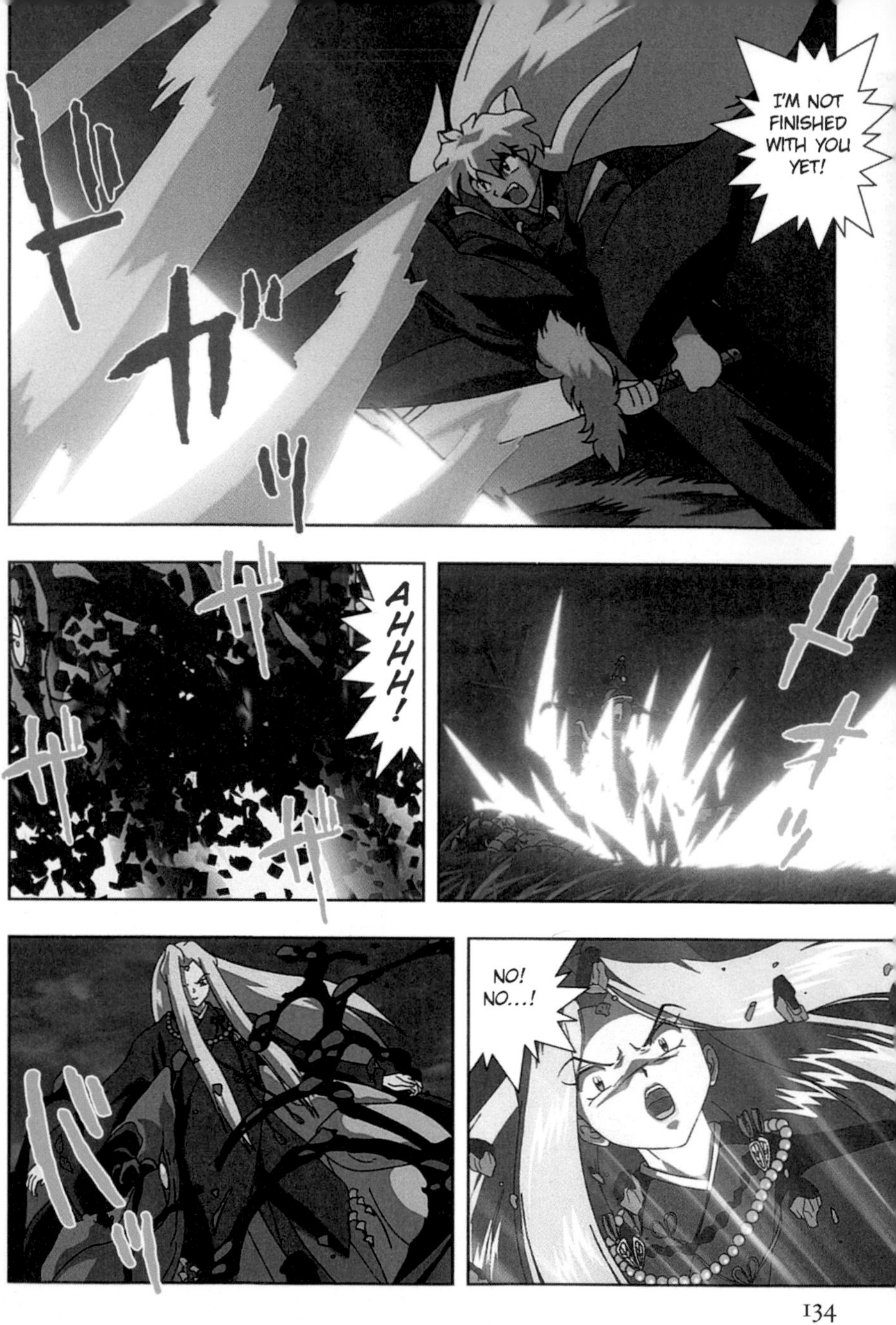

I'M NOT FINISHED WITH YOU YET!
AHHHH!
NO! NO...!

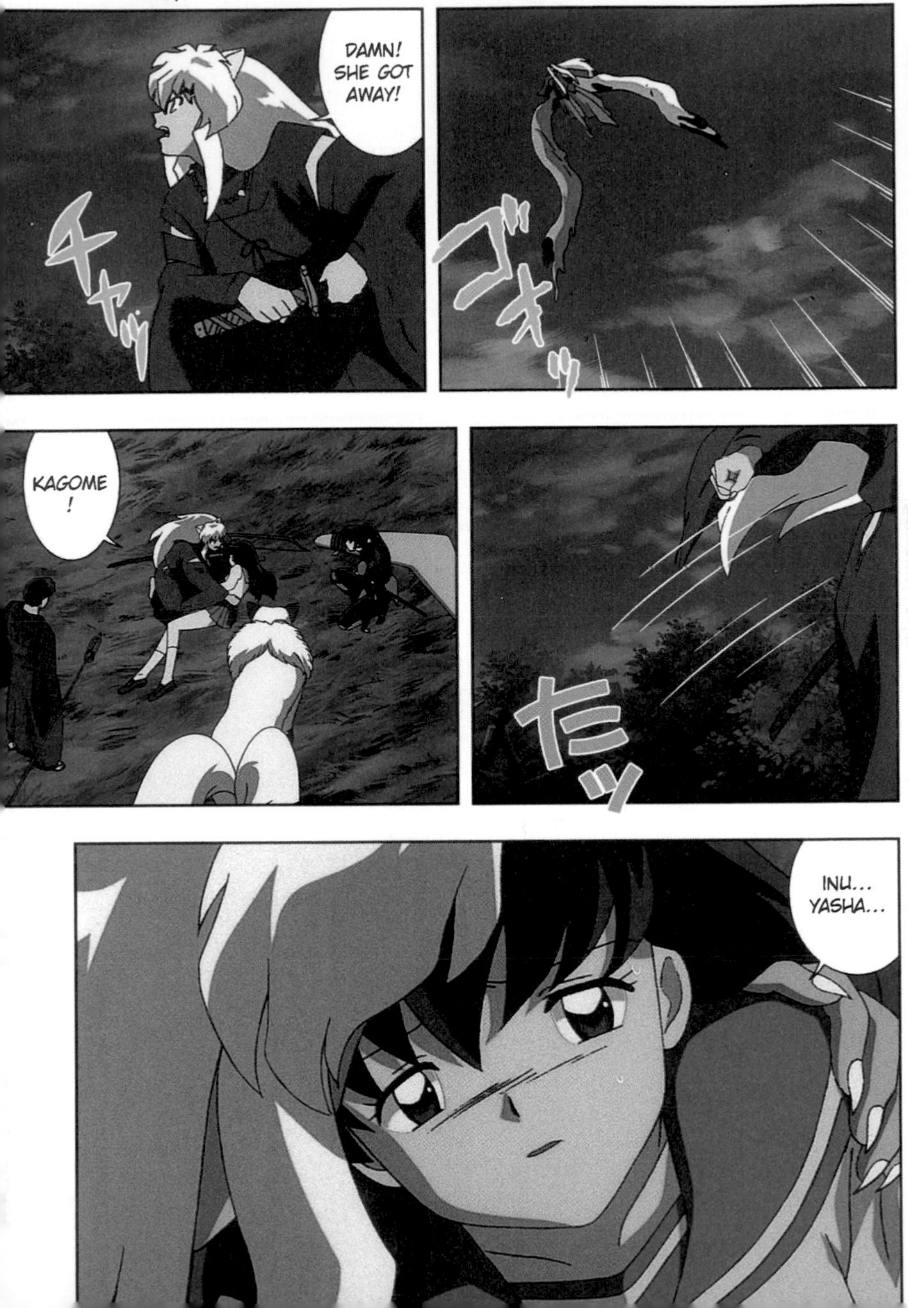
ゴオッ
DAMN! SHE GOT AWAY!
チャッ
タッ
KAGOME!
INU... YASHA...

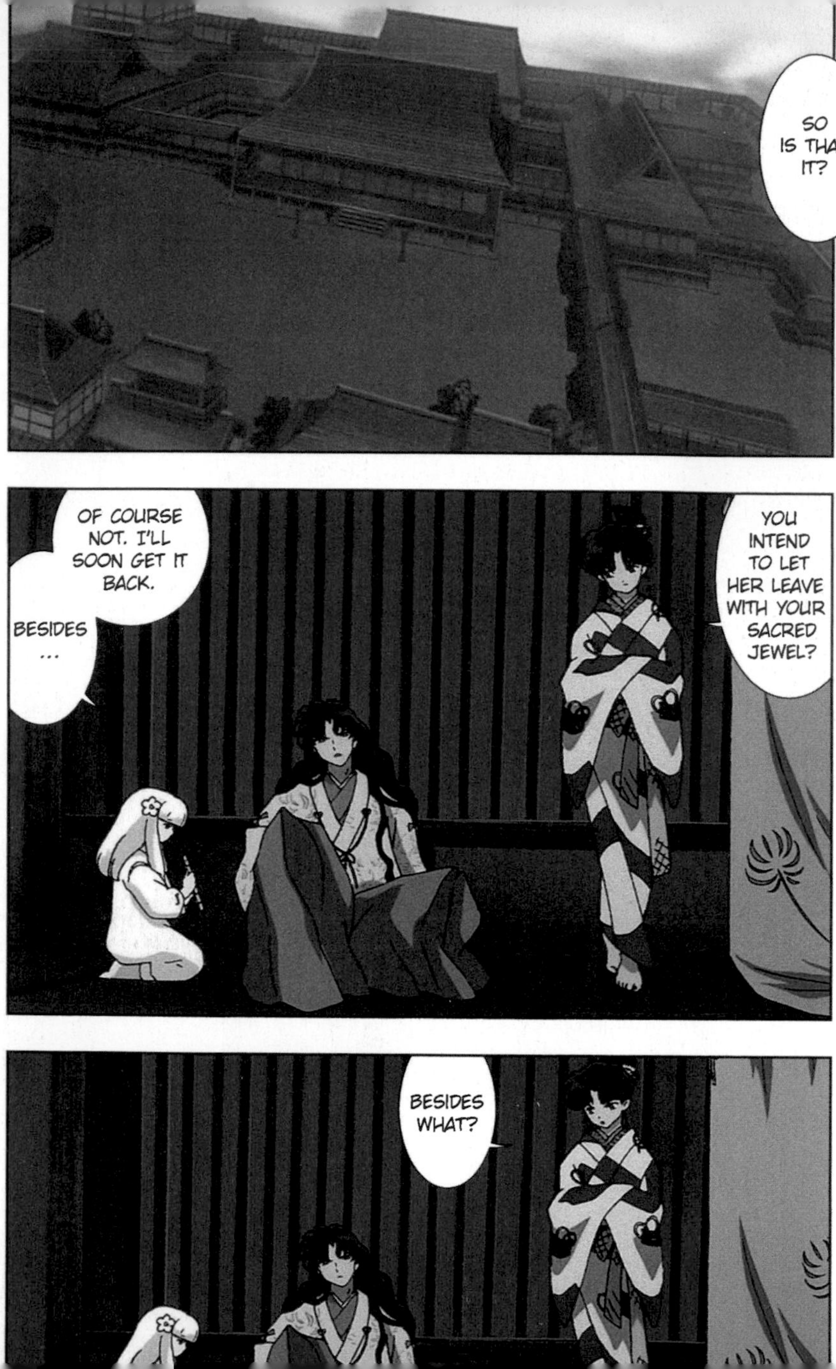
SO IS THAT IT?
YOU INTEND TO LET HER LEAVE WITH YOUR SACRED JEWEL?
OF COURSE NOT. I'LL SOON GET IT BACK.
BESIDES ...
BESIDES WHAT?

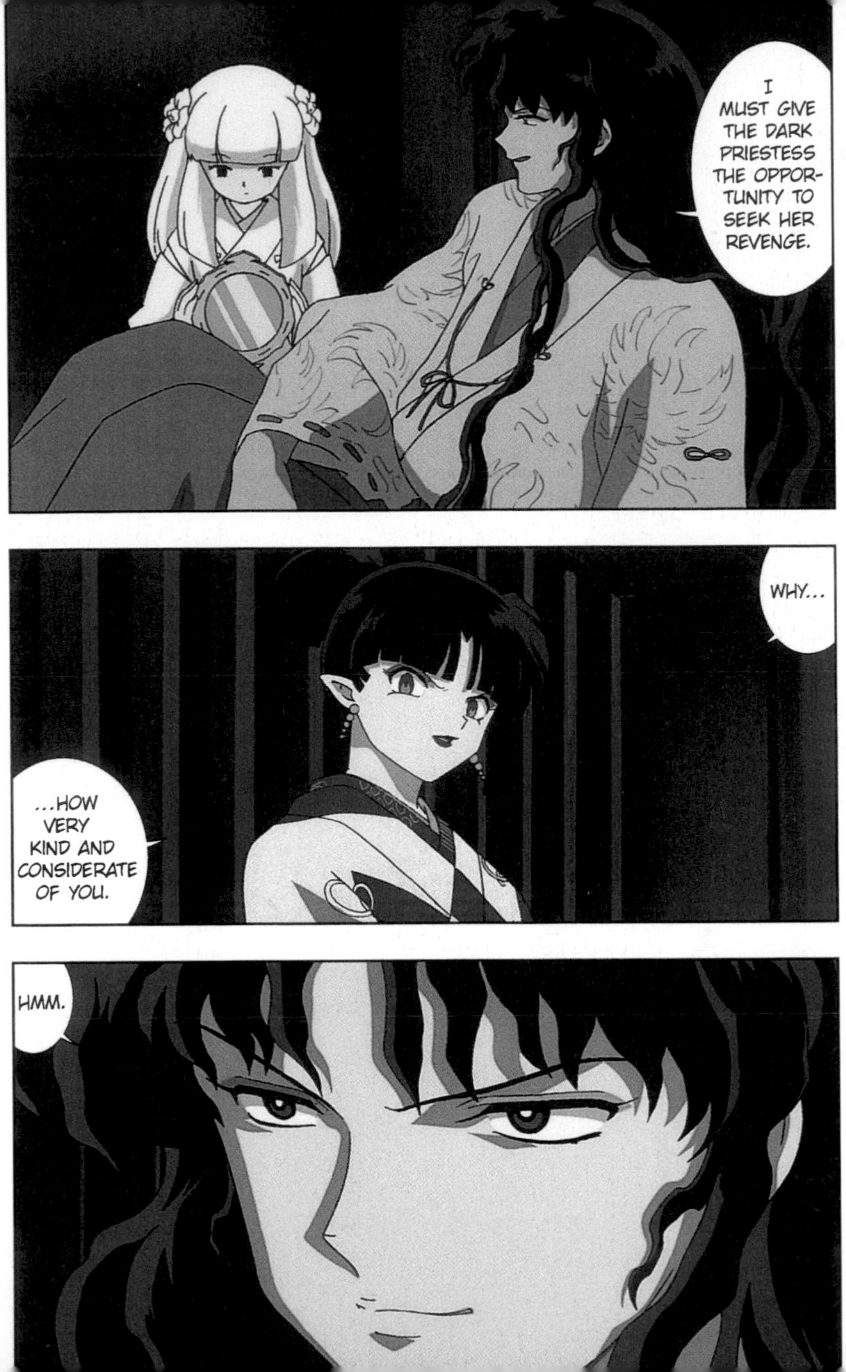
I MUST GIVE THE DARK PRIESTESS THE OPPORTUNITY TO SEEK HER REVENGE.
WHY...
...HOW VERY KIND AND CONSIDERATE OF YOU.
HMM.

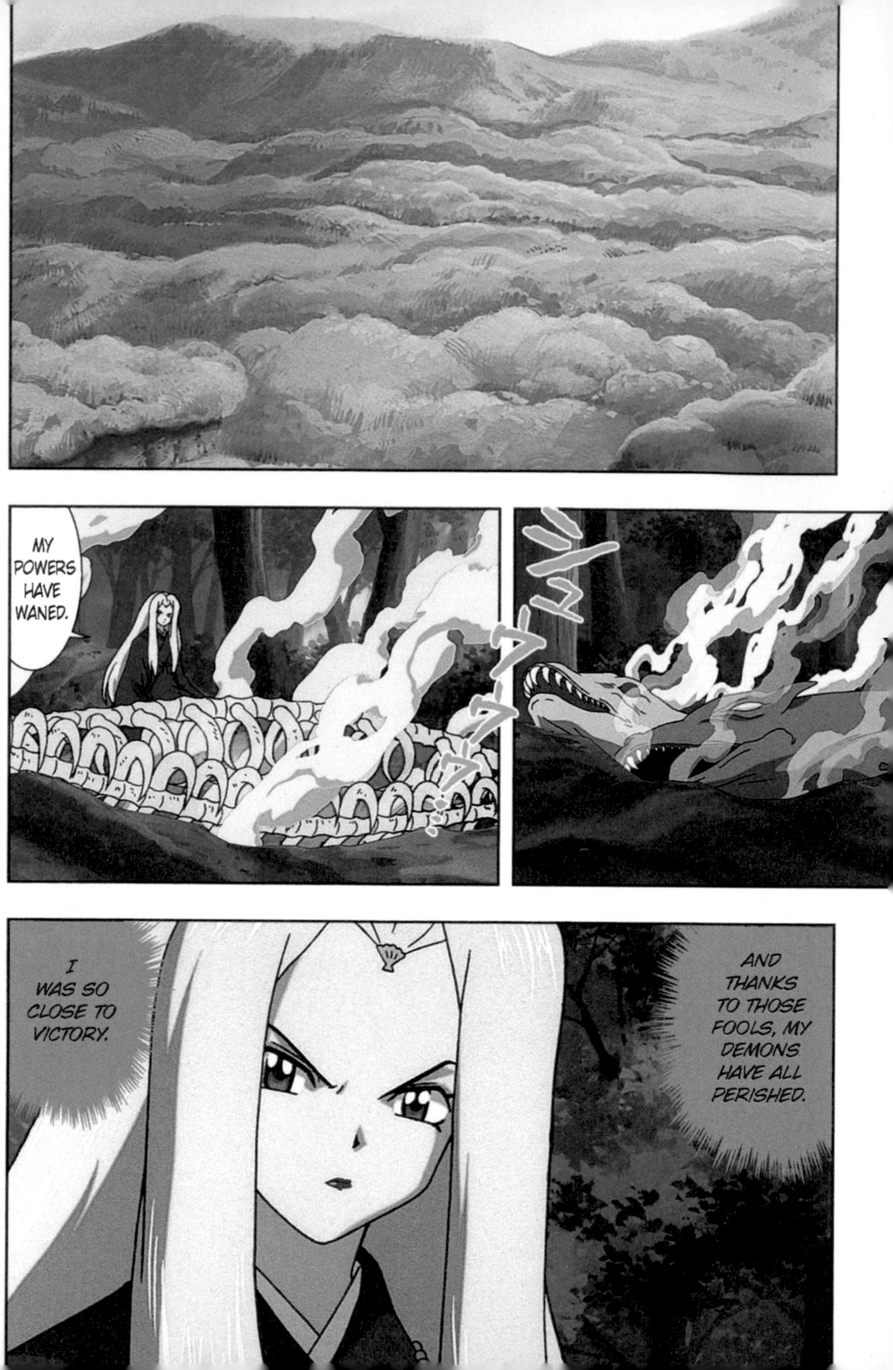
シュワーワーワ
MY POWERS HAVE WANED.
AND THANKS TO THOSE FOOLS, MY DEMONS HAVE ALL PERISHED.
I WAS SO CLOSE TO VICTORY.

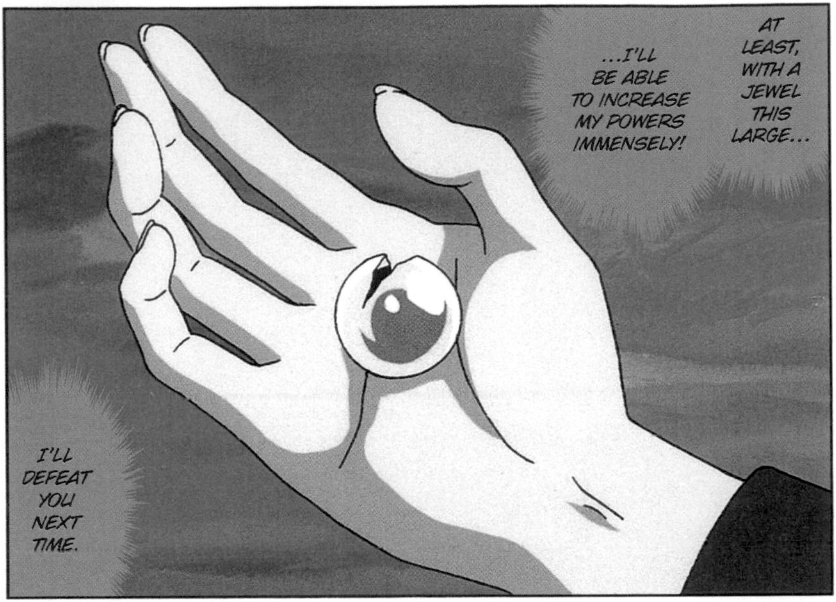
AT LEAST, WITH A JEWEL THIS LARGE...
...I'LL BE ABLE TO INCREASE MY POWERS IMMENSELY!
I'LL DEFEAT YOU NEXT TIME.

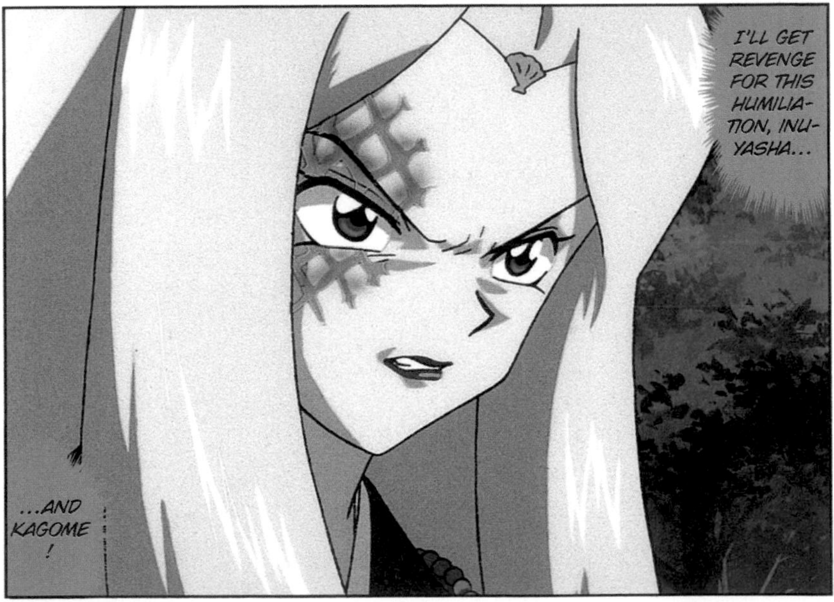
I'LL GET REVENGE FOR THIS HUMILIATION, INU-YASHA...
...AND KAGOME!

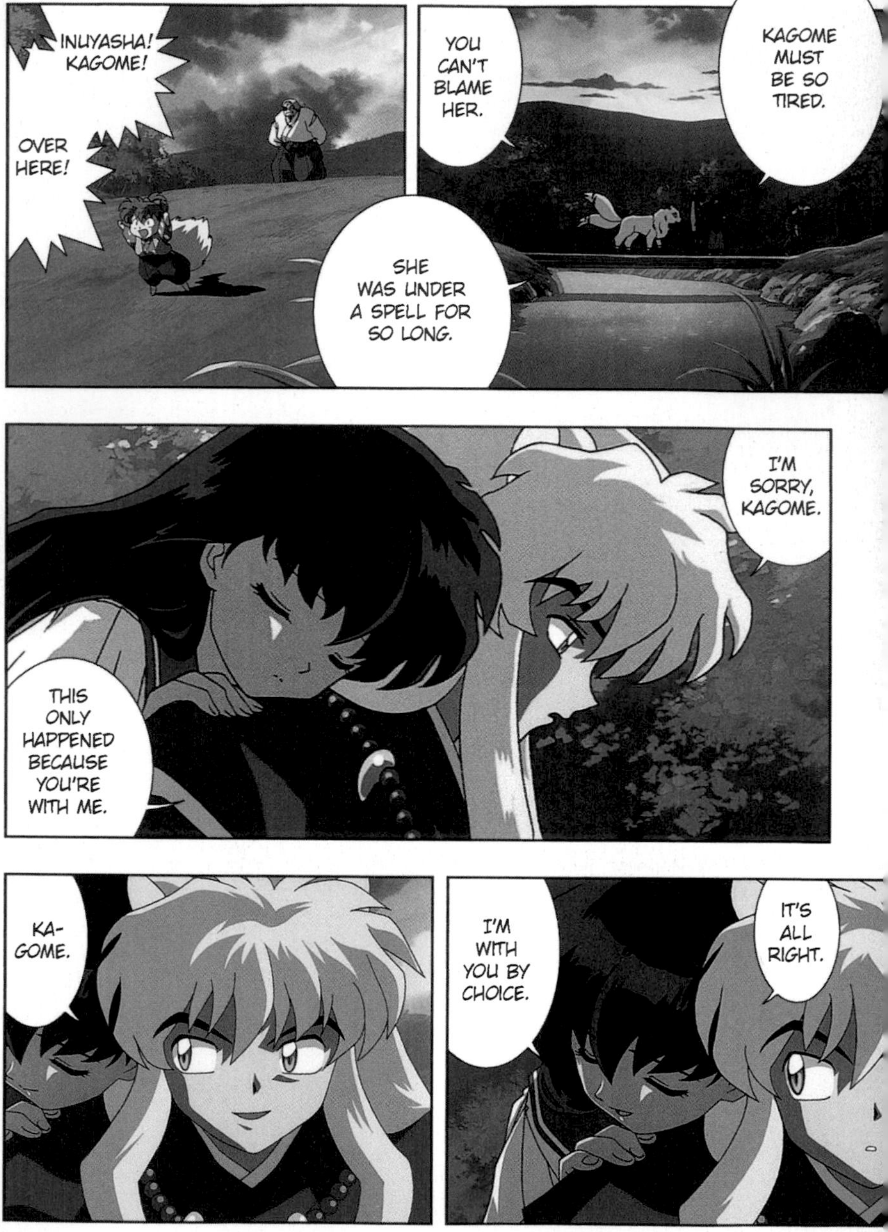
KAGOME MUST BE SO TIRED.
YOU CAN'T BLAME HER.
SHE WAS UNDER A SPELL FOR SO LONG.
INUYASHA! KAGOME!
OVER HERE!
I'M SORRY, KAGOME.
THIS ONLY HAPPENED BECAUSE YOU'RE WITH ME.
IT'S ALL RIGHT.
I'M WITH YOU BY CHOICE.
KA-GOME.

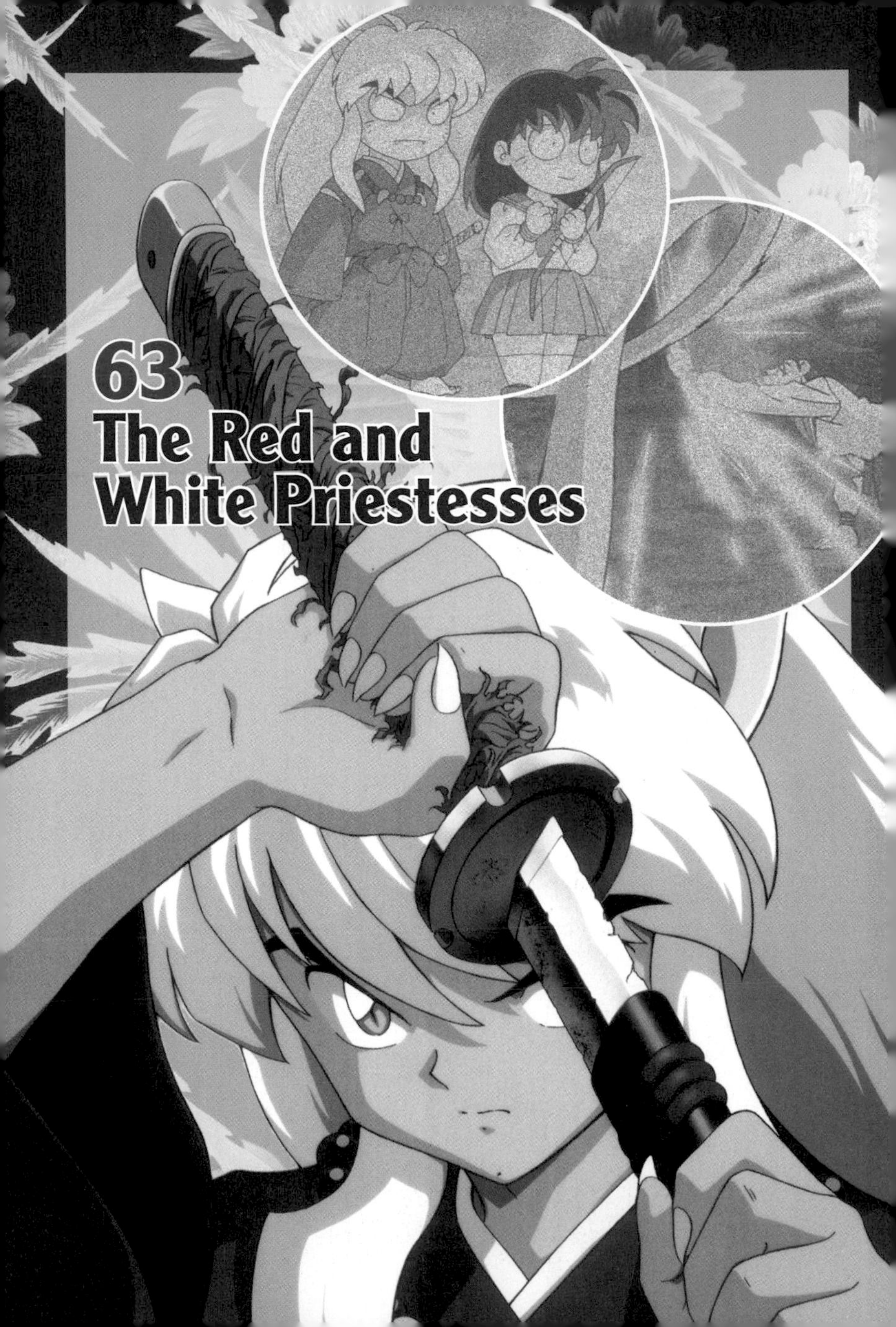
63
The Red and White Priestesses

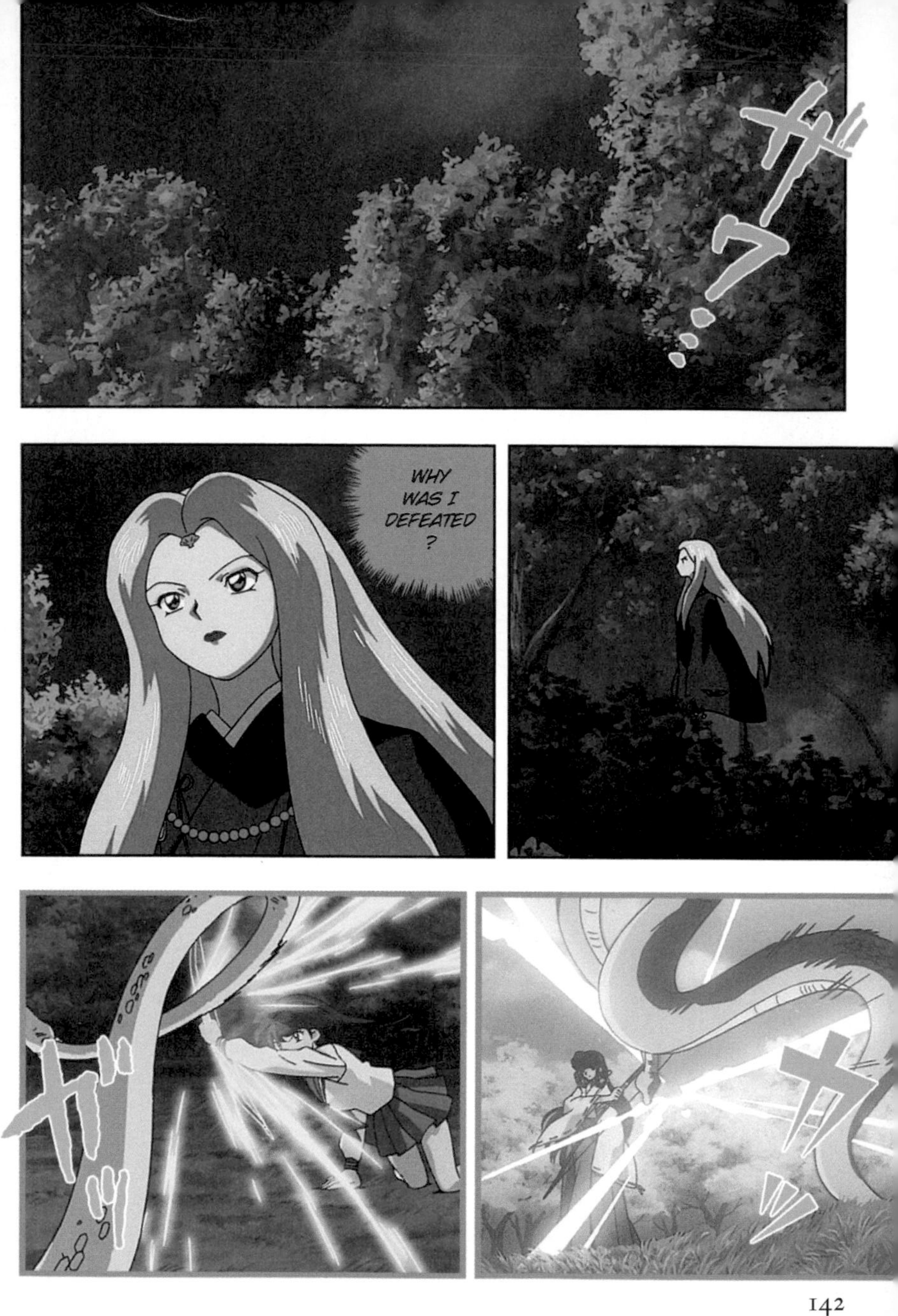
ザワ…
WHY WAS I DEFEATED?
カッ
ガッ

DID I MAKE A MISTAKE SOME- WHERE?

NO, I HAVE MADE NO ERRORS.

...

WHO'S THERE !?

HUH!?

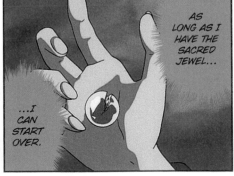

AS LONG AS I HAVE THE SACRED JEWEL...

...I CAN START OVER.

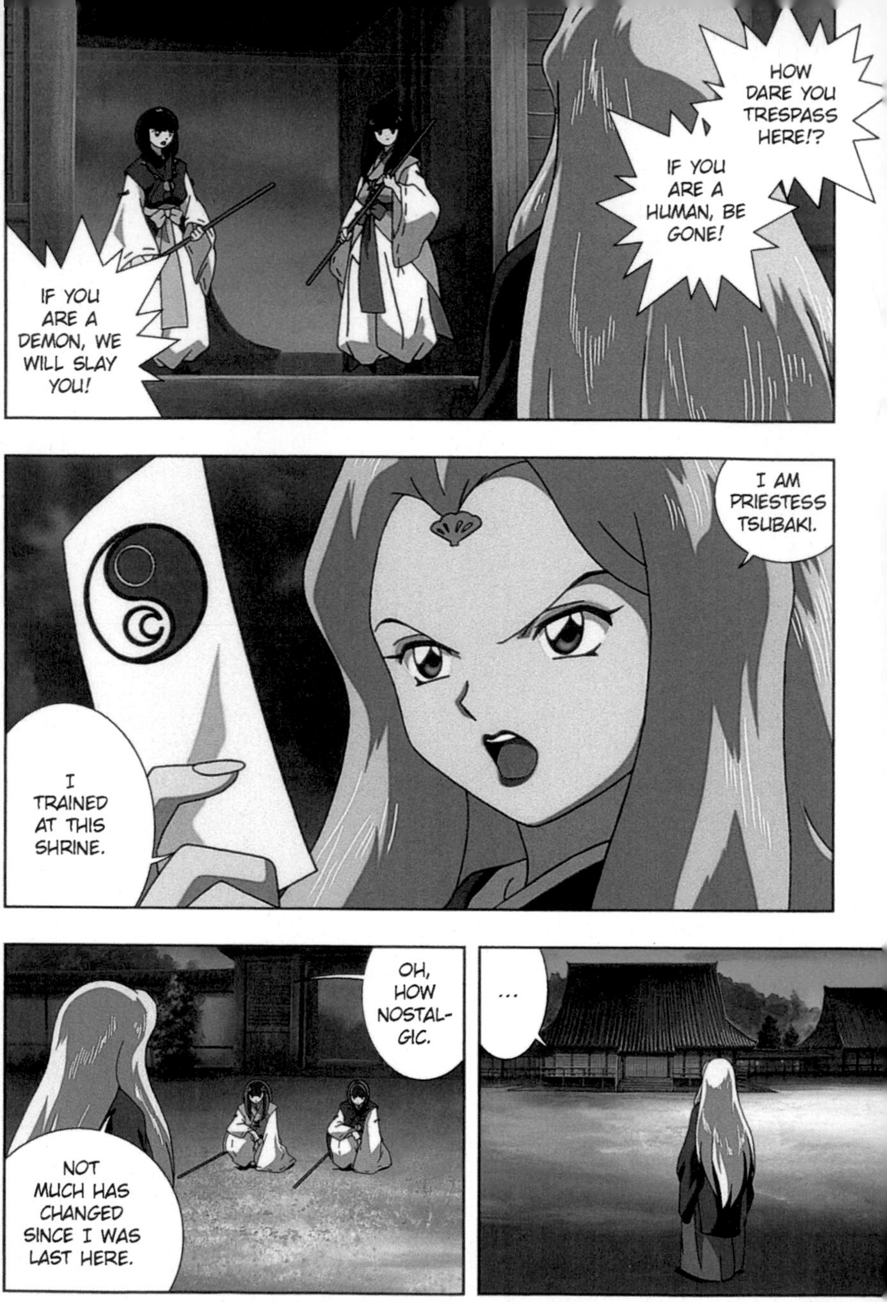
HOW DARE YOU TRESPASS HERE!?
IF YOU ARE A HUMAN, BE GONE!
IF YOU ARE A DEMON, WE WILL SLAY YOU!
I AM PRIESTESS TSUBAKI.
I TRAINED AT THIS SHRINE.
...
OH, HOW NOSTAL-GIC.
NOT MUCH HAS CHANGED SINCE I WAS LAST HERE.

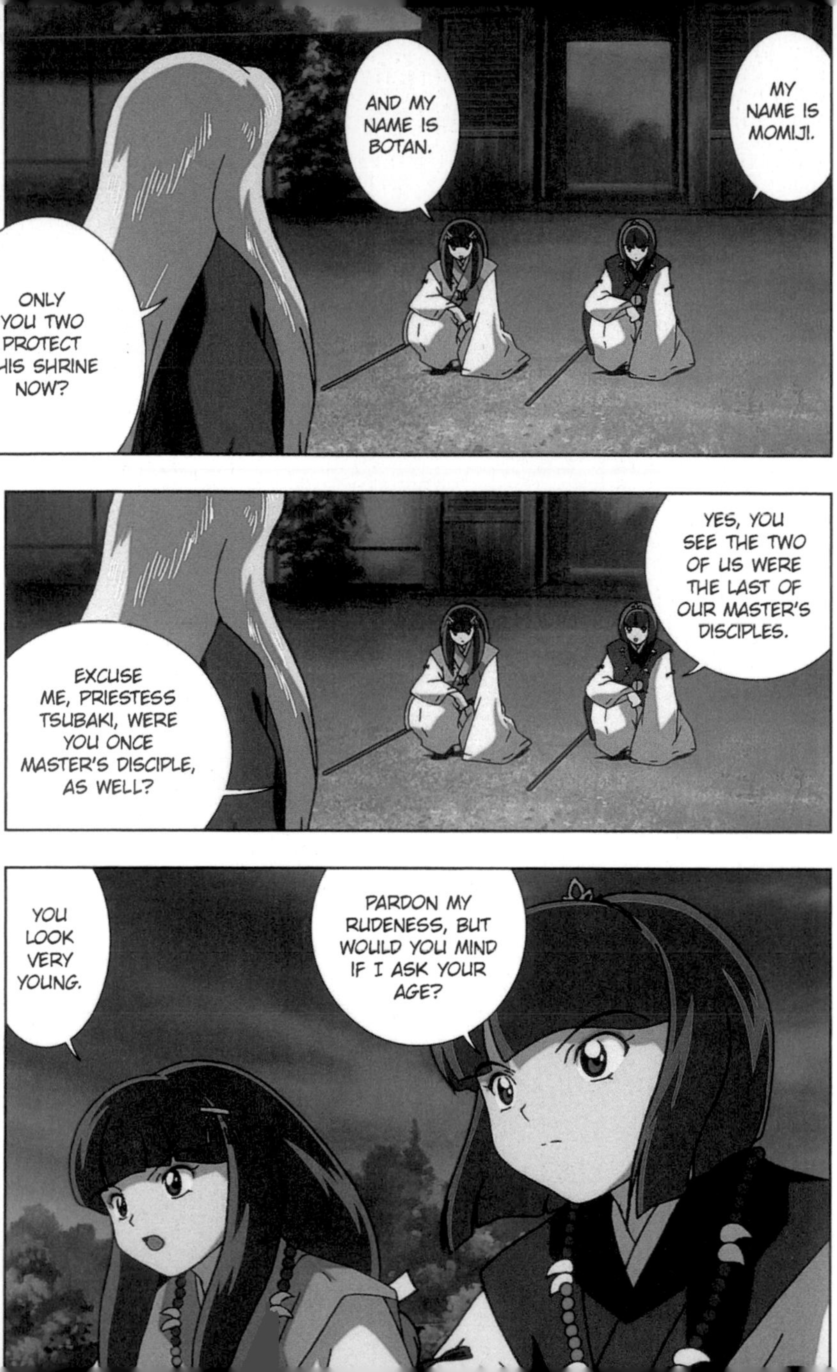
MY NAME IS MOMIJI.
AND MY NAME IS BOTAN.
ONLY YOU TWO PROTECT THIS SHRINE NOW?
YES, YOU SEE THE TWO OF US WERE THE LAST OF OUR MASTER'S DISCIPLES.
EXCUSE ME, PRIESTESS TSUBAKI, WERE YOU ONCE MASTER'S DISCIPLE, AS WELL?
PARDON MY RUDENESS, BUT WOULD YOU MIND IF I ASK YOUR AGE?
YOU LOOK VERY YOUNG.

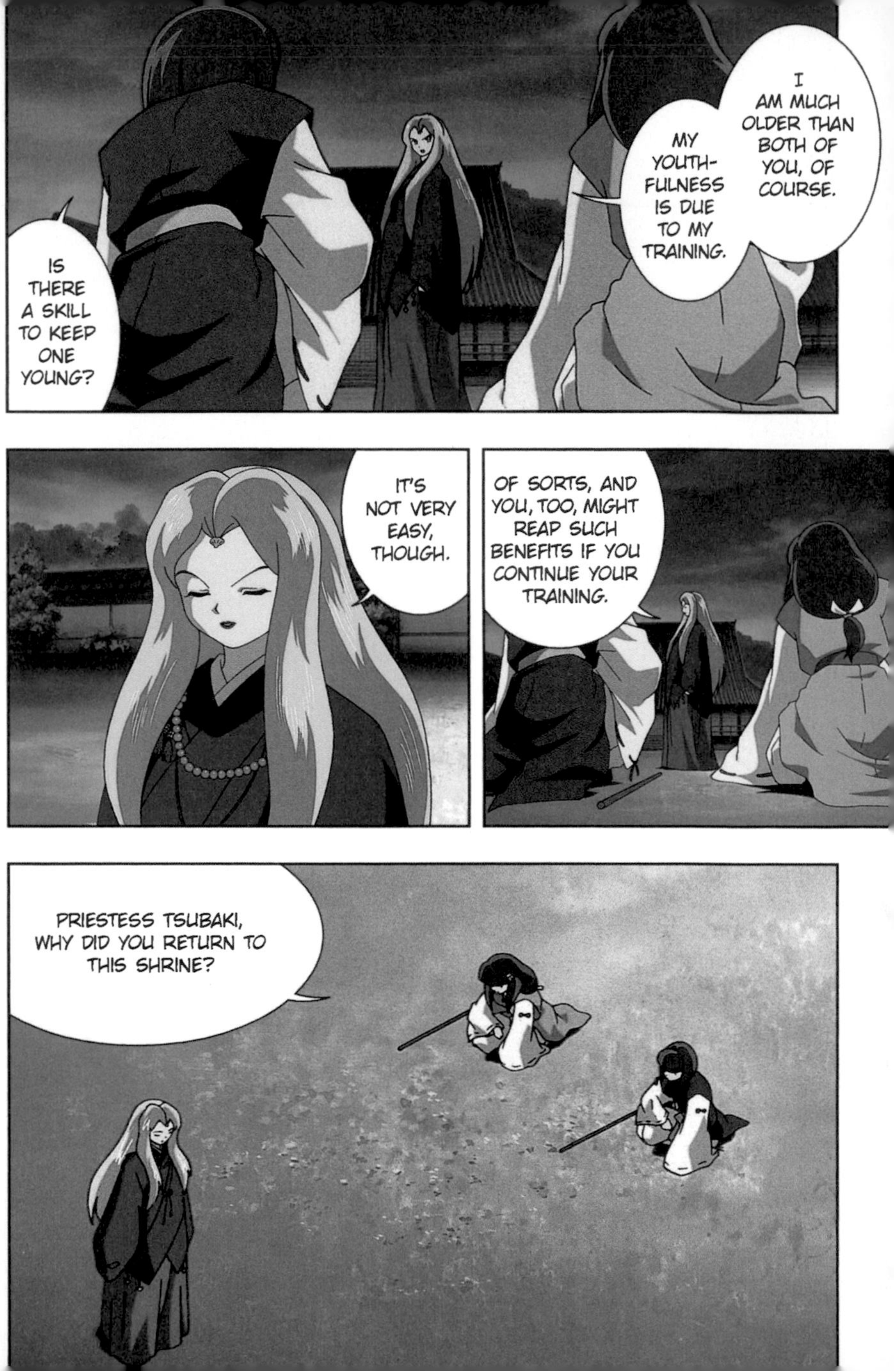
I AM MUCH OLDER THAN BOTH OF YOU, OF COURSE.
MY YOUTH-FULNESS IS DUE TO MY TRAINING.
IS THERE A SKILL TO KEEP ONE YOUNG?
OF SORTS, AND YOU, TOO, MIGHT REAP SUCH BENEFITS IF YOU CONTINUE YOUR TRAINING.
IT'S NOT VERY EASY, THOUGH.
PRIESTESS TSUBAKI, WHY DID YOU RETURN TO THIS SHRINE?

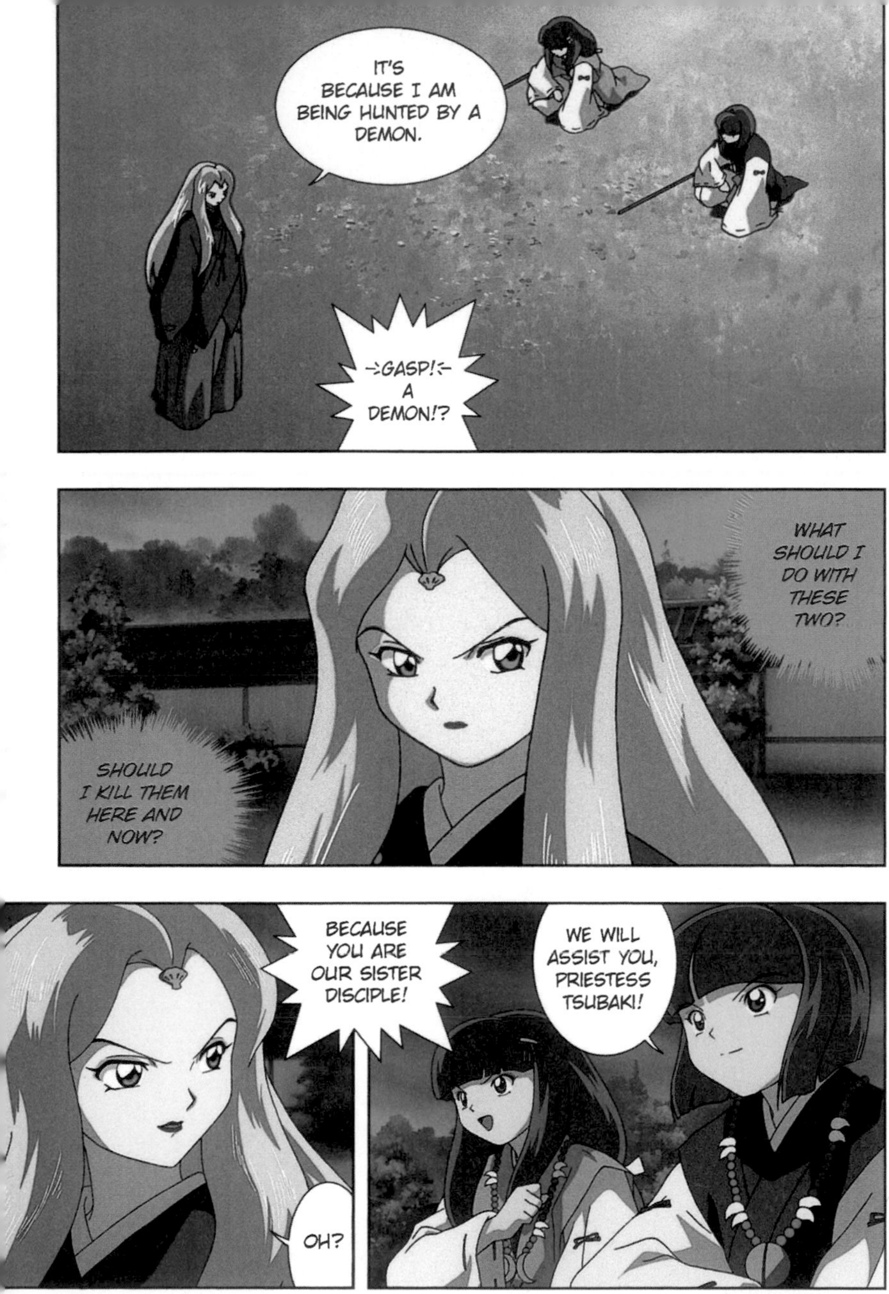
IT'S BECAUSE I AM BEING HUNTED BY A DEMON.
-GASP!- A DEMON!?
WHAT SHOULD I DO WITH THESE TWO?
SHOULD I KILL THEM HERE AND NOW?
WE WILL ASSIST YOU, PRIESTESS TSUBAKI!
BECAUSE YOU ARE OUR SISTER DISCIPLE!
OH?

...!!

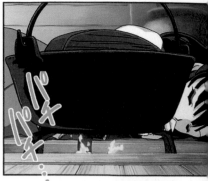

I REMEM-BER...

...WHAT HAP-PENED NOW.

I WAS PLACED UNDER A CURSE BY TSUBAKI.

148

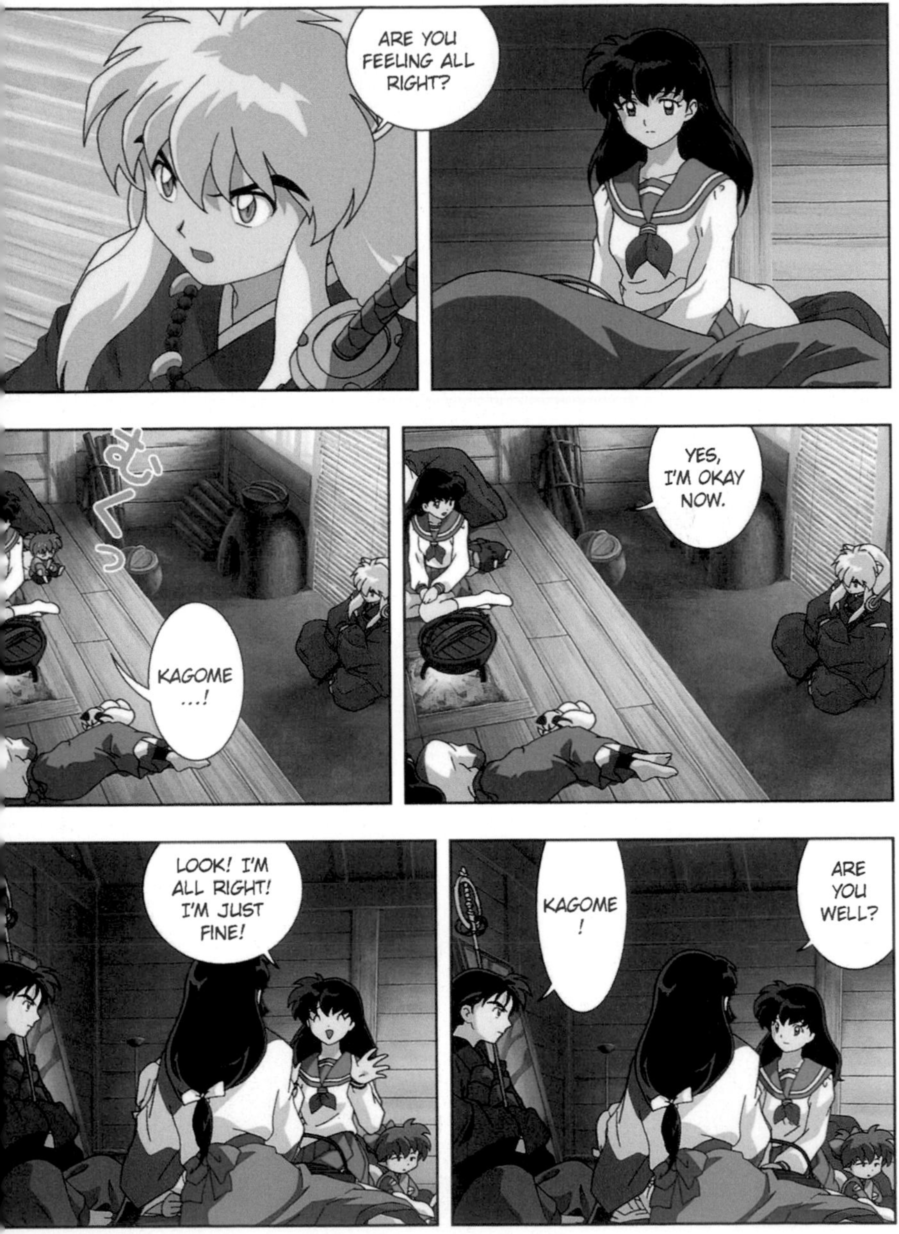
ARE YOU FEELING ALL RIGHT?
YES, I'M OKAY NOW.
むくっ
KAGOME ...!
ARE YOU WELL?
KAGOME !
LOOK! I'M ALL RIGHT! I'M JUST FINE!

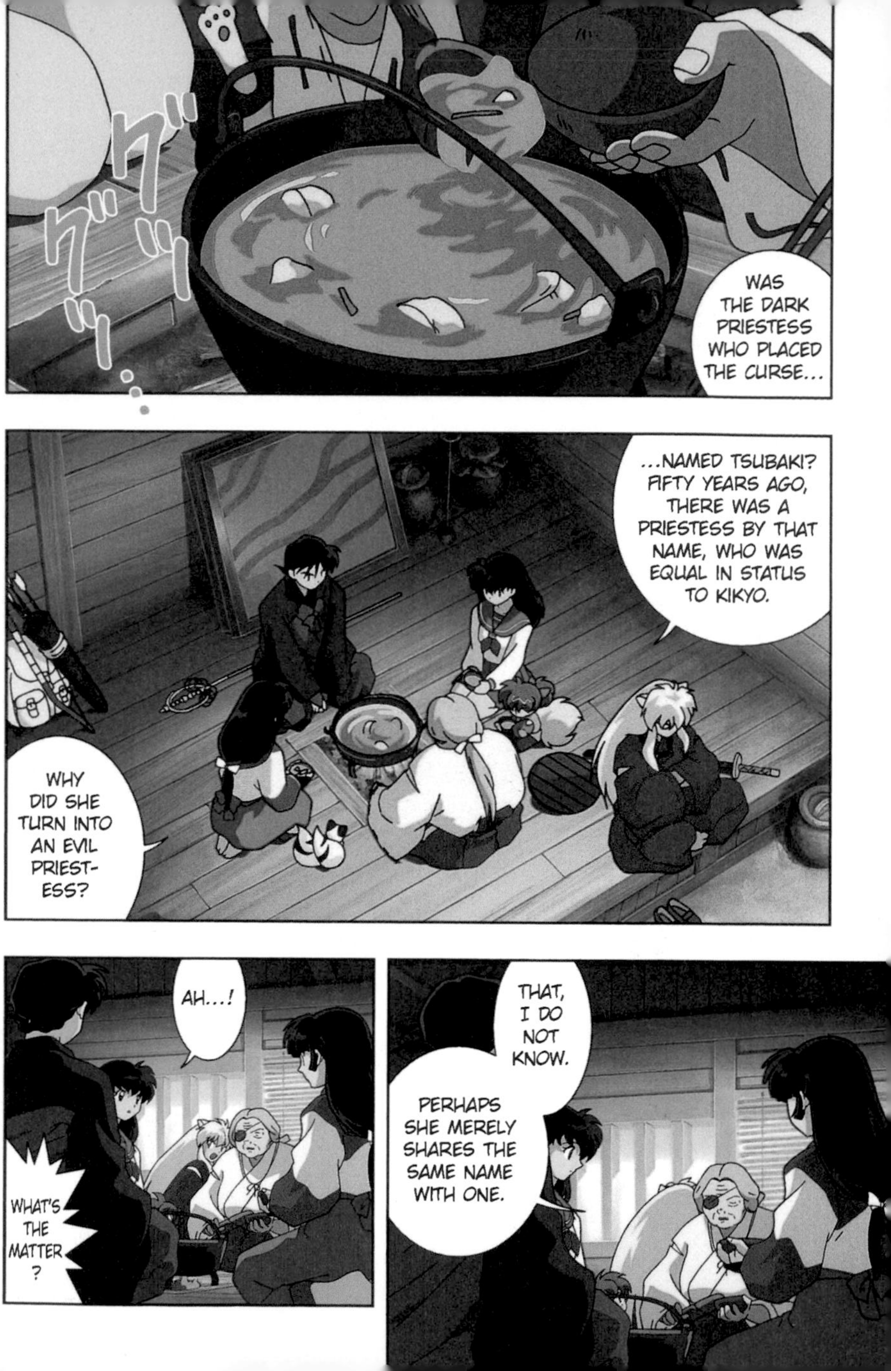
WAS THE DARK PRIESTESS WHO PLACED THE CURSE...
...NAMED TSUBAKI? FIFTY YEARS AGO, THERE WAS A PRIESTESS BY THAT NAME, WHO WAS EQUAL IN STATUS TO KIKYO.
WHY DID SHE TURN INTO AN EVIL PRIEST-ESS?
THAT, I DO NOT KNOW.
PERHAPS SHE MERELY SHARES THE SAME NAME WITH ONE.
AH...!
WHAT'S THE MATTER?

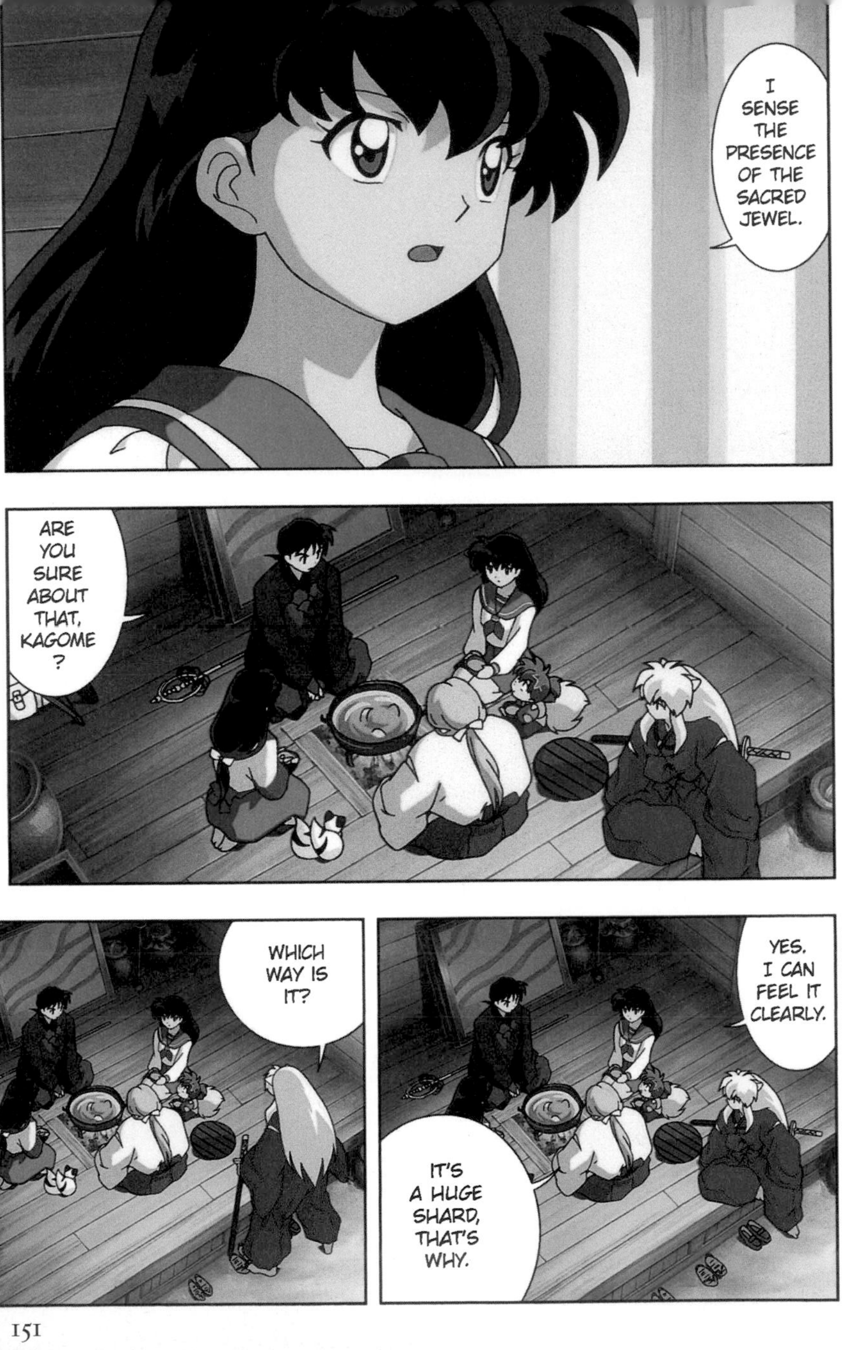
I SENSE THE PRESENCE OF THE SACRED JEWEL.
ARE YOU SURE ABOUT THAT, KAGOME?
WHICH WAY IS IT?
YES. I CAN FEEL IT CLEARLY.
IT'S A HUGE SHARD, THAT'S WHY.

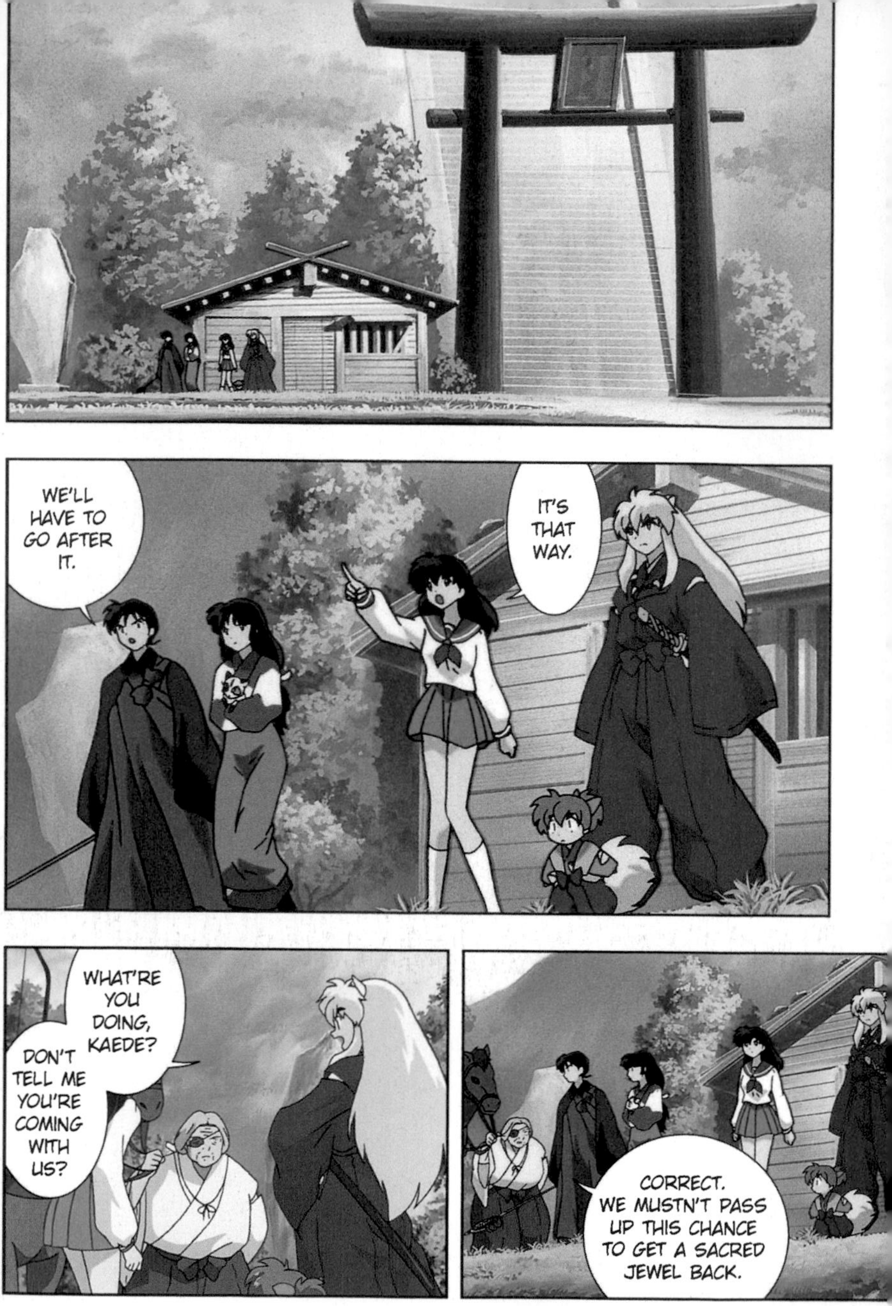
WE'LL HAVE TO GO AFTER IT.
IT'S THAT WAY.
WHAT'RE YOU DOING, KAEDE?
DON'T TELL ME YOU'RE COMING WITH US?
CORRECT. WE MUSTN'T PASS UP THIS CHANCE TO GET A SACRED JEWEL BACK.

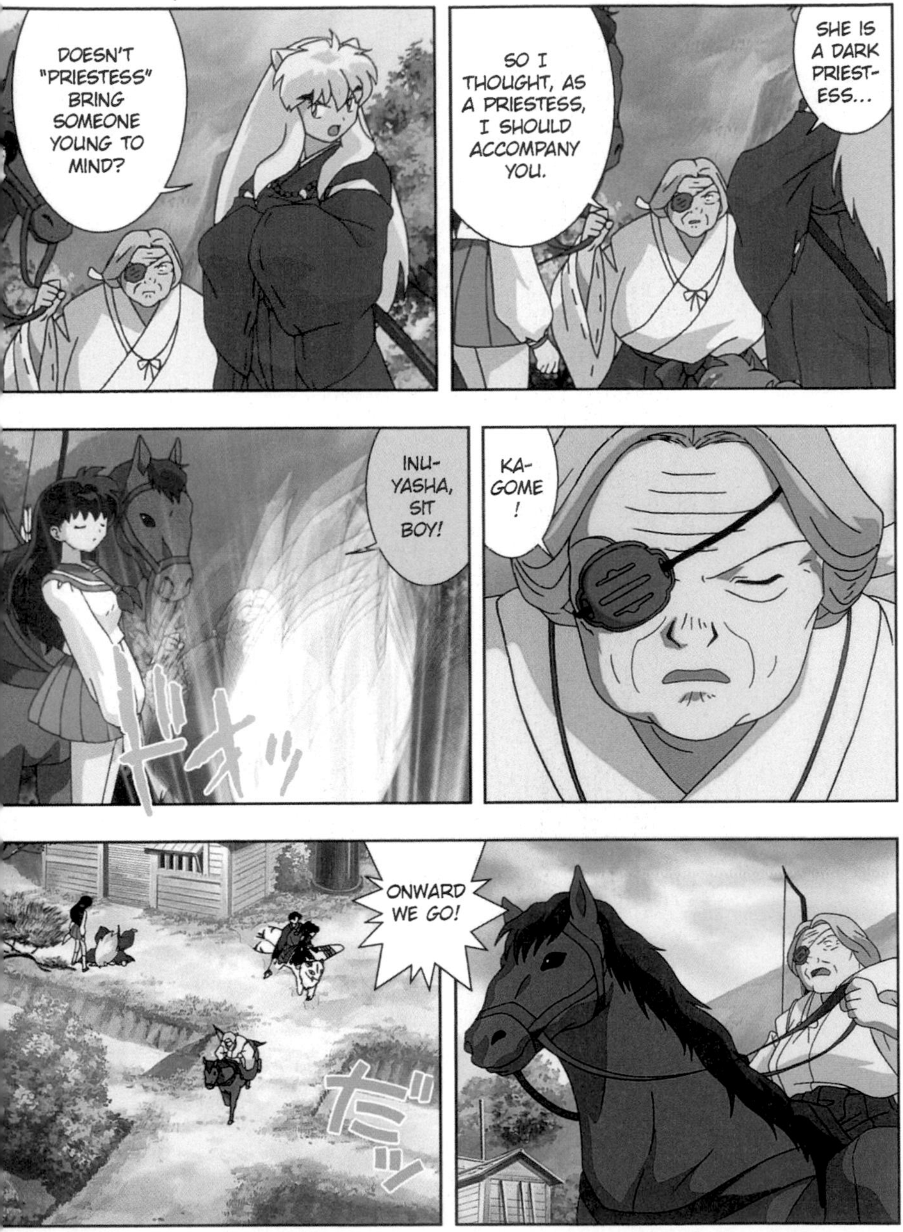
SHE IS A DARK PRIEST-ESS...
SO I THOUGHT, AS A PRIESTESS, I SHOULD ACCOMPANY YOU.
DOESN'T "PRIESTESS" BRING SOMEONE YOUNG TO MIND?
KA-GOME!
INU-YASHA, SIT BOY!
ドオッ
ONWARD WE GO!
だッ

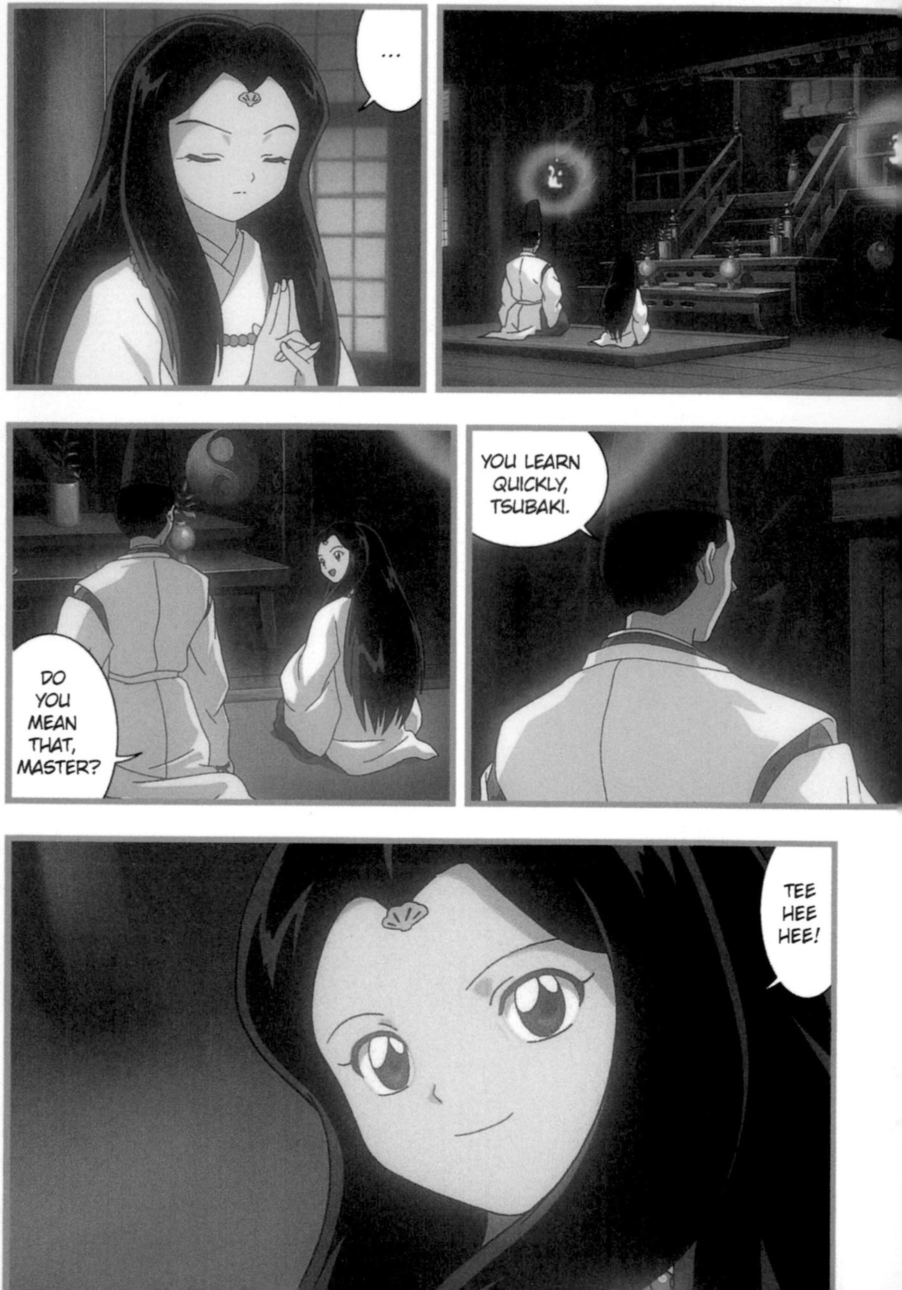
...
YOU LEARN QUICKLY, TSUBAKI.
DO YOU MEAN THAT, MASTER?
TEE HEE HEE!

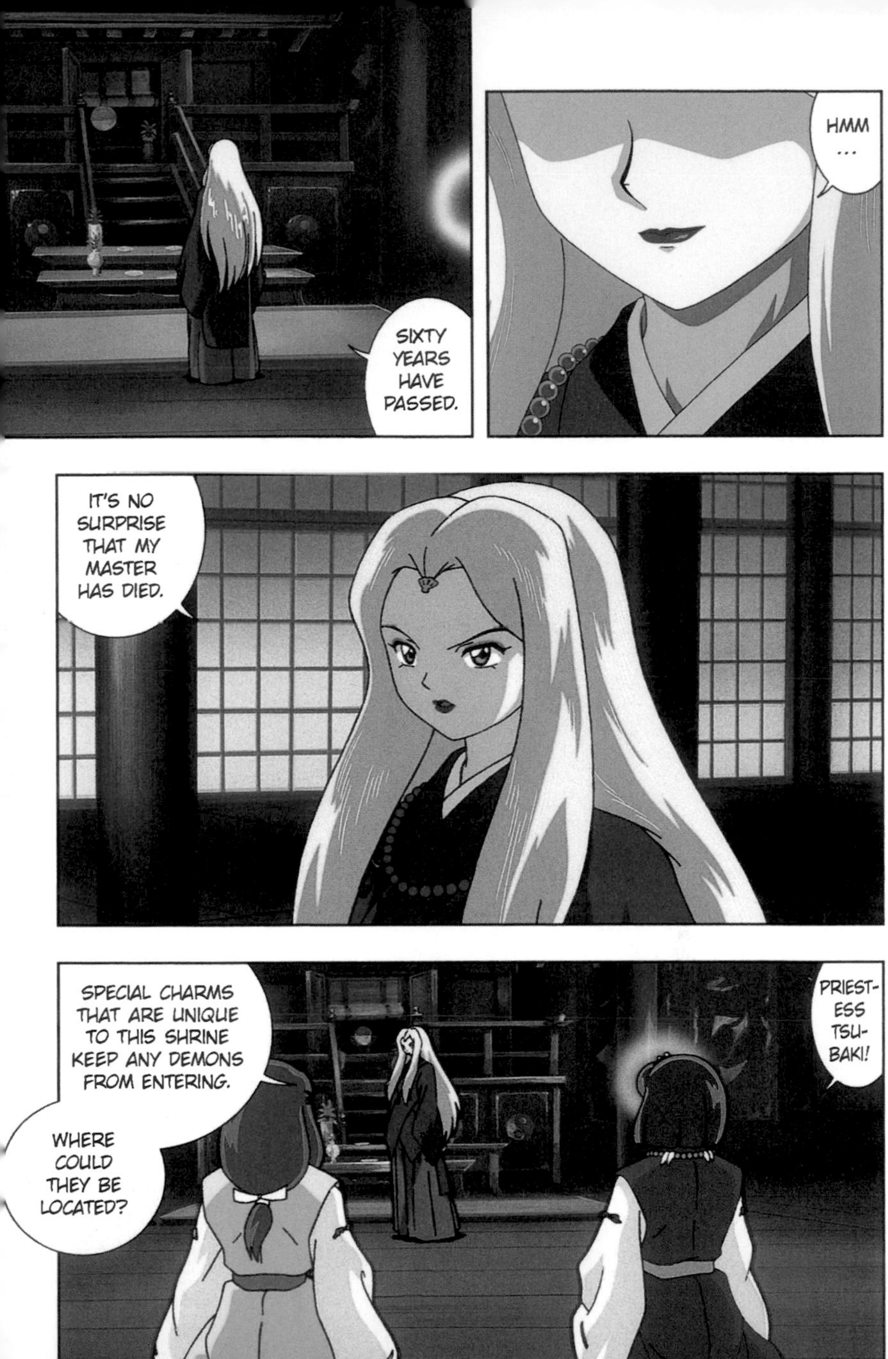
HMM ...
SIXTY YEARS HAVE PASSED.
IT'S NO SURPRISE THAT MY MASTER HAS DIED.
PRIEST-ESS TSU-BAKI!
SPECIAL CHARMS THAT ARE UNIQUE TO THIS SHRINE KEEP ANY DEMONS FROM ENTERING.
WHERE COULD THEY BE LOCATED?

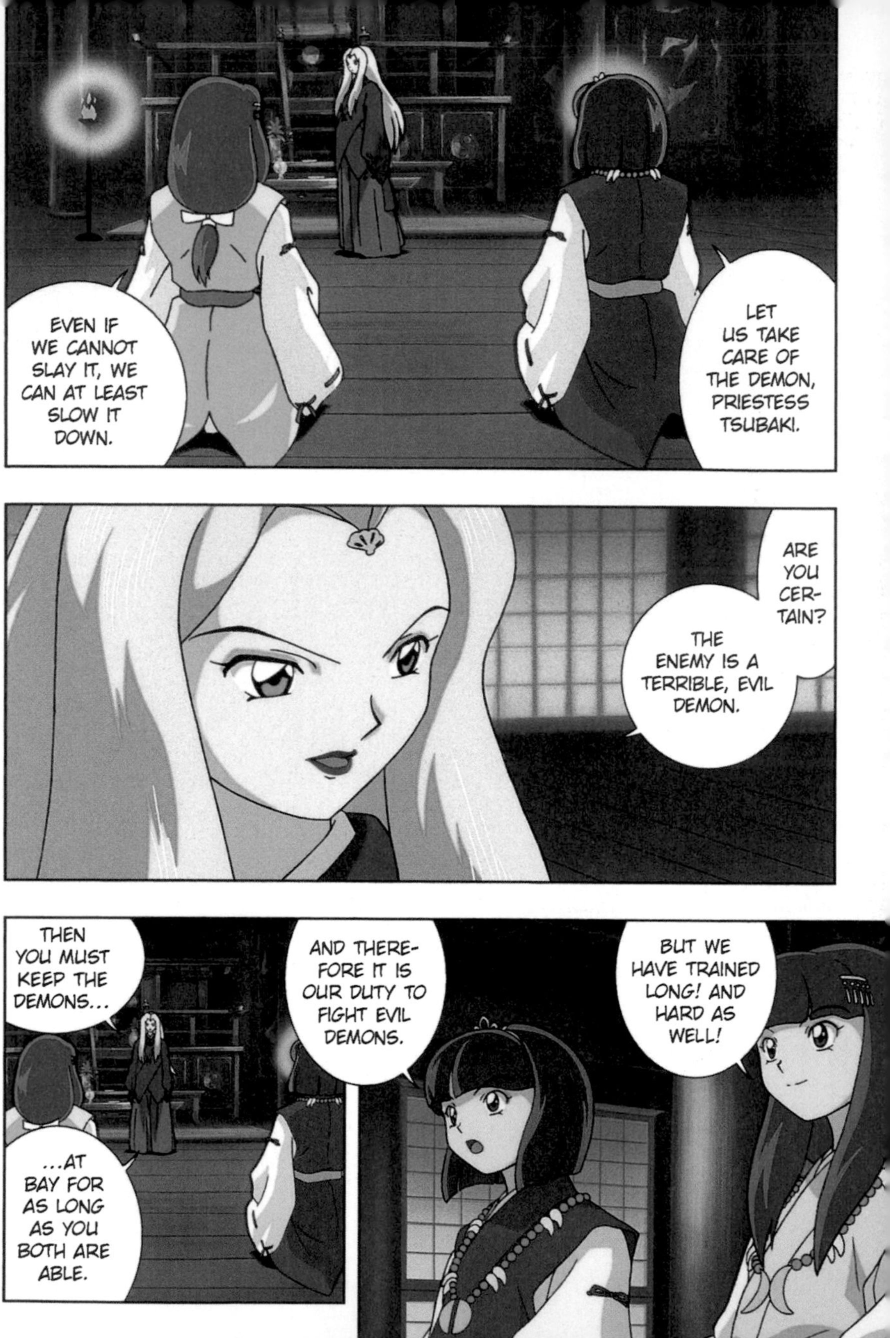
LET US TAKE CARE OF THE DEMON, PRIESTESS TSUBAKI.
EVEN IF WE CANNOT SLAY IT, WE CAN AT LEAST SLOW IT DOWN.
ARE YOU CER-TAIN?
THE ENEMY IS A TERRIBLE, EVIL DEMON.
BUT WE HAVE TRAINED LONG! AND HARD AS WELL!
AND THERE-FORE IT IS OUR DUTY TO FIGHT EVIL DEMONS.
THEN YOU MUST KEEP THE DEMONS...
...AT BAY FOR AS LONG AS YOU BOTH ARE ABLE.

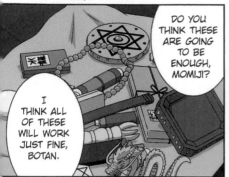

DO YOU THINK THESE ARE GOING TO BE ENOUGH, MOMIJI?

I THINK ALL OF THESE WILL WORK JUST FINE, BOTAN.

IT IS OUR VERY FIRST TIME, THOUGH.

THAT'S ALL THE MORE REASON FOR DOING IT!

YOU'RE RIGHT! IT'S ALL PART OF TRAINING AND EXPERIENCE!

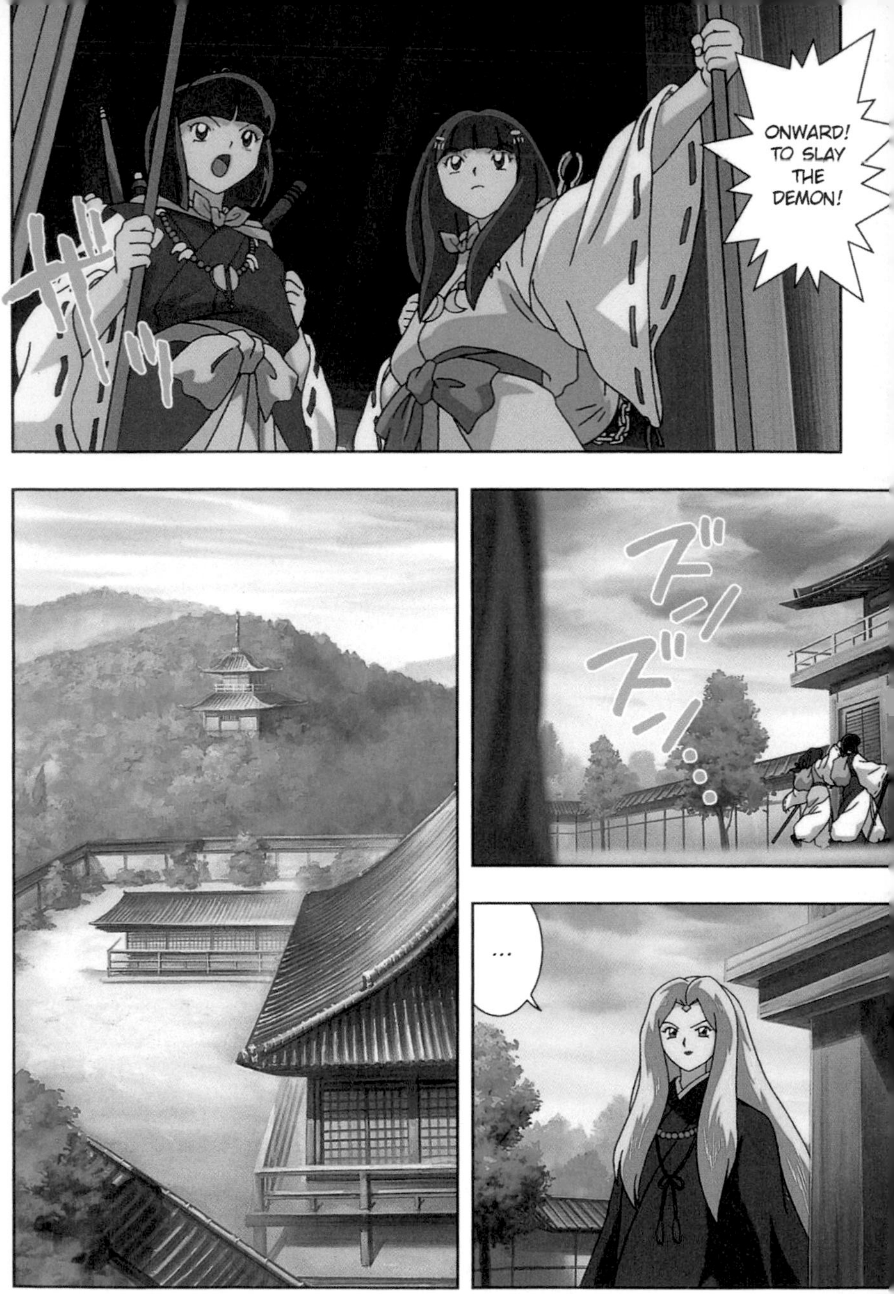
ONWARD! TO SLAY THE DEMON!
ザッ
...

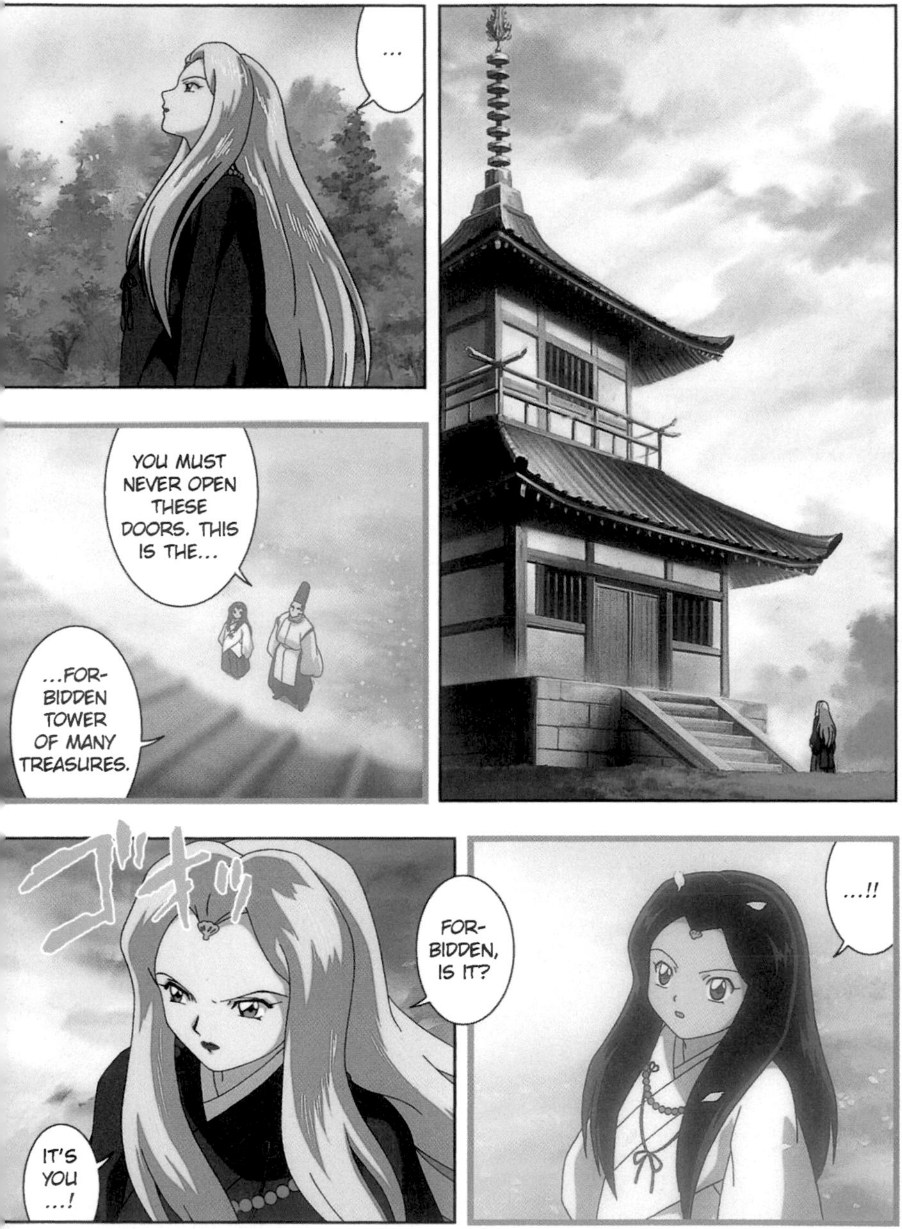
...
YOU MUST NEVER OPEN THESE DOORS. THIS IS THE...
...FOR-BIDDEN TOWER OF MANY TREASURES.
...!!
ゴキッ
FOR-BIDDEN, IS IT?
IT'S YOU ...!

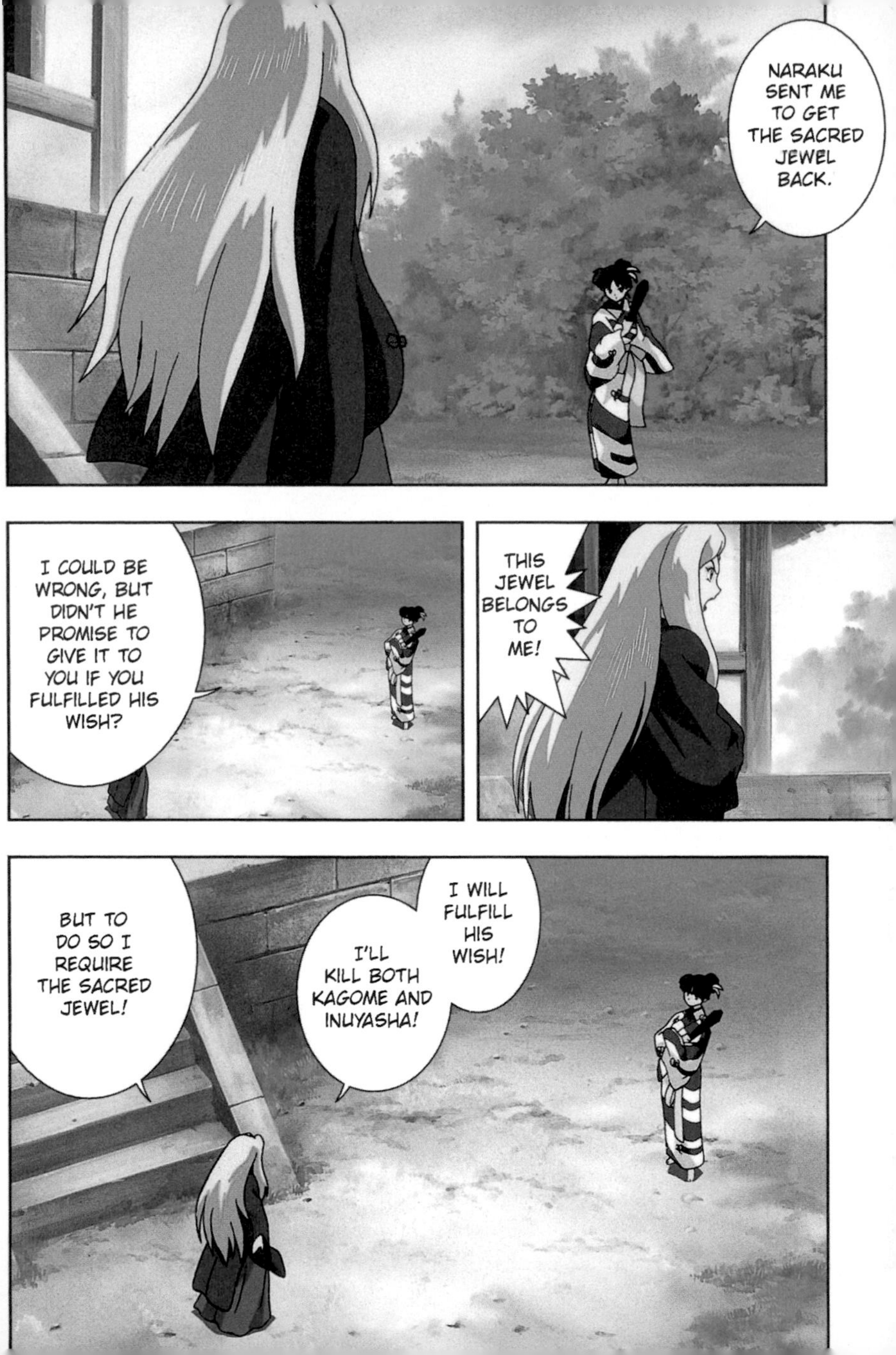
NARAKU SENT ME TO GET THE SACRED JEWEL BACK.
THIS JEWEL BELONGS TO ME!
I COULD BE WRONG, BUT DIDN'T HE PROMISE TO GIVE IT TO YOU IF YOU FULFILLED HIS WISH?
I WILL FULFILL HIS WISH!
I'LL KILL BOTH KAGOME AND INUYASHA!
BUT TO DO SO I REQUIRE THE SACRED JEWEL!

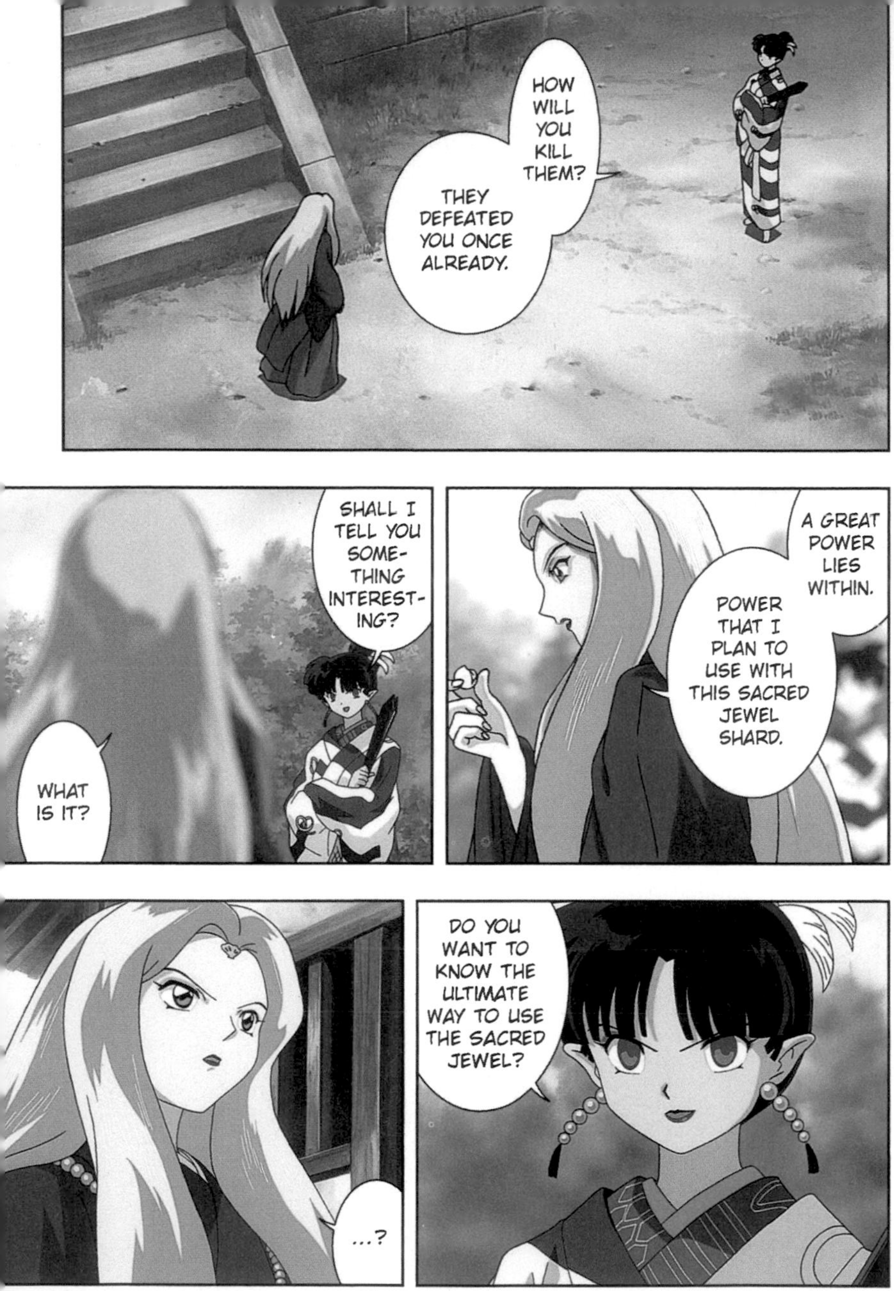
HOW WILL YOU KILL THEM?
THEY DEFEATED YOU ONCE ALREADY.
A GREAT POWER LIES WITHIN.
POWER THAT I PLAN TO USE WITH THIS SACRED JEWEL SHARD.
SHALL I TELL YOU SOME-THING INTEREST-ING?
WHAT IS IT?
DO YOU WANT TO KNOW THE ULTIMATE WAY TO USE THE SACRED JEWEL?
...?

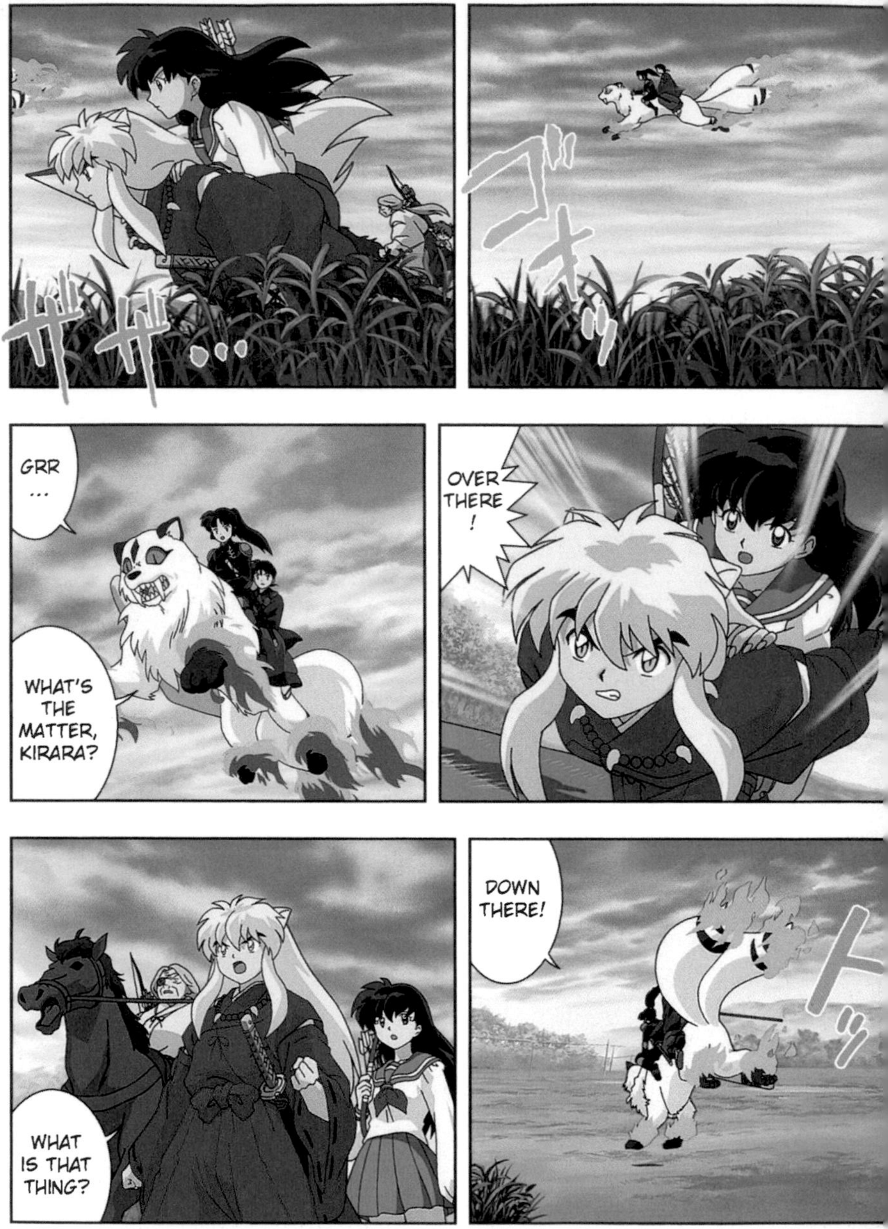
ゴォッ
ザザ…
OVER THERE!
GRR ...
WHAT'S THE MATTER, KIRARA?
DOWN THERE!
トッ
WHAT IS THAT THING?

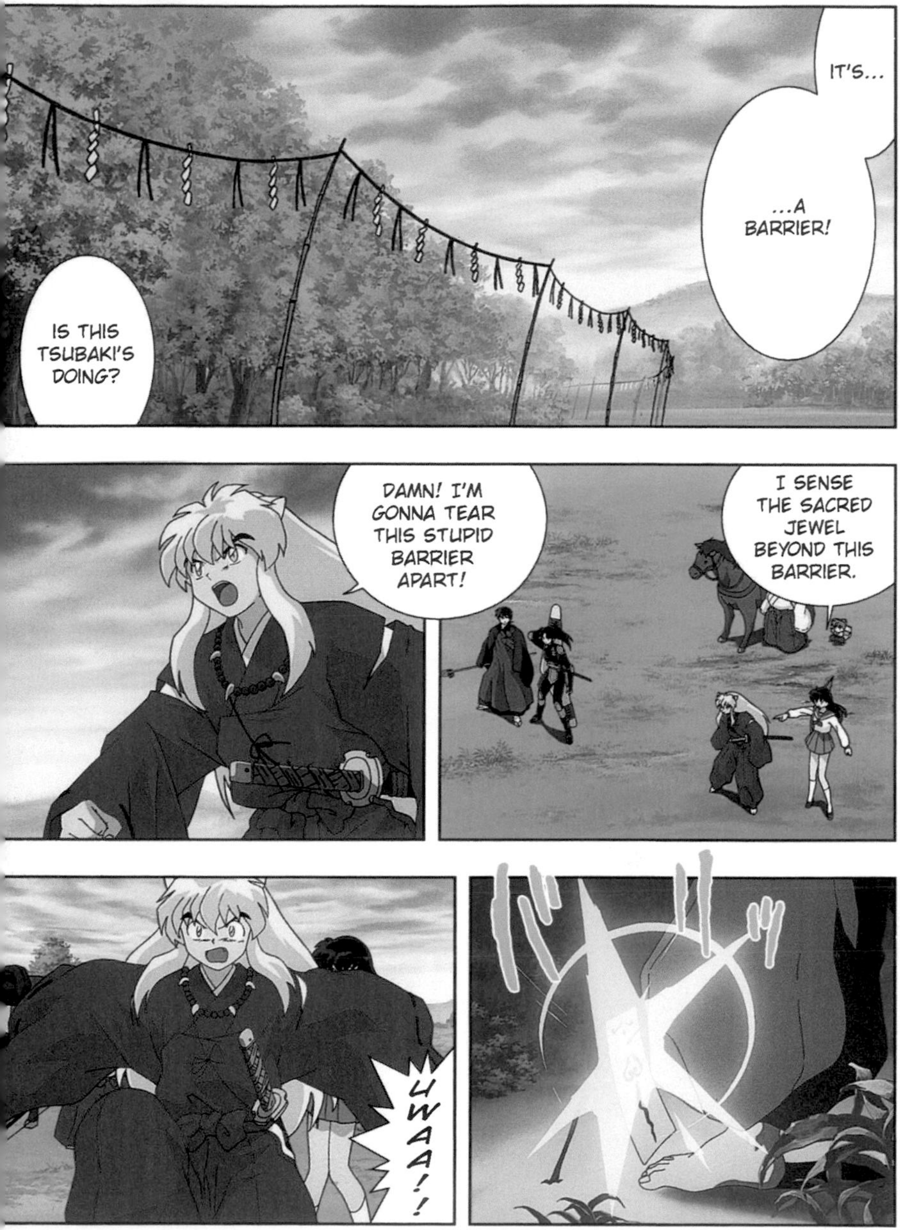
IT'S...
...A BARRIER!
IS THIS TSUBAKI'S DOING?
I SENSE THE SACRED JEWEL BEYOND THIS BARRIER.
DAMN! I'M GONNA TEAR THIS STUPID BARRIER APART!
UWAA!!

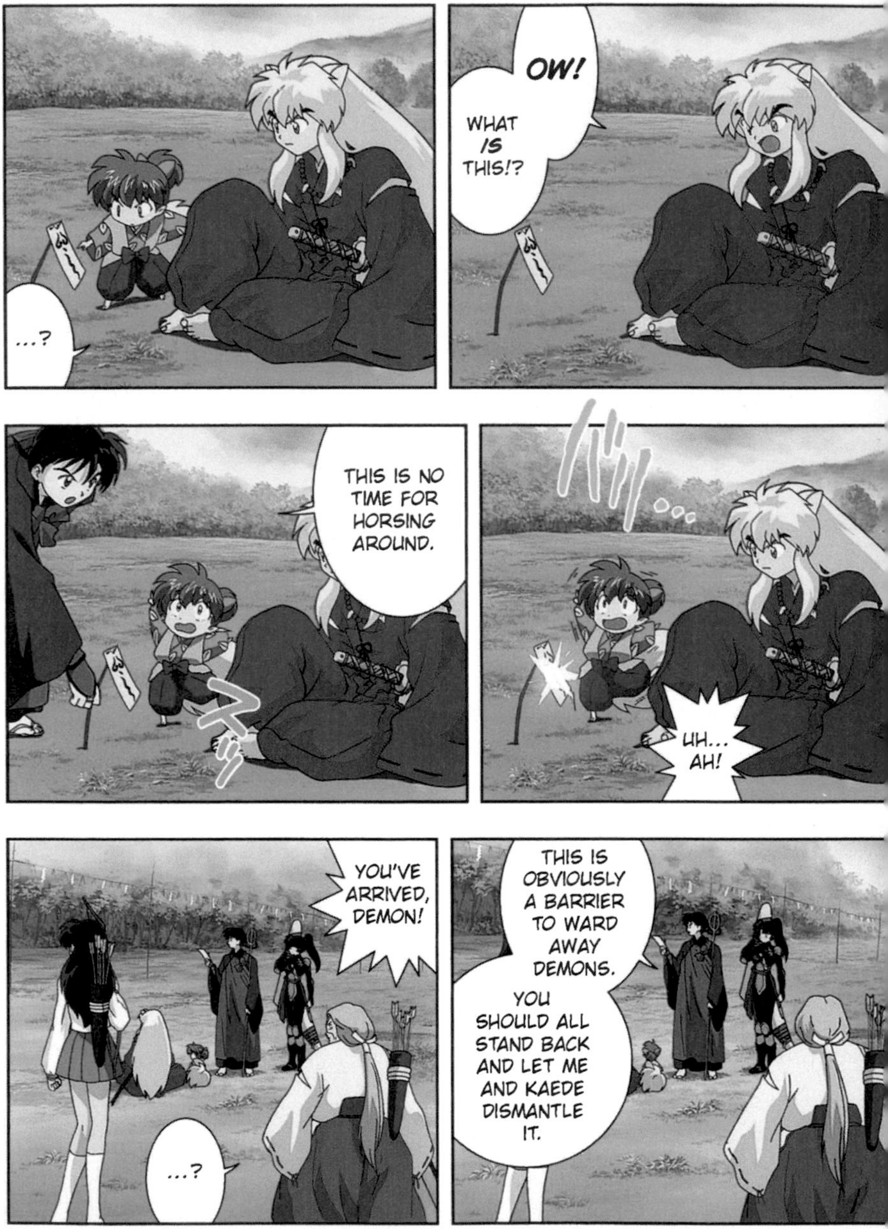
OW!
WHAT IS THIS!?
...?
UH... AH!
THIS IS NO TIME FOR HORSING AROUND.
THIS IS OBVIOUSLY A BARRIER TO WARD AWAY DEMONS.
YOU SHOULD ALL STAND BACK AND LET ME AND KAEDE DISMANTLE IT.
YOU'VE ARRIVED, DEMON!
...?

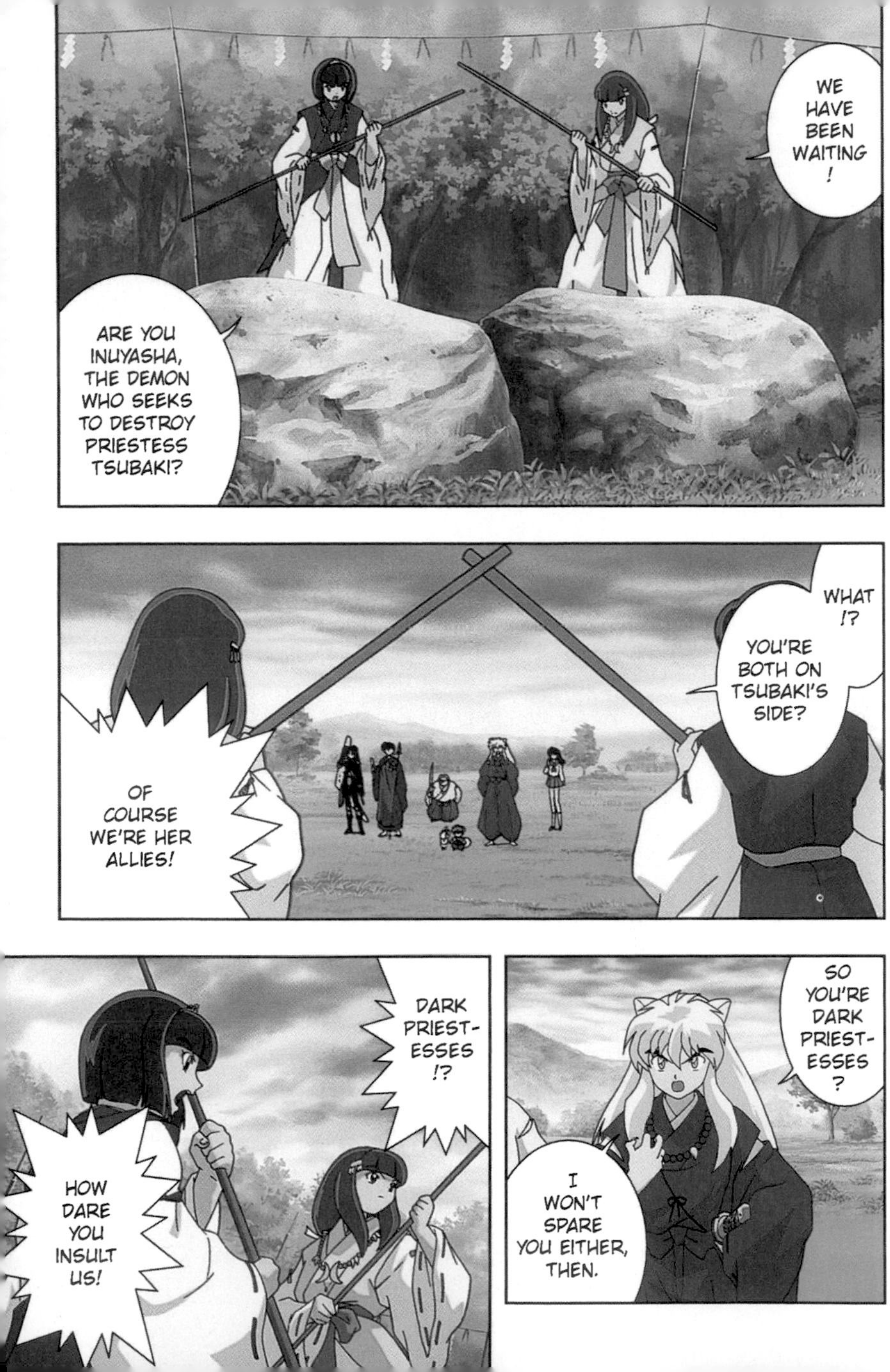
WE HAVE BEEN WAITING!
ARE YOU INUYASHA, THE DEMON WHO SEEKS TO DESTROY PRIESTESS TSUBAKI?
WHAT!?
YOU'RE BOTH ON TSUBAKI'S SIDE?
OF COURSE WE'RE HER ALLIES!
SO YOU'RE DARK PRIEST-ESSES?
I WON'T SPARE YOU EITHER, THEN.
DARK PRIEST-ESSES!?
HOW DARE YOU INSULT US!

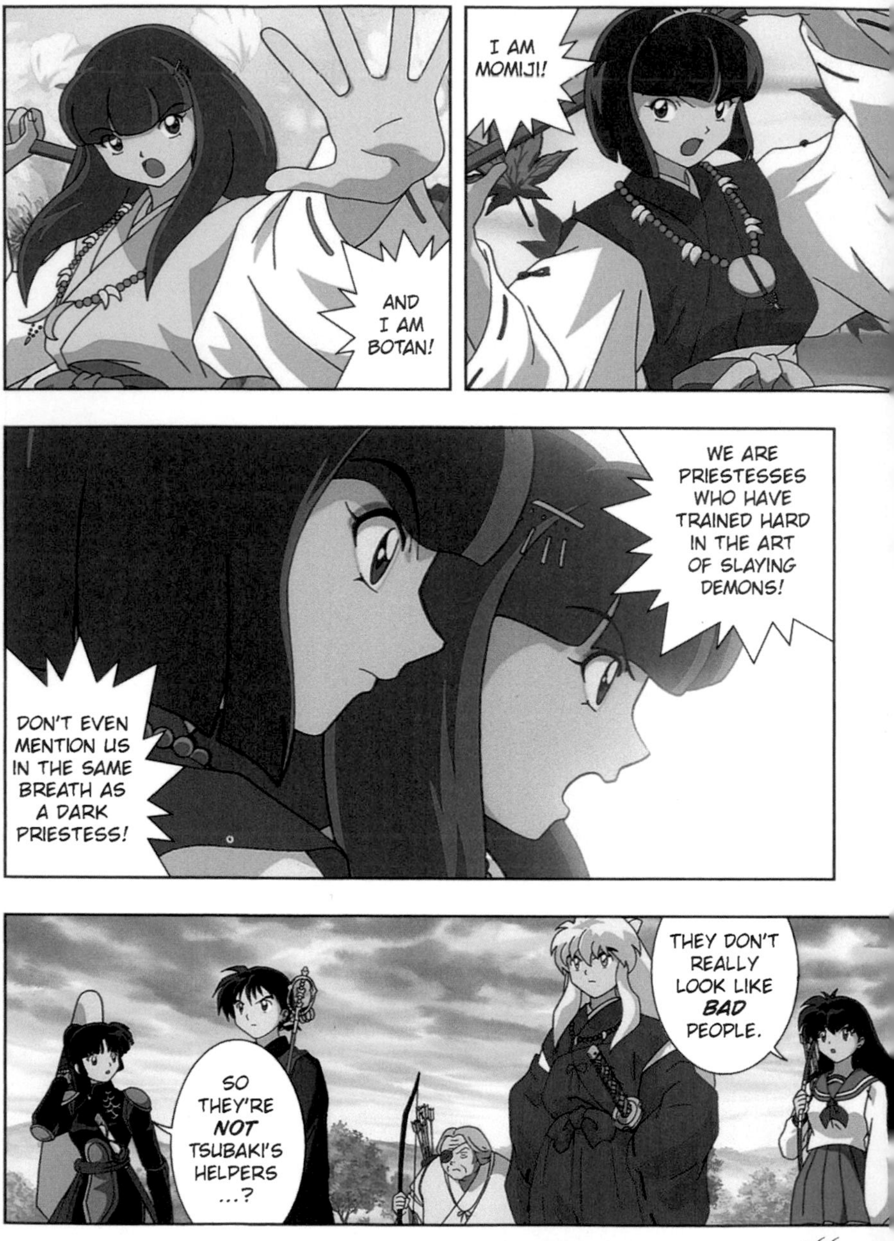
I AM MOMIJI!
AND I AM BOTAN!
WE ARE PRIESTESSES WHO HAVE TRAINED HARD IN THE ART OF SLAYING DEMONS!
DON'T EVEN MENTION US IN THE SAME BREATH AS A DARK PRIESTESS!
THEY DON'T REALLY LOOK LIKE *BAD* PEOPLE.
SO THEY'RE *NOT* TSUBAKI'S HELPERS ...?

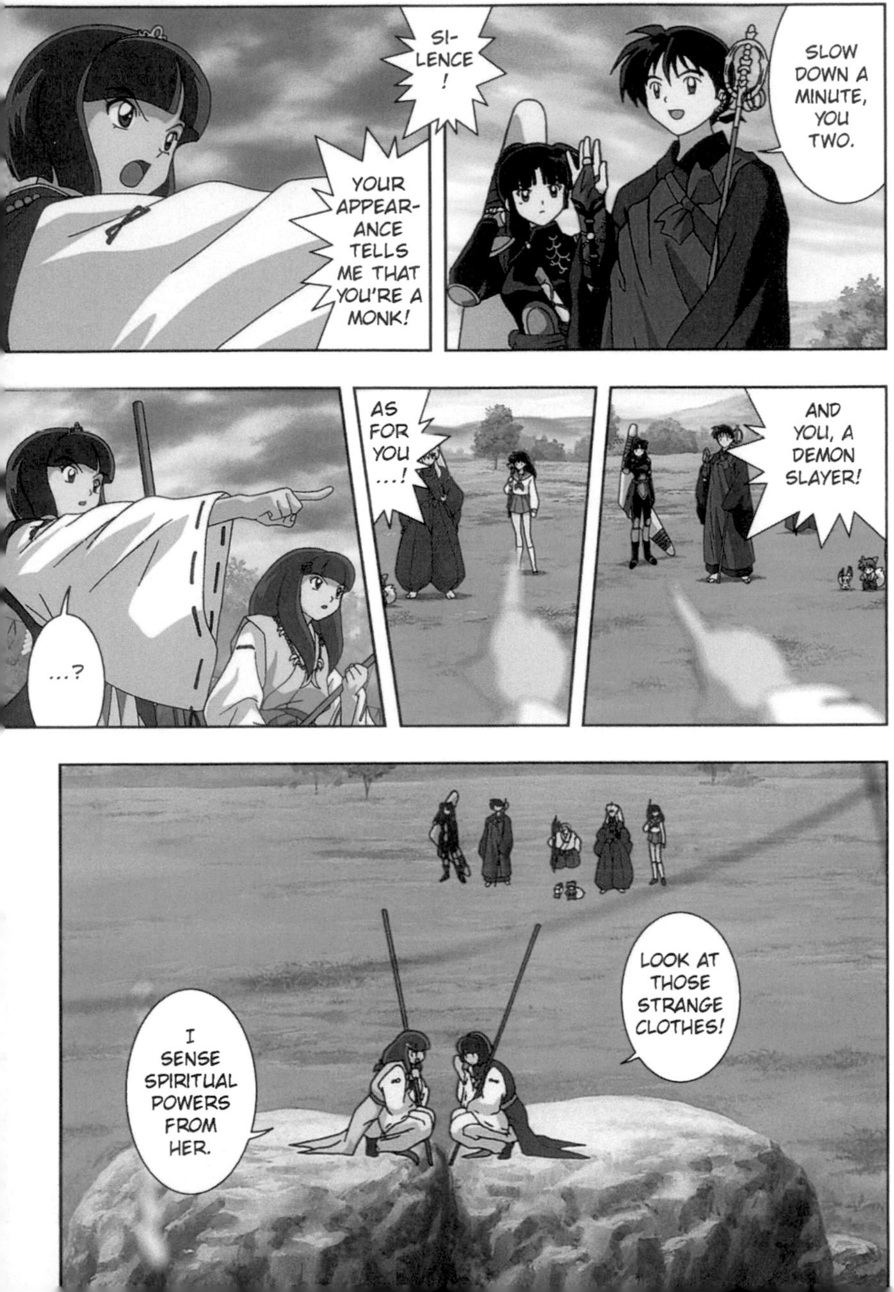
SLOW DOWN A MINUTE, YOU TWO.
SI-LENCE!
YOUR APPEAR-ANCE TELLS ME THAT YOU'RE A MONK!
AND YOU, A DEMON SLAYER!
AS FOR YOU ...!
...?
LOOK AT THOSE STRANGE CLOTHES!
I SENSE SPIRITUAL POWERS FROM HER.

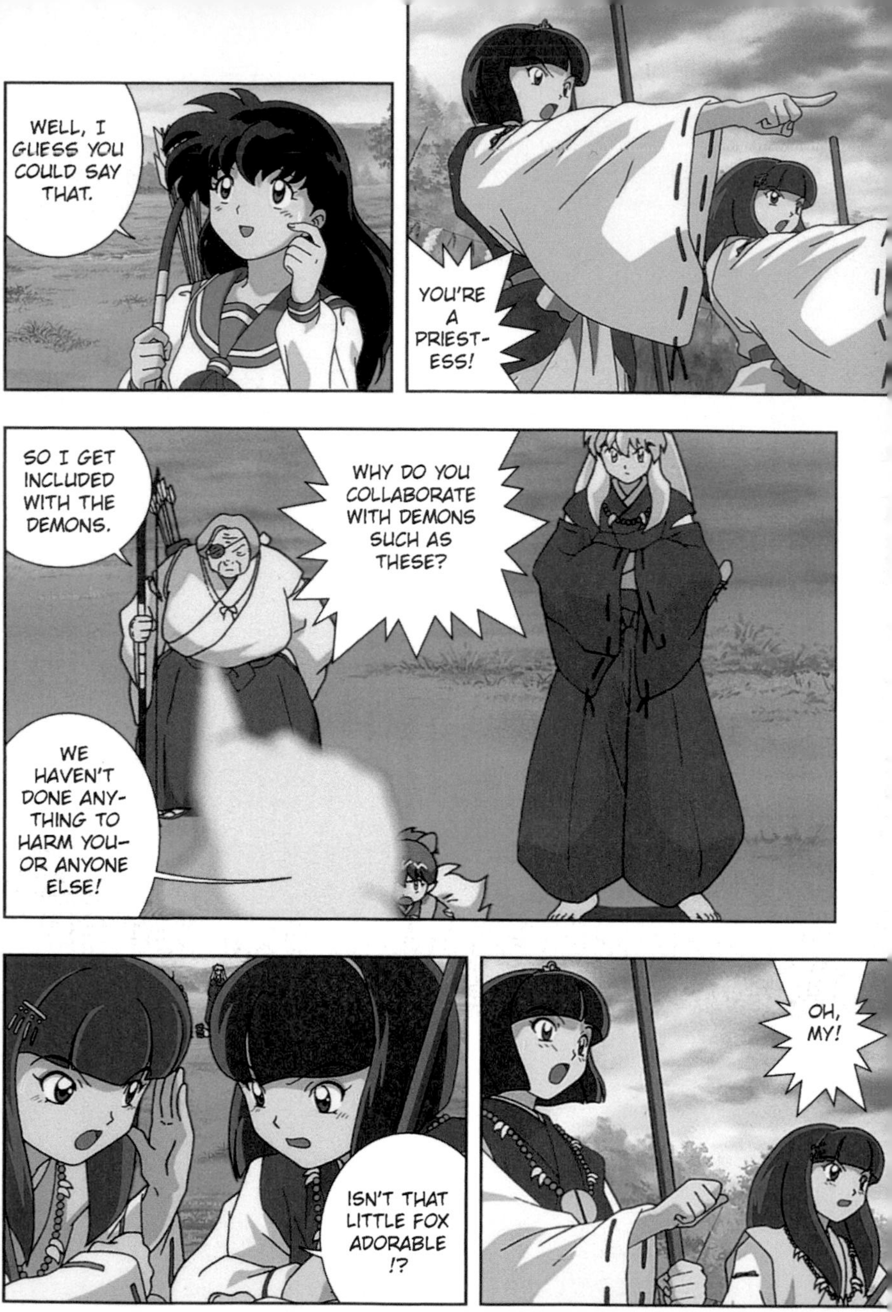
YOU'RE A PRIEST-ESS!
WELL, I GUESS YOU COULD SAY THAT.
WHY DO YOU COLLABORATE WITH DEMONS SUCH AS THESE?
SO I GET INCLUDED WITH THE DEMONS.
WE HAVEN'T DONE ANY-THING TO HARM YOU—OR ANYONE ELSE!
OH, MY!
ISN'T THAT LITTLE FOX ADORABLE !?

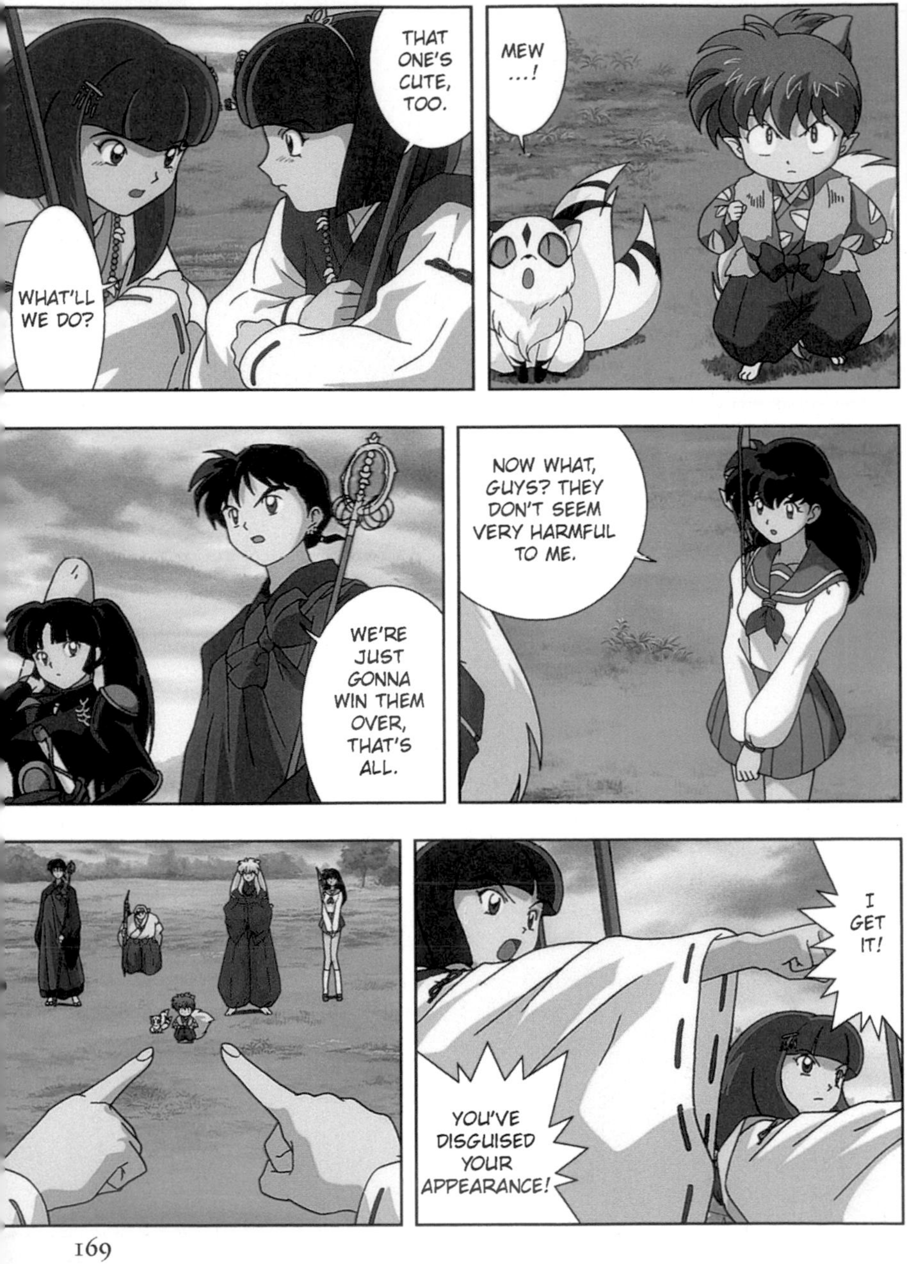
MEW ...!
THAT ONE'S CUTE, TOO.
WHAT'LL WE DO?
NOW WHAT, GUYS? THEY DON'T SEEM VERY HARMFUL TO ME.
WE'RE JUST GONNA WIN THEM OVER, THAT'S ALL.
I GET IT!
YOU'VE DISGUISED YOUR APPEARANCE!

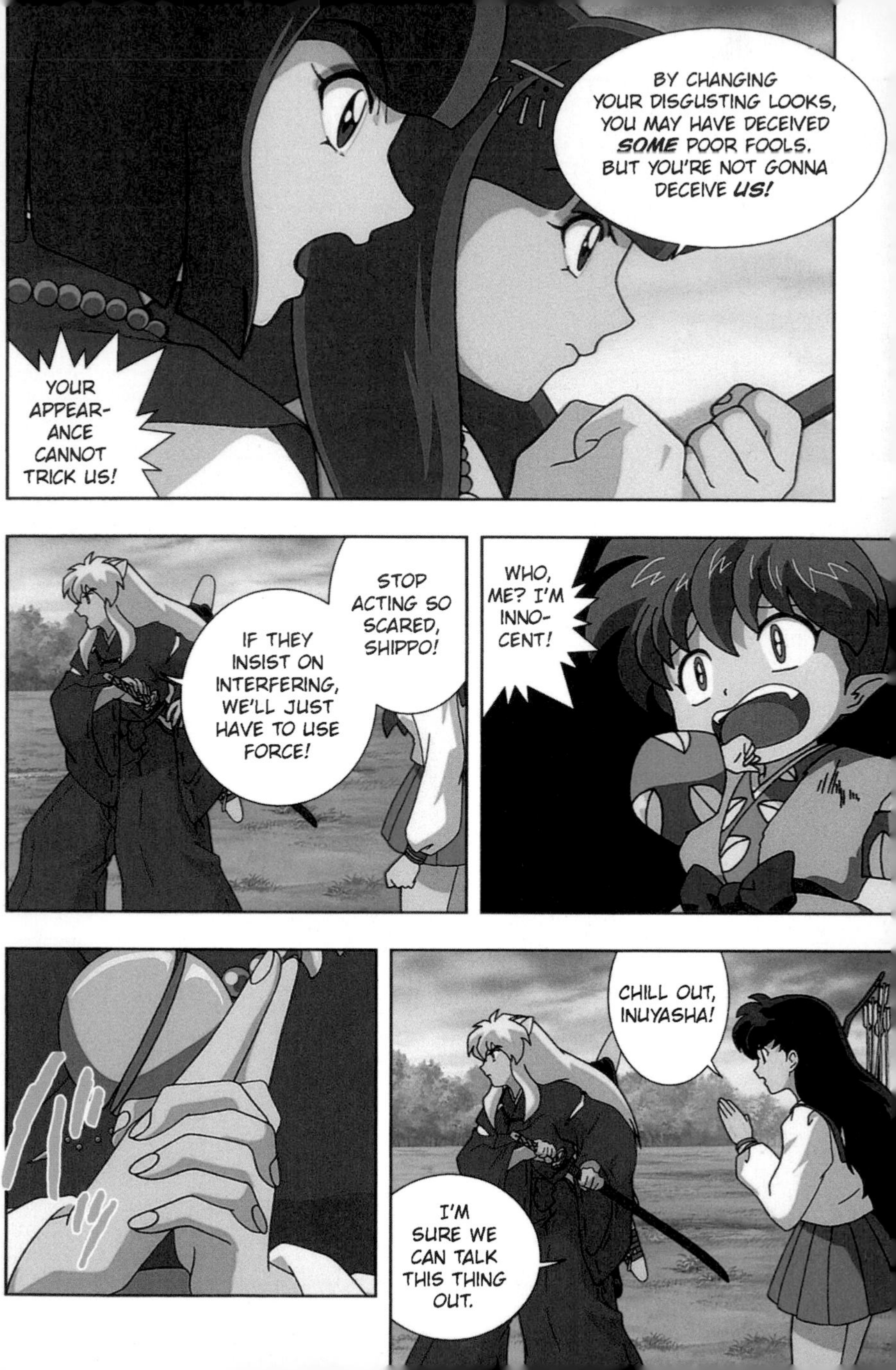
BY CHANGING YOUR DISGUSTING LOOKS, YOU MAY HAVE DECEIVED **SOME** POOR FOOLS. BUT YOU'RE NOT GONNA DECEIVE **US!**
YOUR APPEAR-ANCE CANNOT TRICK US!
WHO, ME? I'M INNO-CENT!
STOP ACTING SO SCARED, SHIPPO!
IF THEY INSIST ON INTERFERING, WE'LL JUST HAVE TO USE FORCE!
CHILL OUT, INUYASHA!
I'M SURE WE CAN TALK THIS THING OUT.

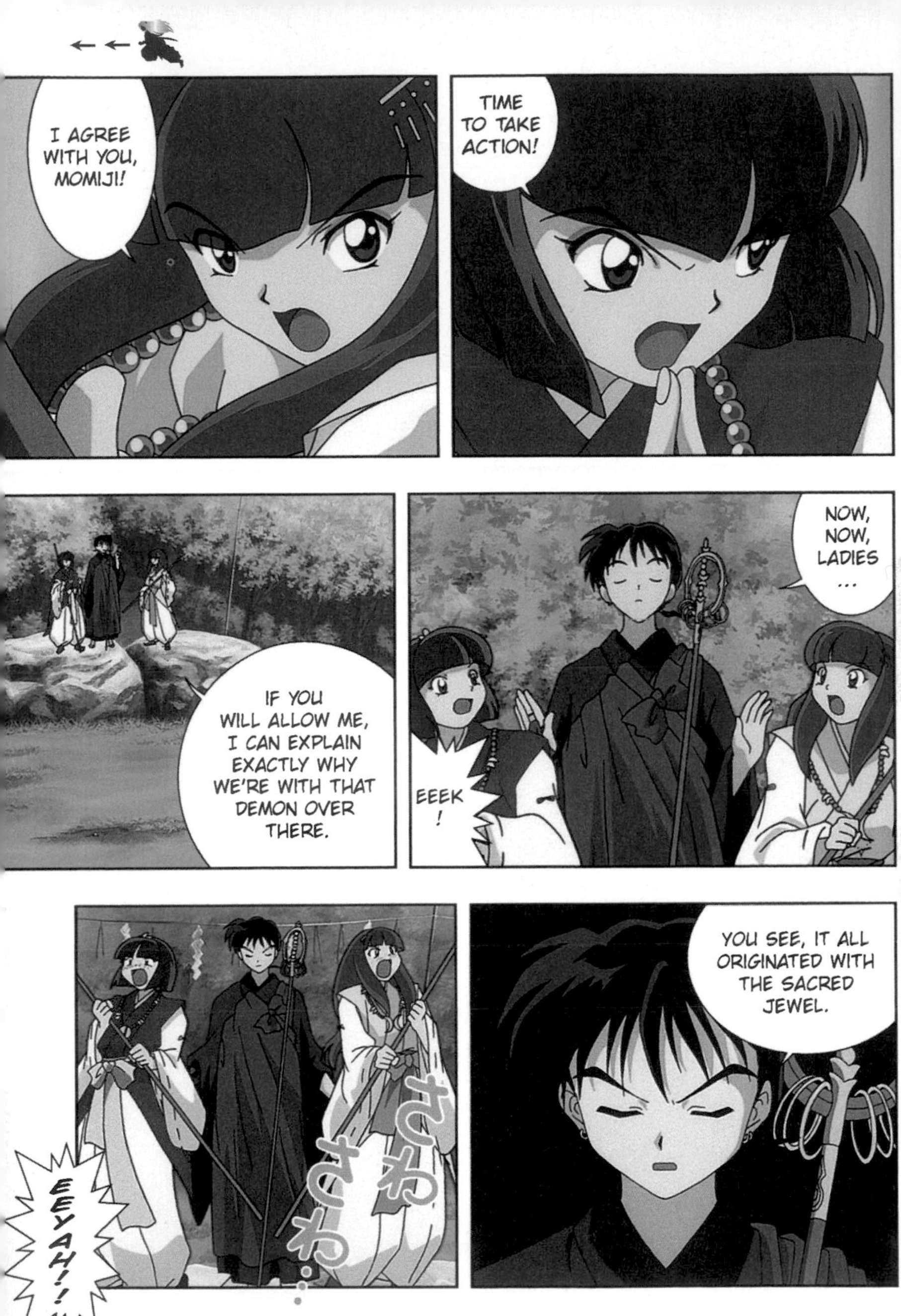
TIME TO TAKE ACTION!
I AGREE WITH YOU, MOMIJI!
NOW, NOW, LADIES...
EEEK!
IF YOU WILL ALLOW ME, I CAN EXPLAIN EXACTLY WHY WE'RE WITH THAT DEMON OVER THERE.
YOU SEE, IT ALL ORIGINATED WITH THE SACRED JEWEL.
さわさわ...
EEYAH!!

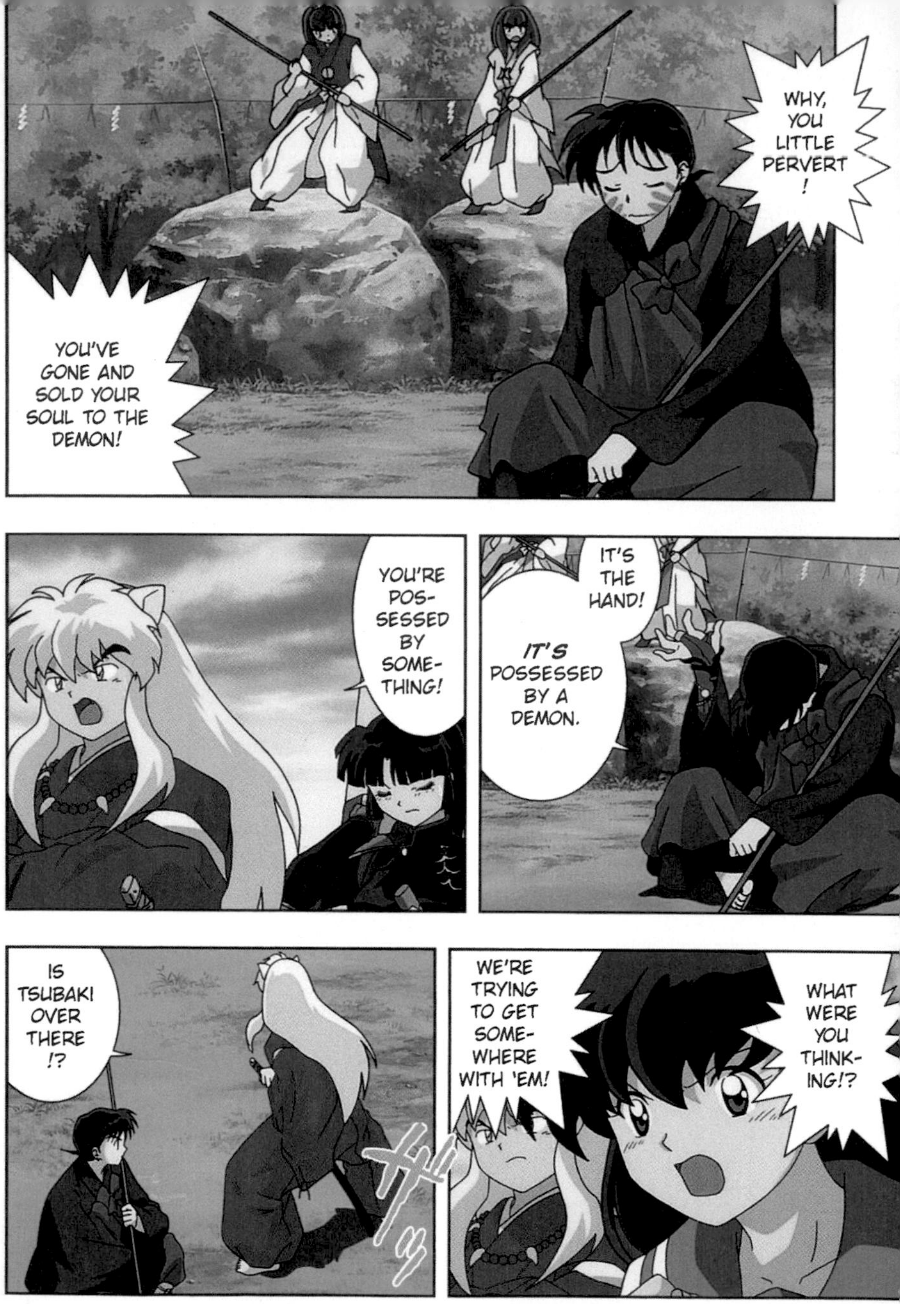
WHY, YOU LITTLE PERVERT!
YOU'VE GONE AND SOLD YOUR SOUL TO THE DEMON!
IT'S THE HAND!
IT'S POSSESSED BY A DEMON.
YOU'RE POS-SESSED BY SOME-THING!
WHAT WERE YOU THINK-ING!?
WE'RE TRYING TO GET SOME-WHERE WITH 'EM!
IS TSUBAKI OVER THERE!?

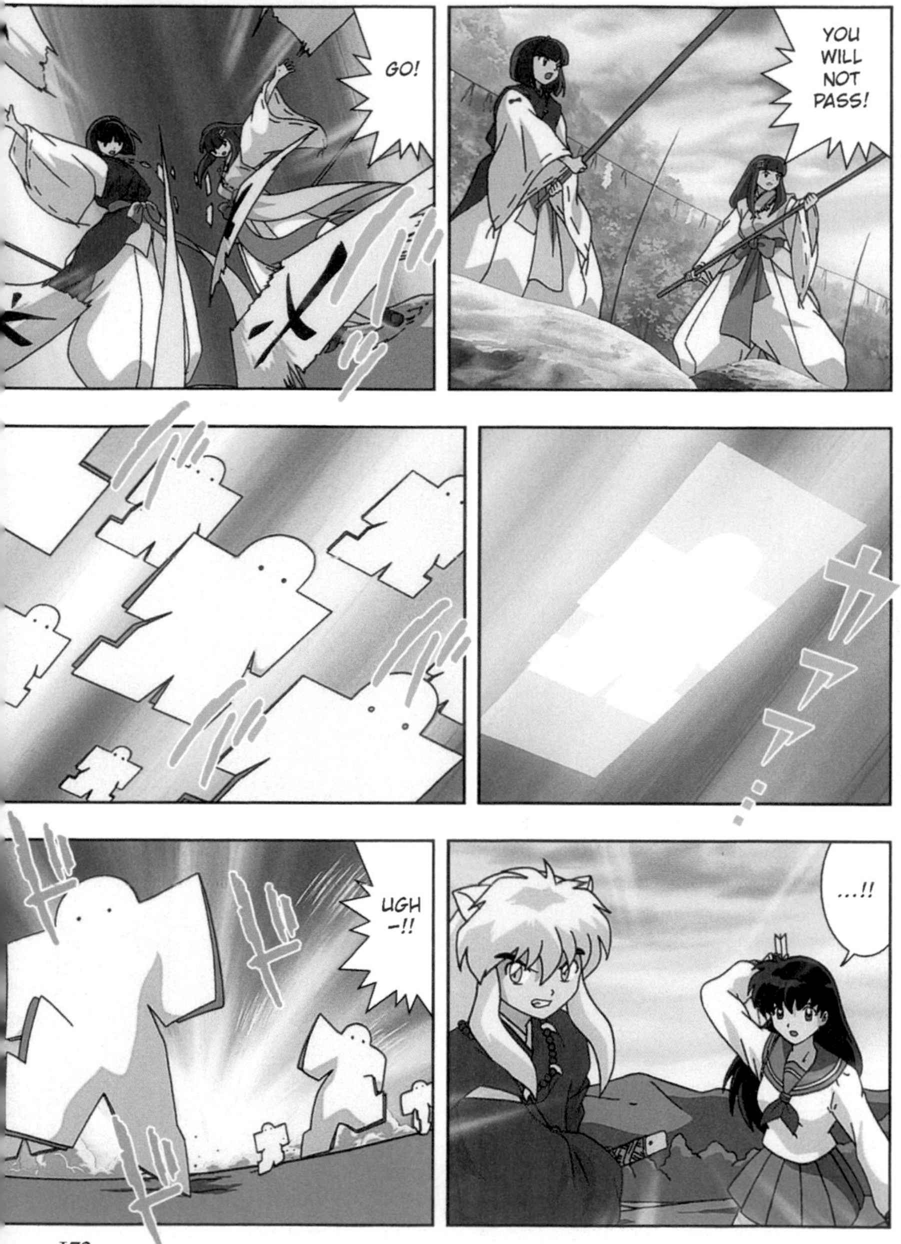
YOU WILL NOT PASS!
GO!
サアア…
…!!
UGH-!!

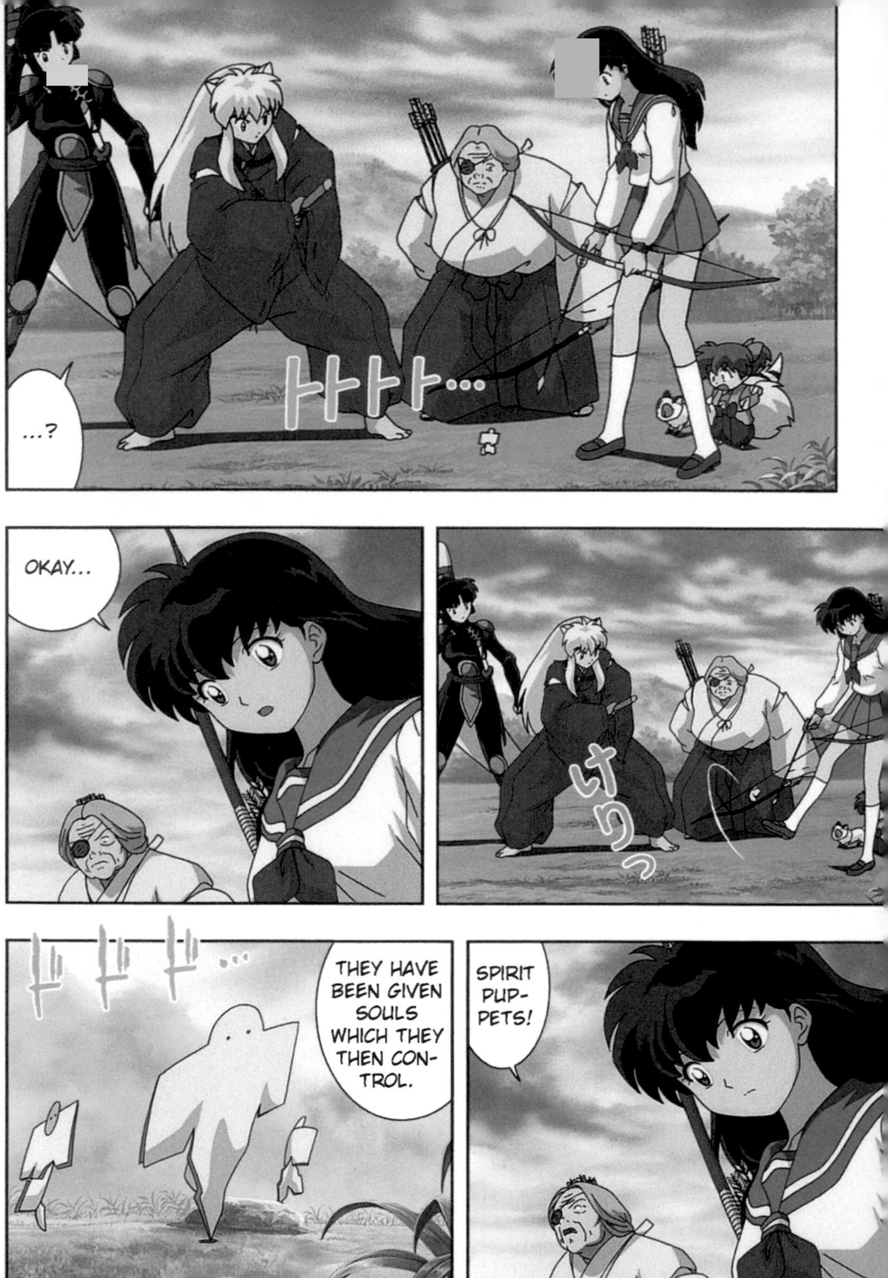
...?
けりっ
OKAY...
SPIRIT PUP-PETS!
THEY HAVE BEEN GIVEN SOULS WHICH THEY THEN CON-TROL.
ドドド…

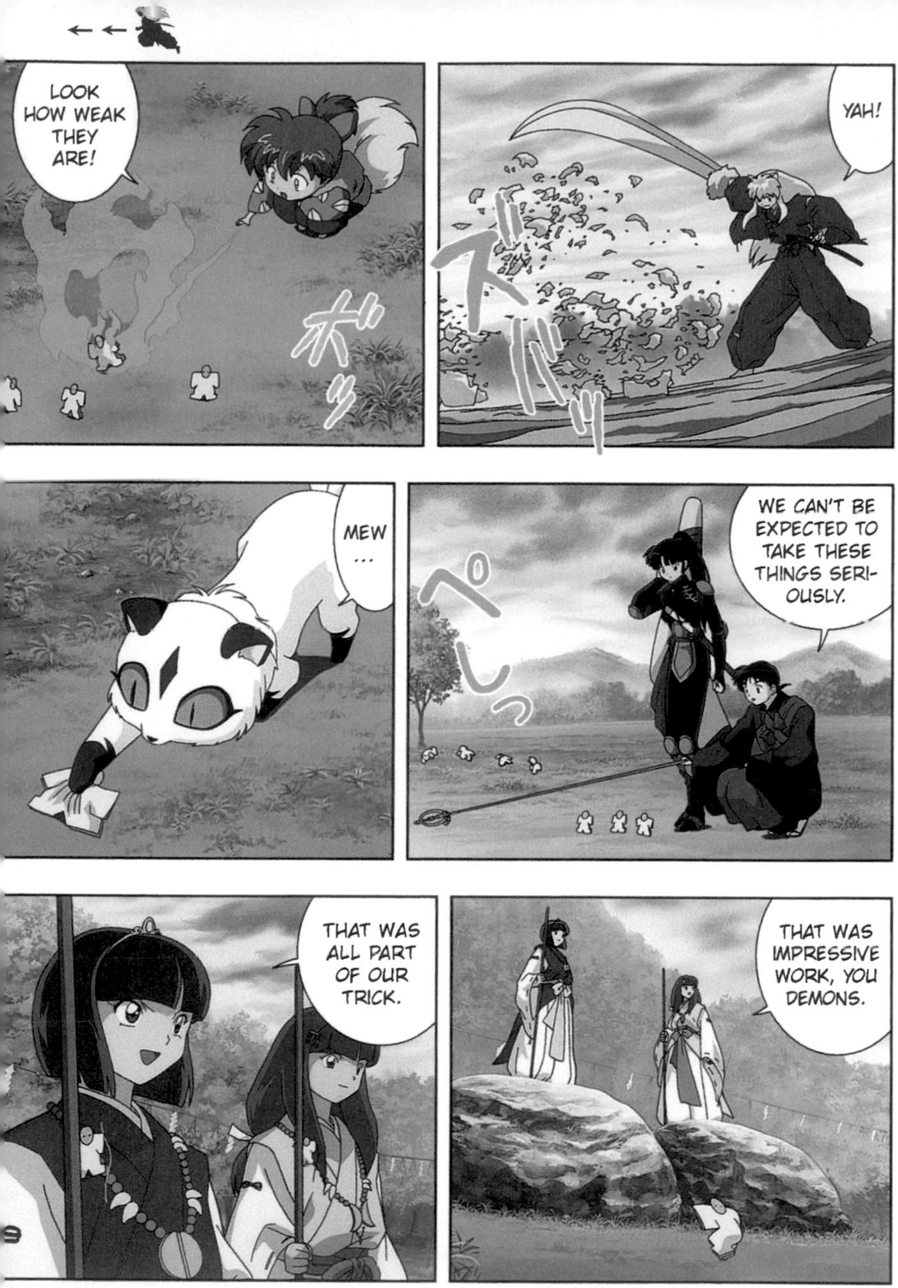
YAH!
ズバッ
LOOK HOW WEAK THEY ARE!
ボッ
WE CAN'T BE EXPECTED TO TAKE THESE THINGS SERI-OUSLY.
ぺしっ
MEW ...
THAT WAS IMPRESSIVE WORK, YOU DEMONS.
THAT WAS ALL PART OF OUR TRICK.

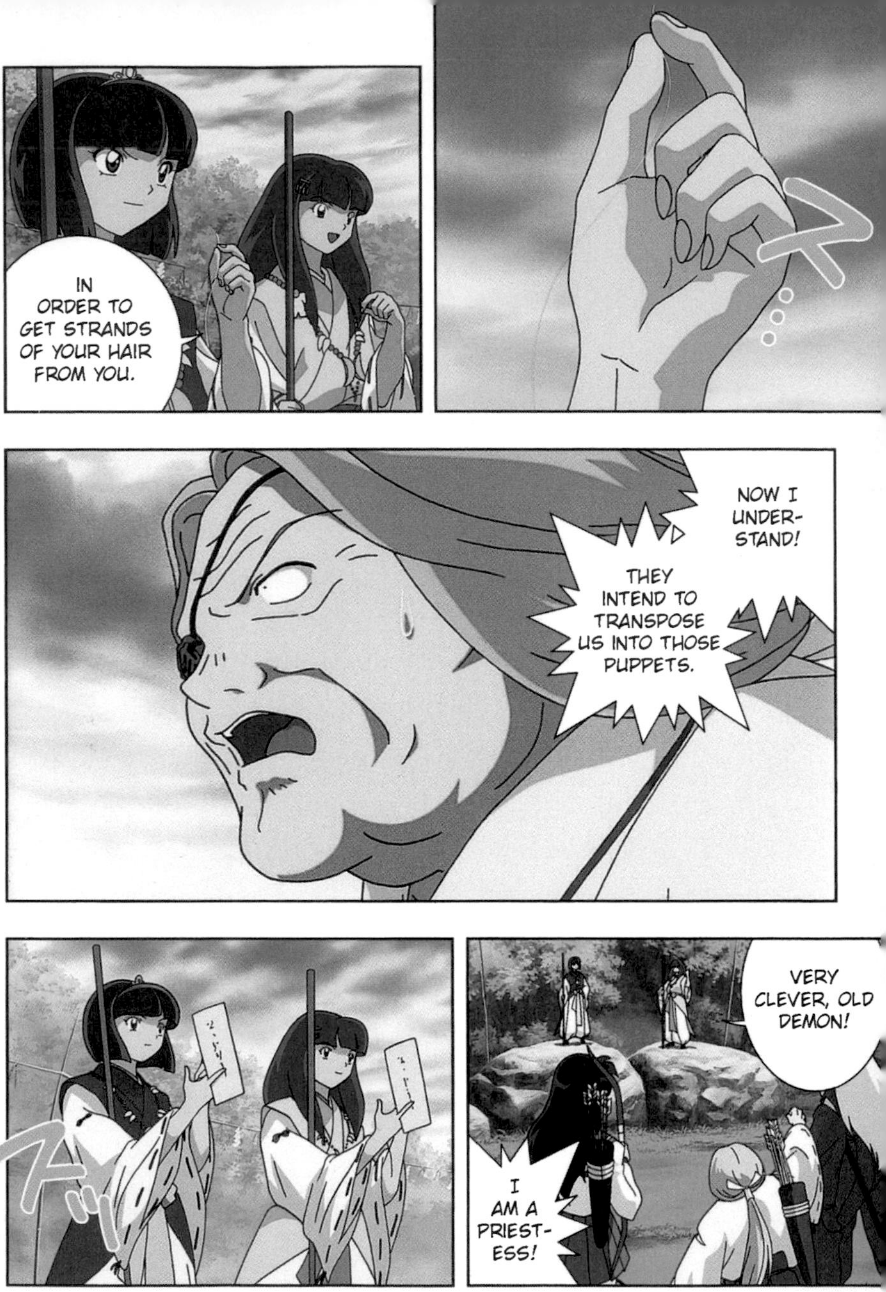
IN ORDER TO GET STRANDS OF YOUR HAIR FROM YOU.
NOW I UNDERSTAND!
THEY INTEND TO TRANSPOSE US INTO THOSE PUPPETS.
VERY CLEVER, OLD DEMON!
I AM A PRIEST-ESS!

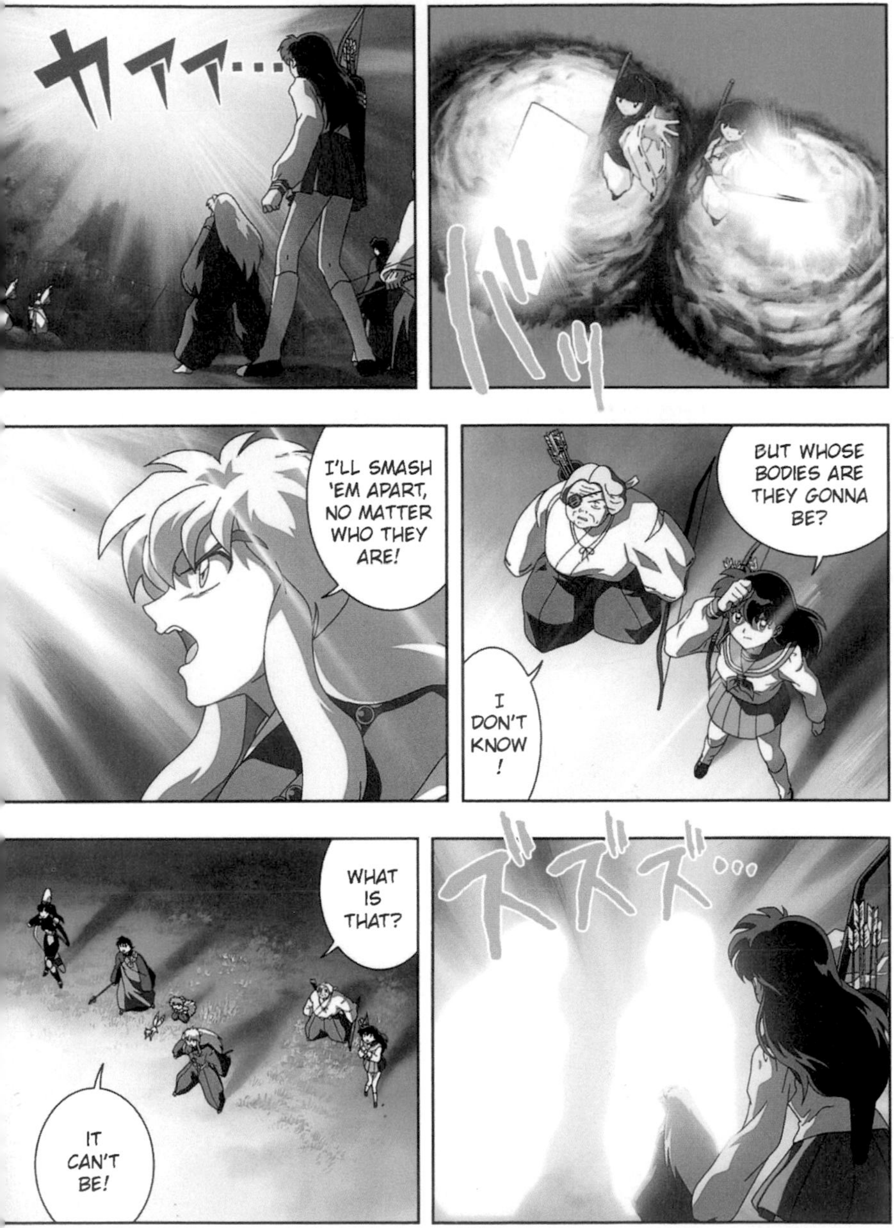
カァァ…
BUT WHOSE BODIES ARE THEY GONNA BE?
I DON'T KNOW!
I'LL SMASH 'EM APART, NO MATTER WHO THEY ARE!
ズズズ…
WHAT IS THAT?
IT CAN'T BE!

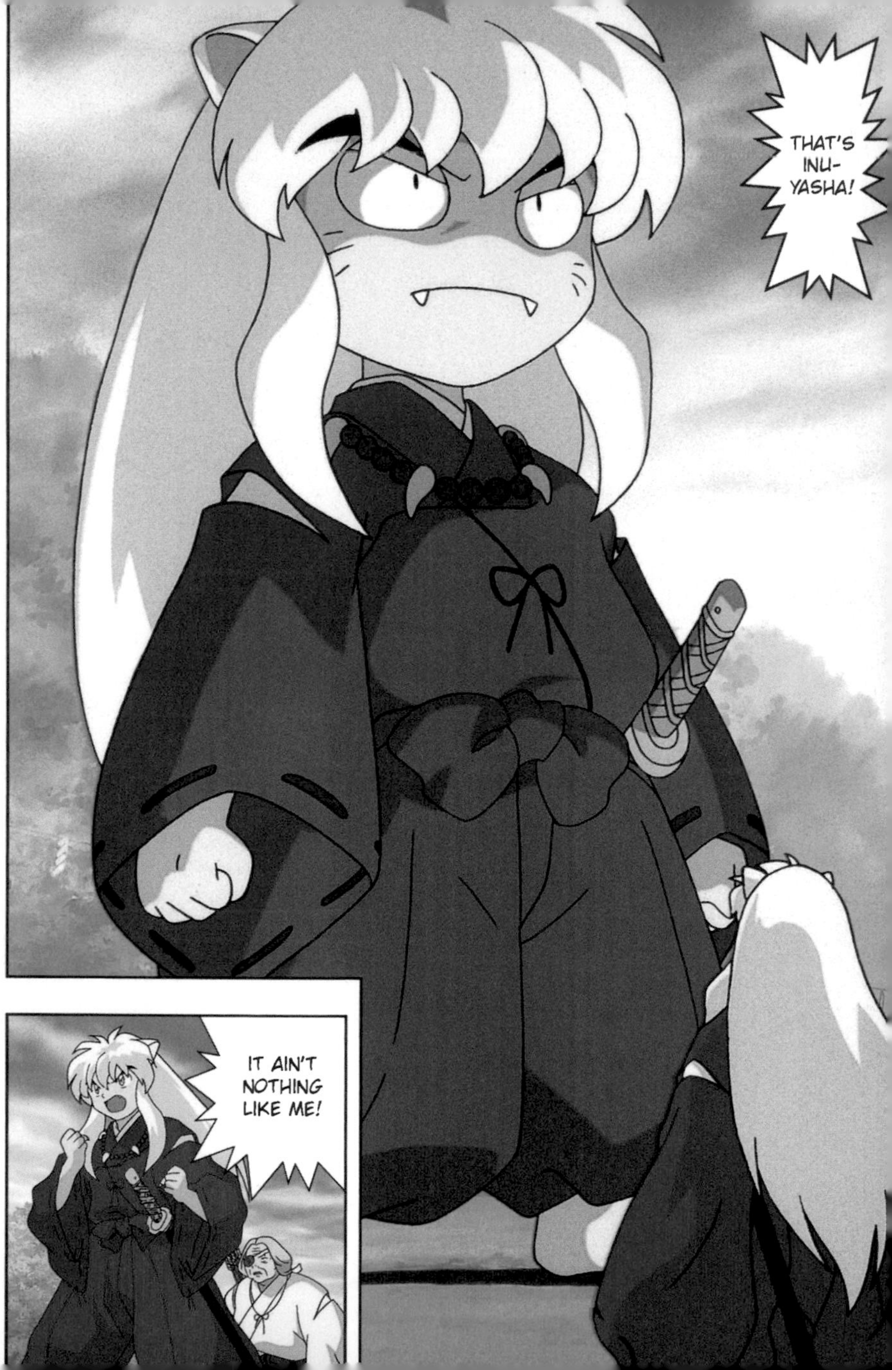
THAT'S INU-YASHA!
IT AIN'T NOTHING LIKE ME!

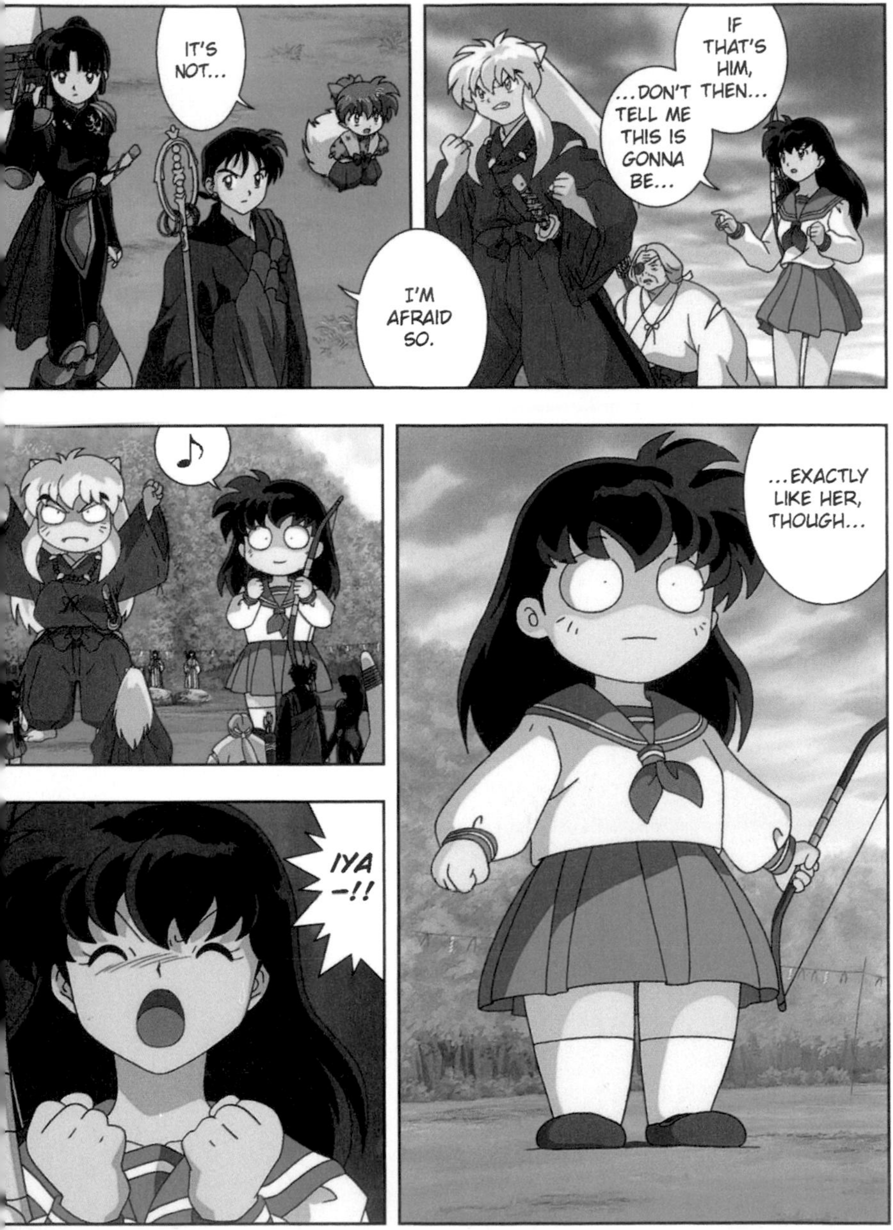

IF THAT'S HIM, THEN...
...DON'T TELL ME THIS IS GONNA BE...
IT'S NOT...
I'M AFRAID SO.
...EXACTLY LIKE HER, THOUGH...
♪
IYA—!!

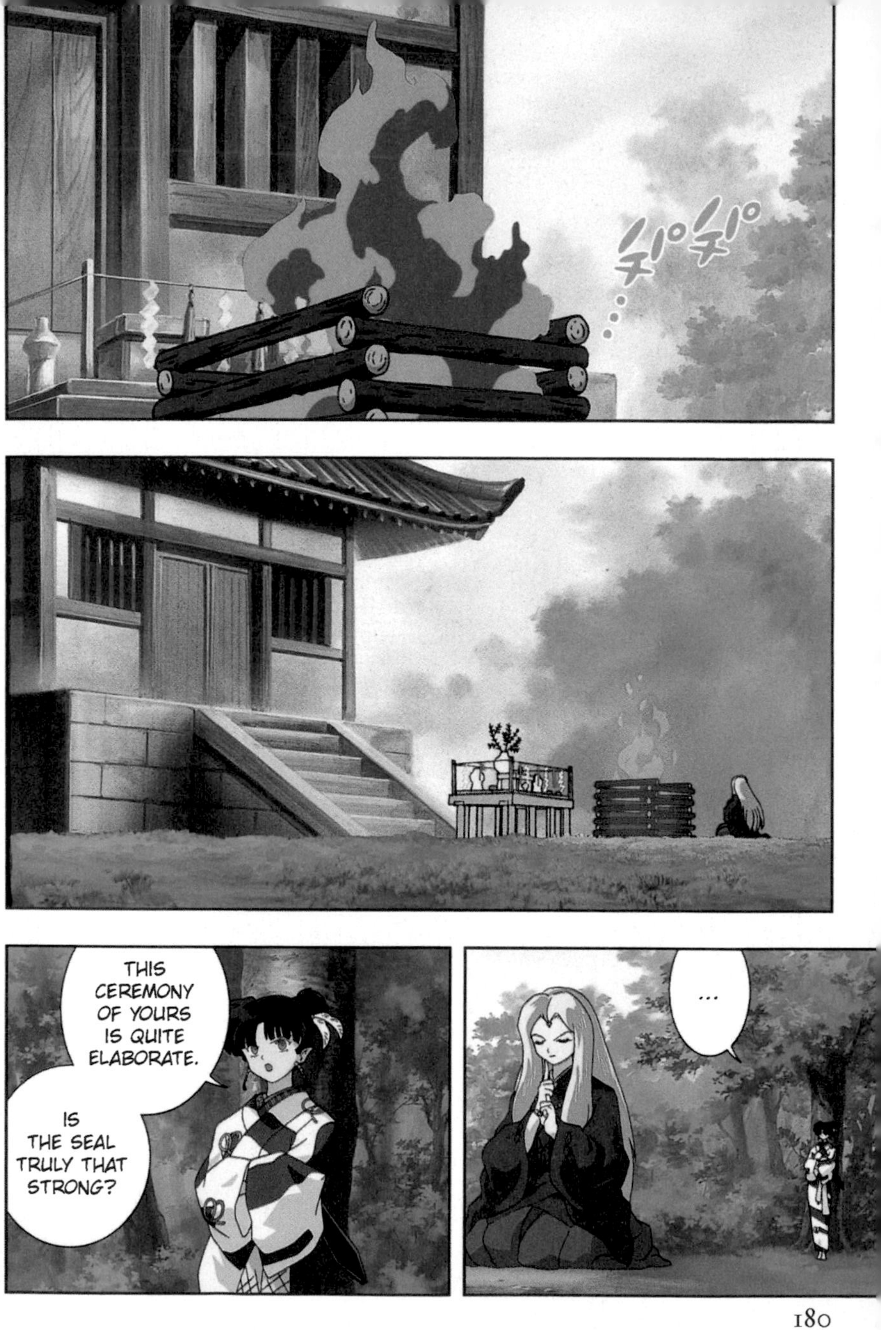
...
THIS CEREMONY OF YOURS IS QUITE ELABORATE.
IS THE SEAL TRULY THAT STRONG?

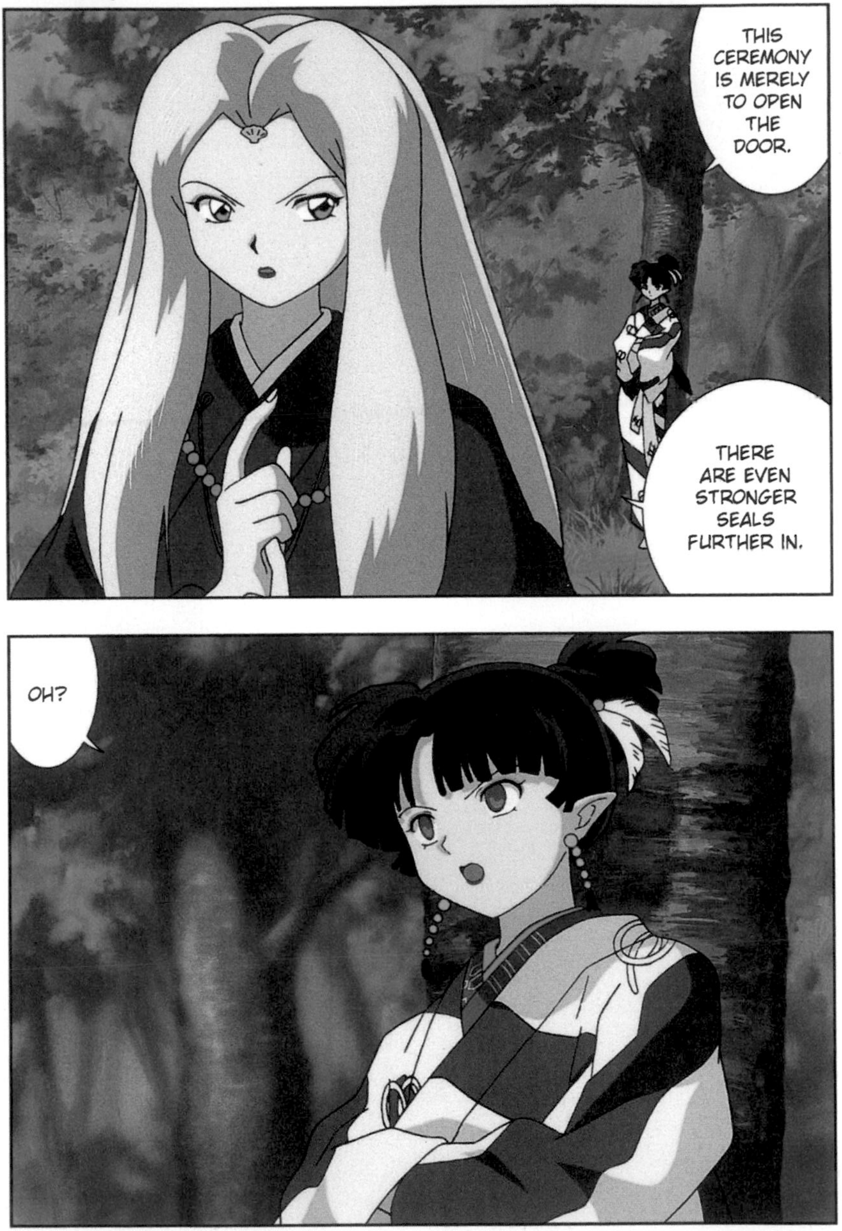
THIS CEREMONY IS MERELY TO OPEN THE DOOR.
THERE ARE EVEN STRONGER SEALS FURTHER IN.
OH?

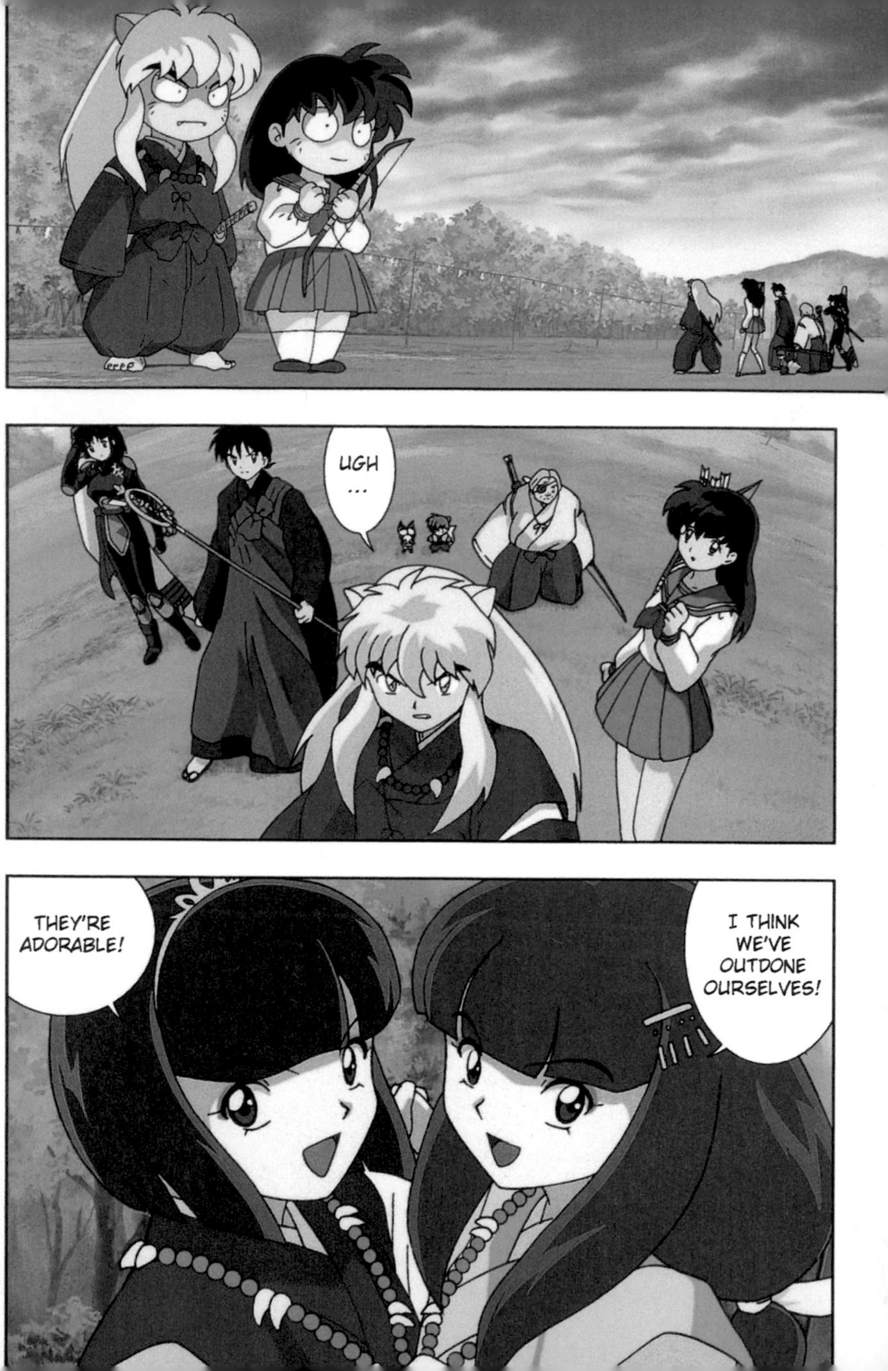
UGH ...
I THINK WE'VE OUTDONE OURSELVES!
THEY'RE ADORABLE!

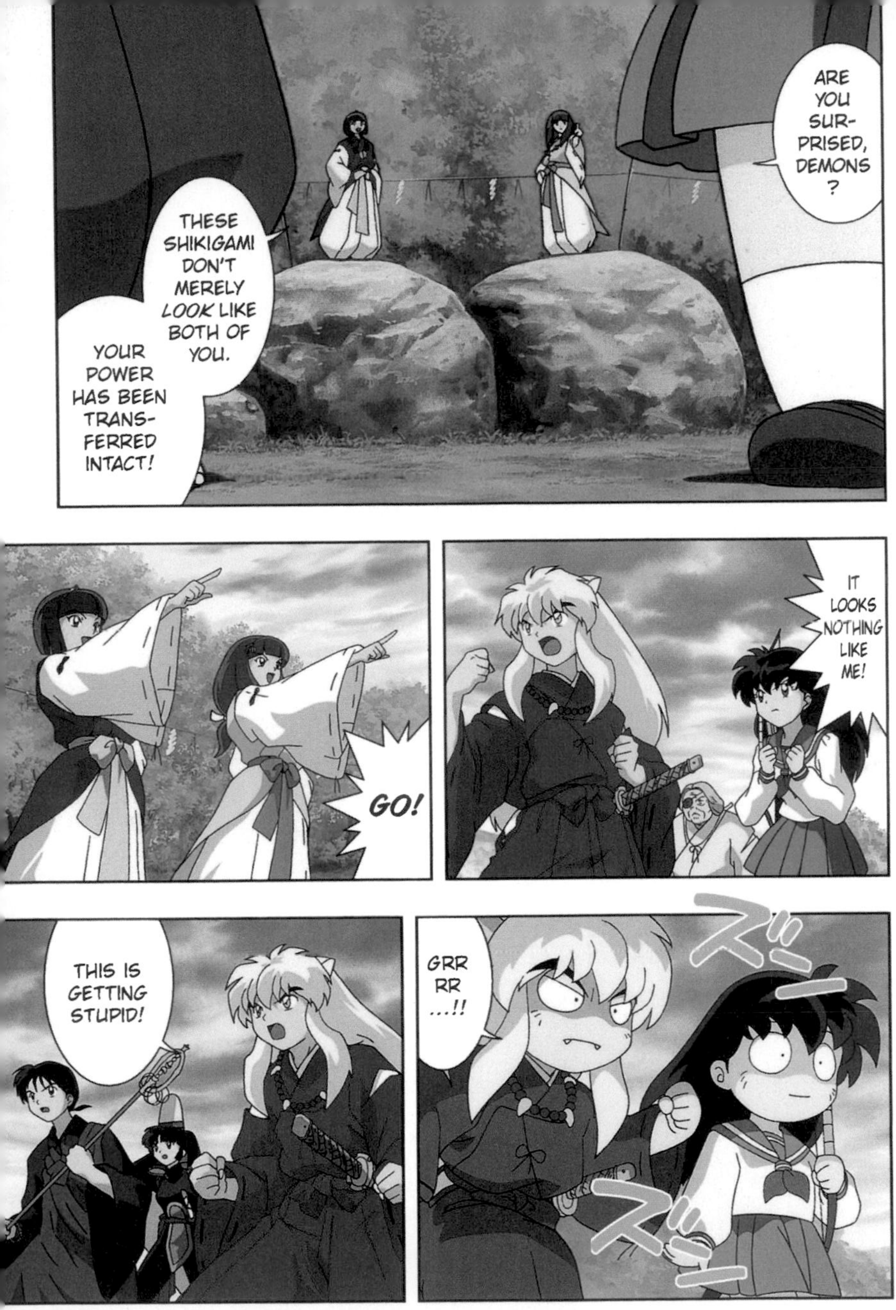
ARE YOU SUR-PRISED, DEMONS?
THESE SHIKIGAMI DON'T MERELY *LOOK* LIKE BOTH OF YOU.
YOUR POWER HAS BEEN TRANS-FERRED INTACT!
IT LOOKS NOTHING LIKE ME!
GO!
ズー
GRR RR ...!!
ズー
THIS IS GETTING STUPID!

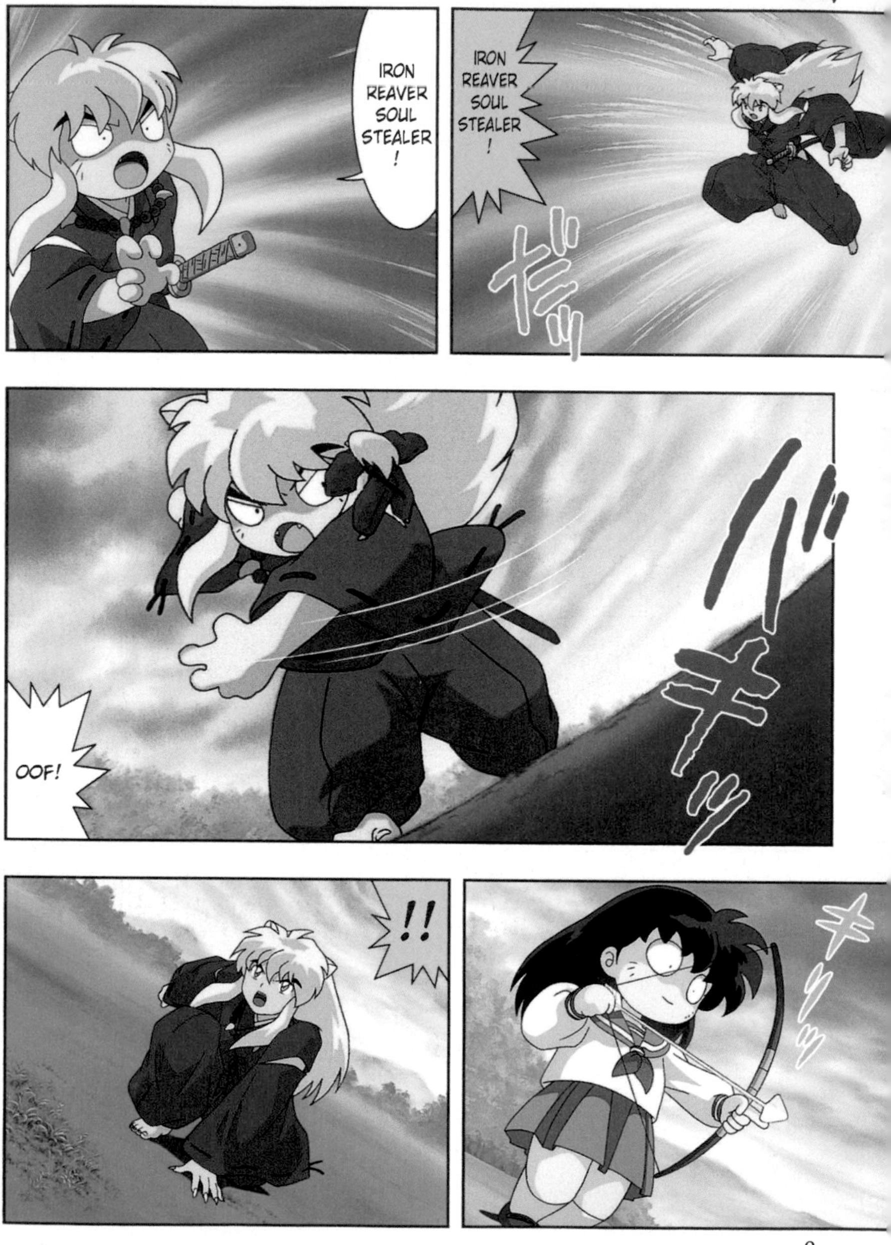
IRON REAVER SOUL STEALER !
ダッ
IRON REAVER SOUL STEALER !
バキッ
OOF!
キリリッ
!!

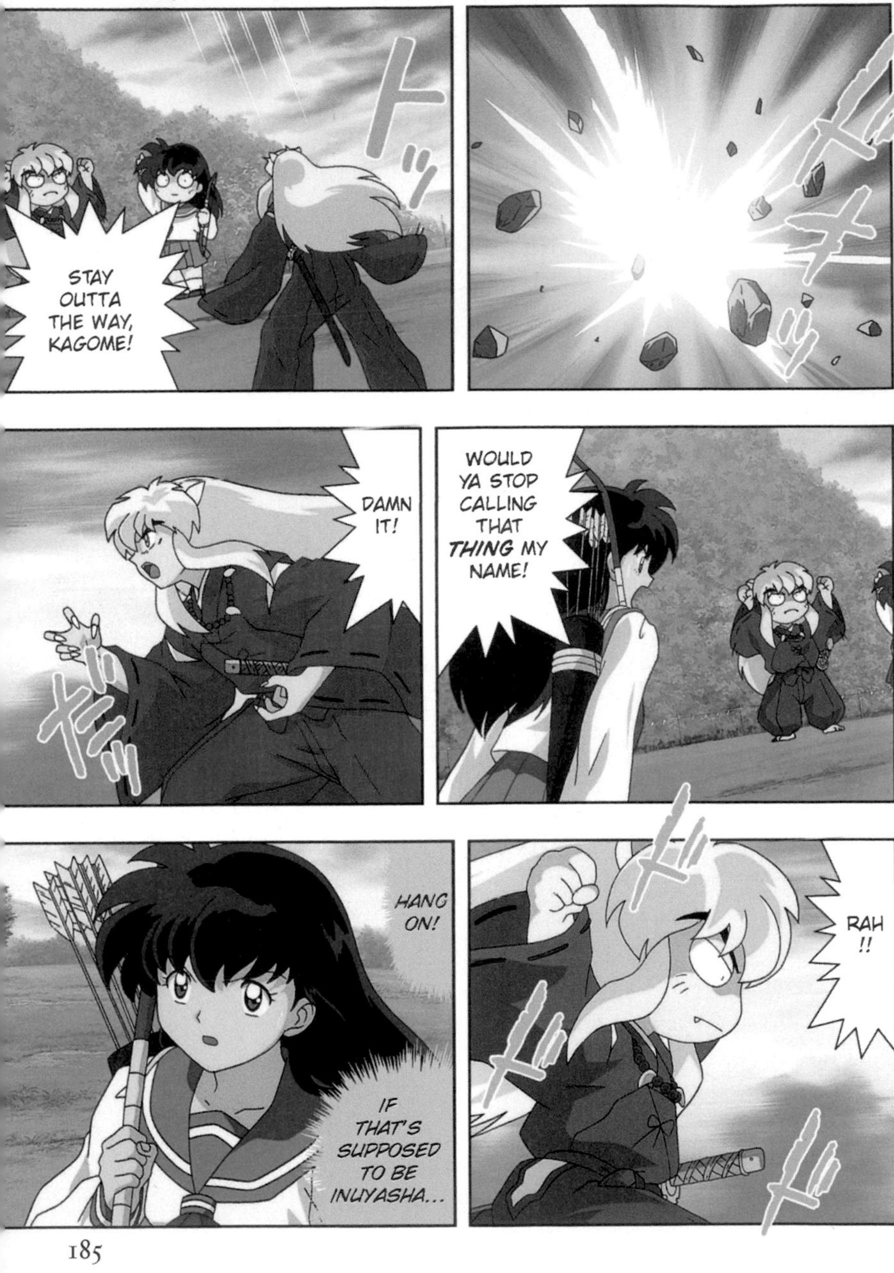
STAY OUTTA THE WAY, KAGOME!
WOULD YA STOP CALLING THAT THING MY NAME!
DAMN IT!
RAH !!
HANG ON!
IF THAT'S SUPPOSED TO BE INUYASHA...

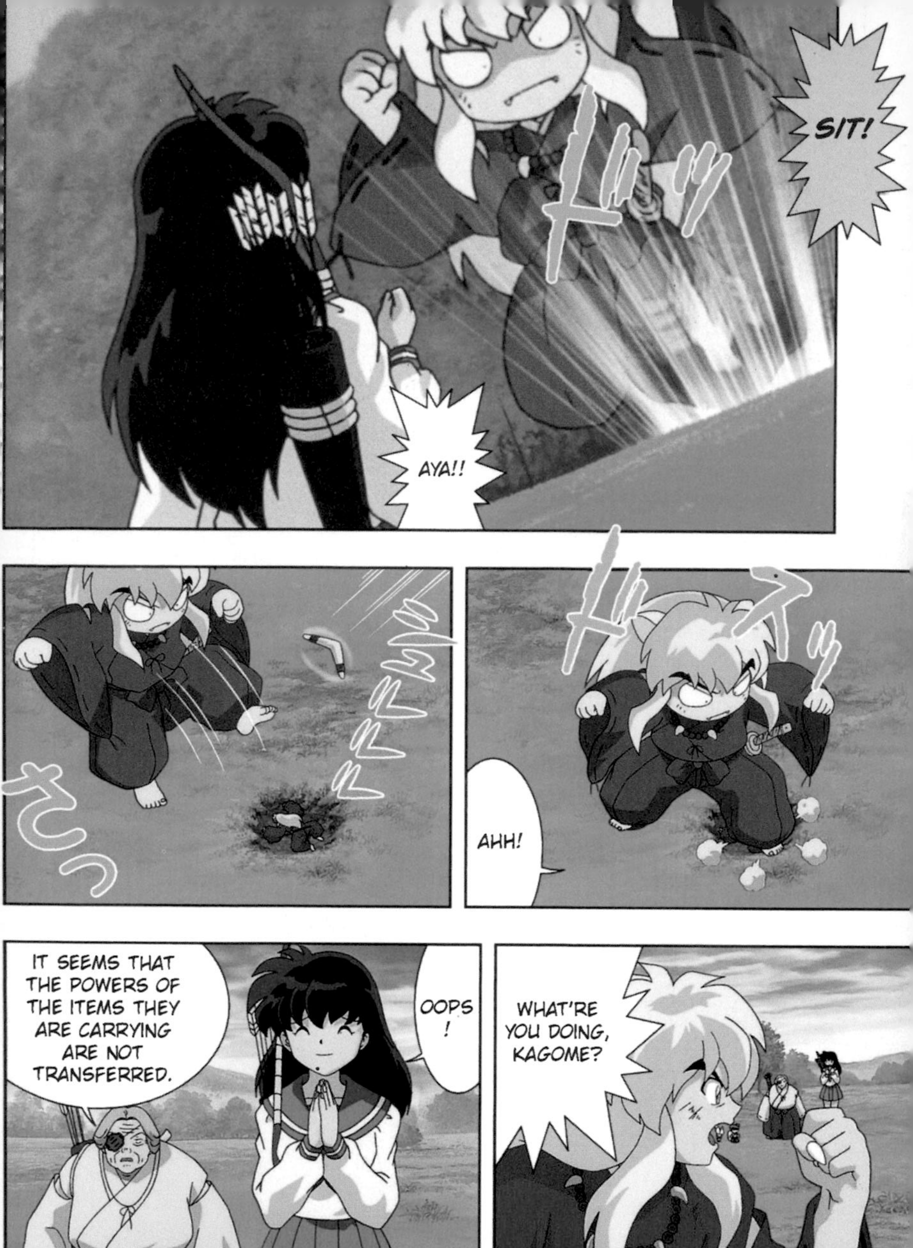
SIT!
AYA!!
AHH!
WHAT'RE YOU DOING, KAGOME?
OOPS!
IT SEEMS THAT THE POWERS OF THE ITEMS THEY ARE CARRYING ARE NOT TRANSFERRED.

GOES TO PROVE THAT THING'S A BIG FAKE.

FAKE, BUT KIND OF ENVIABLE.

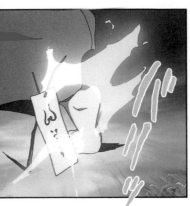

HUH! WHAT'S WITH THAT SWORD !?

♪

UWA-!!

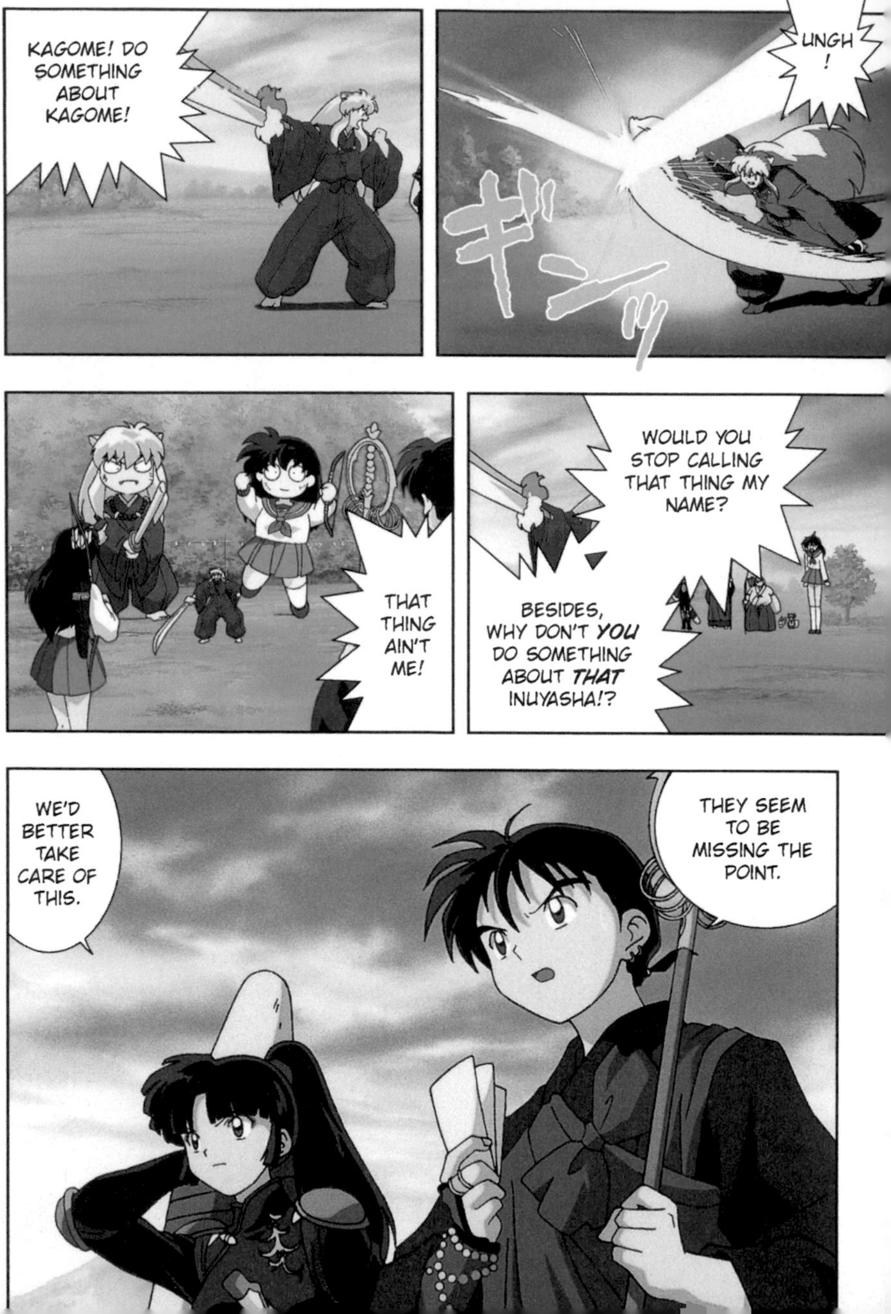
UNGH!
ギンッ
KAGOME! DO SOMETHING ABOUT KAGOME!
WOULD YOU STOP CALLING THAT THING MY NAME?
BESIDES, WHY DON'T *YOU* DO SOMETHING ABOUT *THAT* INUYASHA!?
THAT THING AIN'T ME!
THEY SEEM TO BE MISSING THE POINT.
WE'D BETTER TAKE CARE OF THIS.

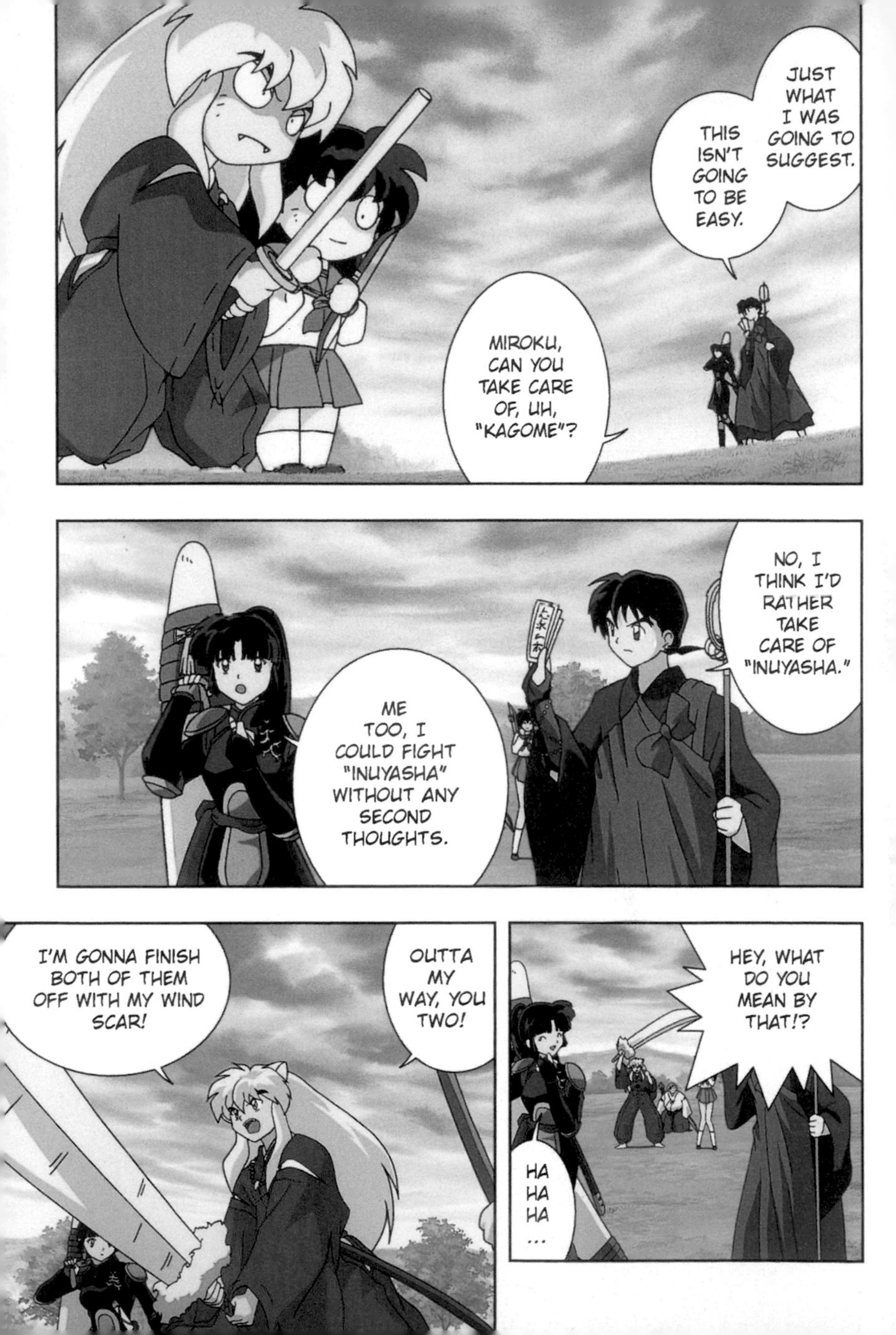
JUST WHAT I WAS GOING TO SUGGEST.
THIS ISN'T GOING TO BE EASY.
MIROKU, CAN YOU TAKE CARE OF, UH, "KAGOME"?
NO, I THINK I'D RATHER TAKE CARE OF "INUYASHA."
ME TOO, I COULD FIGHT "INUYASHA" WITHOUT ANY SECOND THOUGHTS.
HEY, WHAT DO YOU MEAN BY THAT!?
HA HA HA ...
OUTTA MY WAY, YOU TWO!
I'M GONNA FINISH BOTH OF THEM OFF WITH MY WIND SCAR!

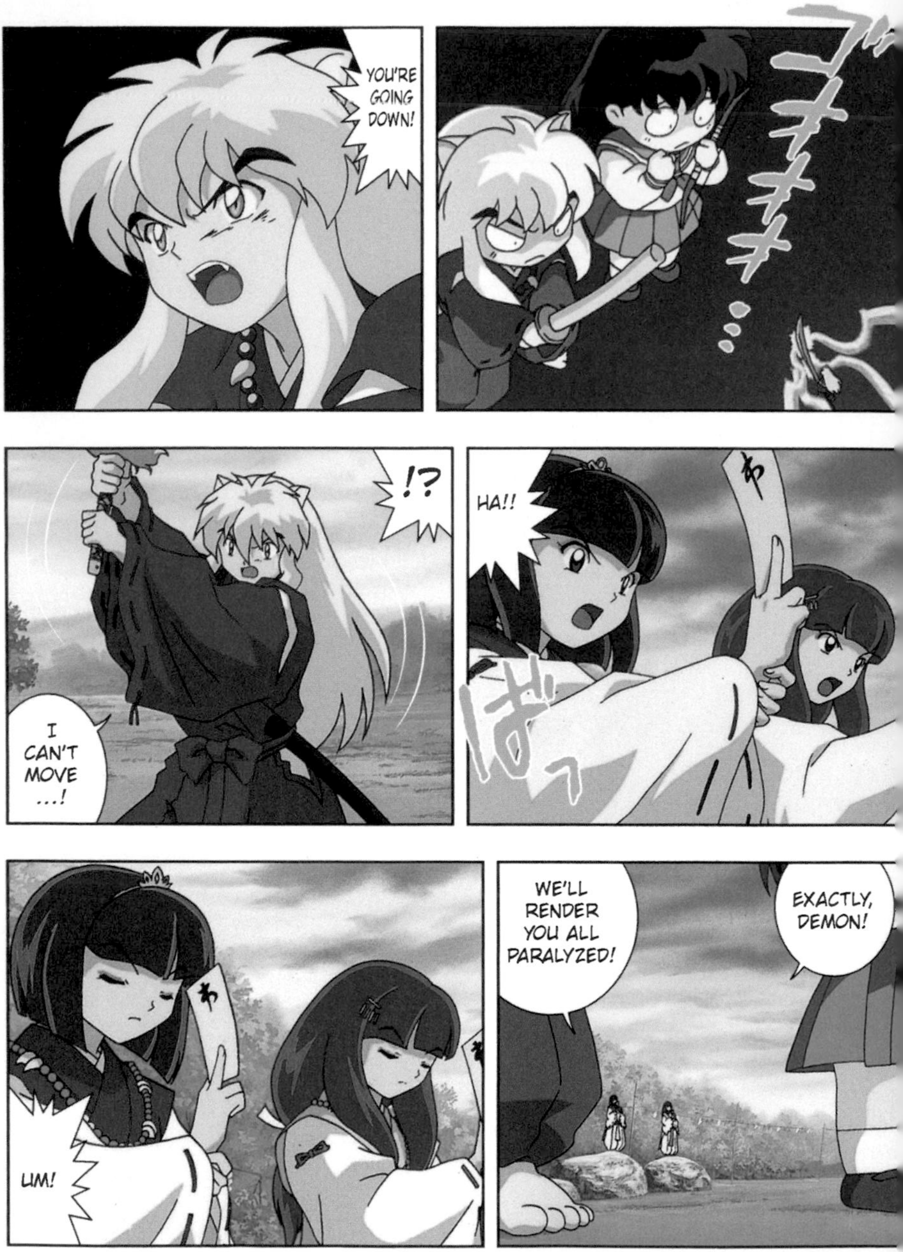

YOU'RE GOING DOWN!
HA!!
ばっ
!?
I CAN'T MOVE ...!
EXACTLY, DEMON!
WE'LL RENDER YOU ALL PARALYZED!
UM!

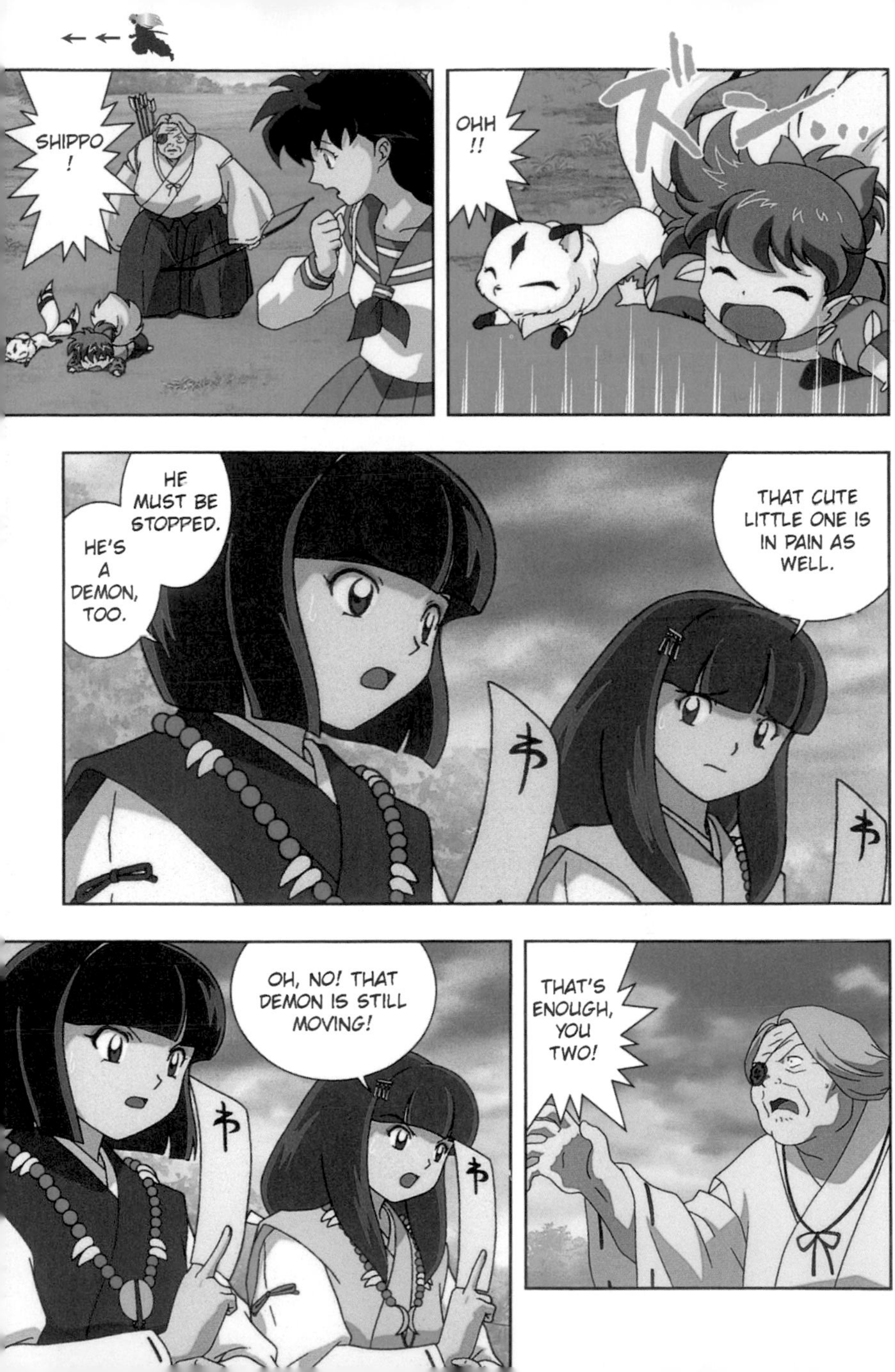
OHH !!
SHIPPO !
THAT CUTE LITTLE ONE IS IN PAIN AS WELL.
HE MUST BE STOPPED.
HE'S A DEMON, TOO.
THAT'S ENOUGH, YOU TWO!
OH, NO! THAT DEMON IS STILL MOVING!

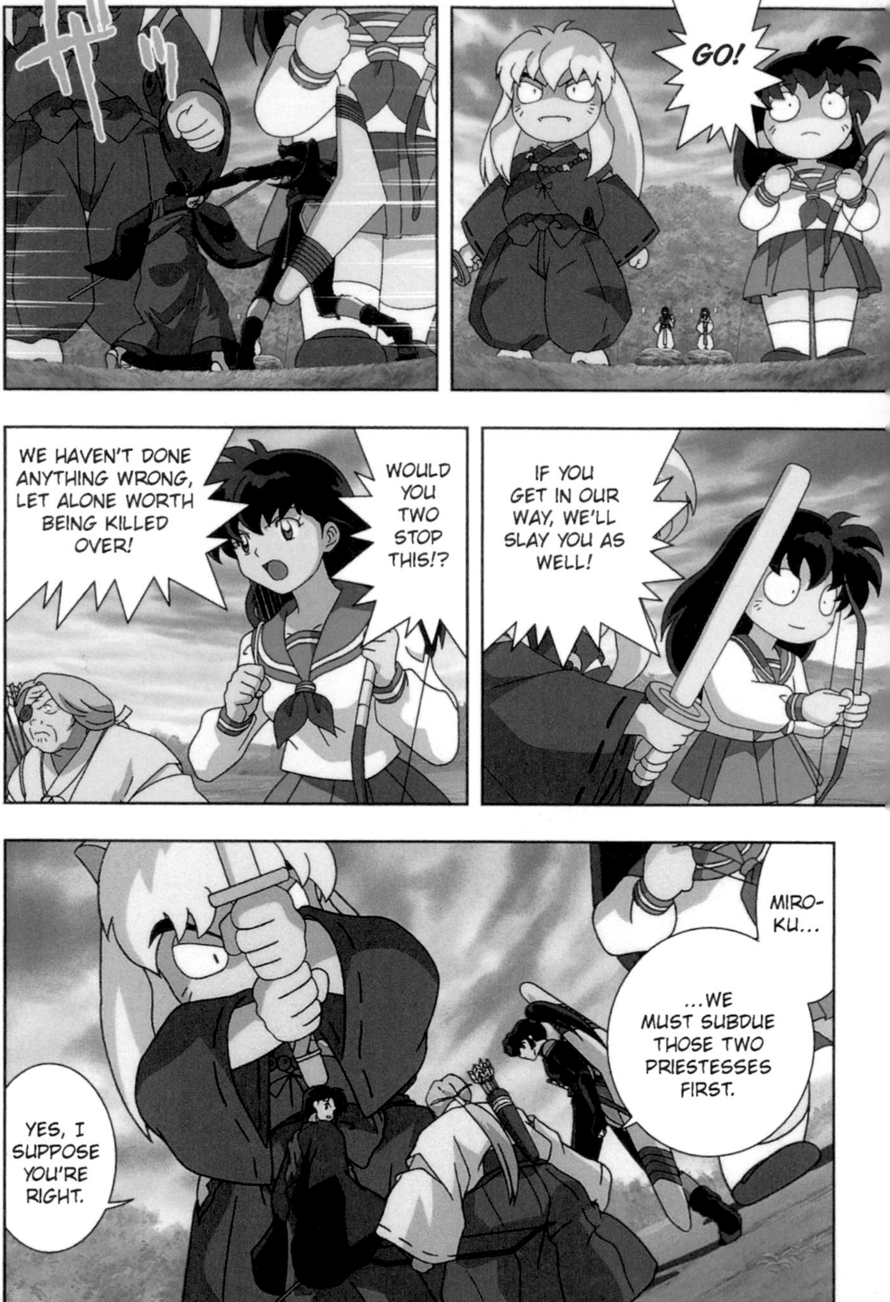
GO!
IF YOU GET IN OUR WAY, WE'LL SLAY YOU AS WELL!
WOULD YOU TWO STOP THIS!?
WE HAVEN'T DONE ANYTHING WRONG, LET ALONE WORTH BEING KILLED OVER!
MIRO-KU...
...WE MUST SUBDUE THOSE TWO PRIESTESSES FIRST.
YES, I SUPPOSE YOU'RE RIGHT.

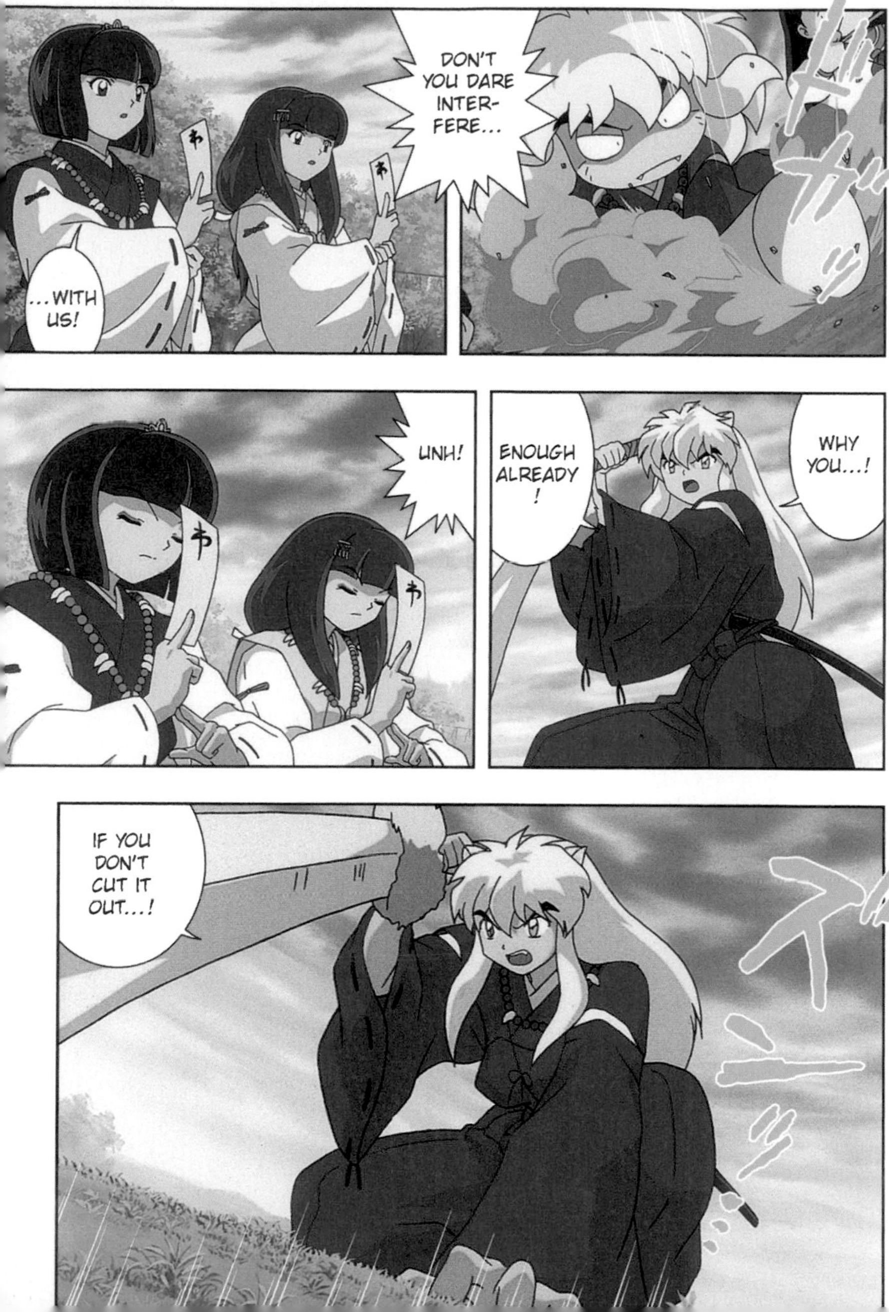
DON'T YOU DARE INTERFERE...
...WITH US!
WHY YOU...!
ENOUGH ALREADY!
UNH!
IF YOU DON'T CUT IT OUT...!

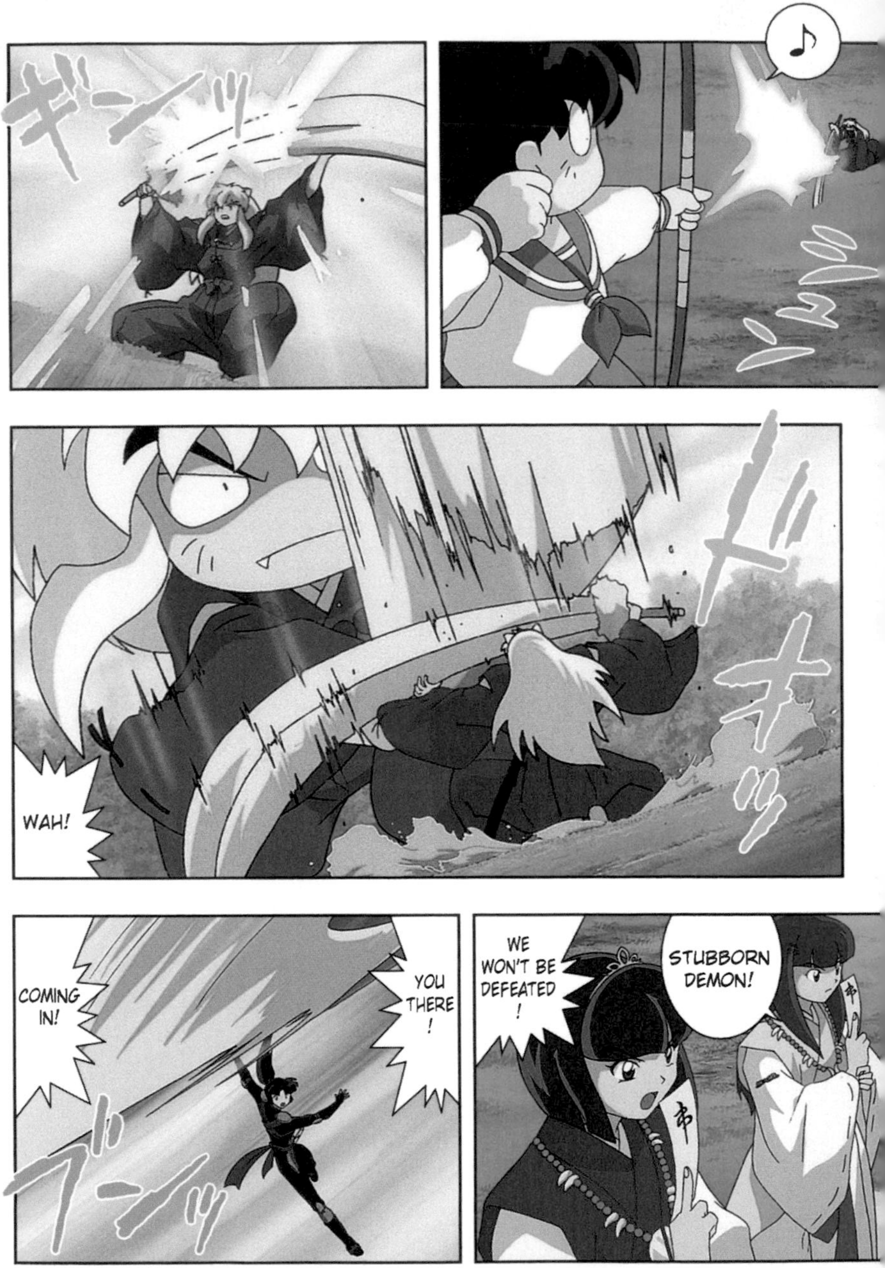
♪
WAH!
STUBBORN DEMON!
WE WON'T BE DEFEATED!
YOU THERE!
COMING IN!

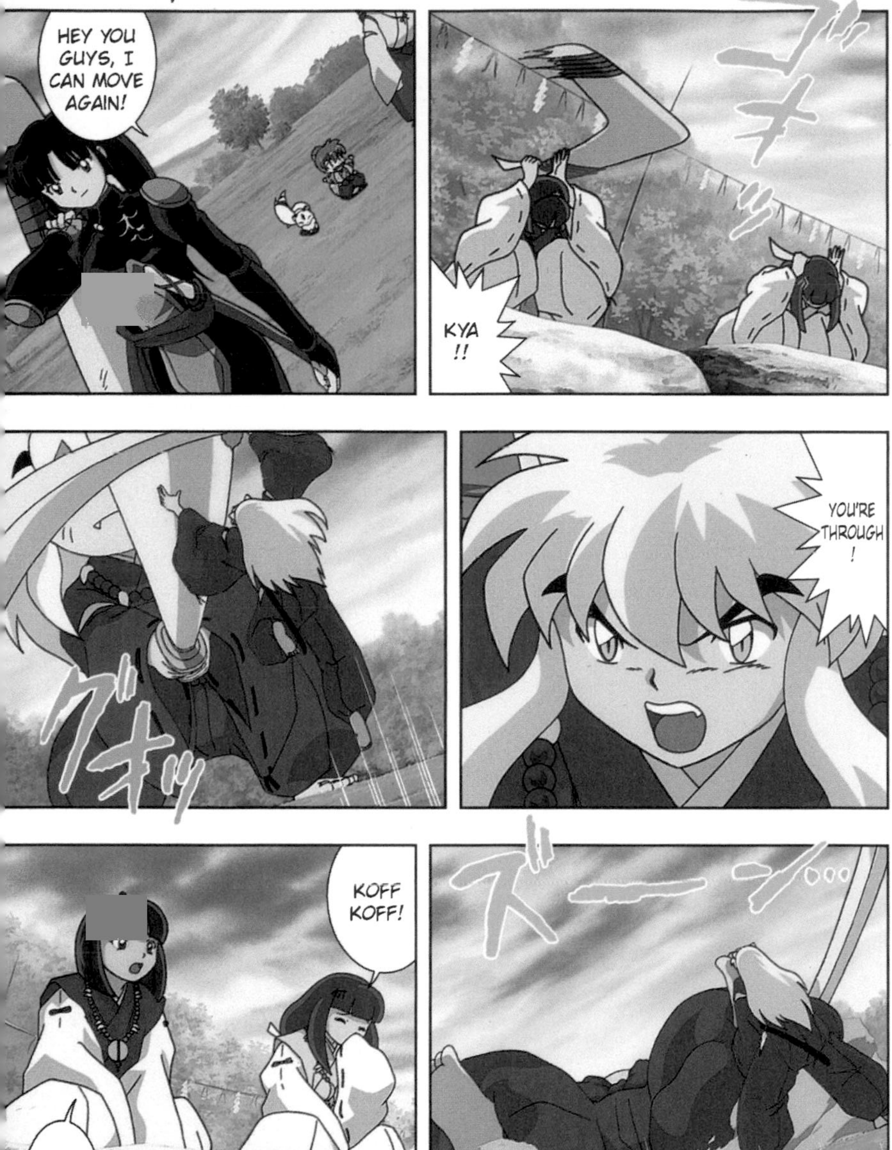
ゴキッ
KYA !!
HEY YOU GUYS, I CAN MOVE AGAIN!
YOU'RE THROUGH !
グキッ
ズーーン…
KOFF KOFF!
...!!

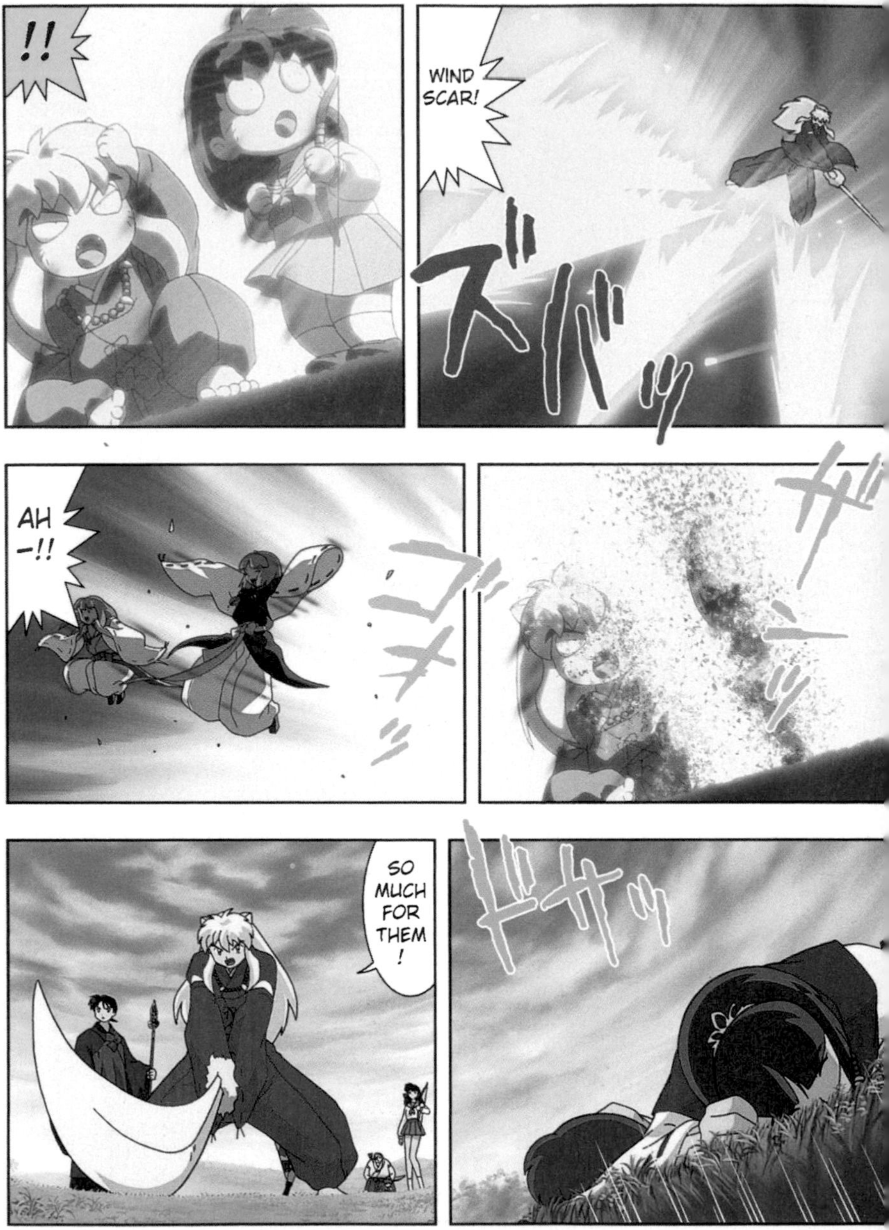
WIND SCAR!
ズバッ
!!
ザーッ
AH—!!
ドサッ
SO MUCH FOR THEM!

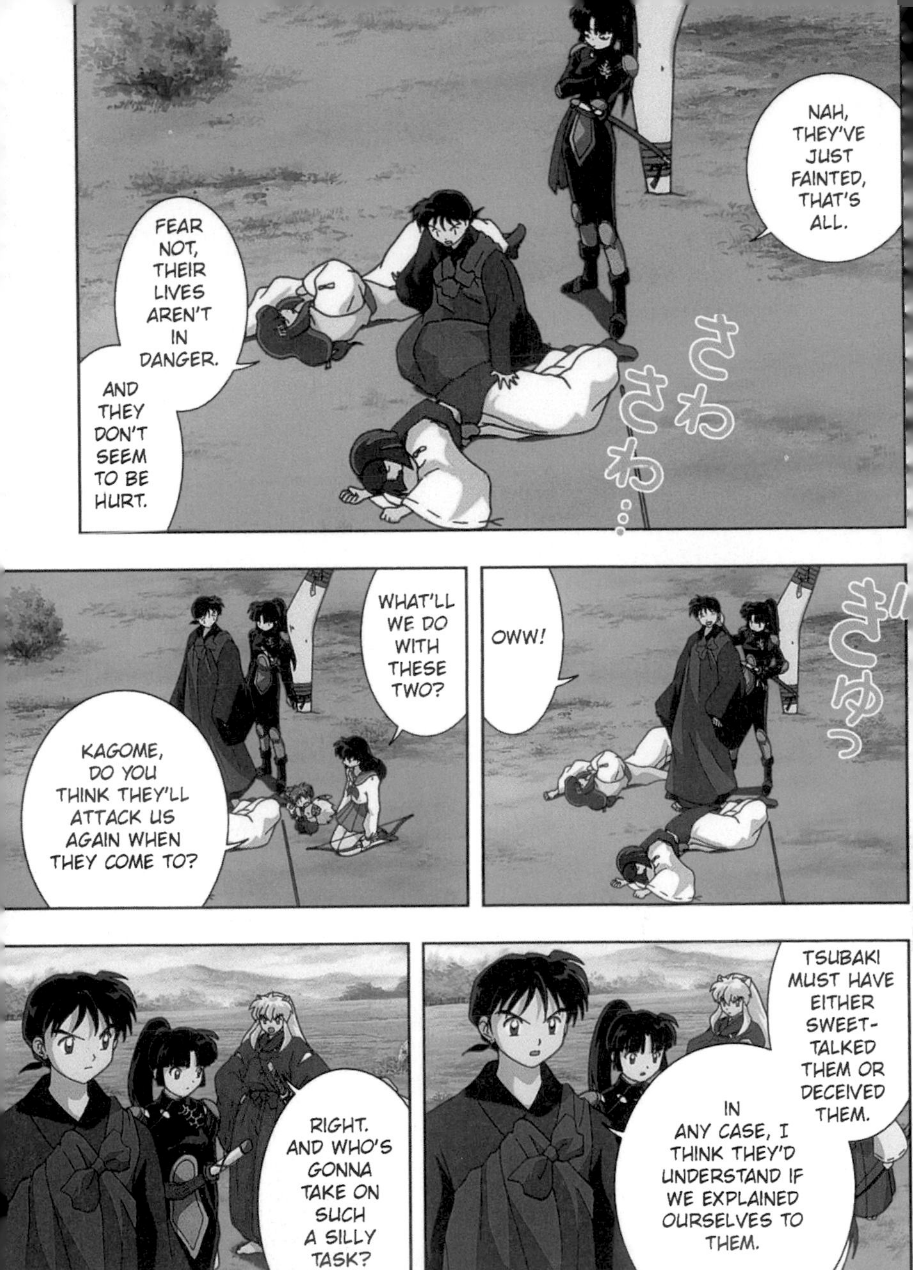
NAH, THEY'VE JUST FAINTED, THAT'S ALL.
FEAR NOT, THEIR LIVES AREN'T IN DANGER.
AND THEY DON'T SEEM TO BE HURT.
さわさわ…
ぎゅっ
OWW!
WHAT'LL WE DO WITH THESE TWO?
KAGOME, DO YOU THINK THEY'LL ATTACK US AGAIN WHEN THEY COME TO?
TSUBAKI MUST HAVE EITHER SWEET-TALKED THEM OR DECEIVED THEM.
IN ANY CASE, I THINK THEY'D UNDERSTAND IF WE EXPLAINED OURSELVES TO THEM.
RIGHT. AND WHO'S GONNA TAKE ON SUCH A SILLY TASK?

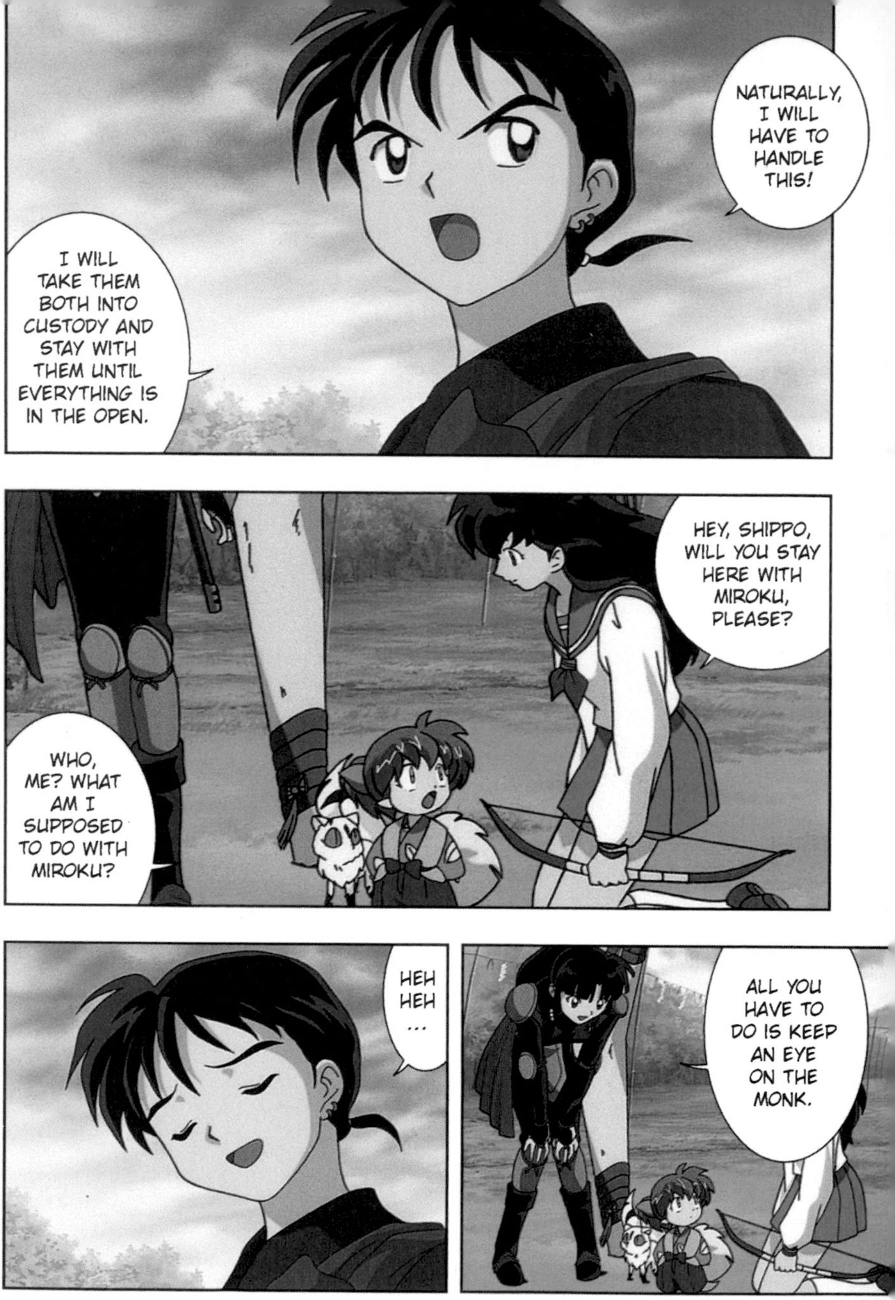
NATURALLY, I WILL HAVE TO HANDLE THIS!
I WILL TAKE THEM BOTH INTO CUSTODY AND STAY WITH THEM UNTIL EVERYTHING IS IN THE OPEN.
HEY, SHIPPO, WILL YOU STAY HERE WITH MIROKU, PLEASE?
WHO, ME? WHAT AM I SUPPOSED TO DO WITH MIROKU?
ALL YOU HAVE TO DO IS KEEP AN EYE ON THE MONK.
HEH HEH ...

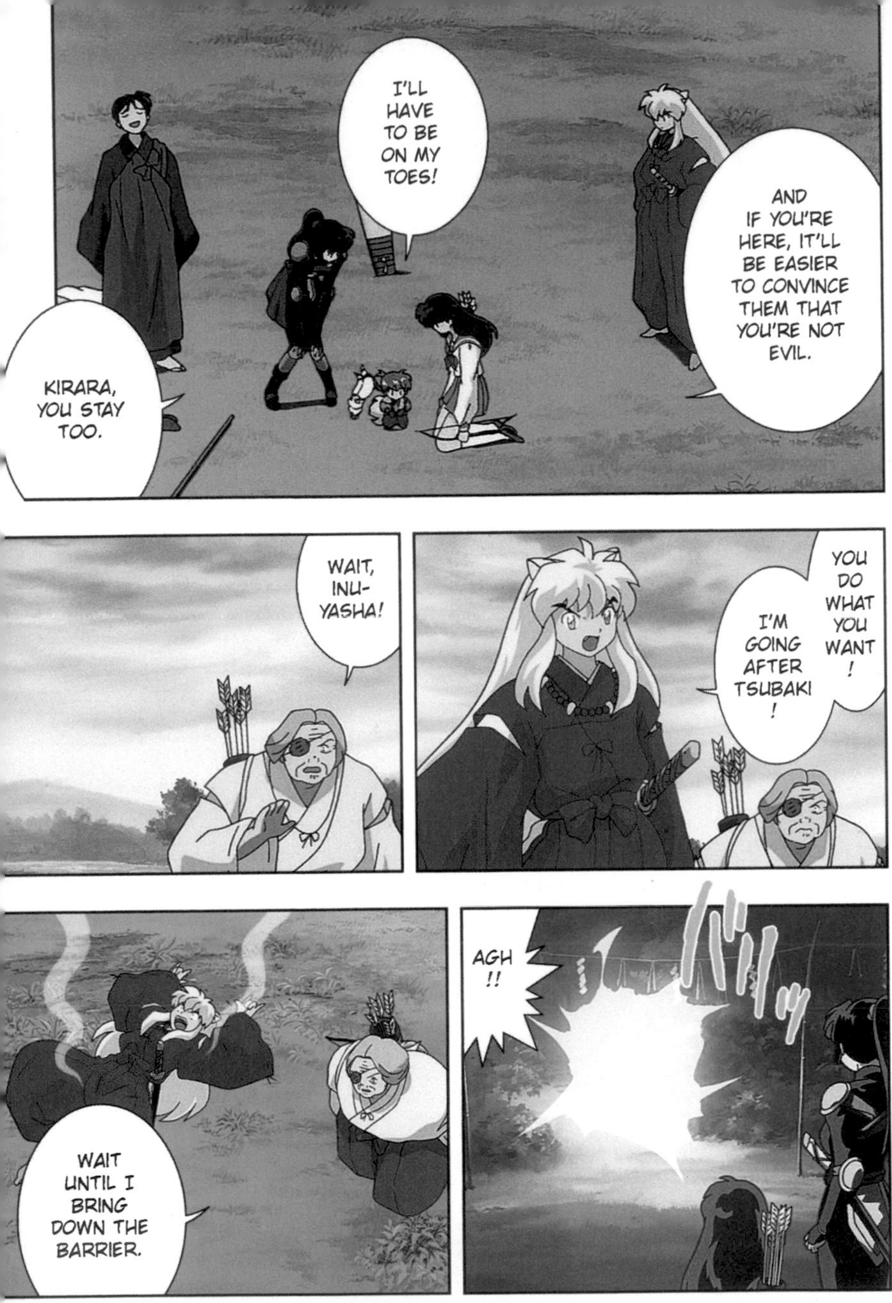
AND IF YOU'RE HERE, IT'LL BE EASIER TO CONVINCE THEM THAT YOU'RE NOT EVIL.
I'LL HAVE TO BE ON MY TOES!
KIRARA, YOU STAY TOO.
YOU DO WHAT YOU WANT!
I'M GOING AFTER TSUBAKI!
WAIT, INU-YASHA!
AGH!!
WAIT UNTIL I BRING DOWN THE BARRIER.

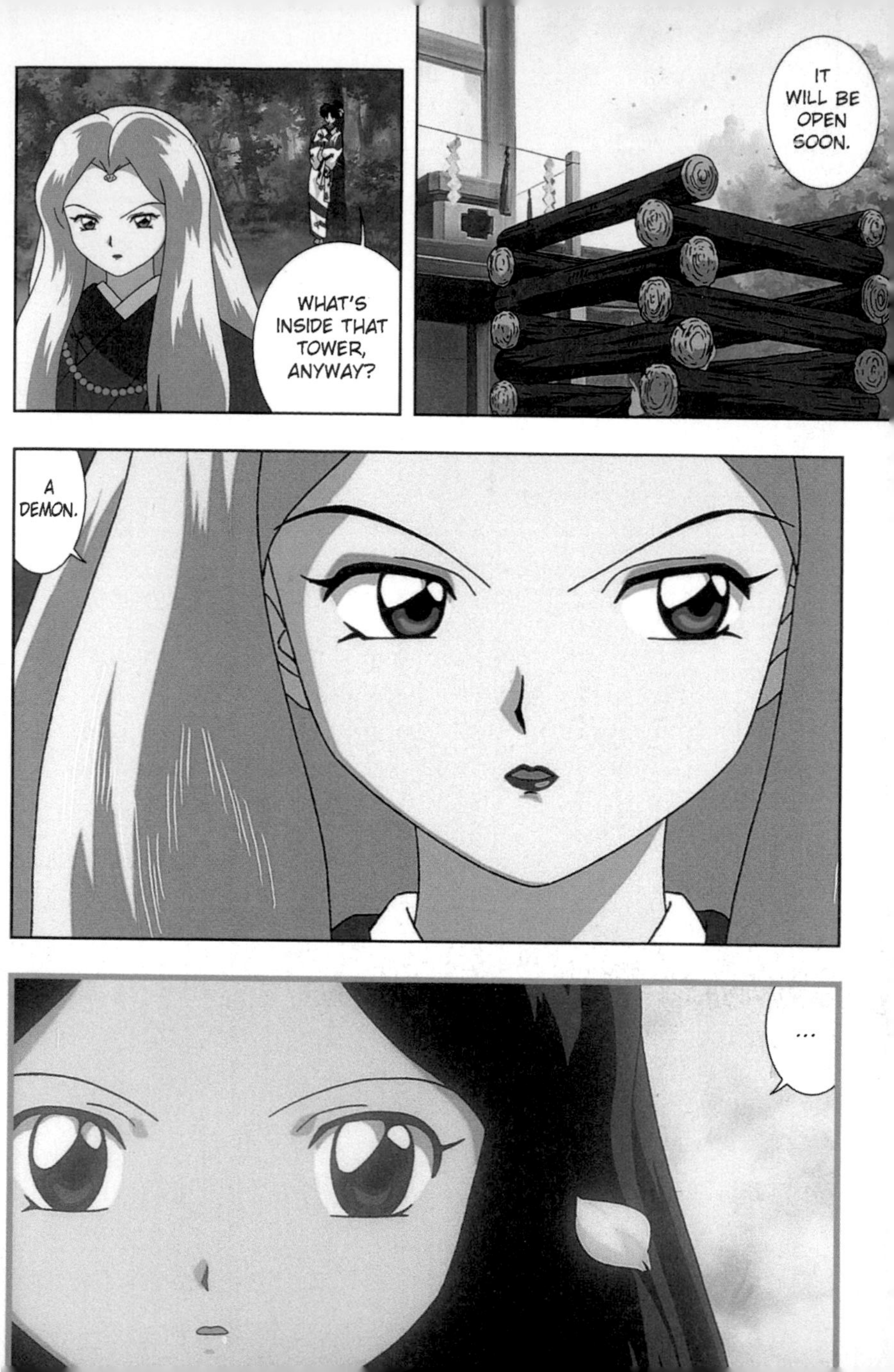
IT WILL BE OPEN SOON.
WHAT'S INSIDE THAT TOWER, ANYWAY?
A DEMON.
...

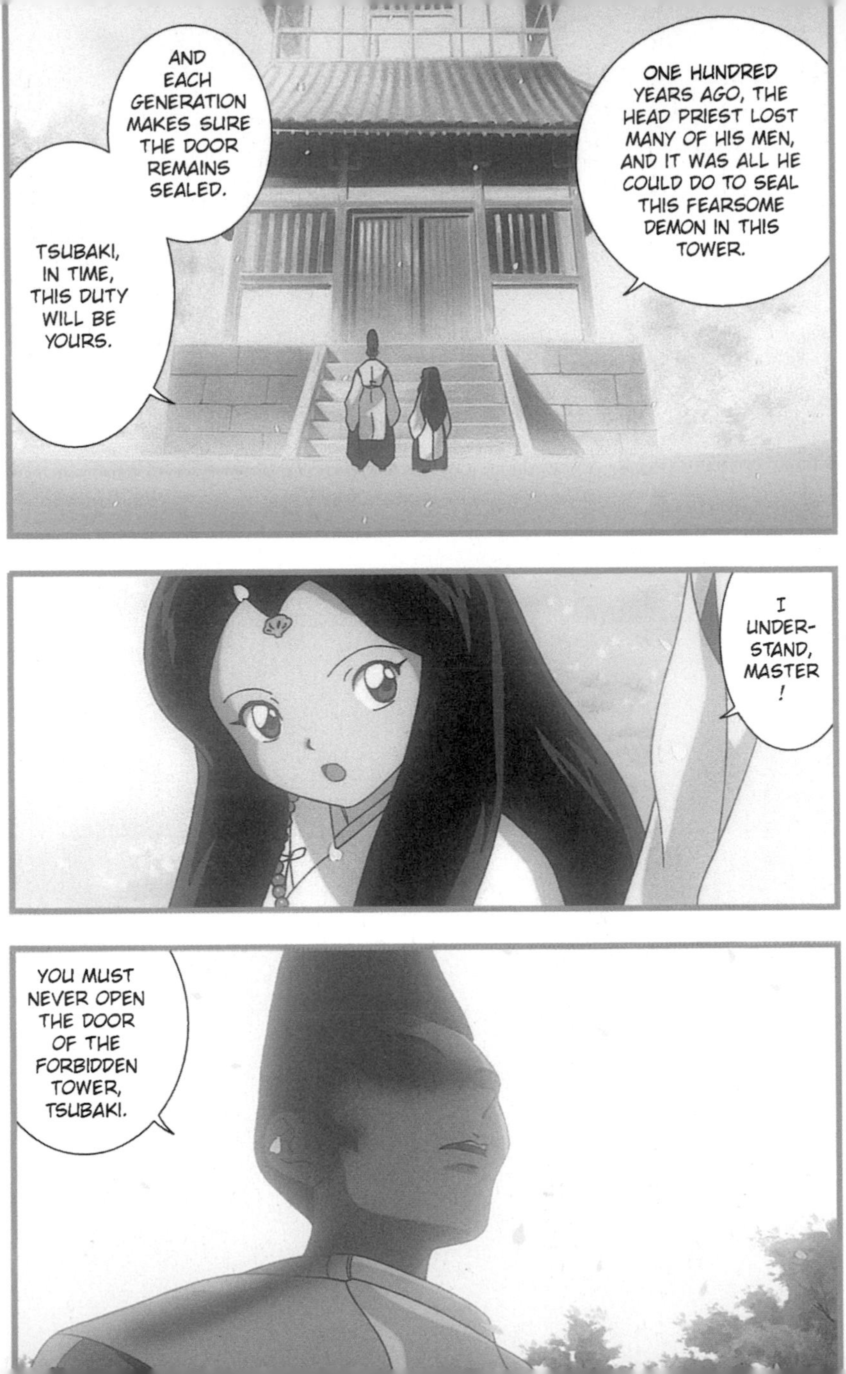
ONE HUNDRED YEARS AGO, THE HEAD PRIEST LOST MANY OF HIS MEN, AND IT WAS ALL HE COULD DO TO SEAL THIS FEARSOME DEMON IN THIS TOWER.
AND EACH GENERATION MAKES SURE THE DOOR REMAINS SEALED.
TSUBAKI, IN TIME, THIS DUTY WILL BE YOURS.
I UNDER-STAND, MASTER!
YOU MUST NEVER OPEN THE DOOR OF THE FORBIDDEN TOWER, TSUBAKI.

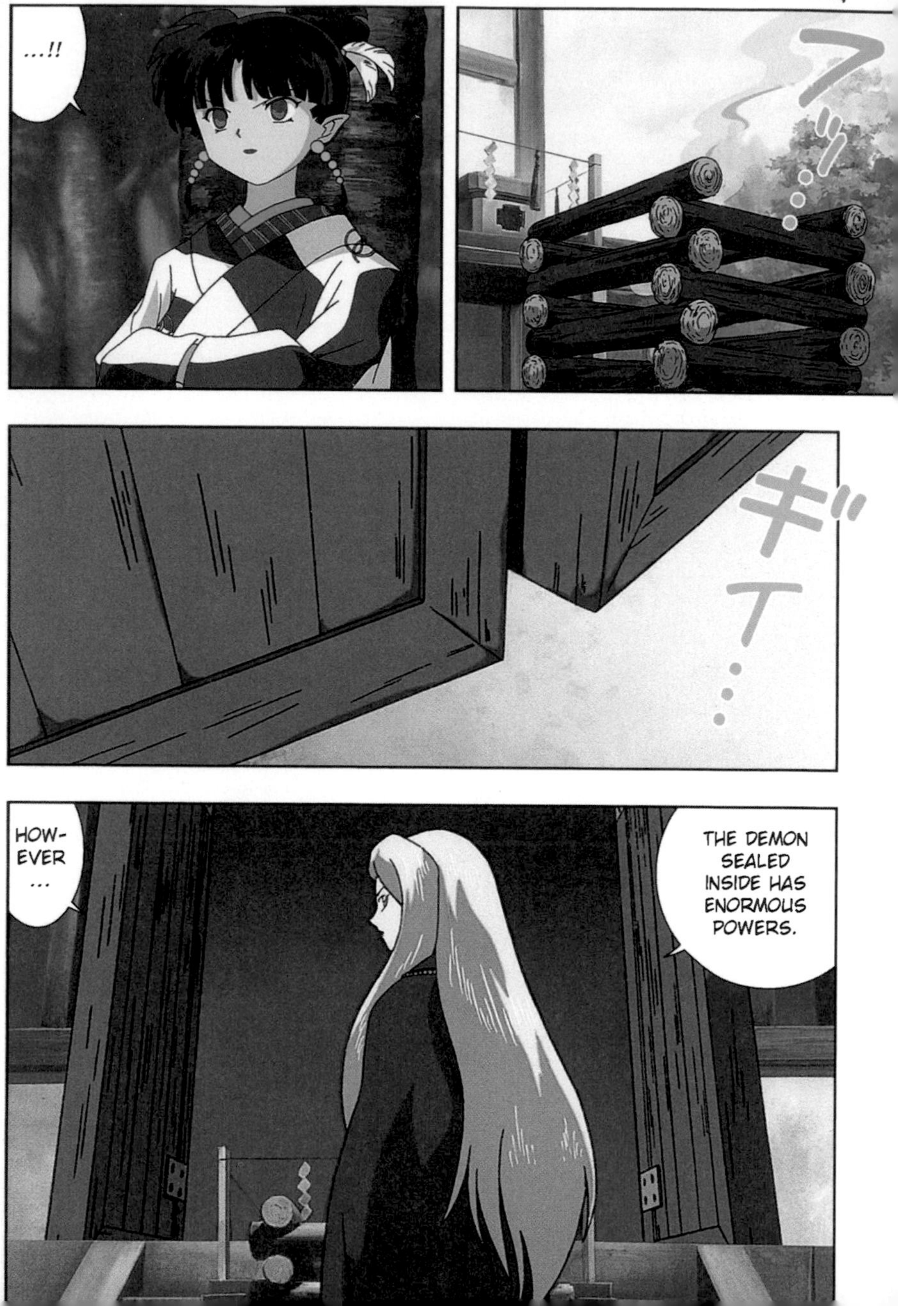

フッ…
...!!
ギイ…
THE DEMON SEALED INSIDE HAS ENORMOUS POWERS.
HOW-EVER ...

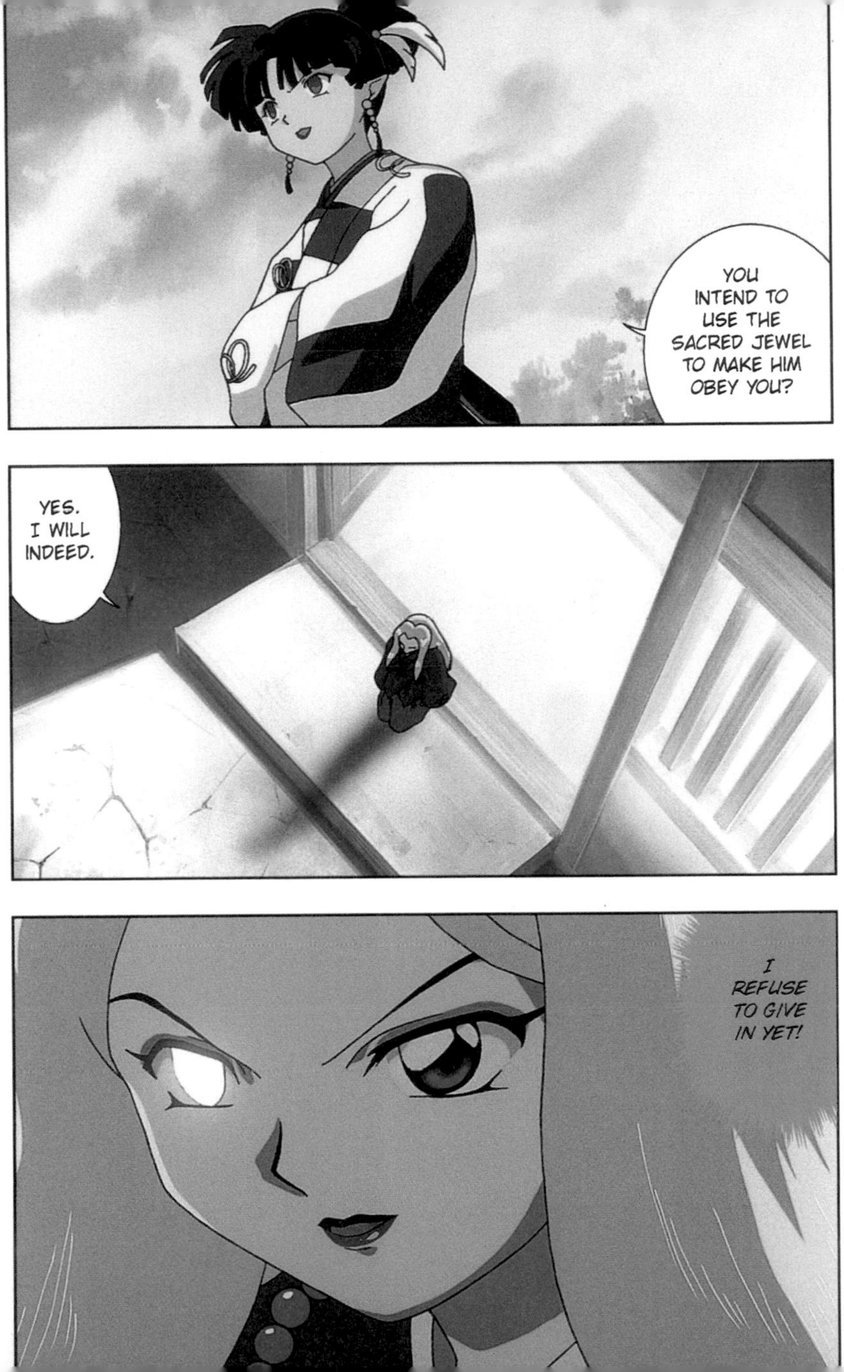
YOU INTEND TO USE THE SACRED JEWEL TO MAKE HIM OBEY YOU?
YES. I WILL INDEED.
I REFUSE TO GIVE IN YET!

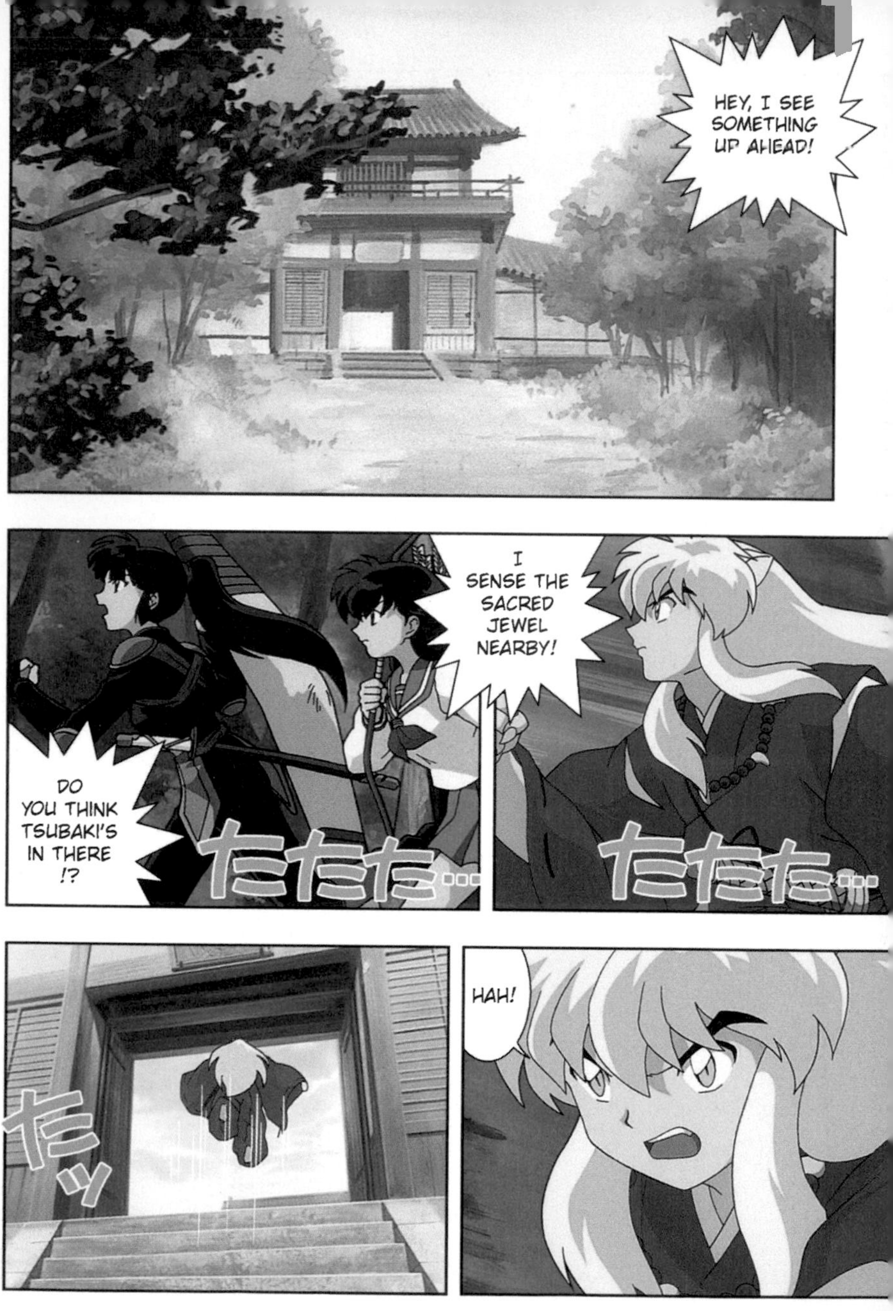
HEY, I SEE SOMETHING UP AHEAD!
I SENSE THE SACRED JEWEL NEARBY!
たたた...
DO YOU THINK TSUBAKI'S IN THERE !?
たたた...
HAH!
たッ

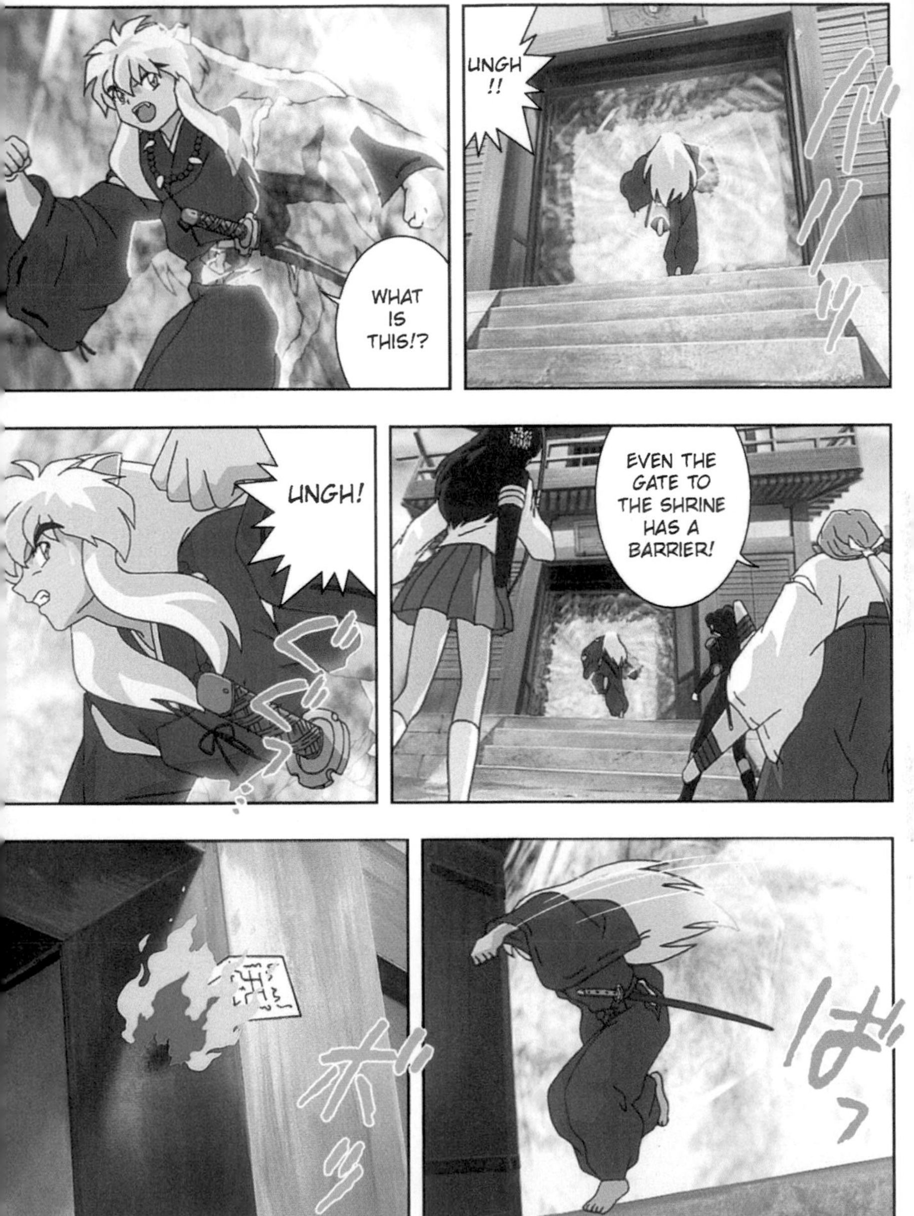
UNGH !!
WHAT IS THIS!?
EVEN THE GATE TO THE SHRINE HAS A BARRIER!
UNGH!

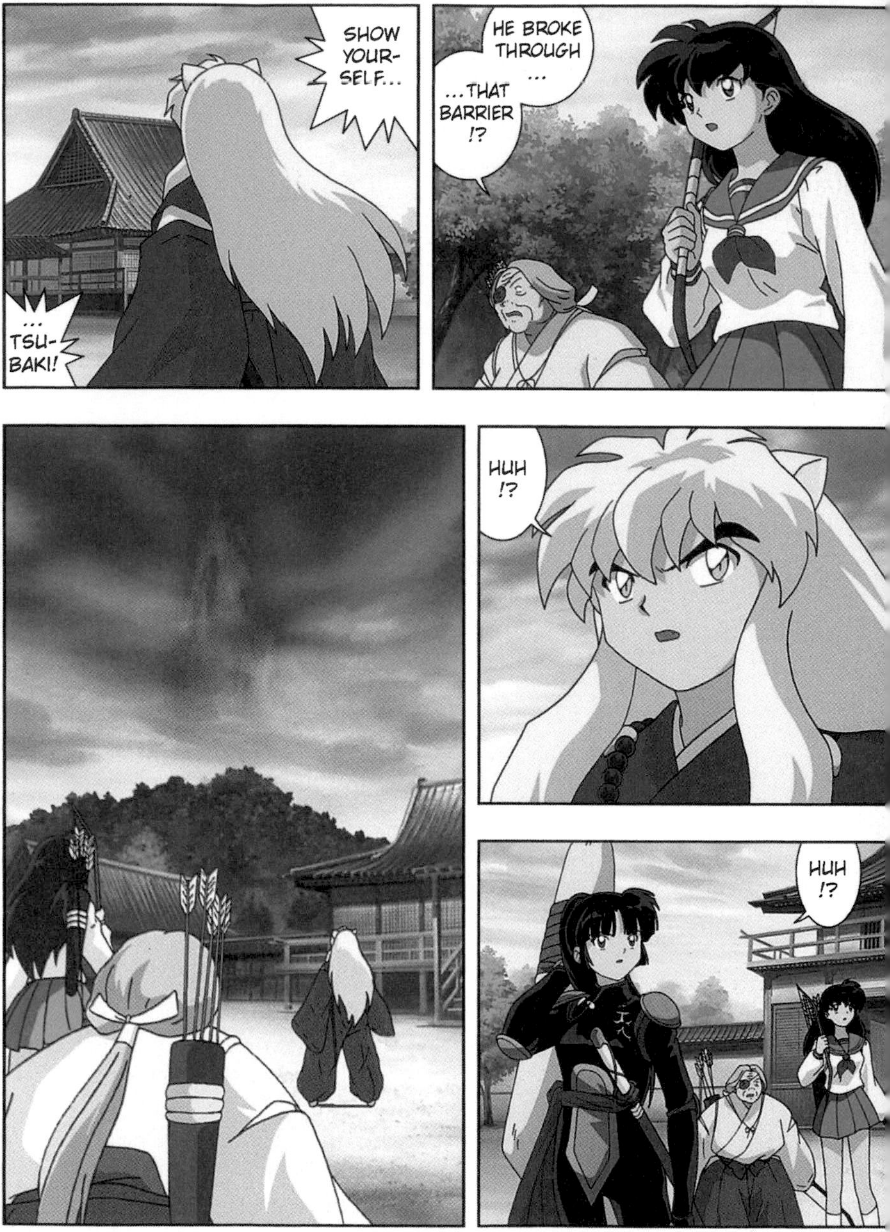
HE BROKE THROUGH ...
...THAT BARRIER !?
SHOW YOUR-SELF...
...TSU-BAKI!
HUH !?
HUH !?

TO BE CONTINUED

Glossary of Sound Effects

Each entry includes: the location, indicated by page number and panel number (so 3.1 means page 3, panel number 1); the phonetic romanization of the original Japanese; and our English "translation"—we offer as close an English equivalent as we can.

34.2 FX: Za (rustling in grass)

35.1 FX: Gaa (here comes the snake) [note: in anime the snake says "Rrrargh!" here]

35.3 FX: Ka (shine from Kikyo deflecting the Shikigami)

40.2 FX: Ta ta ta… (running)

41.1/2 FX: Suuu… (hissing from jewel)

42.1 FX: Ta (Inuyasha leaps)
42.2 FX: Ta ta ta… (running)

43.1 FX: Za (Inuyasha and Kagome see the ominous—looking barrier)

46.1 FX: Giri (bow string stretches)
46.2 FX: Gyun (arrow is shot)
46.3 FX: Ka (shining)
46.4 FX: Zu zu zu (barrier shimmers and disappears)

47.1 FX: Goh (whooshing)

48.1 FX: Doh doh (arrows thunk)

49.4 FX: Za (Kikyo steps on some of Naraku leftover stuff)
49.4 FX: Shuuu… (stuff dissolves and disappears)

50.4 FX: Ba (Tsubaki swipes at Kikyo with arrow)

51.2 FX: Suu… (Kikyo disappears)

Chapter 61
Kikyo and the Dark Priestess

7.2 FX: Doh (thunk of arrow)

8.1 FX: Goh (whoosh)

9.2 FX: Goh (whoos)
9.3 FX: Bari bari (our heroes are deflected by barrier)

11.3 FX: Su… (Kikyo enters barrier)

14.2 FX: Da (Inuyasha runs at Kagome)
14.3 FX: Shun (Kagome fires arrow)

14.4 FX: Doh (arrow strikes)

15.4 FX: Boro (Naraku's demon puppet self is struck down)

18.1 FX: Suuu…
18.4 FX: Fura (Kagome collapses)
18.5 FX: Dosa (Inuyasha catches Kagome)

21.4 FX: Ta ta ta… (running)
21.3 FX: Da (Inuyasha runs)

24.1 FX: Za za za za za… (Inuyasha runs through the forest)
24.2 FX: Za (Inuyasha leaps)

27.2 FX: Goh (whoosh)
27.3 FX: Goh (whoosh)

69.4 FX: Baki (demon deflects Inuyasha's strike)
69.6 FX: Za (Inuyasha skids upon being thrown to the ground)

Chapter 62
Tsubaki's Unrelenting Evil Spell

72.2 FX: Doga (demon lands)
72.4 FX: Zan (demon slashes Inuyasha)

73.4 FX: Za (demon lands, Inuyasha leaps away)
73.5 FX: Ba (Inuyasha slashes)

74.1 FX: Ga ga ga (demon slashed by blades)
74.4 FX: Gu (Tsubaki closes her fist)

75.2 FX: Kaa… (demon's eye glows)
75.3 FX: Shuuuu… (glow disappears)

78.4 FX: Ta (Miroku runs off)
78.5 FX: Ta ta ta… (running)

79.1 FX: Bun (Sango throws boomerang)
79.3 FX: Bashi (demon deflects Hiraikotsu)
79.4 FX: Ta (running)
79.5 FX: Ba (Miroku throws sutras)

80.1 FX: Bashi (sutras are deflected)
80.2 FX: Kaa (demon's eye shines red)
80.3 FX: Boh (sutras burst into flame)

81.1 FX: Guoh (demon roars)
81.2 FX: Zun (demon stamps at Miroku)
81.3 FX: Doga (demon almost squashes Miroku)
81.4 FX: Za (Miroku falls on grass)
81.5 FX: Ba (demon draws back to smack Miroku)
81.6 FX: Goh (whoosh)

82.1 FX: Ta (Inuyasha leaps and pulls Miroku out of the way)
82.2 FX: Zuun (demon's foot slams down where Miroku just was)

52.2 FX: Za (Kirara lands)
52.4/5FX: Zawa (a wind from the creepy temple blows through the grass)

53.1 FX: Gii… (door of creepy temple creaks open)
53.3 FX: Za (Tsubaki is revealed)

57.1 FX: Da (Inuyasha lunges toward Tsubaki)
57.2 FX: Cha (Inuyasha starts to pull Tetsusaiga from sheath)

58.3 FX: Poh… (the jewel purifies)

59.2 FX: Gu (Tsubaki closes her fist around jewel)

61.5 FX: Zu zu zu (Tsubaki gets some snake skin and her eye turns red)

62.1 FX: Goh (whoosh)
62.3 FX: Niya… (Tsubaki flashes evil smile)
62.4 FX: Doh (demon tentacles come out of Tsubaki's eye)
62.5 FX: Goh (demon tentacles go for Inuyasha)
FX: Ta (running)

63.2 FX: Goh (whoosh)
63.3 FX: Za (Inuyasha skids through grass)

64.2 FX: Da (Inuyasha leaps)
64.3 FX: Zan (Inuyasha strikes demon)
64.5 FX: Zu—n… (Inuyasha strikes at demon)

67.4 FX: Da (demon lunges toward Inuyasha)

68.1 FX: Doga (demon pounces)
68.2 FX: Toh (Inuyasha touches down)
68.3 FX: Doh (demon appendage lashes out at Inuyasha)
68.4 FX: Za (Inuyasha skids away)
68.5 FX: Ba (demon pursues Inuyasha)

69.2 FX: Ba (here come the claws)
69.3 FX: Goh (whooshing)

119.1 FX: Ba (Tsubaki's demon lunges to attack)
119.4 FX: Da (Inuyasha lunges for Kagome)
119.5 FX: Za (Inuyasha leaps away with Kagome)
119.5 FX: Doga
(demon pounces where Kagome just was)

120.2 FX: Toh (Inuyasha hops away)
121.2 FX: Ba (demon attacks)
121.3 FX: Da (Inuyasha plants himself between demon and Kagome)
121.5 FX: Zuba (Inuyasha's claws slash)

122.1 FX: Ga ga ga (demon torn apart)
122.2 FX: Ga gu (demon disintegrating)
122.3 FX: Goh (whoosh)
122.5 FX: Zan (Inuyasha finishes off demon serpent)

123.1 FX: Poto (severed demon head hits ground)
123.2 FX: Doh (Miroku punches through head of dead demon with his staff)
123.3 FX: Shuuuu… (hissing)

125.2 FX: Ka (Tsubaki's magic eye shines)
125.4 FX: Goh (whooshing)
125.5 FX: Doh (Inuyasha hit by demons)
126.1 FX: Zuba (slash)
126.2 FX: Doh (tentacle picks up Inuyasha)
126.4 FX: Zuba (slash)
126.5 FX: Doga (slash)

127.2 FX: Bun (Sango throws her weapon)
127.3 FX: Ga ga ga ga
(Hiraikotsu smashes through demons)
127.4 FX: Gasa (Something slithering nearby)

128.1 FX: Za za za… (demon starts to slither)
128.2 FX: Zuru (demon's head reforms)

129.1 FX: Da (Inuyasha leaps toward Kagome)
129.4 FX: Ba (demon lunges ay Kagome)
129.5 FX: Kaaaa… (demon's eye shines)

83.2 FX: Gu (Tsubaki clutches Jewel)

84.1 FX: Jiririririri (alarm clock ringing)
84.5 FX: Pi (alarm clock is switched off)

99.3 FX: Zuki (Kagome gets a pain in her neck)
99.4 FX: Pohh… (things get blurry)
99.5 FX: Dosa (Kagome collapses)

101.3 FX: Su… (Buyo becomes Kirara)

105.1 FX: Doh (arrow hits target)
105.2 FX: Dokun… (heartbeat)
105.4 FX: Ta (Kagome scoots off)

107.2 FX: Koku… (Kagome nods)
107.4 FX: Kiri (arrow string stretches as it is pulled)
107.6 FX: Shu (arrow flies)

108.1 FX: Doh (arrow hits target)

109.6 FX: Zuki (Kagome feels pain in her neck)

110.3 FX: Ba (demon leaps over)
110.4 FX: Doga (demon lands)

112.1 FX: Ka (shining of Kagome's open eye)

112.3 FX: Da (demon slaps his tail at Inuyasha)
112.4 FX: Bun (Inuyasha slashes)

113.1 FX: Doga (demon strikes)
113.2 FX: Baki (another tail strike)
113.3 FX: Za (Inuyasha hits ground and skids)
113.5 FX: Gyun (arrow turns around toward demon)

114.1 FX: Doh (arrow strikes)
114.3 FX: Shu (Kagome shoots arrow)
114.4 FX: Doga (arrow strikes)

118.2 FX: Pohh… (snakes drips venom on Jewel)
118.3 FX: Doh (Kagome collapses)

153.4 FX: Doh (Inuyasha does face plant)
153.6 FX: Da (Kaede gallops off)

158.1 FX: Za (Botan and Momiji slide door open)
158.2 FX: Zun zun… (Botan and Momiji exit shrine, staffs in hand)
159.5 FX: Goh (Kagura's wicked wind whistles and moans)

162.1 FX: Goh (Kirara flies)
162.2 FX: Za za… (Inuyasha runs through grass with Kagome on his back)
162.5 FX: Toh (Kirara touches down)

163.4 FX: Bari (barrier repels Inuyasha)

164.3 FX: Bari… (Shippo gets an electric shock from barrier)
164.4 FX: Su (Miroku casually picks up stick with sutra seal that repelled and shocked Inuyasha and Shippo)

170.5 FX: Ba (Botan and Momiji prepare to do mischief)

171.5 FX: Sawa sawa… (grope, grope)

172.5 FX: Za (Inuyasha skids to a halt)

173.2 FX: Ba (priestesses toss sutra thingys)
173.3 FX: Kaaaa… (sutras shine as them become paper dolls)
173.4 FX: Ba ba ba (cute shikigami paper dolls appear)
173.6 FX: Doh doh doh (dolls storm towards our heroes)

174.1 FX: Toh toh toh toh… (pitter patter of little paper dolly feet)
174.2 FX: Keri (Kagome kicks paper dolly)
174.5 FX: Doh doh doh (paper dolls stalk our heroes)

175.1 FX: Zuba (slice)
175.2 FX: Boh (a poof of Shippo's fox fire)
175.3 FX: Peshi (Miroku knocks some dolls over with his staff)

130.1 FX: Doga (Kagome smacks down the serpent)
130.2 FX: Hyururururu… (serpent falls through the air)
130.4 FX: Doh (demon hits Tsubaki)
130.5 FX: Goh (demon goes in through eye)

131.3 FX: Ga (Kikyo smacks serpent with her bow)

132.2 FX: Doh (Tsubaki collapses)
132.3 FX: Shuuuu… (Jewel hisses as it purifies)
132.5 FX: Kaaaaa… (jewel shines brightly)

133.1 FX: Poro (shards pop out of Kagome's neck)
133.3 FX: Ba! (Tsubaki snatches jewel)
133.4 FX: Za (Tsubaki sits up)
133.5 FX: Goh (demons swarm to Tsubaki)
133.6 FX: Ba (Inuyasha draws sword)

134.1 FX: Doga (Tetsusaiga strikes ground)
134.2 FX: Doh (strike slays demon)
134.3 FX: Za za za (demons disintegrate)
134.5 FX: Ba (Tsubaki takes off)

135.1 FX: Goh (Tsubaki whooshes away)
135.2 FX: Cha (Inuyasha goes to draw his sword)
135.3 FX: Ta (Inuyasha turns toward the others)

138.2/3 FX: Shuuuu… (hissing as demons dissolve)

Chapter 63
The Red and White Priestesses

142.1 FX: Zawa… (rustling of Tsubaki's footsteps)
142.4 FX: Ka (flash of light as Kikyo deflects Tsubaki's curse with bow)
142.5 FX: Ga (whack)

148.1 FX: Pachi pachi (flames crackling)

149.4 FX: Muku (Shippo sits up)

150.1 FX: Gu gu… (stuff bubbling in pot)

176.1 FX: Su… (Momiji holds up hair, displayed between thumb and forefinger)
176.5 FX: Su (Botan and Momiji whip out their sutras)

177.1 FX: Ba (priestess throw sutras)
177.2 FX: Kaaa… (shining as sutras turn into shikiigami paper dolls)
177.5 FX: Zu zu zu… (paper dolls glow as they grow)

180.1 FX: Pachi pachi (flames crackling)

183.4 FX: Zu—n zu—n (fake Inuyasha and fake Kagome stomp toward the real ones)

184.1 FX: Da (Inuyasha leaps)
184.3 FX: Baki (fake Inuyasha swipes at real Inuyasha)
184.4 FX: Kiri (fake Kagome nocks an arrow)

185.1 FX: Doh (arrow smashes into ground)
185.2 FX: Toh (Inuyasha lands on his feet)
185.4 FX: Da (Inuyasha rushes at fake Inuyasha and Kagome)
185.5 FX: Doh doh doh (fake Inuyasha charges)

186.1 FX: Dohh (fake Inuyasha stomps toward our heroes)
186.2 FX: Dosu (fake Inuyasha stomps on real Inuyasha)
186.3 FX: Surururu (boomerang approaches fake Inuyasha)
186.3 FX: Sa (fake Inuyasha removes his foot)

187.2 FX: Da (Inuyasha leaps toward fake Inuyasha)
187.3 FX: Bari (Inuyasha trips on stick with sutra seal)
187.5 FX: Shu (blimpy Kagome shoots arrow)

188.1 FX: Gin (clang)

190.1 FX: Gohhh… (whooshing)
190.3 FX: Ba (priestesses throwing shikigami)

191.1 FX: Zun (Shippo does faceplant)

192.2 FX: Za (Sango runs in front of fake Inuyasha and blimpy Kagome)

193.1 FX: Doga (fake Inuyasha attacks)
193.5 FX: Zun (Inuyasha gets up)

194.1 FX: Shun (arrow flies)
194.2 FX: Gin (somewhere between a clang and a ping)
194.3 FX: Dohh (fake Inuyasha swings at Inuyasha)
194.5 FX: Bun (Sango lets Hiraikotsu fly)

195.1 FX: Goh (whoosh)
195.4 FX: Guoh (Inuyasha defelcts plush toy Inuyasha's sword thingy)
195.5 FX: Zu—n… (fake Inuyasha topples over into dirt)

196.1 FX: Zuba (Inuyasha cuts up the overgrown plush toys)
196.2 FX: Zan (fake Inuyasha split in two)
196.3 FX: Goh (whoosh)
196.4 FX: Dosa (Botan and Momiji land on ground in a heap)

197.1 FX: Sawa sawa… (Miroku gropes the unconscious priestesses)
197.2 FX: Gyu (Sango hauls Miroku up by his ear)

199.4 FX: Bari (blinding crackle flash of light)

202.1 FX: Fu… (fire goes out)
202.3 FX: Gii… (door with creaky hinges opening)

204.2 FX: Ta ta ta… (running)
204.3 FX: Ta ta ta… (more running)
204.5 FX: Ta (Inuyasha leaps up the rest of the stairs)

205.1 FX: Bari (Inuyasha whacks into barrier)
205.4 FX: Gu gu… (Inuyasha struggles to free himself)
205.5 FX: Ba (Inuyasha leaps through barrier)
205.6 FX: Boh (sutra seal burns off with blue flame)

InuYasha™

Rated #1 on Cartoon Network's Adult Swim!

In its original, unedited form!

maison ikkoku™

The b
roma
of err
favori

Ranma ½

The zany, w
of martial arts
best!